AMERICA'S INFORMATION WARS

AMERICA'S INFORMATION WARS

The Untold Story of Information Systems in America's Conflicts and Politics from World War II to the Internet Age

Colin B. Burke

ROWMAN & LITTLEFIELD
Lanham • Boulder • New York • London

Published by Rowman & Littlefield
An imprint of The Rowman & Littlefield Publishing Group, Inc.
4501 Forbes Boulevard, Suite 200, Lanham, Maryland 20706
www.rowman.com

Unit A, Whitacre Mews, 26-34 Stannary Street, London SE11 4AB

Copyright © 2018 by The Rowman & Littlefield Publishing Group, Inc.

All rights reserved. No part of this book may be reproduced in any form or by any electronic or mechanical means, including information storage and retrieval systems, without written permission from the publisher, except by a reviewer who may quote passages in a review.

British Library Cataloguing in Publication Information Available

Library of Congress Cataloging-in-Publication Data Available

ISBN 9781538112458 (hardback : alk. paper) | ISBN 9781538112465 (electronic)

♾ ™ The paper used in this publication meets the minimum requirements of American National Standard for Information Sciences Permanence of Paper for Printed Library Materials, ANSI/NISO Z39.48-1992.

Printed in the United States of America

Thanks to Joe Morello and Cal Tjader and to
Jeffery Hartley, the librarians' librarian.

CONTENTS

List of Figures	ix
Preface	xi
Acknowledgments	xv

PART I: INFORMATION AT WAR WITH HITLER AND TOJO, THEN WITH STALIN — 1

1	The OSS's Unusual Librarians	3
2	Forging an Intelligence System	19
3	A New Information Culture	37
4	Microfilm at the OSS, for War and Profit	55
5	One System for All Intelligence	75
6	CIA's Classification and Automation Battles	97

PART II: COLD WAR INFORMATION POLITICS AND LIVES — 115

7	Ideology and Science Information Policy	117
8	The CIA's Librarians under Fire	137
9	Library and Classification Revolutions?: SAL, Semantic Factors, the Luhn Scanner	153
10	Automation Dreams, Minicard	173
11	The CIA versus the Librarians	189
12	From Microfilm to Computers	203
13	Automatic Translation's Woes	217

CONTENTS

14 A Cold War Information Career   235

PART III: INFORMATION'S TROUBLED GOLDEN AGE TO THE ERA OF OPEN ACCESS   255

15 Sputnik's New Politics of Information   257

16 An American Information Century?   277

17 The Plural Information System Survives, with Difficulty   295

18 A New Information Era: The American Information Century's Challengers   315

19 Another Serials Crisis, Open Access, the Return of Ideology   337

Bibliography   351

Index   363

About the Author   373

LIST OF FIGURES

Fig. 2.1	COI Abstract Card	30
Fig. 2.2	COI-OSS Map System Card	32
Fig. 4.1	Langan Aperture Card	57

PREFACE

This book narrates the development of science, sci-tech, and intelligence information systems and technologies in the United States from the beginning of World War II to the second decade of our century. The story ranges from a description of the information systems and machines of the 1940s developed at Wild Bill Donovan's predecessors of the Central Intelligence Agency, to the rise of a huge international science information industry, and to the 1990s' open access/open culture reformers' reactions to the commercialization of science information. Necessarily, there is much about the people, cultures, and politics that shaped the methods, systems, machines, and protests. The reason for that is simple: the histories of technologies and methods are human histories. Science information's many lives were shaped by idiosyncrasies and chance, as well as by social, economic, political, and technical forces.

This narrative begins in 1941 when the United States was attempting to create its first unified intelligence information system, a struggle that soon became critically important to America's science information efforts. The story shifts from that work at what became the Office of Strategic Services (OSS) to the ideologically laced postwar contests over science and science information policies. Those contests overlapped adventurous information systems efforts at the new Central Intelligence Group that replaced the Office of Strategic Services. The narrative then travels through the Cold War years when science information and university research were defense necessities, as a new type of librarian, the

PREFACE

information scientist, emerged to deal with the unique challenges of sci-tech information, and when there was an incessant search for information methods and machines. The new classification and retrieval methods, such as KWIC, Uniterms, and citation indexing/ranking, and amazing precomputer machines like Intellofax, the Luhn Scanner, and Minicard that laid the foundations for today's systems, necessarily receive much attention.

The story next moves to our century as science information and America's higher education system became major and highly concentrated industries serving a vast global market and when the skyrocketing costs of both became so burdensome that university expenses became a political issue, leading radical information reformers to demand free access to all science information. Soon, young Internet tycoons joined the protests, driven by a strange new egalitarian open culture ideology—but not the Communist or the anti-Communist creeds that were so important from the 1920s through the Cold War years.

This book's attention to information systems, methods, and technologies does not mean this is a limited narrative, one confined to a predetermined and narrow definition of subject matter and permissible content. I began my research at an important starting point and followed where the evidence led. If I had not done that, and had made this book into a traditional monograph or technical report, I would have done a disservice to history. The evidential trails proved that information history involves much more than the technical. Science information's tools and technologies did not arise and live in an idealized and isolated cocoon. Furthermore, information technologies and methods did not follow an ever-ascending linear path. There were many instances of false starts and of massive investments leading to techno dead ends, such as the microfilm Minicard, mechanical language translation, and the semantic factors classification system.

The flow of evidence also demonstrated that information history is a human history. The varied motives, personalities, and beliefs of unique and extraordinary people fashioned science information's past. The important players ranged from a gentleman scholar who led the Office of Strategic Services' information work, to an ill-fated Hollywood movie director, to life mavericks like the science information legend Eugene Garfield, to international financial wheeler-dealers such as Robert Maxwell, and to youthful ultraliberal, ideologically driven Silicon Valley

PREFACE xiii

Internet millionaires like Brewster Kahle. However, although there are no determining laws of information history, social, political, legal, and economic factors were important. After 1940, science information's tools and policies, as well as America's universities, were being molded by the nation's wealth, its role in international affairs, the standoff between left and right politics, and by the intensifying conflict between Soviet and Western interests.

Ideological influences were significant. After World War II, there were recurring policy debates in America, at first spurred by ex–vice president Henry Wallace's call for "Socialist" science information. His demands spread to questions about who was to determine research and educational policies, when his information legacy was passed on to Hubert Humphrey during the 1950s and 1960s and, in an altered form, to the open access advocates, such as Peter Suber, a generation later.

While acknowledging ideological, social, and technological influences, much of this work is organized around the biographies of many previously ignored but important people. In-depth looks at the lives of three unusual men, Wilmarth Sheldon Lewis, Kenneth Addicott, and John Langan, provide new perspectives on the American intelligence community's struggle to organize information (including that for images) and on the origins of important information technologies such as the aperture card and Intellofax. The biographies, especially Langan's, confirm the old saying that history is stranger than fiction.

The career of James Perry, one of the first of a new breed of librarians (documentalists/information scientists), yields an understanding of the changes in American higher education and the information profession during what contemporaries called the American century, when, for almost four decades, it appeared the United States would always be the dominant force in science information—as well as being the world's economic and military powerhouse and the leading science publisher. Perry's information career began when he was a struggling engineer/chemist at the Massachusetts Institute of Technology. Then, he worked for the Central Intelligence Agency and soon became a new type of academic, a wandering "soft-money" professor, whose precarious career depended on grantsmanship.

The CIA's funds and Perry's long and at times painful career touched on the professional lives of almost everyone in a generation of science and technical information pioneers, including such famous professionals as Jesse Shera, Joe Becker, and Allen Kent. They and Perry helped create what seemed to be an American information century. That century proved to be short lived, however. By the 1980s, the nation had to confront threatening economic competition, even in the scientific publishing field. At the same time, it was dealing with the escalating cost of education, research, and science information.

This volume concludes with a short review of the reactions to those threats. They ranged from an acceptance of a new globalized information capitalism and its inegalitarian consequences, to liberals' faith that cost-saving digital technologies would democratize access to science information, to politically charged open access crusades and adventures such as PubMed Central and the Internet Archive, and to the "information guerilla" actions of a strange type of open culture/open society information radical, Aaron Swartz.[1]

While this book features people and is aimed at the fabled but illusive general reader, the nonspecialist, it does contain a few sections, such as the one on the first OSS classification systems, that necessarily include some technical details about library and classification methods and machines. Those sections are not tutorials and a reader does not have to understand the fine points of the methods and technologies to appreciate how difficult it was, and is, to organize and retrieve information.

NOTE

1. A future volume to provide a detailed look at the history of and the amazing people involved in the open access, open societies, and open culture battles that began in the 1990s is envisioned.

ACKNOWLEDGMENTS

After almost ten years on topics related to this work my list of indebtedness is so long that I can only mention a few of those who deserve recognition.

Among the many individuals, the late Peter Dobkin Hall never failed to inform me about the history of nonprofits, and Michael Buckland, Boyd Rayward, and Robert V. Williams gave invaluable help on information history. The staffs at the National Archives in College Park and Washington, D.C., especially Jeff Hartley, often led me to unexpectedly invaluable files, as did those at the Library of Congress and Columbia University. The earlier support from the librarians at the Chemical Heritage Foundation and from Eugene Garfield was invaluable. The gracious archivists at the lovely Lewis Walpole Library deserve a special salute.

There are approximately a dozen librarians and staff members at my university's library who went far beyond the call of duty. The interlibrary loan team filled several requests a week for many years, and the circulation department always found a way to keep books available, even when I could not get to the library for several weeks. The research librarians and the group in the periodicals department probably had their life spans reduced by several years because of their extraordinary efforts on my behalf.

Part I

Information at War with Hitler and Tojo, Then with Stalin

I

THE OSS'S UNUSUAL LIBRARIANS

In the late 1930s, Franklin Roosevelt, the liberal and internationalist president of the United States, began preparing for a possible entry into war. By 1940, he already had the nation deeply involved in preparedness—for conflicts in both Europe and Asia. His planning included building a viable intelligence service.

There was a need to hurry. It seemed that Germany might soon conquer England, as well as the continental nations. Japan's intentions were also worrisome. In response, Roosevelt decided to send a special emissary to Europe to gauge England's ability to withstand an invasion. An extra assignment was to learn how England organized its intelligence services. Roosevelt's representative was ordered to return with suggestions on how to cure America's obvious intelligence weaknesses. Good advice was needed. The United States had a long history of standing aloof from international conflicts and had a rather naïve abhorrence of spying. While the nation had been increasing its surveillance of the world, and of suspected internal enemies, its intelligence organizations remained small, weak, and very disorganized. There were many groups gathering information, but they often were tripping over each other while failing to monitor important targets. Worse, they had habitually refused to share information.

There were too many uncoordinated efforts. The army, navy, and coast guard had intelligence departments, even radio spying agencies. The State Department gathered reports from its overseas offices and had a special, but tiny, intelligence group. The Treasury Department collected world trade and finance information that revealed the intentions of foreign governments. While the Federal Bureau of Investigation focused on internal matters, its files contained much of value to those shaping America's foreign policies. All those efforts did not lead to good strategic intelligence, however.[1] One reason was that the nation's intelligence capabilities had grown helter-skelter. Each organization had its own culture and each protected its bureaucratic turf. The lack of coordination was an irritant to President Roosevelt, especially because there was no one agency putting all the separate intelligence facts together into meaningful reports for him—and there was no office able to direct the various agencies to efficiently focus on significant questions.

There was also a technical problem: none of the agencies spoke the same information language. Each had developed its own terminology and file systems. Gathering information from across the agencies was difficult and costly although good intelligence depends on bringing together thousands of bits and pieces of information from diverse sources.

William Donovan, Roosevelt's special emissary to England, had been instructed to seek ways to solve the coordination problem. In 1941, when he returned from his latest trip to assess England's survivability, he had many ideas and suggestions for a thorough reshaping of the American intelligence community. The grand sweep of his ideas and ambitions was the result of more than his learning the details of Britain's intelligences services' organization and methods—and of more than his professional and personal ties to Britain's covert intelligence group in New York City. Donovan's dynamic personality had much to do with his great ambitions, his initial bureaucratic successes, and the frictions that led to the termination at the war's end of the intelligence organization the president allowed him to create in mid-1941.[2]

WILD BILL, THE POET, AND THE LIBRARY OF CONGRESS AT WAR

Donovan, a first-generation Irish American Catholic, had the energy and intellect to rise from a lower-middle-class background to become a Columbia University graduate, a decorated World War I hero, a powerful New York–based international lawyer-businessman, and a confidant of many of the nation's leaders and intellectuals. But he also made important enemies. His daredevil behavior as a college athlete had earned him the nickname Wild Bill, and that nickname stayed with him throughout his life, partly because he had little hesitation about stepping on political or bureaucratic toes when pursuing his objectives.

On his return from his surveys in the spring of 1941, the almost sixty-year-old Donovan presented the president with a far-reaching idea for a new and comprehensive intelligence organization. It was to be one that, he hoped, would do more than just coordinate the older agencies. He had visions of a service that would have its own secret army for covert operations as well as an espionage capability. Donovan also wanted his own radio-intercept and codebreaking departments, his own little navy, a private communications system, his own national and international propaganda group, and, significantly, a great information center.

Foremost on his list was a new type of unit to bring together and analyze the entire nation's intelligence information. That hub would use its special sources, as well as those of the other agencies, and was to rely on the best brains in the country to develop presentations for the president. His Research and Analysis group was to create strategic reports and plans, as well as summaries of current intelligence. It was even to have a technologically advanced presentation facility where the nation's leaders could see, on large screens, full-color graphic depictions of the world situation.[3]

The worth of that facility and Donovan's other intelligence hopes rested on the creation of a revolutionary information system, something that he had yet to define.

Although Donovan was influential and persuasive, the president did not give him all desired, at least in mid-1941. Roosevelt did not approve a "strategic" service. He only allowed Donovan to create the Office of the Coordinator of Information (COI), one with a budgeted staff of fewer than one hundred that was charged with realizing only the information coordination dream. Donovan was given one advantage, however. The COI began as an independent civilian office attached to the White House, not to a military agency. That allowed Donovan freedom to appoint some unusual intellectuals and academics to help build his organization. Unfortunately, the powers the COI was to have over the military and the civilian intelligence agencies had not been made clear.

The ambivalence continued after the COI was directly linked to the military and became the Office of Strategic Services (OSS) in mid-1942.

Uncertainties about powers and duties and his first meager budgets did not defeat Donovan. He continued to build his dream organization and began flexing all his bureaucratic muscles. He had some successes. Within a year, by mid-1942, his workforce was ten times what he had originally been allocated and he had made overtures to the other intelligence agencies, trying to convince them to give him their full cooperation. The expansion continued. By 1945, he was directing a force of some thirteen thousand men and women.

Growth did not guarantee organizational triumph, however. Wild Bill's dynamism and optimism in 1941 had led him to naively believe he could quickly create a new organization and staff it within a few months. A man in a hurry to do what he could to defeat the Fascist enemies, he took many shortcuts. Lines of authority in his organization were not always adequate or clearly defined, and he allowed personnel recruitment practices that led to great embarrassments. Although Donovan was later known as one of the nation's most vocal conservatives, his organization housed many Communists, fellow travelers, and even Soviet informants. Duncan Lee, his personal assistant, was one of them. Donovan's "think tank" Research and Analysis group had also welcomed the Marxist Frankfurt scholars who were associated with Hede Massing, one of the American-based Soviet espionage controllers. Wild Bill was even willing to recruit hundreds of ex-members of the Communist-directed International Brigades of the Spanish Civil War for his covert operations groups because they were experienced anti-Fascist fighters.[4]

Although his recruitment gaffes were not an immediate issue, most of Donovan's great ambitions remained blocked during 1941 and early 1942, mainly because of the objections and intransigence of the military agencies and the State Department. However, he had been able to launch his plan for his own central information and analysis center—even before July 1941 when he received the president's official blessing as the coordinator.

STRANGE INFORMATION CENTER BEGINNINGS

Donovan was aided in his information and analysis center efforts by Archibald MacLeish. MacLeish was an unlikely collaborator because he was close to many American radicals and because he was a culturally left-leaning poet whom President Roosevelt in 1939 had selected to lead the Library of Congress, despite the opposition of many professional librarians and political conservatives. The Donovan-MacLeish collaboration was strange. While both men were internationalists and anti-Fascists, MacLeish was a very left-wing Democrat and Donovan was a rather hard-liner Republican. Their social backgrounds were also very different. Wild Bill was from an immigrant background; Archibald was the son of an elite Anglo family that had been able to provide him with an elite prep school, Yale University, and then a Harvard Law School education. Donovan had spent his civilian career as a hardworking lawyer-businessman-politician while MacLeish followed his World War I military service with a few years as a college instructor, an editor for the Progressives' *New Republic*, and a fledgling lawyer.[5]

Then, in his early thirties, MacLeish became one of the famous expatriot avant-garde American intellectuals in 1920s Paris. He soon began publishing poetry, something he continued to do after his return to the United States. He also became increasingly alienated from capitalism, penning plays and articles that foresaw its end. By the mid-1930s, he had gained somewhat of a reputation as a fellow traveler. That was an impediment, but it had not prevented Roosevelt from choosing him for the Library of Congress position, or from Donovan calling on him for help in 1941. Nor would MacLeish's leftish reputation block his postwar position as a full professor of rhetoric at Harvard University, or from winning Pulitzer Prizes for his poetry.

Despite their differences Wild Bill and Archibald joined together to create what they envisioned as the heart of the Coordinator of Information's organization. It was to be located within and be part of the Library of Congress in Washington, D.C. A first step was MacLeish's rallying his intellectual and academic friends and the representatives of major academic organizations, such as the Social Science Research Council, to create what he called "an intellectual reserve corps" to support the "front-line troops" of the Donovan organization.[6] MacLeish also made overtures to institutions and corporations with foreign contacts that could supply information, such as the Museum of Modern History and the Singer Sewing Machine Company.[7]

In July 1941, MacLeish signed an agreement with Donovan, creating a Division of Special Information that was to be an integral part of the Library of Congress, with the COI as its only customer. Its staff of experts in all fields was to gather, classify, and index *all* information relative to foreign affairs. Most valued, high-level academics in its Research and Analysis group (that Intellectual Reserve) would prepare reports on "strategic matters."[8] To MacLeish's surprise, just as the first agreements were being finalized, Donovan reworked the COI's organization. He created a bureaucratically stand-alone Central Information Division under his own new Research and Analysis group while the Library of Congress continued using a reduced force in its Division of Special Information.[9] Although the new COI groups were to be housed within the Library of Congress's recently completed annex building, and would heavily rely on all the library's resources and personnel, the library and the Central Information Division became formally independent organizations.

MacLeish accepted the new relationship and helped Donovan recruit many of the nation's leading scholars from the country's elite universities, such as Harvard's historian William Langer, for the new analysis group. Donovan aided the recruiting by convincing the Civil Service Commission to waive its rules on maximum government salaries so the COI could match those at America's most prestigious universities.[10]

THE COI'S CLASSIFICATION AND DATABASE CHALLENGE

Then was the task of finding the people who would be able to create a new type of library, one essential for making intelligence information useful at the highest policy-making levels. A first challenge was to forge a system that could allow gathering together the information that, hopefully, all the nation's intelligence groups would forward to Donovan's organization. That kind of integration called for the development of a new database and a unique classification and indexing system, one that could combine the disparate information coming from the other agen-

THE OSS'S UNUSUAL LIBRARIANS

9

cies, each of which had its own special classifications and terminologies. Donovan decided to call the new service that was to conquer the data capturing and classification challenges the Central Information Division (CID). Eventually, it was placed under Langer's command after he was made the chief of the Research and Analysis group. A logical move to begin the CID's life was to borrow experts from the Library of Congress and leading government libraries who had experience in using classification and indexing systems and who had an appreciation of the latest information technologies such as microfilm and tabulating machines. Robert D. W. Connor, the ex-archivist of the United States, was approached.[11]

There were disappointments. Connor refused the offer. Then, Ernest S. Griffith, who had led the impressive Legislative Reference Service in the Library of Congress, and Walter L. Wright, the Near Eastern scholar who had briefly led the library's Division of Special Information, declined.[12] MacLeish was frustrated but did not give in. He began a new search, one with a rather unusual outcome. There were many in government service who had managed large intelligence files and others in the business world who had worked with massive databases, but MacLeish and Donovan did not focus their new search on FBI, insurance companies, credit rating firms, or information-systems consulting companies. They again looked to the East Coast's elite academia.

THE SURPRISE: A CONSUMMATE LIBERAL AND A MAN NOT OF HIS TIME

In August 1941, MacLeish informed Donovan that the best man for the job was an old friend of his, the forty-six-year-old Wilmarth Sheldon Lewis, someone who had never worked as a librarian, a business information expert, a manager, or an intelligence analyst.[13]

The American public did not and would never know much about Wilmarth Sheldon Lewis although he was a very important behind-the-scenes force in the nation's intellectual, literary, political, and academic realms. He knew and hosted most of the nation's writers, high-level business and political leaders, opinion makers, and scholars. Among many other achievements, he was a trustee of Yale University (even recommending who should be the university's president), a board member of the American Philosophical Society, and a trustee of Princeton University's fabled scholarly Institute for Advanced Study. He was a valued advisor to the Library of Congress as it attempted to become a truly national center for all types of information under the guidance of his close friend Archibald MacLeish. Although a progressive Republican by habit, he became an ally and relative of the Democratic John F. Kennedy family and thus was linked to powerful public intellectuals such as Arthur Schlesinger and his son, Arthur Jr.

Wilmarth's beautiful but unpretentious Connecticut home had and would be visited by intellectual figures like MacLeish and governmental leaders such as Dean Acheson, the secretary of state. Lewis also knew and advised the important library innovators of the 1930s and 1940s like Keyes Metcalf, Luther Evans, and Verner Clapp.

All those connections now seem incongruous because Wilmarth spent a rather physically isolated life, one centered on his restored colonial mansion in rural Farmington, Connecticut. Its gracefully handcrafted library was the home's showpiece. There were some diversions, however. They included visits to his wife's family's vast Newport, Rhode Island, estate and the couple's research trips to Europe. The almost yearly excursions to England were devoted to collecting items on Horace Walpole and the politics of eighteenth-century England and were the greatest exceptions to Wilmarth's isolation.

His family background, his gentlemanly graciousness, his and his wife's personal warmth and charm, and their widespread and voluminous correspondence compensated for being rooted in rural Farmington. However, Wilmarth and Annie Burr Auchincloss, his wife, were never truly people of their own time. He was more like the gentleman scholars of the eighteenth and nineteenth centuries who used their fortunes to support their independent scientific work. Annie was more of a grand lady of a past era of civility. Neither was a twentieth-century American go-getter ostentatiously climbing a social or academic ladder.

One reason for their being able to be so unusual was their wealth. Wilmarth came from a rich California family. His mother was the heir to the great Lux cattle and land fortune. His father was an executive in the state's oil industry. Annie descended from one of the founders of the Rockefeller Standard Oil Company and grew up in a very affluent and socially prominent New York City family. They and Wilmarth's parents could afford to send their children to the best private schools, ones that featured broad humanities curricula and that taught social responsibility to their usually elite students. Wilmarth went to the Thacher Preparatory School, then Yale University. Annie attended the renowned Miss Porter's School in Farmington, Connecticut, that had and would shape the character of generations of the Auchincloss women, including the future Jacqueline Kennedy.

Both Wilmarth and Annie inherited small fortunes in early adulthood and neither had to pursue a career. But they did not become, like MacLeish had for a time, part of the Gatsby "lost generation" of the 1920s that squandered time and money. After graduating from Yale in 1918, spending two years in the U.S. Army in World War I (an experience he never discussed), and working as an editor for a year or so, Wilmarth came into another and sizable fortune, bought the colonial mansion in Farmington (forty miles from New Haven and Yale University) and decided to devote his life to scholarship and to the welfare of the humanities at his beloved Yale. His primary goal was to acquire, edit, and publish everything related to England's great eighteenth-century politician Horace Walpole and his times. Annie, who also had fallen in love with charming Farmington, joined in Wilmarth's lifelong quest of all that was Walpole. She helped Wilmarth locate, catalog, and index thousands of documents and artifacts. By the end of Wilmarth's life the couple and their few helpers had created a file of more than seven hundred thousand index cards related to their Farmington collection. Each card was meticulously indexed and annotated. There was more to their work. Wilmarth led one of the largest private publication efforts in America, Yale Press's some forty-eight volumes of Walpole's correspondence.

Wilmarth was a devoted Yale man, and its alumni and faculty adored him. He taught an occasional class on library methods at the university while always insisting he was not one of those new career professors or a professional librarian who knew or wanted to know the intricacies of Melville (Melvil) Dewey's or other library great classification systems such as the sophisticated Universal Decimal Classification that attempted to be a single worldwide integrated system for all knowledge. That was a point he made when that other Yale graduate, Archibald MacLeish, interrupted the flow of an August 1941 lunch conversation with his longtime friend and asked Wilmarth if he would be willing to move to Washington, D.C., and lead the team to build Donovan's intelligence database system. With Annie's approval, Wilmarth accepted the responsibility—but he demanded the assistance of someone with experience in navigating Washington's bureaucratic mazes. MacLeish promised he would find such a man.

Wilmarth and Annie immediately moved to Washington, D.C., purchased a townhome, and then another next to it. The second purchase was due to Wilmarth discovering they had moved next door to a house of ill repute. Fortunately, he and Annie had enough wealth to be able to persuade the madam to sell her place of business. The Lewises needed a reputable home because they continued hosting intellectuals and officials and because Annie, reflecting her family's reputation and Miss Porter's School's sense of social obligation, was the national volunteer coordinator for the American Red Cross.[14]

AS WE, BUT NOT OTHERS, MAY THINK—THE IRONY OF THE PAPERWORK EFFICIENCY MOVEMENT

Exactly what Lewis had been told of his powers and duties in summer 1941 is unknown, but it soon became clear that he had not been given adequate power to collect all the information the COI was supposed to integrate—and, that the intellectual-classification challenge he faced was greater than he or MacLeish had anticipated. There were no ready-made classifications that fit the COI's needs and there was no uniformity in the systems used by those the COI would both serve and rely upon.

Ironically, one of Lewis's hurdles was the result of a drive for efficiency in the United States government's operations that began shortly before World War I. Because of it there could not be an easy transfer of information to and from the COI's major providers and its customers. In 1910, on the orders of President William Howard Taft, a special commission for efficiency in government was established. The commission's mandate was to encourage the application of the principles of scientific management that had been developed by the engineer Frederick Winslow Taylor and his followers. Science and statistical measurement were applied to all sectors of the economy by those efficiency

THE OSS'S UNUSUAL LIBRARIANS   13

experts, ones often blamed for dehumanizing work and for the "speed-up" that led to many labor protests.

Its near decade-long investigations of procedures in the private sector and government agencies led the commission to admire the index card–based systems for businesses developed by such firms as Melvil Dewey's Library Bureau and by James Newton Gunn, the industrial and managerial expert who had been a leading innovator at Dewey's firm. Gunn had invented the vertical file for organizing and storing materials that could not be placed on shelves, and he had introduced the "tab" for index card systems. Like many new information experts, Gunn had been trained to be one of the new scientific engineers, a type of man who would have great influence on information methods for the next hundred years. [15]

Gunn and the Library Bureau's experts had developed special document classification and indexing systems for many firms, systems typically based on the general concepts in Dewey's hierarchical and subject-oriented Decimal Classification—and using something akin to his numeric notations. However, Gunn and others did not adhere to all of Dewey's methods and goals, or to his taxonomy, in their business applications or, later, during the development of government systems. An example is Gunn's work that led to the State Department's very complex and unique system that emerged in 1910.

There were some good and bad reasons for such deviations from a universal classification system. Dewey's Decimal Classification and card index system had been devised in the mid-1870s when the development of college and public libraries was posing managerial and intellectual challenges. Larger book collections demanded new tools for placement and retrieval. Dewey's and other similar systems allowed for the orderly placement of books and for searching for them by browsing from the most general to the most particular information or vice versa. Such browsing was possible because all books were classified in a well-ordered hierarchal "tree of knowledge," one that made sense to an educated person of the time. The decimal method made cataloging and searching easy by parsing knowledge into collections of ten categories at each level of generality. Dewey-like systems had their limitations, however. Their hierarchical structures and knowledge concepts reflected the needs and intellectual orientations of general-purpose libraries and their typically nonspecialist users.[16] For example, the highest level of the ten most inclusive categories of Melvil Dewey's "tree" included:

000 Generalities (Encyclopedias, Periodicals, Journals, Bibliographies)
100 Philosophy, Esthetics, Psychology
200 Religion
300 Social Sciences
400 Linguistics
500 Pure Sciences
600 Applied Sciences
700 Arts and Recreation
800 Literature
900 Geography, History

The next ten in the decimal division of the Pure Science (500) category were:

500 Pure Sciences
510 Mathematics
520 Astronomy
530 Physics
540 Chemistry
550 Earth Sciences
560 Paleontology
570 Biological Sciences
580 Botany
590 Zoology

Someone searching for information on say, zebrafish, would go to 500, Pure Sciences, then descend to the 590 branch, Zoology, then to 597, Fish, then to the next subdivision, 482, giving the full Dewey number (call number), 597.482. Dewey's system also facilitated browsing by users. It placed subject-related books close to each other on library shelves so a visitor could find other items of interest just by looking at the shelves.

The value and efficiency of such organizations of information depended on a stable and useful taxonomy—and, significantly, one suited to a user's perspectives. However, even when the Belgian Paul Otlet and the American ex-patriot Herbert Haviland Field expanded Dewey's system in their attempts to index all types of information, including scientific and technological literature, their Universal Decimal Classification (taxonomies) reflected the way of thinking, vocabulary, and needs of traditional academics—not businessmen, bureaucrats, specialized scientists, or technologists—or of intelligence organizations.[17] The U.S. Library of Congress's own special version of a decimal classification system shared that limitation.

The two grandest systems (Dewey's and Otlet's) had a goal of a universality implemented by using only terms that were established international standards so that information could be easily and efficiently transferred among people and nations. They had also hoped that the use of purely numeric indicators would transcend any language barriers. Numbers had an additional advantage: they were easier to sort than words. However, achieving such standardization of terms, having fully decimal "ten-division" organization, and being able to use only digits in the card indexes, even in limited fields, was a daunting challenge. To some, they seemed unachievable goals and pursuing them was inefficient. The question of who could wait for worldwide standardization in ever-changing fields, for example, was not just rhetorical. Others pointed out that not everything was or could be well ordered in family-genus-species systems favored by nineteenth-century biologists and Dewey.

Furthermore, general systems such as Paul Otlet's Universal Decimal Classification, and even the Library of Congress's, necessarily became very complex when there were attempts to organize specialized information and to provide precision (pointing exactly to the items desired). Classifying specialized information by just subjects demanded notations that were exceedingly long, hard for users to understand, and expensive to compile. And such work required highly skilled professionals.

Dewey numbers at first were only three to six digits long. By the twentieth century they could contain a dozen or more digits. When a specific book was to be identified, more numbers and letters were needed and such "Cutter numbers" as D775 were appended to the Dewey subject digits to produce a call number.

Even the special extensions of Dewey-like systems, such as those for technologies, were dependent on long, hard to use, and hard to understand classification numbers.[18] The Library of Congress felt so constrained by a numbers-only format that it added letters to its index numbers to allow more combinations. Then its staff went much further by appending English-language subject headings, such as "United States—History—Civil War, 1861–1865—Psychological Aspects," to a number identifier like E468.9.A34 1911 to direct users to desired items.

Despite that and a growing number of objections to decimal systems, the 1910 Taft Commission had let it be known that if any government agency wanted budgetary favors it should immediately begin developing a Dewey-like classification. The commission thought that the decimal method that placed every item within a logically organized and sparse hierarchy, allowing one to easily go from the particular to the more general (or vice versa), outweighed any of the Dewey system's burdens and limitations.

EVERY INTELLIGENCE BUREAU FOR ITSELF

Significantly, the Taft Commission did not ask for the creation of an agency to oversee and coordinate the development of all the government systems. That, the inapplicability of existing classifications, and the desire of agencies to quickly build structures that fit their interests, their vocabularies, and their concepts, led to every government organization devising its unique "decimal" system. Each of the military departments created a special classification. The State Department, the Treasury, and the FBI also had unique versions. The result was a conglomeration of uncoordinated intelligence-related classifications and indexing-number systems, and a range of unevenly detailed systems, all with their own terminologies. Some, like those of the army and navy's intelligence arms, used very refined schema with at least six- or eight-digit subject identifiers (plus country identifiers); others thought three digits were sufficient to guide users to the information they needed. Furthermore, the same bit of information was classified differently in most all systems. Even the army and navy used dissimilar terminologies. As a result, sharing information from one agency to another was very difficult and expensive.

ON CITATIONS

For practical reasons, this work includes a minimal number of endnotes, with priority given to possibly controversial issues. The work does, however, rest upon hundreds of additional sources. The bibliography of utilized secondary sources for this and a related volume may be found at http://userpages.umbc.edu/~burke//.

Abbreviations: CHF, Chemical Heritage Foundation; CWR, Case Western Reserve University Archive; FBI, Federal Bureau of Investigation; FOIA, Freedom of Information Act request; LWL, Lewis Walpole Library; NARA, National Archives and Records Administration.

NOTES

1. On the intelligence problems and the formation of the COI and OSS: Thomas F. Troy, *Donovan and the CIA: A History of the Establishment of the Central Intelligence Agency* (Washington, DC: Central Intelligence Agency, 1988); Rhodi Jeffreys-Jones, "Antecedents and Memories as Factors in the Creation of the CIA," *Diplomatic History* 40, no. 1 (January 2016): 140–54.

2. Douglas Waller, *Wild Bill Donovan: The Spymaster Who Created the OSS and Modern American Espionage* (New York: Free Press, 2011).

3. Barry Katz, "The Arts of War: 'Visual Presentation' and National Intelligence," *Design Issues* 12, no. 2 (Summer 1996): 3–21.

4. Mark A. Bradley, *A Very Principled Boy: The Life of Duncan Lee, Red Spy and Cold Warrior* (New York: Basic Books, 2014); Barry Katz, *Foreign Intelligence: Research and Analysis in the Office of Strategic Services* (London: Oxford University Press, 1989).

5. Scott Donaldson, *Archibald MacLeish: An American Life* (Boston: Houghton Mifflin, 1992).

6. NARA RG226 ai 146 b137 C134cid 8-26-41, MacLeish to Baxter.

7. NARA RG226 ai 146 b137 7-30-41.

8. NARA RG226 ai 146b137 7-30-41, Donovan to MacLeish. The library would soon house other information efforts by the military agencies, ones that employed several hundred civilian professionals throughout the 1940s.

9. NARA RG226 ai 146 b137 7-30-41.

10. William L. Langer, *In and Out of the Ivory Tower: The Autobiography of William L. Langer* (New York: Neale Watson Academic, 1977).

11. Jennifer Davis Heaps, "Tracking Intelligence Information: The Office of Strategic Services," *American Archivist* 61, no. 2 (Fall 1998): 287–308, esp. p. 290.

12. NARA RG226 ai 146 b137 7-30-41 re: Ernest C. Griffith.

13. LWL, Lewis Correspondence files; Herman W. Liebert, "Wilmarth Sheldon Lewis (1895–1979)," *Yale University Library Gazette* 54, no. 4 (April 1980): 198–200; Robin Winks, *Cloak & Gown: Scholars in the Secret War, 1939–1961* (New Haven, CT: Yale University Press, ca. 1996); Annie Burr Lewis, *Dancing on a Sunny Plain*; Wilmarth Sheldon Lewis, *One Man's Education* (New York: Knopf, 1967).

14. Winks, *Cloak & Gown*; LWL, MacLeish Correspondence file 6-3-42; Jennifer Davis Heaps, "Clio's Spies: The National Archives and the Office of Strategic Services in World War II," *Prologue* 30, no. 3 (Fall 1998): 195–207.

15. Bess Glenn, "The Taft Commission and the Government's Record Practices," *American Archivist* 21, no. 3 (July 1958): 277–303.

16. Geoffrey C. Bowker and Susan Leigh Star, *Sorting Things Out: Classification and Its Consequences* (Cambridge, MA: MIT Press, 1999), shows how classification systems have and do vary by needs and cultures.

17. Colin B. Burke, *Information and Intrigue* (Cambridge, MA: MIT Press, 2014); W. Boyd Rayward, *The Universe of Information: The Work of Paul Otlet for Documentation and International Organization* (Moscow: Published for International Federation for Documentation [FID] by All-Union Institute for Scientific and Technical Information [VINITI], 1975).

18. A. C. Foskett, *The Universal Decimal Classification: The History, Present Status and Future Prospects of a Large General Classification Scheme* (London: Linnet Books, 1973).

2

FORGING AN INTELLIGENCE SYSTEM

Wilmarth Lewis knew little of the existing government classification systems when he reached Washington in late August 1941, just four months before the intelligence debacle at Pearl Harbor. The organizational chart for his branch, the Central Information Division (CID), was not finalized and he was unsure what powers he had over the many different offices in Donovan's Coordinator of Information (COI) that were to gather and process intelligence information. He had less of a grasp on his power to obtain data from other government agencies. He knew he had responsibility for the COI's central group that was to handle reports to be used by the experts in the Research and Analysis group, but there was no certainty about his authority over the COI's branches that were to acquire photographs and films, gather maps, compile an international biographic database, and handle information coming from the censorship office. There was also the question of who was to supervise the envisioned traditional library for the use of the Research and Analysis group.

In September 1941, such organizational questions were not Wilmarth's major worries. He focused on the classification problem as he knew he was to be given a helper skilled in bureaucratic turf wars and in dealing with outside agencies. So Wilmarth felt ready to tackle the first item on his agenda, the creation of a classification and indexing system that could coordinate document-based intelligence-related information—at least for major reports such as those the Research and Analysis group would demand.

A GENTLEMAN'S INFORMATION TEAM

Archibald MacLeish had more than kept his promise to Wilmarth to find a Washington-wise bureaucrat. He located a man who thought like Wilmarth and who shared Wilmarth's culture. Lawrence Deems Egbert was a highly educated, cultured, and multilingual expert on international law and economics. He had Harvard University and University of Paris degrees and had taught international law at the university level. He had been the assistant to the law librarian at the Library of Congress, and had served on important governmental commissions. Although he had been only an enlisted man in World War I and had no intelligence experience, he was very bright and a quick study. After serving as Wilmarth's executive assistant at the COI and becoming his friend, Egbert went on to perform important duties at the 1945 Nuremberg trials, even acting as the translator for Justice Robert H. Jackson. Egbert then launched a distinguished career at the State Department and as a legal scholar.

Egbert was not the only member of Wilmarth's 1941 team who was highly educated and who shared his perspectives. Donovan had found two important regular military men to advise Wilmarth on the army's and navy's information systems and needs. Neither was an intelligence expert but both were familiar with intelligence systems and knew how to gain the cooperation of the armed services. Fortunately for Wilmarth, Colonel Frank Ross and Commander Francis Denebrink were not straitlaced martinets who took a condescending attitude toward civilians. Like Egbert, they became Wilmarth's companions and friends, as well as collaborators. Both became important to the war effort after they left the COI in late 1942 for front-line duties.

Wilmarth wanted the others on his first team to be intellectually compatible and to be easy to work with. That meant searching for more humanities-trained college men, not professional librarians, data managers, or tabulating machine experts. Wilmarth and MacLeish did find three men of their type (and of the breed of men on the Research and Analysis team) for the original classification-building group. George Young was the son of a Yale professor and received his undergraduate and history Ph.D. degrees at Yale and then, in 1939, began teaching at Columbia University's Barnard College. Hubert Howe Bancroft, relative of the famous California historian (Berkeley's great Bancroft Library was named after him), would have graduated from Stanford University with a history major but for a foolish mistake when he was twenty years old. He was arrested for reckless driving. He made some amends but did not return to the university. He then worked as a reporter on local newspapers for a few years, eventually securing a job as an editor and economics researcher at the Department of Agriculture in Washington, D.C. The third young man in Wilmarth's original band was Archibald MacLeish's son, Kenneth. The young MacLeish had been schooled in elite private schools and then graduated from Harvard where he did advanced work in anthropology with the illustrious Clyde Kluckhohn.

HUMANISTS FOR SURE AND A LIBRARIAN INCUBATOR FOR SOME, A MAYBE SPY

Lewis, his three young helpers, and the two military men wasted no time in tackling the information coordination challenge. They may have received some hints from one professional librarian, Jesse Shera, who was in the Library of Congress's Special Information unit at the time. Shera was not a typical vocationally trained librarian. He was of the same academic and intellectual culture as Wilmarth's crew. After gaining his undergraduate degree at Miami University in Ohio, he earned a master's degree in history and literature at Yale in 1927. Needing some income, he took a temporary job in Miami University's library and then spent more than a decade as a researcher, librarian, and bibliographer at the Scripps Institute in Ohio, helping with major research projects on population and demographics. At the same time, Shera began building an impressive record of publications about library matters—but not about narrow technical issues, partly because he was searching for a position as an English instructor. He became a prolific author of academic works even though he was blind in one eye, had a total sight of 22 percent, and had strabismus, a rather off-putting malady that causes the eyes not to seem to be looking in the same direction. Shera took a temporary break in 1938 to finally seek a library degree—but of a very, very special type. He entered the University of Chicago's Ph.D. program in library science, one that was more philosophical and sociological than technical. Fittingly, Shera's doctoral research would be broadly historical. The Chicago connection and his work at Scripps led him to gain, finally, a well-paying job. In 1940, before completing his dissertation, he was hired by the innovative international census (demographic) project at the Library of Congress.

A year later he was shifted to the COI-related Special Information Division. The near-seamless relationship between the library and the COI soon put him in close touch with Wilmarth Lewis. Shera supervised much secret research at the library and, in January 1943 after an increase in Wilmarth's budget, he brought Shera into the COI's new incarnation, the Office of Strategic Services, to lead its library research unit. By then, Lewis had already become Shera's mentor and would become a lifelong friend.

There were other unusual librarians who played a significant part in the history of Donovan's information efforts and who, like Jesse Shera, became highly influential librarians who reshaped science information systems during the Cold War's years. One was Vernon Tate, who had a University of California Ph.D. in history. His microfilm facilities at the National Archives became a major resource for Donovan's men. Another nontypical librarian was Frederick Kilgour, a Harvard graduate in chemistry who drifted into a library microfilming project at Harvard and then became a leader in one of Donovan's organizations, the Interdepartmental Committee for the Acquisition of Foreign Publications (IDC). It was secretly acquiring foreign documents at a rate of some 270,000 pages a year, including such important items as guides to minefields in Japanese waters. It cooperated with Britain in securing copies of Germany's published science books and journals.[1] The next librarian was John H. Ottemiller. He worked under Kilgour at the IDC as its chief of analysis and abstracting. Like Kilgour, he became a Yale University librarian—although he had only a bachelor of science degree in librarianship, not a Ph.D. Another librarian (with a doctorate in physical geography) became very important to science information after the war. Burton Adkinson led the map sections at the Library of Congress and, then, at the Office of Strategic Services (OSS). He later headed the National Science Foundation's science information program. There was a fifth unusual librarian, Philip Keeney. He worked in the COI's library for published materials. He did not have much contact with Wilmarth Lewis, but in later years the revelation that he was a Communist and a

FORGING AN INTELLIGENCE SYSTEM

Soviet "source" proved another embarrassment for Donovan's organization.[2]

INNOCENTS IN CLASSIFICATION

Despite having those professional librarians in the COI, all the significant work on the first new COI classification-indexing system was done by Lewis and his three nonlibrarian helpers. They worked hard and within less than a year had created what they believed was a groundbreaking classification and information retrieval system—one, Wilmarth declared, that avoided the shortcomings of those created by "librarians" like Melvil Dewey.[3] Wilmarth and his military advisors were so pleased with their progress they returned to a more scholarly-like pace, often retreating to Wilmarth's office to "blacken their pipes" and discuss world affairs. Meanwhile, Egbert and the other new Central Information Division's managers began recruiting a staff of classifiers and data clerks, ones with high intelligence and foreign language skills.

With the completion of the classification the original tight-knit group dispersed. Kenneth MacLeish went to active naval duty. George Young joined the navy but remained within the COI. Assigned to new duties, he later became an integral part of the new management team of the Office of Strategic Services. Hubert Bancroft moved to the Office of Emergency Management. Wilmarth remained as the Central Information Division's chief but his attention turned to establishing a London branch of the division, to leading a rescue mission to rebuild Peru's national library, and to a new high-status advisory committee he had formed to help Archibald MacLeish turn the Library of Congress into a social force. That committee's goals seemed so important to Wilmarth that he asked for and gained permission to work on the Library of Congress project during many afternoons. Wilmarth was especially proud to have hosted 1942's meeting of the nation's library leaders who devised the Farmington Plan, a sharing agreement among libraries to ensure America had at least one copy of all significant foreign publications.[4]

DEWEY, MOSTLY NO—

Wilmarth was also proud of the uniqueness of the COI's 1942 Central Information Division's classification and retrieval system for the center's main files. It was different from any other, although not quite deserving of the term "revolutionary." After the center began receiving top secret materials, separate files and systems were created for them. Only specially cleared personnel were allowed access to those most secret collections.

Wilmarth's system was not mechanized in any way, either for input or retrieval. It used stock paper index cards, storing them in typical containers, with only a few tabs in a file to ease locating a particular card. As well, there was only one copy of the index to the files and it was in the COI's offices. The system's guide was even less revolutionary and less helpful to users than Melvil Dewey's early guide, the Relativ Index. The COI's guide seems to have been done in such a hurry that it was more of a collection of reminders to those who had created the system than a resource for new staff members.

The COI's main system was unique but not intellectually elegant, and it was not a reflection of Donovan's dream of an independent intelligence role for the COI. As expected, it had been impossible to match concepts or the identifier numbers in the COI classification with those in other schemes, such as those of the Office of Naval Intelligence and the army. The navy for example, used 400 for Industrial and Industrial Relations; the COI's closest category was 2 for Economics. Costly reinterpretation and reindexing of incoming documents was inescapable.

Of importance, the system was slanted to the needs of those forming high-level policy, although to a degree it anticipated the information needs of those engaged in covert operations. Important to Wilmarth, and to the other designers of the COI's system, it avoided using complex hierarchies, long identifiers, and the unfamiliar terminology of most Dewey-like systems.

AS WE, BUT PERHAPS NOT YOU, MAY THINK

Wilmarth Lewis did not know Vannevar Bush, but he and Bush shared a common dislike of traditional libraries and their methods. Bush, who began his career as an engineering instructor at the Massachusetts Institute of Technology (MIT), progressed to become perhaps the most powerful man in the history of American science and technology. He rose to head the powerful grant-dispensing Carnegie Institution of Washington, D.C., in 1938. In 1940, he gained much more power. He convinced President Roosevelt to create a new government organization to coordinate, guide, and fund defense-related scientific and technological research in universities. Within a year, Bush became more influential when his National Defense Research Committee became the cash-rich Office of Scientific Research and Development (OSRD). Work on OSRD projects forever altered faculty and administration expectations about funding and career paths. It was a major force in creating what became known as big science and what became known as an entrepreneurial university.

Since the 1930s Bush had been expressing his dislike of librarians' methods and their old information technologies. While at MIT he began work on his Rapid Selector, an ultra-high-speed microfilm machine he believed would replace the library card catalog and the hierarchal organization of information. He also began sketching his ideas for a personal version of the Selector, calling it the Memex. At the same time, he was developing his own classification and indexing concepts, "associations." He waited until the end of World War II to publish his "As We May Think," an article that became legendary in information science and brought international attention to idea of his associations.[5]

There were many ideas in that July 1945 article, but the one that became foundational was his call for replacement of indexing and specialized classification with individual readers creating links from one item to another, thus avoiding the need for all the complex numbers and specialized terms imposed by others (librarians) in traditional systems. Unfortunately, Bush was never specific as to the definition of "association," and he never confronted an obvious and serious problem. The "we" he had in mind might well have special and unique ways of thinking, making retrieval of information more difficult for others than when using the systems librarians had based on what they believed were universal concepts and terms. As a result, Bush-like systems had a rather ironic potential: they could become systems that "thought as we, but not you."

WILMARTH'S WAY OF THINKING

Wilmarth Lewis may not have known of the proposals for advanced information systems such as Bush's, but he developed his own version of "as we may think" in 1941 as he and his team sought to avoid using the strange language of Dewey-like systems. They did not do anything as radical as creating a system based on associations, or tags, or footnote references (à la the later Science Citation Index) but they went far toward creating a non-Dewey system.

They did it by devising a unique blend of approaches. They chose a combination of a method of shallow rather than deep numeric classification; they relied more upon subject terms than did other systems; and, their classifications and subject terms were based on the concepts and vocabulary of intelligence analysts, not on universal terms and concepts. As well, despite intelligence work requiring the integration of individual facts, Wilmarth and his team decided that it was better to have general terms and short numeric identifiers that pointed to rather large groups of reports (information items) than long ones that brought a user to a fact.

The "we" Wilmarth seems to have had in mind were the strategic thinkers in William Langer's intellectually high-powered Research and Analysis group, not the analysts preparing reports. That short-identifier decision fit with another feature of Wilmarth's system. The COI's materials were to be labeled, stored, and retrieved by a serial number rather than, as in a Dewey system, by the numeric subject identifiers (call numbers). Wilmarth and, later, those who used "term" systems were not concerned that a serial-number system scattered similar documents over the shelves and file cabinets of a library, unlike a Dewey system that grouped like documents together.

So, instead of seven to a dozen digits, the Central Information Division's (CID) system used no more than four to point to subjects of interest. There were only a few general categories, and the number of subdivisions in any one category was quite limited. The basic classifications very rarely went to any depth and the system was not completely decimal (hierarchal). The CID's system had a rudimentary and (incomplete) hierarchal organization, with seven, not ten, highest-level categories.

The seven categories Wilmarth chose reflected the pressures to serve immediate needs and the politics of intelligence information rather than a desire to create a fully integrated and comprehensive information system for an independent intelligence agency. The CID's classification reflected an uncomfortable fact: Donovan's information branch was serving the military branches and the State Department as much or more than it was serving the COI.

The seven highest-level categories were:

0 General
1 Political
2 Economic
3 Military
4 Naval
5 Aviation
6 Psychological and Sociological
7 Subversive and Counter Subversive

The subdivisions in each category were few and they were frequently uneven in the range of items they pointed to. For example, the 0 category had nine subdivisions, ranging from the very broad 0.15 Individuals: Generals, Politicians, Diplomats, Businessmen, to, 0.16 League of Nations, and to the very narrow 0.21 View of New Zealand Government Controlling A—Energy. In the 2 category subdivisions, 2.16 covered all Transportation and Communication, while 2.17, Industry, had one subordinate (2.17.1), Power and Light. Power and Light's special attention was probably because power systems were valued targets for bombing raids and saboteurs. Reflecting Donovan's hopes for his own covert operations, category 7, Subversive and Counter Subversive, had numerous subdivisions.

The press of time on Wilmarth's small team and the then current concepts of warfare are indicated by what was missing. There was no general category for science and technology. Wilmarth's customers had not yet realized that war had become scientific. Later, America's Cold War intelligence agencies realized that, and their systems had to devote much special attention to science and scientists, especially those related to atomic energy and ballistics. Arguably, the Central Intelligence Agency and the air force's intelligence units became "the" science watchers in America after World War II.

PAPER CARDS AND NUMBERS, OK, SUBJECT TERMS FOR SURE, ABSOLUTELY ABSTRACTS

Something else was missing in Wilmarth's system: technological innovation. His system was built on the then somewhat old-fashioned paper index card. Later in the war some tabulating machines would be used—but only for a few of the OSS's files.

Wilmarth and his team did not worry that sparse indexing would make retrieval of information too costly and time consuming because they devised what they believed were sensible alternatives to long Dewey numbers. They had great faith in the use of what they called "subject terms," such as Japan–Chemical, or Abbas Hilmi–Egypt, and they created three versions of the card file to ease retrieval. One copy was arranged (sorted) by name, one by subject, and the third by country. The subject identifiers played a very subordinate role. They were used as secondary items to arrange cards within each name, subject, or country. Another technique they relied upon was a very generous policy of multiple classifications of a document. The many classifications led to very large card files, however. One investigation reported an average of eight cards per incoming document, and by mid-1943 just the main file contained more than 350,000 cards. By the end of the war the branch's combined files contained over three million cards.[6]

Although Lewis had great faith in his alphabetic subject-term system, it was not even as orderly as the subject terms used by the Library of Congress. Because the terms were selected to reflect immediate interests, it was impossible to logically group them or to record them sensibly in the system's guide. Yet, those alphabetic terms, like Czechoslovakia—Silk, fit the needs, concepts, and vocabulary of Donovan's researchers and their military customers.

WILMARTH'S BELOVED ABSTRACT SYSTEM'S LIMITATIONS

The innovation that Wilmarth believed provided the critical path to efficient and precise document retrieval was his summaries of documents (abstracts). He called them "précis." Abstracts had not been used with most formal classification and indexing systems, but he thought they were the only sensible means of allowing researchers to decide whether to call for a document. Wilmarth was half-right in putting so much faith in his précis. Abstracts saved indexing effort, but they were a burden on Wilmarth's division. Every indexer was expected to read a document, assign one or more of the general classifications, and then compose and type a short summary of the contents of the document on the index cards.[7]

Composing those abstracts called for as much, sometimes more, knowledge and skill than assigning the numeric identifiers—and usually much more time. To be useful, a précis had to contain all the important items in a document. That called for knowledge of countries, people, events, and technologies. So, Wilmarth's indexers had to be well educated, skilled, and energetic writers—not just clerks. When the flow of documents into Wilmarth's OSS section increased (estimates for mid-1942 range well over twelve thousand a month), composing abstracts proved a block to processing by some thirty indexers. Serious backlogs developed.

YOU DON'T THINK AS WE, WILMARTH—A BABBLE OF TONGUES

There was another classification problem at the COI's information center. It is uncertain whether it was caused by poor management, the inability of Wilmarth's classifications to work for other than the documentary reports, or just the impossibility of one system handling all types of intelligence information. Whatever the reasons, the COI developed its own babble of classification tongues, despite the organization being mandated to coordinate information. The COI soon became burdened with separate systems for maps, pictures, films, items from the censorship office, and biographic data and for the books and serials in

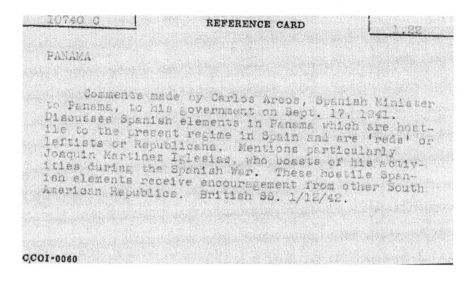

Figure 2.1. COI Abstract Card NARA RG226

its growing traditional library. None of those classification systems shared a common language or structure, and some proved to be very inadequate.

The thirty biographic researchers who were building a file on politically prominent foreign nationals had gathered thirty thousand biographies—indexing only by country name and personal name seemed adequate for their biographical file. No samples of the initial classification system for the COI-OSS's huge collection of films and pictures have been located, but Wilmarth Lewis's comments on it reveal that it was not integrated with his reports' system and that it was so hastily designed that it became useless. It would take a major reworking in 1943 and 1944 to make the almost three hundred thousand photos accessible. The COI's methods for its traditional library remain unknown. It is known the library grew very quickly, had a large staff (twenty-five in 1943), and held a large collection. One estimate gave fifty thousand books and 350,000 journal items by the war's end. The Library of Congress's system was not applied and it is certain Wilmarth's reports' classifications would not have been able to effectively organize or retrieve books and articles.

MAPS AND CENSORS AND OVERLOAD

In contrast, information exists on two other COI-OSS systems. Both were based on deep indexing. They were developed for maps and for materials from the censorship office. Neither relied on, nor was integrated with, Wilmarth's system. In contrast to the reports, maps were intensely indexed. There was a fundamental technical (subject-matter) reason for the map system (eventually indexing some 2.5 million pages) being different.[8] The COI-OSS's group of academic geographers, and the librarian-administrator Burton Adkinson, already knew that no existing classification system, even the special ones of the army or the Library of Congress, or those of geographic societies, could manage the wide range of materials to be gathered from around the world—many times by covert means. Some of the COI's geographers had begun studying the map classification problem since the 1930s after it had been demonstrated that traditional hierarchal systems did not and could not provide the detail needed for effective information retrieval from map collections.[9]

As a result, the COI's geographers created a system that was very detailed and that was more like an aspect or colon system than a hierarchal or even a subject-term system. In such aspect systems, items are indexed and retrieved by sets of characteristics (place, date, color, size, etc.) rather than by a classification (call) number or just a few broad subject terms. Necessarily, the cards in the map indexing files were quite detailed and did not look much like a typical index card. As well, the terms and concepts and abbreviations were unique, not matching those in Wilmarth's system. The map group was quite pleased with its work, but by 1944 its members found a need to mechanize the system, which meant a redoing of some of their classifications.

The COI's maps required a unique system, but another collection could have been, but was not, integrated with Wilmarth's in terms of vocabulary, depth of indexing, or identifiers. Wilmarth was, however, quite proud of the COI's classification methods for the organization's censorship office materials. He lauded it as the only good index for intercepted letters and cables in the nation, perhaps the world.

With the United States' independent censorship office understaffed, Donovan had agreed to take on the job of ensuring that the bits of information in the thousands of intercepts could be accessed by all

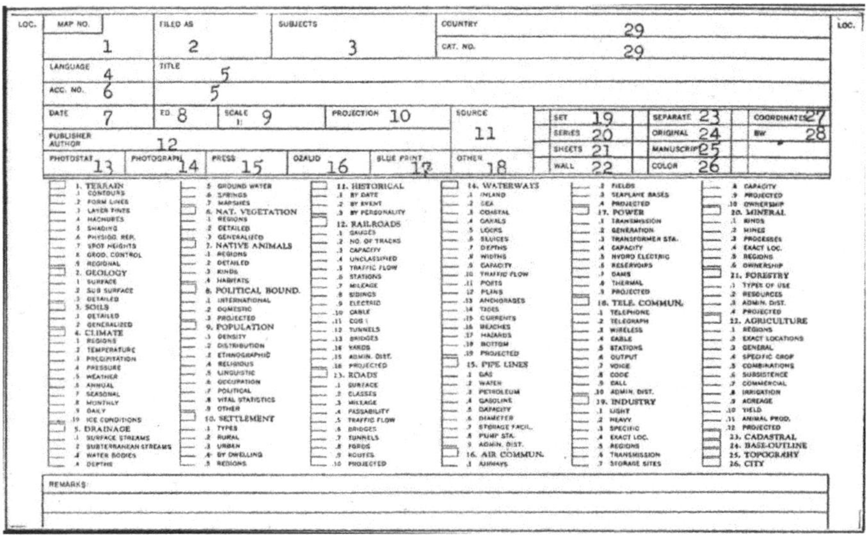
LOC. | MAP NO. 1 | FILED AS 2 | SUBJECTS 3 | COUNTRY 29 | CAT. NO. 29 | LOC.
LANGUAGE 4 | TITLE 5
ACC. NO. 6 | 5
DATE 7 | ED. 8 | SCALE 1: 9 | PROJECTION 10 | SOURCE 11
PUBLISHER AUTHOR 12
PHOTOSTAT 13 | PHOTOGRAPH 14 | PRESS 15 | OZALID 16 | BLUE PRINT 17 | OTHER 18
SET 19 | SERIES 20 | SHEETS 21 | WALL 22
SEPARATE 23 | ORIGINAL 24 | MANUSCRIPT 25 | COLOR 26
COORDINATES 27 | BW 28

1. TERRAIN .1 CONTOURS .2 FORM LINES .3 LAYER TINTS .4 HACHURES .5 SHADING .6 PHYSIOG. REP. .7 SPOT HEIGHTS .8 GEOD. CONTROL .9 REGIONAL
2. GEOLOGY .1 SURFACE .2 SUB SURFACE .3 DETAILED
3. SOILS .1 DETAILED .2 GENERALIZED
4. CLIMATE .1 REGIONS .2 TEMPERATURE .3 PRECIPITATION .4 PRESSURE .5 WEATHER .6 ANNUAL .7 SEASONAL .8 MONTHLY .9 DAILY .10 ICE CONDITIONS
5. DRAINAGE .1 SURFACE STREAMS .2 SUBTERRANEAN STREAMS .3 WATER BODIES .4 DEPTHS .5 GROUND WATER .6 SPRINGS .7 MARSHES
6. NAT. VEGETATION .1 REGIONS .2 DETAILED .3 GENERALIZED
7. NATIVE ANIMALS .1 REGIONS .2 DETAILED .3 KINDS .4 HABITATS
8. POLITICAL BOUND. .1 INTERNATIONAL .2 DOMESTIC .3 PROJECTED
9. POPULATION .1 DENSITY .2 DISTRIBUTION .3 ETHNOGRAPHIC .4 RELIGIOUS .5 LINGUISTIC .6 OCCUPATION .7 POLITICAL .8 VITAL STATISTICS .9 OTHER
10. SETTLEMENT .1 TYPES .2 RURAL .3 URBAN .4 BY DWELLING .5 REGIONS
11. HISTORICAL .1 BY DATE .2 BY EVENT .3 BY PERSONALITY
12. RAILROADS .1 GAUGES .2 NO. OF TRACKS .3 CAPACITY .4 UNCLASSIFIED .5 TRAFFIC FLOW .6 STATIONS .7 MILEAGE .8 SIDINGS .9 ELECTRIC .10 CABLE .11 COG .12 TUNNELS .13 BRIDGES .14 YARDS .15 ADMIN. DIST. .16 PROJECTED
13. ROADS .1 SURFACE .2 CLASSES .3 MILEAGE .4 PASSABILITY .5 TRAFFIC FLOW .6 BRIDGES .7 TUNNELS .8 FORDS .9 ROUTES .10 PROJECTED
14. WATERWAYS .1 INLAND .2 SEA .3 COASTAL .4 CANALS .5 LOCKS .6 SLUICES .7 DEPTHS .8 WIDTHS .9 CAPACITY .10 TRAFFIC FLOW .11 PORTS .12 PLANS .13 ANCHORAGES .14 TIDES .15 CURRENTS .16 BEACHES .17 HAZARDS .18 BOTTOM .19 PROJECTED
15. PIPE LINES .1 GAS .2 WATER .3 PETROLEUM .4 GASOLINE .5 CAPACITY .6 DIAMETER .7 STORAGE FACIL. .8 PUMP STA. .9 ADMIN. DIST.
16. AIR COMMUN. .1 AIRWAYS .2 FIELDS .3 SEAPLANE BASES .4 PROJECTED
17. POWER .1 TRANSMISSION .2 GENERATION .3 TRANSFORMER STA. .4 CAPACITY .5 HYDRO ELECTRIC .6 RESERVOIRS .7 DAMS .8 THERMAL .9 PROJECTED
18. TELE. COMMUN. .1 TELEPHONE .2 TELEGRAPH .3 WIRELESS .4 CABLE .5 STATIONS .6 OUTPUT .7 VOICE .8 CODE .9 CALL .10 ADMIN. DIST.
19. INDUSTRY .1 LIGHT .2 HEAVY .3 SPECIFIC .4 EXACT LOC. .5 REGIONS .6 TRANSMISSION .7 STORAGE SITES .8 CAPACITY .9 PROJECTED .10 OWNERSHIP
20. MINERAL .1 KINDS .2 MINES .3 PROCESSES .4 EXACT LOC. .5 REGIONS .6 OWNERSHIP
21. FORESTRY .1 TYPES OF USE .2 RESOURCES .3 ADMIN. DIST. .4 PROJECTED
22. AGRICULTURE .1 REGIONS .2 EXACT LOCATIONS .3 GENERAL .4 SPECIFIC CROP .5 COMBINATIONS .6 SUBSISTENCE .7 COMMERCIAL .8 IRRIGATION .9 ACREAGE .10 YIELD .11 ANIMAL PROD. .12 PROJECTED
23. CADASTRAL
24. BASE-OUTLINE
25. TOPOGRAPHY
26. CITY
REMARKS:

Figure 2.2. COI-OSS Map System Card NARA RG226

analysts in the intelligence community. The task was assigned to Wilmarth's office, and by 1943 twenty indexers were using a hierarchal system that indexed by country and by as many as six digits for subjects. The systems' type of organization suggests that it was created by a traditional librarian, but although Jesse Shera once remarked that he worked on the censorship problem, the creator remains unknown. The subjects of interest for the censorship materials were the same as those in the reports system but used different terms and groupings. For example, Wilmarth used one category for Psychological and Sociological (6, with few subdivisions). It was so encompassing that it included such things as "radio reception." In contrast, the censorship system used two main categories (200 and 500), for just the Morale and Sociological topics, each with many subdivisions.

The lack of integration of the various sections within the COI was perhaps due to Wilmarth's Central Information Division taking on too many tasks too quickly. That overload problem was compounded. In 1942 another new group, the Documents Intelligence Section, was established and placed under the CID. Its assignments were to gather and organize all the "cover" documents needed by covert agents working in foreign, even enemy, nations.

THE BIG CHANCE FOR "AS WE ALL MAY THINK," AN INTEGRATED INTELLIGENCE DATABASE DREAM

There soon was a greater challenge and opportunity for Wilmarth's division and its reports system. In late 1942, after the COI became the OSS and received more money and much greater supervision by the military's Joint Chiefs of Staff, a request (order?) from General George V. Strong, the head of army intelligence, arrived at the Central Information Division. Strong wanted Wilmarth to build and maintain one central index for all army, navy, and OSS intelligence-related documents.

The request was somewhat ironic because Strong had been one of the most active opponents of Donovan's two organizations, the COI and the OSS. Even the newly expanded powers of the military over the OSS had not fully satisfied Strong.[10] For example, just a few months before he issued his integrated index request, Strong made Donovan shut down his radio-intercept/codebreaking facilities at Bellmore, New York, and Reseda, California, because they impinged on the army's codebreaking turf. In February 1942, Strong went much further. Reflecting his and the State Department's distrust of Donovan's organization, he secretly established his and the State Department's own espionage and covert action organization. Part of its mandate was to keep a watch on the OSS's Communist ties. Commonly called the Pond, it was led by Colonel John V. "Frenchy" Grombach, who later fed information about Communists to the House Un-American Activities Committee and to Joseph McCarthy, as well as to those opposed to the postwar successor to the OSS, the Central Intelligence Agency.[11]

Given General Strong's distrust of the OSS and the information he was receiving about its penetration by fellow travelers and perhaps Soviet agents, it remains a puzzle as to why he asked the OSS to handle so much more intelligence information in late 1942.[12]

In September 1942, Wilmarth Lewis knew nothing of Grombach, the Pond, or the accusations about Communists in the OSS. On his way to London with other top-level Donovan men to establish better relations with Britain's intelligence services, Wilmarth signaled General Strong of his willingness to take on the responsibility for the massive database implied in Strong's communications. Busy preparing for the trip to England, he handed the responsibility for negotiations with Strong and the Joint Chiefs of Staff over to Lawrence Egbert. A very tactful bureaucratic, but a perhaps financially naïve administrator, Egbert immediately followed through. He wrote to General Strong that the Central Information Division was ready to take on the job and that it already had the nation's best classification and indexing system with a staff that had a year's experience in dealing with all types of intelligence materials. He did not immediately request a significant budget increase from the Joint Chiefs although he and Wilmarth foresaw a vast expansion of the amount of information they would have to process if Strong meant what he said. While having great faith in their newly developed reports system, Egbert and Wilmarth also knew they might have to modify it to make it "think" more like everyone in the intelligence community thought to gain its acceptance.[13]

How far the negotiations went is unknown, as is how many new documents flowed into the center. How much was invested in remaking Wilmarth's reports system into "the" answer to the classification coordination problem is also unknown. There seems to have been no major changes to the system's structure or terminology, and the army and navy (and the State Department) did not change their systems. There also is no sign of a major increase in the Central Information Division's budgets. It would not be until the Cold War unleashed torrents of money, and when the more powerful Central Intelligence Agency was created, that a significant attempt to create and impose a universal intelligence information classification appeared.

THE END OF A GENTLEMAN'S INFORMATION CULTURE?

It is certain that by the time Egbert indicated willingness to assume the workload implied in Strong's request the Central Information Division was already overburdened and facing serious problems. Documents were lost because they were being given to analysts before they were indexed. Those documents were not returned. Sometimes reports were never logged into the system. As serious, indexers and abstractors in

Washington were falling behind. Delayed processing of information that usually had a short useful life span was leading to complaints from researchers. The problems went deeper. The huge section in New York City that was gathering pictures, films, and maps seemed especially dysfunctional. There were heated complaints from the military that pictures and maps needed for the planning of the invasion of North Africa were not reaching their men.

Tensions were also mounting inside the Central Information Division's indexing group. Personal frictions were developing and they increased as the reshaping of the COI into the military-controlled OSS led to new types of men being assigned to Wilmarth's group. The days of the humanities-educated gentlemen seemed to be ending. With changes in personnel, especially at the managerial levels, a new culture was emerging. People seemed to be competing for power, even undermining Wilmarth's authority. There was also a change of pace. Retreating to offices to discuss world affairs became unacceptable. As well, the old campus-like informal relationships among the staff were being replaced by more efficient ones between boss and worker and between officer and enlisted man.

Wilmarth became frustrated and dissatisfied, even experiencing what, for him, was anger. Within less than a year the old group was no more. Lawrence Egbert and Wilmarth Lewis left with bitter feelings, soon followed by Jesse Shera.

There was one bright spot, however. By almost chance a new man had appeared. He wasn't of Wilmarth's social or educational background, he had no intelligence experience, and he was not an engineer or efficiency expert as were others among the new arrivals. As well, he came to Washington at a moment of personal crisis. Yet, he became a close lifetime friend of Wilmarth's, he brought modern technology to the CID, and he became a resource for much of the intelligence community.

John Langan also made a critical contribution to the grandest information technology hope of the era: microfilm. He invented a means for changing the unruly microfilm on rolls that frustrated Vannevar Bush's engineers into a useful memory device.

NOTES

1. On the cooperative effort with England, see, for example, Pamela Spence Richards, "Aslib at War: The Brief but Intrepid Career of a Library Organization as a Hub of Allied Scientific Intelligence, 1942–1945," *Journal of Education for Library and Information Science* 29, no. 4 (Spring 1989): 279–96.

2. Rosalie McReynolds and Louise S. Robbins, *The Librarian Spies: Philip and Mary Jane Kenney and Cold War Espionage* (Westport, CT: Praeger, 2009).

3. NARA RG226 ai 146 b137.

4. LWL, Lewis–MacLeish Correspondence file 6-3-42.

5. James M. Nyce and Paul Kahn, eds., *From Memex to Hypertext: Vannevar Bush and the Mind's Machine* (Boston: Academic Press, 1991).

6. Jennifer Davis Heaps, "Tracking Intelligence Information: The Office of Strategic Services," *American Archivist* 61, no. 2 (Fall 1998): 287–308.

7. The army also used an abstract system for some of its intelligence files; see NARA RG165 entry 58.

8. Leonard S. Wilson, "Lessons from the Experience of the Map Information Section, OSS," *Geographical Review* 39, no. 2 (April 1949): 298–310.

9. S. Whitmore Bogg, "Library Classification and Cataloging of Geographic Material," *Annals of the Association of American Geographers* 27, no. 2 (June 1937): 49–93.

10. NARA RG226 as 146 b137 9-24-42, Egbert memorandum.

11. FBI FOIA NO.1119956-000, John "Valantin" Grombach, release date 2-27-2015; NARA n.d. RG263, Records of the Grombach Organization ("The Pond"), esp. series 12.

12. Michael Warner, "Salvage and Liquidation," CIA Library, April 15, 2007, updated June 27, 2008, https://www.cia.gov/library/center-for-the-study-of-intelligence/csi-publications/csi-studies/studies/96unclass/salvage-and-liquidation.html.

13. NARA RG226 ai 146 b137 9-42, Egbert to Baxter; and 8-24-42, Egbert re: Strong request.

3

A NEW INFORMATION CULTURE

When the military's Joint Chiefs of Staff gained supervisory control over the Office of the Coordinator of Information (COI) in June 1942 and renamed it the Office of Strategic Services (OSS), Wild Bill Donovan acquired a much larger budget, a go-ahead for most of his covert operations, and the power to request that military personnel be assigned to his organization. In return, the military demanded, and achieved, oversight of his operations. That included more than just suggestions of who he should employ and how the business of intelligence information should be conducted. New men, with new attitudes and new types of social and cultural backgrounds, began to be assigned to the Central Information Division (CID) just as Wilmarth Lewis was struggling to solve a serious problem in the OSS's New York City branch, and as he was trying to ease the strains caused by the growing workload at the main Washington, D.C., offices of the CID.

The problems in the New York City center were especially serious and were embarrassing to Donovan, as well as to Wilmarth who had recently been ordered to supervise it. The center had a strange beginning and history. One of the obligations Donovan had accepted in 1941 was to supplement the military's picture archives of both still and moving pictures. Pictures or film clips of any town or landscape the Allies might bomb, invade, or penetrate with covert operatives were invaluable. Atherton Richards, one of Wild Bill's old friends and a dollar-a-year COI advisor, had assured Donovan that he could build a visual media operation that could access and organize photos and films obtained from the public, as well as from movie companies, news services, and publishers. Richards also had a vision of a futuristic strategic briefing complex for America's leaders.

He presented his ideas for what was called the Presentation Branch in 1941, then stepped back and returned to his role as a high-level advisor and secret overseas operator for Donovan—and with one of the highest salaries of anyone in the well-paying OSS.[1] Richards did not need the money. He was independently wealthy, very much so. He was heir to and protector of the great agricultural and trading interests begun in the early nineteenth century by the families of the first American Protestant missionaries to Hawaii. Richards was not, however, one of the idle rich. Despite his many pretentions, such as living in the most elite New York City hotels during and after World War II, he was always engaged in important activities.

After coming to the mainland, graduating from Wesleyan University in 1915, and serving in the army, he returned to Hawaii. He worked hard and became a major figure in banking, utilities, and international commercial agriculture. His business interests were not confined to Hawaii, however. He was active in the United States. For example, he was on the board of directors of the Intercontinental Hotels Corporation and he ran the Fijelen Research Corporation, which invested in developing innovative technologies.[2] Richards also seems to have always been in touch with America's intelligence agencies and of course, influential American bankers. He often visited the United States on business, becoming known as the Pineapple King after his successful campaign to convince the American public that pineapple was not only an exotic but healthful food. His entrepreneurial drive never stopped, nor did his search for labor-saving inventions for agriculture. In short, Richards was a rich, powerful, innovative, and influential man.

Richards's influence with Donovan and his range of prewar social contacts (including Merian Cooper, the onetime intelligence officer and director of the famous *King Kong* film) was reflected in the generous budget and staffing for the Presentation Branch's Pictorial Records Section established in New York City in 1942 (with a secondary office in Washington).[3] Two hundred people were hired for the New York center, picked by what Wilmarth Lewis described as "journalists on the fringe of the movie magazine world."[4] Besides having a staff larger than Wilmarth's Washington-based CID, the Pictures section had a more

A NEW INFORMATION CULTURE   39

generous annual budget: $10 million.[5] The staff solicited pictures and postcards from the public and persuaded publishers and film companies to open their archives. They also dealt with materials sent by the OSS's agents and by the military.

At first glance, the Pictorial group's efforts seemed an overwhelming success. Hundreds of thousands of photos and postcards were received each month. That, however, was a deceptive indicator. Many, perhaps most, of the items were worthless. The time required to weed them out was interfering with the group's main assignments to develop a classification system for pictorial information, efficiently organize the materials, quickly respond to requests for specific items, and find ways to reproduce items with the image fidelity required to make the copies of photos and maps useful.

Unfortunately, the New York center was not meeting any of those goals. Wilmarth was receiving complaints from the military that the photo group's classification and indexing system (developed in New York without coordinating with Wilmarth's report system, or with the OSS's Map Information Section)[6] did not, could not, guide anyone to desired materials. There was more. Pictures were stacked in piles on the center's floor with no one knowing quite sure where an item might be located. After items were found, there were further problems. Preparing copies was one of them. Although Wilmarth had hired the innovative photographic and microfilm experts Dudley Parker Lee and Richard W. Batchelder, and had made arrangements with Vernon Tate, the highly regarded microfilm and reproduction expert at the National Archives and Library of Congress, the pace and cost of production, as well as the quality of copies, remained seriously deficient.[7]

Wilmarth thought the fundamental weakness at the Times Square facility was the workforce's attitudes. He evaluated the staff as lacking devotion, as well as skill, and told one friend that the head of the branch never missed a Broadway theater matinee.[8] By early 1943, Wilmarth was convinced something had to be done. He consulted William Langer who agreed that much of the center's work was superfluous and allowed Wilmarth to cut the staff to ten, to slash the overall budget to one-fifth of what it had been, and to shift most of the work to Washington and its twenty-three Pictures section employees.[9]

WILMARTH'S FRUSTRATIONS

The problems in the other departments in Wilmarth's center were not as serious as those in New York City, but they were embarrassing and stressful. The workload was growing without a significant increase in line personnel. The reports' indexers/abstractors continued to be behind in their work. The censorship office was overwhelmed and had to stop publishing its bulletin advising other agencies of what it had discovered. The biographic group was going full steam but seemed to be unable to justify the worth of its thousands of biographies.

One of the difficulties was that special emergency projects often pulled critical CID employees away from their regular work. Jesse Shera, for example, had to travel to Philadelphia on a special mission although his research group was short-handed. In a clever solution to the search for possible contacts in occupied Europe, he had been sent with a microfilming team to mine the records of one of the most important international relief organizations of World War I. The Quakers' American Friends Service Committee had continued its European relief work well after the end of the war and its well-kept files seemed a possible gold mine of information. They proved to be valuable—but any time off from regular duties in Washington added to the backlogs and to the growing number of complaints from the military's and the OSS's analysts. [10]

NEW KIDS ON WILMARTH'S BLOCK

The challenges at the CID included more than the number of workers. There were new cultural differences, ones that added to Wilmarth's distress. Although short of clerical staff and researchers, Wilmarth discovered he had been assigned two new managers (in addition to Lawrence Egbert), ones he had not had an opportunity to approve. They came labeled as branch chiefs and were listed as under Wilmarth's direction, but he soon realized they were not quite his subordinates. As well, they were different types of people than he, Shera, Egbert, or the young men who had helped him create the reports classification system in 1941.

A NEW INFORMATION CULTURE

The two early 1943 arrivals were William Applebaum and Louis Ream. Both were college men—but ones with life experiences and perspectives distinct from Wilmarth's or Shera's. Applebaum was Russian born, coming as a teenager with his family to live in the then small town of Spokane, Washington. After high school, the trilingual young man chose to attend the University of Minnesota, but had to take leave from the college for two years because of family and personal needs. He persevered, however, going on to earn a Ph.D. in geography at Minnesota (with an economics minor) in 1933, at the old age of twenty-seven. Although his parents had been naturalized in the 1920s, for safety, he became a naturalized citizen in 1941.

Applebaum's college education, outlook, and career were not like Wilmarth's. Applebaum was a practical and business-oriented man. That, not the Great Depression that caused such high unemployment in academia, led him to use his applied geographic knowledge in business. He worked in the new grocery supermarket industry and applied the tools of statistical geography to marketing. He became a rather well-paid expert in store location and administrative techniques. Although deeply oriented to the business world, he remained in contact with academic geographers. When Donovan's men called out for help from the college geographers' association in May 1942 Applebaum was recruited to be the assistant chief of the COI-OSS's geography division. The division's job was to collect, organize, and, when needed, create maps for the army's and the OSS's own operations.

Applebaum played a role in devising the division's elegant map classification scheme, but he soon became known more as an excellent administrator and efficiency expert than a geographer. Within less than a year he was a confidant of William Langer and was given a commission as a lieutenant (soon captain) in the marine corps so that he had enough status to deal with the military. Then, Langer assigned him as a branch chief under Wilmarth.

Applebaum quickly became a vocal critic of the way the CID was being run. He was so abrasive that in mid-1943 Wilmarth complained about him to William Langer. Lewis's protests did not harm Applebaum's career, however. He was, to Wilmarth's surprise, given more authority. In 1944, Applebaum was pushed "upstairs." He traveled to the CID's outposts in England, Italy, Algeria, Egypt, India, Ceylon, Burma, and China on a whirlwind tour and reorganized all their operations and improved their ability to gather scientific information, something that had finally become a priority for the OSS. He was awarded the Bronze Star for his achievements. He returned to become even closer to Langer. After the war, Applebaum returned to the business world and became known as the founder of the field of marketing geography, and a respected author. [11]

Louis Ream was the other new man who so irritated Wilmarth Lewis. Ream was as or more of a business and efficiency man than Applebaum. The son of one of the multimillionaire founders of the giant United States Steel Corporation, Louis was an Ivy League graduate, Princeton 1908. Although he had a liberal arts degree, he spent thirty-five years as a manager and then owner-executive in major steel corporations. During his World War I naval service he was recognized as an outstanding administrator.

After the war, he came in direct contact with some of the most powerful and influential men in America. He was a right-hand man of the leaders of U.S. Steel and for many years traveled throughout Europe on their behalf. He also knew Wild Bill Donovan and in the early 1940s was regarded as one of his deputies. By the end of the war he had moved from the CID to the top of the OSS's hierarchy. He was so admired as an administrator that he was appointed the deputy director of the covert operations remnant of the OSS when it was moved into the army's intelligence branch at the war's end. [12]

HOW LONG CAN A GENTLEMAN REMAIN A GENTLEMAN?

By mid-1943, as might be expected given Ream's and Applebaum's backgrounds and personalities, and their ties to William Langer, both were acting more like the CID's directors than branch chiefs following Wilmarth's orders. That, and the production problems and personnel shortages at the center, led the usually gracious Wilmarth to lose his composure. After his requests for budget increases were rejected, in June 1943 he wrote an angry letter to William Langer, his superior—and close friend. Wilmarth railed about his budget and complained about his group being treated as lowly unskilled workers. He reported that Jesse Shera felt the same way. Wilmarth demanded an indepen-

A NEW INFORMATION CULTURE

dent status for the CID and threatened to resign unless he was given more resources and powers. Langer also lost some of his self-control. He responded to Wilmarth with a rejection of the reorganization demand—but with a postscript indicating he wanted Wilmarth to stay on. Wilmarth relented and apologized, but was not happy. He sensed that he was probably a lame-duck CID director with his powers being drained by his new assistants.

He was not the only one of the old CID crew who was discontented. Lawrence Egbert, Wilmarth's first and trusted administrative aid (and acting chief when Wilmarth was away), became so frustrated that he resigned in May 1943 and took on regular army work as a legal advisor.[13] Jesse Shera was also very upset and made plans to leave. He began concentrating on completing his University of Chicago Library School Ph.D. dissertation so that he might immediately take a job there.[14]

Although the CID's budget situation improved somewhat, while its workspaces were enlarged when the Research and Analysis group moved to new buildings, and while it gained more technical help from the National Archives, Wilmarth's organization remained, at least in Langer's and Ream's view, in a "state of chaos." Langer soon took an independent step. He asked for and was allocated another new special assistant in April to survey all the CID. In August, after James A. Montgomery, the Philadelphia lawyer, made his report, Langer began looking for what he diplomatically called another "assistant" for Wilmarth. He quickly found one, had him meet with the CID staff for a preliminary interview, and waited for reactions. Langer soon received word of them, but he was not pleased.[15]

WHERE IS ALASKA? EFFICIENCY TAKES CHARGE

Langer's choice, Raymond Deston, was a thirty-seven-year-old graduate (at a rather late age of twenty-four) of Maine's Bowdoin College, a highly respected liberal arts school. Deston, however, did not leave Bowdoin in 1930 to become a man of letters or to become a teacher or professor. He had selected a business major and immediately went to work, becoming recognized as an efficiency expert. When called by the OSS he was an executive at the John Hancock Mutual Life Insurance

44   CHAPTER 3

Company in Boston, describing himself as a specialist in sales promotion.

Deston's preliminary interview with Wilmarth and Jesse Shera had not gone well. Wilmarth disliked Deston's "character" and Jesse thought him "superficial."[16] Wilmarth did not protest to Langer directly, however. He asked for evaluations from his new branch chiefs. Reflecting the informal but real hierarchy at the CID, Louis Ream then wrote to Langer, stating that both Lewis and Shera had strong objections to appointing Deston as Wilmarth's assistant but that Wilmarth would be willing to have, if need be, William Applebaum as the assistant with Deston taking Applebaum's old job. Langer, at Ream's suggestion, rejected Wilmarth's plan and Deston immediately came on board as Wilmarth's supposed assistant. Then within two months he took Wilmarth's old title, chief of CID, and began applying efficiency to all aspects of the divisions work.

Wilmarth soon backed away from the CID entirely, accepting a secret mission to Canada during October and November. He then returned to Farmington, claiming ill health as the reason for not returning to the CID. Wilmarth would never again return to the OSS. He remained a gentleman throughout his life and refrained from making any public statements about how he had been treated at the CID, but he did tell at least one close friend that although he had made some good friends while in Washington, all he really had was bad memories of the CID experience. When he was later asked to join an OSS alumni organization that William Casey, the future director of the Central Intelligence Agency, was forming, Wilmarth responded that when he had handed in his badge in November 1943 it "was for keeps" and that he wanted nothing more to do with the organization. He wrote another friend that he "looks back in horror on his years at the CID."[17]

In 1943, Jesse Shera also became increasingly distressed as Deston began "distorting" the CID's culture. Among other things, Deston's efficiency drive meant reducing work activities to their smallest components and making all work at the CID part of a production system that could use low-skilled employees. That meant the CID could no longer share in the OSS's prestige, especially that of its Research and Analysis group, the home of famous "brainiacs."

Jesse Shera did give Deston some high marks for reorganizing the desk arrangements and work flows at the CID, but he had sharp com-

A NEW INFORMATION CULTURE

ments about Deston's attitude toward information work, relations between management and workers, and how Deston had encouraged the staff to become oriented to competing for advancement. In one of the first of a lifelong stream of letters to Wilmarth Lewis, in November 1943 Shera bemoaned how quickly Deston had changed the organization. Shera told Wilmarth there were no more intellectual discussions of world affairs, that Deston pushed the staff to advertise and "sell" the CID's products, and that he had told all the staff they needed business experience.

Shera wrote that what bothered him the most was the "the unblushing contempt for education and culture" that had emerged. Shera reported that one of the new crew said that if all the years of education of the old staff were added up they would average to forty-five per person. After looking at the CID's research collection, another man remarked that "France fell because the Frenchmen were all busy writing books." Shera was stunned by the statement by one of Deston's men that while he never used libraries he could get more books on a shelf if they were arranged by size, not subject. Other comments, such as "Say, what is the Luftwaffe, anyway?" and "Where is Alaska?," convinced Shera that he should try to do something to save the old work culture.

SHERA RETREATS TO ACADEMIA

Shera acted. He went to Ream, then Langer, and protested. But he was rebuffed with the statement that the problems, if any, were due to personality conflicts.[18] With that, Shera made his final decision to leave the OSS. Wilmarth, knowing since mid-1943 that Shera was unhappy, had negotiated for a standby replacement for him. Wilmarth had selected Warren Smith, a young Yale man who had been working on Wilmarth's Walpole project since the early 1930s, to step in if Shera did leave. Warren Smith's arrival did not endanger Deston or his efficiency soul mates, however. One old-fashioned scholar could not undo the changes at the CID, nor could John Ottemiller, a young librarian from Brown University who took over Shera's position.

Shera wasted little time. He had been able to finalize his doctoral dissertation and was prepared to pass his Ph.D. examination. Although he felt some guilt about abandoning his war work, in February 1944 he happily reported that he was on his way to a managerial job at the University of Chicago's library.[19] He quickly rose to prominence at the university and in the library and information world. He made a reputation as a philosopher of information, as an adept manager, and as an advocate for advanced library and information technology. In 1952, he left Chicago to head a great information adventure at Western Reserve University in Cleveland, Ohio, where he created a new doctoral program and, with the encouragement of the university's entrepreneurial president, established a hopefully great moneymaking center that would automate science information retrieval. That brought him in contact with James Perry and Allen Kent, two new information scientists who played roles in the first postwar attempts to redo the methods and technologies of intelligence information. Their intelligence roles were in the future, however. It was another man who created a technological revolution at the CID's center.[20]

HOORAY FOR HOLLYWOOD

During the frictions and frustrations at the CID during 1943, almost by chance a shining star appeared: John Francis Langan. John was a different type than either Wilmarth Lewis or Raymond Deston, but both soon adored him. Although he described himself as an "impossible Irishman," he could work with Deston, became a close lifetime friend of Wilmarth's, and made singular contributions to intelligence processing. Given his long history of unwise personal and career choices, all that was unlikely. In fact, by the time he was asked to join Donovan's organization he had become such an "impossible Irishman" that it is difficult to understand how he was hired for any security-sensitive position.

Langan began life in 1905 in the cold and forbidding deep-shaft mining town of Iron Mountain in Michigan's far north. His father, apparently a not too successful merchant, was forty-two years old when John was born and was of undistinguished Irish heritage. John's young, twenty-three-year-old mother was a first-generation American of German-speaking, immigrant Polish parents. Although having two young children, his parents divorced before John reached kindergarten age. John's early life was troubled although his mother moved to South

A NEW INFORMATION CULTURE

Bend, Indiana, where the good Catholic John attended a parochial school. When he was approaching his teenage years, his mother settled in Brookline, Massachusetts, a suburb of Boston, telling her friends she was a widow.

While his father struggled for a living in St. Louis, Missouri, his mother Claire fought to keep the family respectable. But she was unable to pay for high school for John. The fourteen-year-old had to take work as a laborer in a local electrical plant just to pay for a few courses. Claire and John wanted more, however. They were ambitious and intelligent and both desired to share in the American middle-class dream. Claire knew she would never be able to pay for college for John but thought she found a route to his higher education.

In 1920 John Francis lied about his age (he was only fifteen) and enlisted in the United States Navy. He was clever enough to gain an assignment to the navy's preparatory school in Annapolis, Maryland. The school was designed to feed deserving young men into the Naval Academy for four years of higher education and a commission as an officer. John, being smart and very, very charming, did well at the school but, perhaps because his real age was discovered, received only an honorable discharge after just two years of his enlistment. But he was not defeated. He returned to Brookline, transferred educational credits from the prep school, and within a year obtained a high school diploma.

While attending high school he became enamored with the entertainment industry and began working as a stage manager, at what he identified as the Beacon Hill Theater in nearby Boston. It was known as more of a movie theater than a theatrical house, but during the early 1920s John made some show-business friends who would be important to him later in life. Among them were two young Boston-area men, Richard and Louis de Rochemont. Unlike John, they were from a well-to-do family and were college educated. Richard, a Cambridge-Latin and Harvard University graduate, became a lifetime friend of John. Both Richard and Louis also became involved with the theater, but with a special new variety of it. They entered the news-film industry in both New York and Hollywood. The brothers became, among many other achievements, the guiding hands for the famous *Time* magazine's *March of Time* award-winning film documentaries.

Meanwhile, in the mid-1920s Langan, while not having much experience, decided that show business was his future. He bravely went to New York City and worked as a lowly paid assistant stage manager. Fortunately, during his first jobs he made significant contacts, such as the famous actress Jane Cowl. John soon became more than an assistant. He developed into a respected New York Broadway stage manager for the likes of Richard Bennett, Grace George, and Alice Brady. Those Broadway stars were also important figures in the Hollywood film industry, a link that, along with his gift of Irish blarney, soon led John to California.

In 1929, it seemed that the twenty-four-year-old was to be one of Hollywood's wunderkinds. He immediately began work at Paramount Pictures as a director, not a stage manager, and at a very generous salary. Although not receiving screen credits for the films he worked on, he seemed to be on his way. Then, the Great Depression struck the film industry. He was out of work in 1931 and struggled to make a living acting as a private dialogue coach and by producing minor documentaries, ones, sadly, the major studios refused to distribute. John also began a life of moving from one apartment to another, wondering if he would be able to pay the rent for any of them.

GREAT MISTAKES

John soon made one of several very bad decisions in his life. In 1931, when he was working as a dialogue coach for Neil Hamilton, then one of the great matinee idols of film (later Commissioner Gordon on the *Batman* television show), John was foolish enough to become involved in a distasteful affair. He agreed to meet with Lorna Brown, a young and very attractive British actress from South Africa who was demanding a large sum from Hamilton to keep from telling his wife about her sexual relations with him. John met Lorna on a street corner and arranged for the payment and her promise of silence. Surprisingly, John began to date her, to live with her, and to marry her in order that she would not be deported because she had overstayed her visa.

Lorna soon changed her stage name to Joan Manners (also Lorna Langan), played in a few films, and got pregnant. A girl was born in 1933. John assumed it was his, gave her the name Joan Langan, and

A NEW INFORMATION CULTURE

promised support. Joan Manners did not want to live with John and later claimed little Joan's father was really a six-foot, blue-eyed scriptwriter named John Manners. The elder Joan was also building a reputation as "easy." Despite all that, John Langan continued to believe the little girl was his and that she deserved his support.

Providing support was difficult. John faced hard times for the next four years. He found some part-time jobs as a dialogue director, then tried for work in Hawaii, then returned to Hollywood to accept a job as a supervisor of the Federal Theater Project's stage presentations at a wage that was one-twentieth of what he made in 1929. Even that job did not last, and he agreed to accept a percentage of the ticket receipts for the Hollywood version of an off-Broadway play. It folded within two months.

Despite his financial situation, his lower-class background, and Hollywood's highly active Communist movement, John did not drift into the party or even become a fellow traveler. Perhaps that was because his luck changed. He landed a contract as a test director at Warner Bros. Studio. The job was in the "B" movie division that produced such undistinguished films as *Nancy Drew: Reporter*. The work paid only one-fifth of his pre-Depression income but it was a job, a seemingly permanent one and, given the average income of the 1930s, he seemed to be on easy street. But, unwisely, he returned to his old habit of living too well.

Just then, Joan Manners, whose film career had plummeted and who was working as a waitress, appeared in court, reversed her previous statements, and demanded full support for herself and little Joan. In reaction, John (who had gone through a second marriage ceremony with Manners to, he thought, ensure that little Joan would not be taken by the authorities while her mother was away in New York) demanded a full divorce and visitation rights with the child. The divorce hearing was more than unpleasant. Big Joan became hysterical and was taken to a hospital to recover. That, and the custody hearings, appeared in the local papers. Joan soon brought John and herself to national attention—and back to poverty.

She had a sandwich-board sign created with the accusation that John was failing to pay the required alimony and child support now that he had his first full-time job in five years (and after she had supported him for all that time, she claimed) and that he was trying to take little Joan from her now that he had some money. She put the sign over her shoulders and paraded back and forth in front of the main gate of Warner Bros. Studio. The studio bosses were furious and called the police. Joan was arrested. At the court hearing, the judge, aware of the agreement reached during the divorce hearings that prohibited Joan or John from harassing each other, ordered her to jail for five days for contempt of court.

If that was not enough to bring John to the front pages of newspapers across the country, Joan's next actions ensured national attention. She refused to cooperate at the jail and was put into solitary confinement—in a padded cell. The drama did not end. Joan gained help from the American Civil Liberties Union, was released from her cell after three days, and obtained a ruling that her right of free speech had been denied and that, if she wanted, she could resume picketing. She might have done so had she not been arrested a short time after her release because she was an illegal alien. She had spent nine years in the United States on a short-term visa.

She again made the national news. She sought sympathy by declaring she had been made a woman without a country because, she stated, she had lost her British citizenship by marrying an American and, thus, could not return to South Africa or England even though she was being forced to leave the United States—and without her daughter. While the immigration authorities pondered the situation, Joan was released, only to again face the ire of Hollywood's family court. After both she and John admitted they had so little money (he was down to his "last twenty bucks") the judge declared little Joan a ward and sent her to an orphanage, then to a foster home.

John was devastated. He could do little for the child because, as the Irish would say, he was "down on his uppers." Joan's picketing had led Warner Bros. to let him go. He was scrambling to make a living as a private drama coach and was embarrassed by having to work in defense plants.[21] Joan was also up against it. She was again arrested, this time on vagrancy and bunko charges. She was giving rides to people on Wilshire Boulevard and then demanding they give her money to be donated to British War Relief. She managed to avoid jail, but the episode added to John's concerns about little Joan's welfare.

John soon made another rash and dangerous move. He snatched little Joan from her foster home and flew her to Brookline, Massachu-

A NEW INFORMATION CULTURE

setts, to stay with his mother, who had remarried into a wealthy family. John returned to Hollywood to face the fury of big Joan and the courts. He was forced to surrender little Joan, and he and Joan Manners were ordered to court to determine a final custody agreement. Private charities were contacted and agreed to pay for a Los Angeles probation officer to fly little Joan back to Hollywood. At the new hearings, big Joan was more restrained than was typical. With her finances somewhat better (she said she now had a good waitress job paying $350 a week) and with John promising one-quarter of his income for support, the judge gave little Joan back to her mother, but granted John weekend visiting rights.

That, however, did not end the drama. There was a fight during one of John's first visits. Big Joan called the police, claiming that John had beaten and kicked her. John was brought to court. But after the judge listened to him, and to an again hysterical Joan, he dismissed the charges against John and then made a decision that ran against the American legal traditions that favored mothers. He gave John full custody of little Joan, at least temporarily.

That did not signal an end to John's personal or financial problems. In late 1941, he was still working at low-paying and temporary drama coaching jobs and again filling in at defense plants. There was a bit of hope in John's life, however. He found a new girlfriend and future wife, Florence Bremen, but she could not provide much help besides caring for little Joan. There also was the worry that big Joan might succeed in reclaiming the girl. As worrisome, it seemed that the major studios now regarded him as a pariah.

Then old friendships came to the rescue. John had a chance for a new steady job and, possibly, a means of getting away from Joan Manners.

WHAT'S A NOT-NICE KID LIKE JOHN DOING IN A HIGHLY CLASSIFIED JOB?

Richard de Rochemont had been John's buddy since their Boston years and had thought of having John index his *March of Time* films. Richard had connections to the COI-OSS's pictures project and thought that John might be a good man to serve as a Hollywood liaison, especially

CHAPTER 3

because John knew documentary filmmakers and producers who probably had valuable prints stored away in their vaults. De Rochemont was also a friend of the famous writer Robert Sherwood, who was helping Bill Donovan with propaganda/public relations work. De Rochemont also knew Atherton Richards, the Pineapple King and founder of the COI's Presentations-Picture group.

Following de Rochemont's suggestion, John quickly contacted the Pictures group. He got a response. In early 1942, he was sent the application forms needed for a security check and employment screening. Positive words reached Washington, D.C., before his applications did, and it seemed certain that he might finally have a steady job. He felt sure his friends' recommendations would override any problems due to his spotty work history and his marital problems.

They did, and he was hired. But whether he would be based on the East or West Coast remained uncertain. His exact duties were also not well defined. Important to his later life, he did not inform Washington that while he was unemployed he had been experimenting with ways to classify and index films, ways to use microfilm to store film clips, and ways to retrieve information by using tabulating machines. When John later applied those ideas to the Pictures group's problems, Wilmarth Lewis thought he had found a miracle worker and John thought he had entered what he believed would be a pathway to riches.

NOTES

1. Barry Katz, "The Arts of War: 'Visual Presentation' and National Intelligence," *Design Issues* 12, no. 2 (Summer 1996): 3–21.

2. Neil MacKay, *The Hole in the Card: The Story of the Microfilm Aperture Card* (St. Paul: Minnesota Mining & Manufacturing, 1996).

3. NARA RG226 ai 146 b137, James A. Montgomery.

4. This quote suggests that Richard and Louis de Rochemont of the *March of Time* films had much to do with the center.

5. In 2006 dollar value.

6. Leonard S. Wilson, "Lessons from the Experience of the Map Information Section, OSS," *Geographical Review* 39, no. 2 (April 1949): 298–310.

7. LWL, Lewis–Langan Correspondence; Robin Winks, *Cloak & Gown: Scholars in the Secret War, 1939–1961* (New Haven, CT: Yale University Press, ca. 1996), 106.

A NEW INFORMATION CULTURE

8. The on-site manager at the time was Colonel I. E. Norris.

9. NARA RG226 air 146 b137, Montgomery report.

10. NARA RG226, ai 146, Central Information Division Budget folder.

11. William L. Langer, *In and Out of the Ivory Tower: The Autobiography of William L. Langer* (New York: Neale Watson Academic, 1977), p. 196; NARA RG226, OSS Personnel files.

12. LWL, Lewis–Shera Correspondence; NARA RG226 146 b75, Central Information Division.

13. NARA RG226 OSS Personnel files, Egbert.

14. LWL, Lewis–Shera Correspondence 2-28-44.

15. NARA RG226 ai 146 b137.

16. LWL, Lewis–Shera Correspondence 11-23-43.

17. LWL, Box dr 2 Langan folders; LWL, Lewis–Shera Correspondence 12-15-43; LWL, Lewis–Langan Correspondence 5-16-61.

18. LWL, Shera–Lewis Correspondence 12-28-44.

19. LWL, Shera–Lewis Correspondence 11-23-43.

20. CWR, Papers of Jesse Hauk Shera.

21. John failed to mention the defense work in his OSS job application, NARA, OSS Personnel files.

4

MICROFILM AT THE OSS, FOR WAR AND PROFIT

In mid-1942, the OSS's Pictures group decided that John Langan should be assigned, at least for a time, to its East Coast centers—although his formal assignment was to obtain travelogue and documentary films usually found in Hollywood's archives.[1] Listed as only a film technician, with a salary less than he had made during his last full-time job at Warner Bros. Studios, and having no savings, John may have worried about the expense of moving from Hollywood. But going east had a great advantage. He could take Joan, his nine-year-old daughter, far away from his bitter ex-wife Joan Manners (aka Lorna Langan). So, John and Florence Bremen took little Joan eastward—without telling her mother where she would be!

The evidence is not clear about John's destinations. He may have first gone to the OSS's Pictorial Records office in New York City, but he was working in Washington by early 1943 when Wilmarth Lewis reduced the New York center to a handful of staff and transferred most of its operations to Washington, D.C.

John, although still a lowly technician, soon became a star, and not just in the Pictures group. He also became a favorite of Wilmarth Lewis, so much so that Wilmarth allocated scarce funds for John's ideas of how to finally bring order to the Pictures section. John had convinced Wilmarth that he could implement the radical ideas he had been toying with since 1940, and quickly so. John promised to create a new classification and indexing system for pictures and to automate the retrieval of desired items.

With a budget for expenses larger than his annual salary, John was given the resources he needed to create an innovation, his microfilm-tabulator "aperture" card system. He also was permanently assigned to the CID's Washington office. With this career boost John reverted to some of his old personal habits. Although he had a salary less than one-half that of Wilmarth's, he decided to move into a home in the new and very posh Washington suburb of Chevy Chase, Maryland. He did not neglect his project, however.

A PICTURE DESERVES A THOUSAND WORDS

John's first task was to devise a new classification system for still pictures and films, ones that would fit the needs of the CID's special customers. From his thoughts about how to classify and index stock motion picture films for Hollywood producers who wanted to avoid shooting new scenes, he already had a long list of what would be required. He seems not to have felt it necessary to research the methods used by newspaper and magazine photo archivists, or those of commercial services such as Otto Bateman's. After becoming familiar with intelligence needs, he added more features to the two systems he was devising. Both classifications contained a great deal of information and, perhaps to Wilmarth's disappointment, had little overlap with the CID's reports system.

John thought precise and deep indexing and unique concepts were essential to providing his users the specific items they needed as quickly as possible. And, he was determined to create an automated system. His system for still pictures was not hierarchal. It had fourteen categories for aspects of a picture. The most important, country, province, industry, subject, communications type, supplementary, military type, topography, latitude and longitude, date, and the accession (file location) indicator, all had numeric codes. John also left room for words to describe the "place" of a picture. All that called for fifty-six digits, a length far too long for a conventional classification system. Important, however, all the Langan codes fit on an electric tabulator/sorter card—and with extra spaces left over. Using the multicoded cards and the tabula-

MICROFILM AT THE OSS, FOR WAR AND PROFIT

tors would, John believed, eliminate expensive search time by skilled librarians and avoid the construction of a huge index file.

Langan's way of identifying frames taken from stock films was necessarily more innovative and complex than his one for still pictures. It reflected his practical experience in the film industry. He had twenty-nine categories that identified the location and subject of a film (even the weather and background when it was shot) and all the technical details needed for someone who might want to reproduce an item. He created numeric codes for each item; altogether they required sixty-four digits.

Wilmarth quickly approved both systems and the use of International Business Machines' (IBM) tabulators, deciding they would finally bring order to the pictures' collections. He concluded the labor involved in the deep indexing was well worth the expense. So did William Langer and so would (after some flare-ups) Raymond Deston, the efficiency expert. He eventually saw Langan's system as a step toward automating all the CID's files.

The CID's customers also found the Hollywood man had a knack for classification in general and that John "thought as they did." He would soon be lent to other branches of the OSS, military agencies, and the civilian bureaucracy. John helped with the OSS's map system's revisions, aided the navy's photo section, and assisted the marine corps, the war crimes commission, and the Bureau of the Budget. The Bureau of

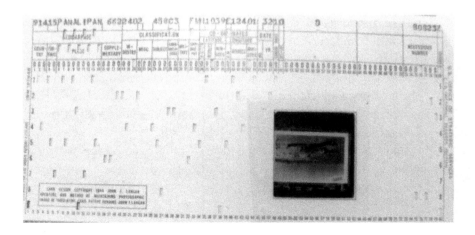

Figure 4.1. Langan Aperture Card NARA RG226

Ships, the Army Transport Corps, and the Public Health Service also called on John's advice.

John's initial work for the navy was very innovative. He was instrumental in creating an early version of a mechanical language translation system. The navy's George McSpadden, a Stanford University linguist and Spanish literature scholar, had been drafted and ordered to compile translation dictionaries for foreign military communications. John helped build a classification system that identified the foreign language's word, the proposed English translation, the navy's equivalent meaning codes, the parts of speech, and the document the term had come from.

THE UNIT RECORD

Langan brought other innovations to the CID, ones that astounded his colleagues. His indexing of each item on a separate tabulator punchcard (a "unit record") was important for more reasons than saving space. It allowed the electromechanical devices to select the cards that contained the desired code combinations and sort them into separate packets. With an electromechanical sorter it was possible to quickly recombine cards in any desired order. Although the tabulators of the era were rather unsophisticated and called for repeated runs of a deck of cards to find desired items, tabulators were much faster than other retrieval technologies such as book indexes or paper index cards.

Separate unit record cards had another advantage. Unlike paper lists, the individual cards could easily be arranged in different ways because they were not locked into a fixed serial order as were items on rolls of tape or in books. That freedom was especially important for the navy's translation project. It allowed the creation of dictionaries on-the-fly, each arranged in different ways, and automatically printed by an advanced tabulator.

However, because no libraries had used tabulators to replace their catalog card files, the CID took a leap of faith when it accepted Langan's punch-card system.[2]

A PICTURE *WAS* WORTH A HOLE AND A THOUSAND WORDS, THE GREAT MICROFILM OPPORTUNITY, APERTURES

The most innovative of John Langan's contributions is difficult to appreciate without an understanding of the long and tortured history of microfilm, the "memory" technology that many in the 1930s believed would revolutionize libraries, information systems, scientific communications, and codebreaking.[3] John's proposal that a microfilmed miniature copy of a picture, a map, or a document be inserted into a unit record card, then selected by a tabulator using the codes punched into the card, was revolutionary—and courageous. If his plan worked and if he was correct in his belief that the cards' microfilms could be used to produce full-scale copies of pictures, maps, and documents, there would be a substantial savings of storage space for photos and a significant reduction in the time needed to produce copies for the CID's users. It would also serve as a means, as did Wilmarth's précis, of determining with more precision if a selected item was one that users wanted. There were more advantages. For example, using the microfilm inserts, the navy's language system allowed translators to instantly see the context of a word's usage.

JOHN'S FAITH IN A DEVELOPING BUT UNSURE TECHNOLOGY

John was asking Wilmarth and the CID to take the chance of wasting time and money because he was moving into immature and, in one case, untested technical territory. Microfilm technology had been rapidly advancing but still had failings in the 1940s. The ability to reduce the size of text or a picture through reverse photography (by factors of at least twenty or thirty), place it on a film, and later reproduce the image in its original size had been known since the early nineteenth century. The process had been used for sending secret messages during the Franco-Prussian War and World War I and, with technical improvements in cameras and film technology, it was possible to place large amounts of text on tiny "microdots" that a spy could hide under postage stamps.

Espionage was not the only application of microphotography. Its use began to migrate to the business and educational worlds in the 1920s. The first major business application came in late in the decade when the American George L. McCarthy invented a new camera allowing the continuous microfilming of bank checks. His invention soon led the huge Eastman Kodak Company to absorb his Recordak firm and to put more of its own resources into developing better film stock for microfilming. The reduction in the cost of high-quality film was hastened by the demands of the moving picture industry. Significant, by the late 1930s the old fire-prone nitrate film stock was being replaced by the safer and longer-lasting cellulose acetate film. But even the new film had problems such as tearing and developing spots that blemished images.

The possibilities for using microfilm in libraries and for academic publication had been explored since the early 1900s, with the Belgian Paul Otlet being one of its most famous advocates. There were few practical results until the technical improvements of the 1920s hinted that microfilm might become "the" solution to the evils of crowded library shelves, expensive copying, decaying newspapers and books, and of the escalating cost of science publications. During the mid-1920s, the United States' Library of Congress launched a decadelong, path-breaking project to microfilm books at the British Library for preservation purposes, but few other major library or academic efforts appeared until the mid-1930s when further technological advances, including innovations such the Draeger camera (specifically designed for library use) appeared.

With the cost of copying by microfilming becoming lower than by other methods, academics and friendly businesses sponsored a few large academic projects. Harvard University, with help from the Rockefeller Foundation, launched a major venture for the preservation of foreign and fragile newspapers. Eastman Kodak microfilmed and sold copies of the *New York Times*. Dissertations were filmed and sold to libraries, and the Library of Congress and the National Archives established reproduction centers. As well, with the United States' Department of Agriculture and the American Documentation Institute–aligned Science Service taking the first steps, plans were laid for a centralized system to replace expensive science periodicals with microfilmed copies of individual articles. Soon, private companies, such as

MICROFILM AT THE OSS, FOR WAR AND PROFIT

R.W Batchelder's Microfilm Corporation, began offering microfilm solutions on a contract basis to academic as well as commercial customers.

One of the most interesting academic microfilm adventures began when Germany's Nazi government forbade non-Aryans from contributing to Germany's *Zentralblatt für Mathematik*, the international mathematics abstract journal. In reaction, the United States' Rockefeller and Carnegie Foundations generously founded an American-based version at Brown University, *Mathematical Reviews*. The project, begun in 1939, was unique for several reasons. Among them was the use of microfilm and a small handheld viewer developed with the help of the National Research Council's Scientific Aids to Learning project. Subscribers were sent microfilms of the journal as well as a low-cost viewer. There was an announcement that they could soon order copies of desired individual articles from the center. The *Reviews* was also unique because the Rockefeller Foundation broke with its post–World War I policy of not funding science journals or bibliographic publications and because the publication was able to get copies of almost all the world's mathematics journals during World War II—probably with the help of the OSS.

In the United States during the 1930s and early 1940s many other groups began advocating for projects that would allow the widespread use of microfilm and other "micro" formats (such as microcards) in libraries and universities. The American Documentation Institute, the American Library Association, the Social Science Research Council, and the National Research Council led efforts to improve technologies and set uniform standards that would allow sharing of microfilmed documents. Led by Frederick Keppel, its technology-friendly leader, the Carnegie Institution, which typically focused on educational problems, funded a major effort that amply supported research into microfilm's basic technologies by the young Vernon Tate at the National Archives (he was previously at the Library of Congress) to develop inexpensive microfilm readers, film printers. It also supported a journal, the *Journal of Documentary Reproduction* (later, *American Documentation*), that served as an international platform for the application of microfilm in libraries and schools.

Despite all those achievements, when John Langan made his proposal to Wilmarth Lewis in the mid-1940s, microfilm continued to be a worrisome technology. High-quality copying from microfilms remained a challenge, but the major problem was with the fundamentals of the medium. The greatly reduced size of text or graphics meant that a human could not easily locate a desired item, whether it was on a roll of film or in another form such as a microcard, a chip, or a microfiche. That had not been regarded as a great problem when microforms were used by businesses as an archive tool for rarely used items, or when items had been microfilmed and used in serial order, such as checks' cashing dates.

For frequently used materials, or for searches by subject, all existing microforms had weaknesses.[4] When rolls (the most common form) were used, a search had to proceed serially, one item at a time, with a searcher looking within each of them to see if it was the desired one. With all microform reading devices having stubborn deficiencies, continuous reading led to eyestrain and headaches. Rolls of film, of course, had their contents locked in their original order so that rearranging them or adding new items was nearly impossible.

Innovators, such as Germany's Emanuel Goldberg and the United States' Vannevar Bush, had tried to overcome that "serials problem" by devising machines that combined identification codes implanted in each microframe with very high-speed optical searching and, in Bush's case, flash reproduction of selected items on another roll of film. The technical problems with such devices were intransigent, however. It took hundreds of thousands of research dollars (including investments in Bush's microfilm machines to aid codebreaking) and a wait of almost two decades after World War II to produce a working, reliable, and affordable but stripped-down version of such machines.[5]

All other microforms had weaknesses. When rolls of film were cut into individual frames, so files were not serial but were unit recorded, they suffered from an identification problem and they were easily lost due to their tiny size. Small sheets of film (microfiche) had room for a few visible identifiers but were not suited to automation and they were prone to deterioration from hard use. The paper microcard, another form that seemed an answer to many problems, was only in the design stage in the 1940s. Fremont Rider, the techno-savvy American librarian, had proposed a microcard system that combined microphotography with the usual paper library catalog card so that readers would have the text of an article or book in hand when they found its index card. The front of a microcard was to have the typical identifiers; the back was to have the text printed in greatly reduced size—as many as twenty-seven pages per card. Unfortunately, Rider's card could not solve the challenge of avoiding massive files if multiple access identifiers were desired. It was not automation friendly, and it was difficult to prevent the cards from being lost or stolen.

THEY SAID IT WAS A SILLY DREAM: THE APERTURE CARD

John Langan probably never heard of Atherton Slidell, the chemist and leader of the American Documentation Institute, who had suggested another solution to microfilm's limitations. In 1934, Slidell announced it would be a good idea to combine microfilm frames with tabulator cards. That, he thought, would allow many code identifiers to be linked to each frame and the frames easily filed, retrieved, and copied. A microframe implanted in a card would overcome the serial organization problem. But Slidell never implemented a system—John Langan would.

In 1940, when John was in Hollywood and exploring the stock-film problem and hoping for employment, he had sketched his ideas and presented them to the IBM and Remington Rand Corporations, the two major manufacturers of tabulating machines. According to John, they laughed at him, remarking that their highly precise machines could not work with any films and would be damaged by cards with "implants." They also pointed out there were no adhesives that could anchor the films and even if they did, the machines would scratch or warp the films as the cards passed through the code-sensing and transport stations. Despite such warnings, Langan stood by his dream.

By early 1943, and with Wilmarth Lewis's backing, John began working on his aperture card system for the CID's picture division. After gaining advice on microfilm reproduction from Vernon Tate at the National Archives, whose microfilm section, like the Library of Congress's, had become a near appendage of the OSS, Langan calculated the thickness of microframes and the thickness of the IBM cards. He found that if a portion of an IBM card was removed, an inserted frame would not exceed the card's thickness and, thus, could pass through a tabulator's processing stations without clogging the machine. (The standard card was 6.7th of an inch thick, a microfilm frame 5.5th of an inch thick, which left room for an adhesive to bind the film to the card.) [6] Then, John used a trial and error method on the few IBM tabulators the OSS was operating and found spaces where the code-sensing metal brushes and the transporting rollers did not touch the cards. That indicated the films would not be scratched or pulled from the cards. With the help of the mechanics at the National Archives, he explored how to precisely slice the aperture in the tabulator cards so that light could flow through the film. He also determined how to efficiently and precisely cut the individual frames from the rolls of microfilm that came from the large cameras that photographed pictures and documents. John also set himself the task of creating a reading station for his unique cards.

While John and the mechanics were developing devices for cutting, implanting, and viewing the cards, he gained permission to set a crew to work cutting the films and the apertures in the cards by hand using razor blades. John wanted to have a deck of at least three hundred cards ready for testing as soon as possible because Wilmarth Lewis needed successful demonstration runs to convince both the OSS's hierarchy and the tabulating companies that Langan's ideas were feasible. A stumbling block remained. John could not find an adhesive strong and thin enough to anchor the films to the cards. Again, the National Archives came to the rescue. While in the archives' basement, John discovered a film adhesive the archives' conservationist had developed for preserving endangered documents. With that, the test deck could be completed.

Wilmarth Lewis gave Langan the go-ahead to approach IBM for permission to use its machines and cards. John was again the object of some laughter. The IBM men once more said his idea would never work. Wilmarth's influence, and John's charm and perseverance, saved the day. IBM agreed to rigorously test the cards. The company's experts were surprised: the system worked! IBM agreed to allow the cards to be used on its devices and it later agreed to manufacture cards with precision-cut apertures if John wanted them. With that, the CID soon got busy turning the OSS's piles of photos and films into an orderly collection of aperture cards.

There had been more good news for John. His new wife, Florence, presented him with a beautiful baby boy, one the ten-year-old little Joan adored.

MIXING TECHNOLOGY WITH BUSINESS

Before John Langan and Wilmarth Lewis received the go-ahead from IBM and the OSS for John's aperture card adventure, John had been busy turning his ideas into patents and, hopefully, a business and a new career. With Wilmarth's (and the rest of the OSS's leaders') approval, John began meeting with patent attorneys in mid-1943. By late 1944, after a year and a half's consultations, he was sure that he would have the fundamental patents for aperture cards and related machines. The OSS did not object to his securing the patents, although the development of the systems had used government resources and had taken place while he was a government employee. Letters from the CID's administrators stated that since the aperture work was not part of his job description he deserved to have the patent rights. All the government wanted was royalty-free use in exchange for a payment of $1.

John had been doing more than seeking patent rights. Believing he would be guaranteed control over all forms of aperture cards, not just the tabulator card form, he began exploring other techno-alternatives. Over time he realized that apertures could tap a market much deeper than companies that could afford the expensive tabulating machines. Desktop versions of his system might find a place in small businesses and libraries. Over the years, John's and related companies would offer microfiche-like, microcard-form, and edge-notched card products. Edge-notched cards, such as those by the McBee firm, were large and thick cards that had spaces on their edges with each of the spaces standing for a code category. If an item was coded for "Russia," the appropriate edge space would be punched. When a long needle was inserted into a pack of cards, those with a punch in the "Russia" space would fall out and be selected.

As soon as he thought his patents applications would be approved, John began laying the foundations for a company in what he later called the business of "information retrieval." He quickly gained help. Wilmarth agreed to act as a trustee for Langan's patent-related affairs and arranged to have his wealthy Auchincloss stockbroker relatives advise John on his personal finances. Then, John found someone who promised to back the expensive development of new machines, provide business advice, and support his proposed Film'n File company during its early developmental years.

66 CHAPTER 4

That someone was the OSS's Atherton Richards. He soon brought in a rather silent junior partner, Bill Casey, the London-based chief of OSS's European operations, influential corporate lawyer, and future head of the Central Intelligence Agency.

ALL IS LOST? A KIDNAPPER?

In late 1943, just as the aperture card business seemed to be John's road to wealth, his world was almost destroyed. His ex-wife had learned where he was, then hired lawyers to take little Joan from him. John, with no savings, needed aid. His first thought was of Wilmarth Lewis. John phoned Farmington and reached Annie Burr only to discover that Wilmarth was still away in Canada on his special trip for the OSS. Annie sympathetically listened to John, then contacted Wilmarth, who immediately provided financial aid, help that John later declared "saved" little Joan.

John contacted a lawyer and prepared for whatever his ex-wife Lorna (aka Joan Manners) might try. The ex–movie actress, now running, surprisingly, a profitable girls' school in Hollywood, made her move in early 1944 and took John to court. In late February, John's, and even little Joan's, pleas were ignored. A federal judge in Maryland awarded full custody to Lorna. Little Joan seemed on her way back to Hollywood. John then made another of his rash moves. The same day as the judge's decision, at a hotel in Washington, D.C., where Lorna had taken little Joan, John seized his daughter, hid her with friends in Washington, D.C., and called Lorna warning her not to interfere. That led to Lorna declaring that little Joan had been stolen, gaining a court order demanding her return, and issuing a threat of a kidnapping charge against John.

John, an employee of one of the nation's most secret agencies, again became a national news item. However, he had made so many friends in the OSS that he did not fear for his job and, even if it was in jeopardy, he decided he would continue to try to save his daughter from what he now believed was an insane woman. After he obeyed a Washington, D.C., court order to present little Joan, he pressed his case. To John's relief, the kidnapping charge was not pursued and the judge was willing to hear another round of custody arguments—but only if John and Lorna were searched for weapons before entering the courtroom.

The hearings made their own national headlines. Lorna tried to outflank John's attorney by declaring, again, that John was not little Joan's father and that despite two ceremonies, she had never really married John. When the judge objected to smearing little Joan's name with illegitimacy, Lorna declared that the handsome Hollywood scriptwriter John Manners had been the real father. Lorna then testified she was glad that Manners had never had any significant contact with little Joan—although now admitting that she had married Langan. When she sensed she was painting herself as a "slut," and perhaps as an unfit mother, she reversed her testimony and declared she had married John Manners. Quite soon, Lorna became hysterical in the courtroom and even John had a tearful breakdown while testifying. Matters became more complex when Claire, John's mother, who had married into a wealthy Boston family, petitioned the court to prevent Lorna or John from gaining custody of little Joan.

The judge ordered blood tests and had a long, private conversation with little Joan. The tests showed John could have been the father. Little Joan's statements suggested that Lorna had and would be a parental risk and that John and his new wife had been good parents. With that, the judge reversed the Maryland court's decision, granted full custody to John, and forbade Lorna from seeing Joan. Lorna announced she would abide by the ruling—then she reneged. John kept little Joan but had to wage rounds of court battles until July 1945 when an appeals court ruled in his favor. The new trials added to family pressures that soon led to John and his new wife Florence separating, then divorcing. There was more bad news for John. By the end of 1944 John was no longer living in stylish Chevy Chase. He had to move into an apartment in the government-built Naylor Gardens development in one of Washington, D.C.'s, less than prestigious neighborhoods.

ON TO RICHES, JOHN HOPES

The legal battles, the financial pressures, and the related emotional anguish did not stop John from seeking "gold" in microfilm. Although he was a full-time OSS employee during 1944 and most of 1945, he filed more patent applications and even visited the Yale and Harvard libraries and various businesses seeking future customers, including magazine companies such as *Look*. Atherton Richards was also busy. At first, he tried negotiating with IBM for its purchase of the patents and for a full-time consulting position for Langan. That fell through and Atherton decided to develop an independent company. By early 1945, well before the victory over Germany, he had a Boston engineering firm designing and manufacturing sophisticated versions of John's machines, with expectations they would be ready by February 1946. Within just a few years Atherton had invested more than a half million dollars in the machines' development.

In 1945, as the war was ending, John Langan made no requests to stay on with the intelligence agency. It would have been futile to do so. The OSS and its CID were doomed. The reports of Communist infiltration of the OSS and accusations about lack of security in the agency by men such as Frenchy Grombach were just two of the reasons President Harry Truman ended the OSS in late September 1945. The OSS's covert operations group was transferred to the army, the research group was sent to the State Department, and any central library/information center functions were piled into an ill-defined and underfunded new Central Information Group (CIG).

John Langan did not move back to Hollywood or seek work in the film industry. His luck seemed to have permanently changed. He had secured a full-time and well-paying job at *Look* magazine in September 1945. He had been hired to create an aperture card archive of all its photos, but he and Atherton continued to develop their Film'n File company. Atherton Richards then arranged to have the *Wall Street Journal* publish a long complementary article in 1946. In addition, with the help of R. W. Batchelder's New York micrographics firm, John sought more private and government customers, and he and Richards laid plans for a great pre-Google book and periodicals copying program. They envisioned using their planned version of a Fremont Rider library microcard to film books and periodicals in major libraries, then selling copies to other libraries in America and Europe. John also kept inventing. Atherton was impressed enough with John's new idea for replacing addressograph mass-mailing systems to supply more money to Film'n File.

John recharged his optimism and returned to his old habit of spending all he had. He took a home in the upscale New York City suburb of White Plains, New York, hired a governess for little Joan, and searched for private college preparatory schools for her while he courted another beautiful woman. He soon remarried and, like a good Catholic boy, planned the ceremony for St. Patrick's Cathedral in New York City—with Wilmarth Lewis as the best man. John soon had two more children and arranged for his little Joan to attend the elite Seven Sisters, Smith College.

THE END OF A MICRO DREAM, THE COWBOY'S LIFE FOR ME?

Unfortunately, the Film'n File business did not prosper during the 1940s and John was not becoming an overnight millionaire. One reason was that a few technical difficulties persisted (the adhesives tended to stick two cards together) and marketing and distributing proved difficult for a small company. Also, personal frictions developed. By 1949, Atherton and Langan had lawyers battling each other and John was no longer seeing Richards as a savior, but as an enemy. In 1950, John sold all his rights to Atherton and decided to start a new life and to seek his fortune in what he predicted to be a booming new industry. His next project was not in the emerging television industry, however. It was cattle raising in the Old South. With the proceeds from the sale of his patent rights he bought an old plantation near rural and isolated Madison, Georgia, stocked it with cattle, and began to live the kind of life he had always wanted. He named his new girl child and the eight-hundred-acre plantation Mallory as he, the once poor Irish boy, became a gentleman farmer in a town famed for its historic antebellum mansions.

LANGAN, NO—RICHARDS AND THE COLD WAR, YES— THE MISSING DOLLAR

To John's surprise and displeasure, just as he was moving to Georgia the Film'n File company began to prosper. Richards had made alliances with the Dexter Folder Company of Pearl River, New Jersey, for technical aid and business advice and with the McBee and Eastman Kodak Companies for help in marketing and distribution. A wise move of his was to change the company name to Filmsort to gain some distance from Film'n File's reputation for unreliability.

Those business changes came at the right time: the emergence of the Cold War meant sales of aperture cards boomed. Tens of millions of the cards were being sold each year, with the best customers being the American military and its contractors. They found the cards to be "the" solution for storing, retrieving, and transmitting technical documents and drawings. It would be decades before computer graphics were developed enough to provide a substitute. The cards soon became a standard within the American government and for its NATO allies.

That did not make John Langan happy. He had no share in Filmsort's good times and his personal fortunes were declining. His cattle operation, which had used up all the monies from the sale of his patent rights, had gone bust within five years. By 1954, the plantation was up for sale. John bounced back, however. With his usual optimism and charm, he and his family moved five hundred miles to Atlanta, Georgia, where he found work as a stockbroker. Then, it seemed for a moment that he might have revenge on Atherton Richards who, John wrote Wilmarth in 1958, had "skinned him"[7] when he bought John's patent rights in 1950 and was now trying to "skin" the U.S. government. The FBI had just searched John's house because Atherton had been refusing to grant the government the royalty-free use of aperture cards it had negotiated when John was with the OSS. That meant an extra cost of about a penny a card, a fee that was substantial because the government was purchasing tens of millions of cards a year.

John was not sad about Atherton being in a bit of trouble; perhaps that is why he did not exploit a weakness in his old contract with the government, a weakness that would have saved Atherton further problems and might have made John some money. The government had forgotten to fulfill its part of the agreement. It had never paid John the promised $1. John played the role of nice guy. He wrote to Wild Bill Donovan, who arranged to have a check sent to John. John framed it and put it on his wall. The old agreement was rescued and the government saved thousands upon thousands of dollars.

AN IMPOSSIBLE IRISHMAN'S IMPOSSIBLE LIFE, INFORMATION RETRIEVAL

At the same time, Langan thought he was going to return to the information business. There were two new opportunities that made him believe he would again find riches in microfilm. The first was bittersweet. As it seemed that microfilm would remain "the" memory technology and that sales would remain high, the giant 3M Company of Minnesota decided to enter the microfilm business, and in a big way. It purchased the rights to John's old patents for some $15 million. The company laid plans to invest much more in perfecting his aperture cards and in creating advanced systems, ones that could even serve traveling businessmen by having automated workstations in hotels. John did not receive anything from the patent transfers, but 3M hired him on as a part-time consultant. The second opportunity held more promise. John had continued inventing and had built a portfolio of patents. Among them was one he thought was going to return him to being the leader of the aperture world and, he admitted, allow him to get even for being negotiated out of his old invention by Atherton Richards. John had found a way to make aperture cards without using any adhesive, as well as a less expensive method of manufacturing the cards. That meant faster production, much lower cost per card, and a very high profit margin.

John joyfully reported that if successful, the new card and the new manufacturing process meant the demise of the companies using his old patents. His only competitive worry was a new huge microfilm machine Eastman Kodak was designing, the Minicard. John said it made his type of system look like an "old sailing ship." Despite the Minicard threat, John was able to attract investors and to have Eastman Kodak agree to act as his distributor and hands-on technical advisor. His investors usually were old friends like Richard de Rochemont and Bill Casey. John felt lucky to have Casey act as the brains behind the new Langan Aperture Cards Inc. and the new Langan Information Retrieval Corporation. That was especially true because Casey was running his own very lucrative and influential legal, information, and intelligence service for large international corporations. However, there was some irony in Casey's involvement with John's new adventure. Casey had piloted the legal team that, in John's words, had "skinned" him in

1950. But Langan now trusted and respected Casey, even writing Wilmarth Lewis how much he admired Casey's behind-the-scenes running of the staunch anti-Communist Richard Nixon presidential bid.

In 1960, John was sure that he would finally become a millionaire. He believed he could sell his holdings in the new company for at least $10 million. He was so upbeat that he decided to take another poke at Atherton Richards. He sent Richards a letter offering him the opportunity to buy a few shares in the new corporation. Langan was, typically, overly optimistic. It took several years and hundreds of thousands of dollars to develop the machinery for his nonadhesive cards and to locate and construct manufacturing plants, including one in Marietta, Georgia, just twenty-five miles from his home.

The "impossible" then hit John once again. In 1969, when his company was producing its first cards, the machines malfunctioned. They could not be coaxed to work at the speed necessary to meet orders. The company went bankrupt, just as John began succumbing to the ills of old age. He retired in Nevada, sans any millions, passing on in 1982 but remaining (as he had continued to tell Wilmarth Lewis) an upbeat "impossible Irishman."

Meanwhile, while John had been trying to conquer microfilm, the successor to the OSS had been having its own new information organizational and classification battles as America's intelligence agencies began facing the challenges of what became the Cold War. As early as 1943, America's radio spies had initiated a watch on the Soviets and the late 1945 successor to the OSS would immediately make Russia its prime objective.[8]

NOTES

1. On Langan's involvements and systems, see his extensive files in NARA, RG226, and those at the LWL as cited in previous chapters. Photo and films also came from Europe and Asia. For example, OSS "stole" copies of German newsreels being shown in neutral Portugal and forwarded them to the OSS's photo section.

2. Robert V. Williams, "The Use of Punched Cards in US Libraries and Documentation Centers, 1936–1965," *IEEE Annals of the History of Computing* 24, no. 2 (April–June 2002): 16–33.

MICROFILM AT THE OSS, FOR WAR AND PROFIT

3. Alan Marshall Meckler, *Micropublishing: A History of Scholarly Micropublishing in America, 1938–1980* (Westport, CT: Greenwood, 1982).

4. R. W. Batchelder, "The Scope and Value of the Microcard," *Special Libraries*, May–June 1952, 157–61.

5. Eugene Garfield and Emik A. Avakian, "AMFIS—The Automatic Microfilm Information System," *Special Libraries* 48 (1957): 145–48; Charles P. Bourne and Trudi Bellardo Hahn, *A History of Online Information Services 1963–1976* (Cambridge, MA: MIT Press, 2003); Richard A. Condon, "Mechanized Image Systems," in *Data Acquisition and Processing in Biology and Medicine*, ed. Kurt Enslein with John F. Kinslow, vol. 4, *Proceedings of the Rochester Conference* (Oxford: Pergamon, 1966), 179–88.

6. Neil MacKay, *The Hole in the Card: The Story of the Microfilm Aperture Card* (St. Paul: Minnesota Mining & Manufacturing, 1996).

7. LWL, Lewis–Langan Correspondence, Langan to Lewis, 8-2-58.

8. Michael Peterson, "Before Bourbon," NSA Center for Cryptologic History, n.d.

5

ONE SYSTEM FOR ALL INTELLIGENCE

In 1945, as an Allied victory became certain, the United States' leaders began planning for a peacetime America, one they hoped would have full employment and freedom from the economic agonies of the Depression era. They urgently sought ways to use government programs to prevent a resurgence of the frightening labor and ideological unrest of the 1930s. The plans they were formulating were usually positive, such as the GI Bill to subsidize higher education and the commitment to use the government's fiscal powers to stabilize the economy. Such initiatives fit with the administration's continuing commitment to the New Deal's reliance on big government. In contrast, the plans also included dismantling two very important institutions: Vannevar Bush's Office of Scientific Research and Development (OSRD) and Bill Donovan's Office of Strategic Services (OSS). Bush's OSRD had done much to make big science's well-funded research in universities at least a temporary American reality. Donovan's organization was the nation's first attempt to establish an integrated intelligence system and a permanent cloak-and-dagger capability.

Those two proposed reductions in the role of the federal government led to protests. Scientists called for a massive peacetime replacement for the OSRD so that America's universities could become world-class institutions. They and university administrators demanded federal support for what Bush called the "endless frontier" of science, with scientists, not government bureaucrats, determining how tax dollars would be spent. An implicit part of Bush's and his admirers' arguments was that science and the technologies it spawned would be the new version of Frederick Jackson Turner's socioeconomic "escape valve," with scientific and technological innovations preventing further Socialistic radicalism. The academics' demands also included substantial subsidies for science and technology information systems.

At the same time, Donovan and his allies lobbied for the creation of another and permanent central intelligence agency with, finally, a coordinated information capability, arguing that such an organization was vitally needed because of America's new role as the world's superpower and because of the threat of international Communism.

Frustrating the academics, the OSRD was left to die as Bush's and his university colleagues' proposals were put on hold while Congress debated other postwar policies. Meanwhile, as a temporary substitute, the professors hoped they could continue to shape science and information systems through the newly created Joint Research and Development Board that was to advise the military on science and technology policies and, importantly, on the state of technology in threatening countries. One of the board's most important chores was to provide strategic warnings of the possibility of a new type of Pearl Harbor surprise attack, a Soviet atomic one. Although the Vannevar Bush–led board was only advisory, its university and industry members had great influence and important responsibilities. The navy, for example, immediately followed the board's recommendations for massive subsidies for research in America's universities.

While the scientists hopefully awaited congressional action on a new sweeping federal science program, Donovan's plea for a permanent central intelligence agency, one independent of the military, received an unambiguous rejection. In September 1945, the OSS was split into pieces and President Truman had visions of those remnants soon dwindling away. The OSS's Research and Analysis group and its library and files were given to the State Department while the espionage and action groups went to the army's intelligence branch.[1]

THE CIG, WHAT WAS IT TO BE?

However, the old goals of coordinating the nation's intelligence activities and providing the president with strategic warnings and integrated

ONE SYSTEM FOR ALL INTELLIGENCE

estimates of the world situation were not entirely abandoned. A National Intelligence Authority, which included representatives of the army, navy, State Department, and the White House, was created. In turn, it established the Central Intelligence Group (CIG), its own version of a bureaucracy, to carry out its policies. The CIG was a very small and unusual organization and it was dependent on the army, navy, and State Department for its funds and personnel. Worse, it began, as had the CID, with no one sure of its duties and powers. Its vague mandate was to coordinate but not supplant other intelligence activities, but there were no clear lines of authority over the other agencies, each of which wanted to maintain or expand its intelligence information domains. The CIG's only specific objectives were to watch the new adversary, the Soviet Union; prepare world-situation summaries for the president; and help ready the nation for a new type of war, one based on science and technology.[2]

The CIG's birthing difficulties were compounded by its staff being newcomers to centralized intelligence and to information processing. There had been, by design, a clean sweep, with no high-level OSS leaders being hired by the new agency. Even those in the Office of Research and Estimates, the CIG's replacement for the OSS's Research and Analysis group, were relative beginners as were those in the organization's library-information center. None of Wilmarth Lewis's Central Information Division's leaders were called back, not even John Langan. John Ottemiller, who had moved with the OSS's library to the State Department, did not return, even after the CIG finally gained some control over the old OSS library books and data files.

GREAT EXPECTATIONS, BUT NO WILMARTH

The CIG was not satisfied with the OSS's information system and decided it would be necessary to create a completely new one. The process began with a young leader, Kenneth Addicott, in charge. The thirty-five-year-old Addicott was an unlikely choice for guiding the redoing of Wilmarth Lewis's work, for arranging President Truman's daily intelligence briefing, or for dealing with the reactions of the federal bureaucracy to the CIG's attempts to define itself as a major intelligence organization. Although Addicott had a bit of intelligence experience during World War II, he had no library training, his academic credentials were weak, he never held high military rank, and he was from a less than prestigious family. Educationally and culturally, he was not of the Ivy League background of the OSS's early wartime leaders such as Lewis or William Langer.

Kenneth had only a respectable lower-middle-class background. Edwin, his father, had begun his career as a teacher and amateur historian in rural California, then rose through the ranks of the evolving educational bureaucracy of the early twentieth century to become the principal of one of San Francisco's newest high schools, Polytechnic. It was in a then lower-middle-class neighborhood on the edge of the city's Golden Gate Park, and "Poly" was not of the academic stature of college-prep Brooklyn Polytechnic or of San Francisco's Lowell High that was located a few blocks from Addicott's school. As well, Poly, and Kenneth's father, faced some academic hard times in the 1920s when Poly's student culture seemed to have led so many of its students to ignore their studies that the senior Addicott felt it necessary to suspend some seventy of them.[3]

That action led to Poly becoming a well-publicized San Francisco political football. Edwin Addicott was fired, but soon accepted a reinstatement with back pay. Despite those troubles, Edwin sent his three boys to Poly, perhaps because he could not afford private schools or be able to move to a new neighborhood so his sons could attend better public schools.[4] He desired a college education for his children but neither he nor his boys saw any possibility of moving too far up the academic or social ladders. One son entered the nearby low-tuition and not yet high-status Stanford University. After years of teaching, researching, and academic publishing, Frederick became a well-regarded professor of applied botany at California's "farm" college in the Sacramento agricultural area that became the University of California at Davis. The other Addicott boys had a somewhat different history. Kenneth and his brother James attended California schools just beginning to emerge from the status of teachers' colleges. James went to Fresno State (Teachers) College in California's central valley farm belt then, after teaching school for a few years, he followed his brother to Stanford—but not for a degree in the sciences. He obtained a master's in education then began a long and successful tenure as a school administrator.

Kenneth, in contrast, had a rocky career after high school. He took his time in graduating from San Jose State (Teachers) College and then, like James, decided to follow in his father's footsteps. But he went to the University of Iowa, not Stanford, for a master's degree in education, writing a thesis on the not too exciting topic of assembly programs in schools. He then returned to California to work as a curricular advisor and as an adult education instructor. Both jobs were insecure and neither seemed a pathway to a satisfying career like James's or Frederick's. The adult education work interested Kenneth, however, partly because it had a social mission of helping those who could not afford college. So, in 1940 Kenneth decided to enter a doctoral program at Nicholas Murray Butler's temple of Progressive education, Columbia University's Teachers College in New York City. To support himself while he worked on his Ph.D. dissertation, "Museums for the Army," he took a position as an instructor at the American Museum of Natural History. Although employed at the museum for less than three years, and not known to be working on statistical problems, he claimed to have gained experience using tabulating equipment.

Then, at age thirty-one, he was drafted into the army. He served in its intelligence branch for a year before being shifted to the OSS. He worked for the OSS's Contacts branch in the San Francisco area where he located and interviewed people likely to have information on the Far East. Kenneth was congratulated on his ability to obtain precious documents that could help agents sent into areas such as Manchuria. He was also recognized as a good administrator, being promoted to chief of his section and sent to the East Coast.

At the war's end, Kenneth realized he liked intelligence work and Washington, D.C. He had no career to return to so he was one of the few OSS men to accept a position with the small CIG. He became one of its first administrators and received a great honor: he was selected to be the CIG's representative on the military/State Department team that prepared the president's intelligence reports. That was the beginning of his new career as a lifelong intelligence man, later including service in the Central Intelligence Agency's clandestine action group.

THERE WILL BE MECHANIZATION, THERE WILL BE ONE CLASSIFICATION SYSTEM!—BUT NOT WILMARTH'S!

Kenneth's 1946 stint on the presidential briefing committee was interrupted after just three months when the CIG received orders to create an advanced and mechanized information system that was to serve all (repeat, all) of America's foreign intelligence agencies. It was to integrate their information systems and handle all types of information. Who revived General Strong's idea and ordered the attempt to construct a radically new mechanized system in unknown, but Vannevar Bush, the influential advisor to the military and its intelligence services, had been attempting to craft an automated library since the 1930s through his work at MIT and through the Carnegie Foundation–funded Scientific Aids to Learning (SAL) project. After World War II, other agencies, such as the Army Medical Library and the Atomic Energy Commission, also began considering ways to automate bibliographic methods, but their efforts at the time were only tentative explorations.

That left the new, small CIG facing a daunting challenge, but one that could not be avoided. The CIG had its orders and an attempt to fulfill them had to be made—despite the absence of advanced information technology, despite the forces aligned against the centralization of America's intelligence capabilities, and despite the formidable intellectual challenge of creating a single coherent classification system that could serve all types of intelligence "customers."[5]

LITTLE KENNETH AND FRIENDS VERSUS THE INTELLIGENCE GOLIATHS, EVEN VANNEVAR BUSH

Because Kenneth Addicott claimed to have had tabulator experience, and because the CIG was short-handed, he was asked to launch the group's new library program. To his later dismay, his acceptance involved him in more than technological matters. The politics of intelligence information was deep, complex, and difficult. Bureaucratic turf battles were inescapable. Taking on the CIG's new information challenge meant bargaining with the military's branches, the State Department, and the Atomic Energy Commission over what role the CIG was

ONE SYSTEM FOR ALL INTELLIGENCE

to have in determining who would, and would not, collect, organize, and disseminate information.

Kenneth began with optimism and naïveté, but with little political power or social statute. He started with the assumptions that the CIG had a mandate and a clear path to becoming the central library and data center for all foreign intelligence matters. He also thought that every agency would gladly supply any data the CIG requested. Furthermore, he assumed the military services and State Department would not regard the CIG as a rather bothersome appendage, that all the other agencies would cooperate in creating a uniform intelligence classification system, and that the CIG's new library could easily fulfill its responsibility to provide services to every customer. He was convinced that he could, at minimum, create an index to all foreign intelligence information so that if his agency was unable to fulfill the utopian vision of a one-stop source holding all documents it could efficiently point to where they were.

However, those objectives were impossibilities. Frictions quickly developed, then intensified, especially after the CIG was changed in September 1947 from being an agency dependent on the military to the relatively freestanding Central Intelligence Agency (CIA). The CIA's new leaders made Kenneth's task more difficult. They were determined their agency would collect and interpret its own information and be able to dictate goals rather than respond to the requests of the other members of the intelligence establishment. The CIA was also in a hurry. Its leaders knew they had to quickly develop the tools to win the battles between Communism and liberalism.

But even before the demise of the CIG and the establishment of the CIA, Kenneth was under pressure—and he had found only one consistently true bureaucratic ally. Unfortunately, it was a very demanding one. Vannevar Bush's Joint Research and Development Board, that served all the military services and that hoped to direct their research programs, wanted the CIG to do a thorough job of collecting and indexing all science-related information so it could advise the military and the president on such vital matters as the Soviet's atomic capabilities. The Bush group was also a constant and aggressive advocate for the use of advanced information technologies and methods. Its demands would be one of the most important forces driving the intelligence community to aid the development of a "science of information," one focused on new methods of information retrieval for the Cold War's sci-tech institutions.

YOU WILL MECHANIZE NOW, BUT WITH DEWEY? THE ISC

In 1946, despite early hints of coming political problems, Kenneth immediately began his work. His first move did not seem to threaten anyone. He began with the CIG's Bush-mandated advanced information technology goals, ones that did not appear to antagonize any other organization. By the end of the year he had finalized a contract with machine specialists from the International Business Machines Corporation (IBM), then had its men cleared for secret consulting work. Addicott tasked them with helping design what he hoped would become the government's first thoroughly automated information service. However, the CIG's small machine design team and its IBM helpers soon realized they had been asked to do too much, too quickly. The project slipped behind schedule.

Kenneth's other 1946 explorations did touch some sensitive bureaucratic nerves. Believing Wilmarth Lewis's classification was inadequate, he began the process of creating a brand-new scheme, one that would serve and please all the intelligence agencies. Kenneth soon concluded that a much better and purer version of a Dewey hierarchical would be needed—he thought his customers agreed. Quite soon, however, the other intelligence agencies began to worry they would be forced to abandon their classification systems, or, at minimum, to significantly modify them if Addicott's proposed Intelligence Subject Code (ISC) ever came to life.

THE BECKER FACTOR, PRECIOUS FOREIGN SCIENCE INFORMATION, THE FDD

In the summer of 1946 Kenneth formed a small group within the agency to explore the possibility of a new classification scheme. Because the CIG had a limited budget, and had been unable to hire any new professional librarians, Addicott needed to rely on people within the agency.

ONE SYSTEM FOR ALL INTELLIGENCE

He searched for anyone who had library experience. There were few. After some months, he found Joseph Becker, a young man (twenty-four years old) who would later become one of the most innovative and influential figures in Cold War information science, and in the computerizing of America's colleges.

Joe Becker was from a solid but not prosperous Russian immigrant family in New York City's Bronx section. His father and sister worked in the garment industry, earning respectable but not high wages. The family could not afford private schools, and attending even public high school meant the loss of family income. But Joe was so bright that he was honored by being selected, at a very young age, to attend Brooklyn Polytechnic, the old elite high school that had attained collegiate ranking and that had become one of the most expensive colleges in the nation. Joe's parents found the honor hard to resist as Poly had gained international stature because of its record of training imaginative engineers.

Joe was the first of this family to go to college, or even high school, and he had ambitions much greater than being, like his father, a pattern maker. He majored in aeronautical engineering, taking many courses at night, while helping to support his family by working as a stack boy and clerk at the New York Public Library's science and technology division.[6] Although he was doing well at the library, earning as much as half what his father did, Joe had little time to begin a career as an engineer or a librarian. Soon after graduating from Poly he was drafted. Then, a mistake by one the bureaucrats running the army's personnel tabulator database led to a critical juncture in Becker's life. Because it was believed that Joe could read and write Japanese, he was assigned to the army's Far East military intelligence section. He did well and although he did not have a traditional bachelor's degree (he had a bachelor of arts in engineering) he was given the rank of first lieutenant. At the end of the war he was sent to Japan to help collect the tons of industrial, military, and scientific documents being seized by the United States under the military and FIAT programs. Then, he accompanied the documents to the military's Washington Documents Center (WDC) where five hundred tons of enemy documents from Asia were processed by American, British, and Canadian personnel.[7] Lt. Commander John Bagnall, another American who would play a significant role at the CIG and CIA, oversaw the sections of the WDC that were turning documents into intelligence, with a focus on Russian and scientific and technical matters. The Japanese collection contained much about the Soviet, as well as Japanese, sci-tech and cryptanalytic capabilities.

Because of its postwar intelligence value, it was one of the first large data collections turned over to the CIG's Foreign Documents Division (FDD) that oversaw acquiring all foreign materials—by open or covert means. Joe Becker, then the WDC's chief librarian, went with the collection. He soon became one of the FDD's most significant figures as it grew into one of the vital offices in the CIA.

Being transferred to Addicott's library team in 1947 did not end Joe's connections to the FDD, or to the Central Intelligence Agency's great efforts to acquire, by all means possible, both open source and secret foreign documents. As the Cold War developed, that became increasingly difficult as the Soviets became more restrictive. Although they allowed their scientists to appear at international meetings, allowed the export of several hundred of their scientific journals, and joined groups such as the International Federation for Information Processing, they kept the most important science and technology information to themselves.

Joe Becker, despite later becoming the CIA's chief librarian, continued to be recognized as an expert on obtaining foreign books, periodicals, and other documents, especially those of the Soviet bloc. With his guidance, the ever-expanding FDD sent teams to America's universities, private foundations, and businesses with foreign connections to gain promises of providing materials to the agency. Using the resources of the State Department and the military, but also relying on its own covert actions, the FDD forged its version of World War II's Interdepartmental Committee for the Acquisition of Foreign Publications (IDC) and acquired hundreds of foreign publications each month, then surveyed, broadly classified, and cataloged their contents.[8] By 1950, the FDD was regularly acquiring, for example, 150 Soviet scientific journals and large numbers of other foreign periodicals and newspapers. In addition to all that, the FDD eventually housed the old Foreign Broadcast Information Service that monitored the world's open source radio stations.

Consequently, the FDD became one of the largest translation centers in the nation. It soon had 120 translators working in sixty-eight languages, but its workload was so great it had to hire outside contractors, including personnel at the Library of Congress. It also became one of the CIA's strongest advocates for the development of machine (automated) translation. The FDD's role in the translation of scientific publication was so important that until the late 1950s it ran the nation's clearinghouse for sci-tech translations, an operation that saved millions of dollars by preventing duplication of effort by some four hundred federal agencies and their contractors.[9]

Joe Becker's 1946 transfer to the CIG's classification project was not the result of his being an experienced and formally schooled librarian-classifier. He had been selected for Addicott's Intelligence Subject Code team primarily because of his knowledge of foreign documents, his engineering background, and his intelligence experience. Joe wanted to be a true librarian, however. While working full-time at the agency, in 1947 he enrolled at the nearby Catholic University in Washington, D.C., and finally, in 1955 after eight years, earned a master's degree in library science. His thesis, not surprisingly, was on the use of IBM tabulating machines in libraries. His part-time education and his full-time job at the CIA did not prevent him from becoming a valued member of the American library community and a library technology visionary. The American Library Association and the American Society for Information Science awarded him high honors later in his life.

ANOTHER TRY FOR THE ONE CLASSIFICATION SYSTEM

Well before then, in early 1947 Joe Becker and Kenneth Addicott's small staff of eight continued their attempt to fulfill the command to create a new all-inclusive intelligence classification system, one that could serve as the foundation for a one-stop data center at the CIG. They had begun with a logical first step. They examined all the other agencies' systems, hoping to meld them into a single, logically consistent arrangement. That was not an easy task and it was not until August 1947 that a preliminary draft of their scheme was ready.

As soon as the CIG's "group of eight" had submitted their initial offering, Addicott held more rounds of consultations with the military agencies, the State Department, the atomic energy groups, and the Joint Research and Development Board. He also talked with the CIG's new team of analysts who prepared the agency's strategic papers. He asked for their views on the proposed classification system and estimated what their demands for information would probably be. After notifying his team of the initial comments, modifications to the first draft of what became known as the Intelligence Subject Code (ISC) emerged. Kenneth then took the revised version back to his customers and solicited more comments.

The responses were not encouraging. The services demanded more and more additions. They wanted ones that fit their special needs. The Atomic Energy Commission (AEC) had its own intelligence aims and already was angry over what it saw as Addicott's encroachments on its turf because the CIG, not the AEC, had inherited the intelligence files of the Manhattan Project, as well as Henry S. Lowenhaupt (the lead investigator for the project) because General Leslie Groves had distrusted the civilian-led AEC. The AEC and the military services informed Addicott that he had to agree to extensive lists of changes. They demanded many very long and specific classifications, ones that undermined the hierarchic coherence of the initial ISC. They also indicated they were hesitant about altering their own systems. The State Department was the least cooperative.

Only Vannevar Bush's Joint Research and Development Board was pleased, probably because it had no independent information organization and because Addicott and his team had accepted Norman T. Ball, the Joint Board's information expert, as one of their own. He served without cost to the CIG and his influence assured the acceptance of science and technology as major items in intelligence agendas. Luckily for Addicott, Ball quickly became more of an agency man than an advocate of Bush's radical information ideas. He also became a long-term friend of the CIA, a link between science information and the intelligence community, and one of the leaders in moving science information into the era of the Cold War's big science.

NORMAN BALL, THE MAN WHO KNEW AND WOULD KNOW EVERYONE

Although not a librarian, being a career wanderer for much of his life, and never becoming famous, by 1947 Norman Tower Ball had become one of the more influential policy makers in the postwar era's new

ONE SYSTEM FOR ALL INTELLIGENCE

science information efforts. He also was one of the most important men in moving science information providers from focusing on the needs of the traditional university scientist to those of the new sci-tech institutions of the Cold War. [10]

No one could have predicted Norman's importance from his beginnings as the son of a not too prosperous middle-class salesman in Toledo, Ohio, who had barely completed two years of high school. Norman was the family's firstborn, in 1905, when both his parents were in their early twenties and struggling to establish a household. Two other boys were born, Philip in 1909 and Gordon in 1912. Soon, there was a tragedy that strained the family: Gordon died when he was five. Later, there would be a divorce, but with the boys' mother always insisting, as had John Langan's mother, that she was a "widow." Fortunately, with the help of their mother's family Norman and Philip completed high school. After that, Norman received a great honor, a 1924 regular appointment to the United States Naval Academy at Annapolis. He made many friends, edited his class's yearbook, and was noted for his inquisitiveness and energy. He even won a large cash prize for being the "frosh" midshipman with the most knowledge of world affairs. He was on the way to a career as a naval officer.

Norman was, however, also noted for his youthful dislike of regimentation. That was one of the reasons why he surprised his classmates and resigned from the academy after three years. The twenty-two-year-old had not hastily abandoned education, however. He had devised a plan before he decided to leave the academy. He had made connections and immediately enrolled in France's historic and beautiful University of Poitiers. He had a short stay at Poitiers, probably because he was in France on a short-visit exchange program administered by the Quakers' American Friends Service Committee. Within a year, he was back in Toledo and in an educational setting more in tune with his lower-middle-class background. He decided to finish his education, but not in one of Ohio's many high-status colleges. Instead, he chose the struggling city-financed Toledo University, a school housed in downtown business buildings and an old automobile mechanics training facility. The school certainly was not high in the national collegiate rankings. Norman's choice of the Toledo college was unusual as he had been and would always be good at making friends who could provide him with special opportunities. His ability to deal with bureaucrats was reflected in his obtaining a promise of a job in far-off Washington, D.C., as soon as he obtained his degree.

In 1928, Norman began his lifelong career in the federal bureaucracy as an assistant patent examiner, with a specialty in aeronautics. At first, he wasn't sure that patent work would make a rewarding calling. He thought of joining the diplomatic corps and enrolled in the influential foreign service training program at Georgetown University headed by the Jesuit Father Edmund A. Walsh. Walsh had become the Catholic Church's most dynamic anti-Communist spokesman in America, and he and Georgetown University would become one of the CIA's best friends during the Cold War.

Norman did not, however, use his new bachelor of foreign service degree to move into the State Department. He stayed at the Patent Office hoping for advancement through obtaining a law degree at Washington, D.C.'s, George Washington University. He was again an outstanding student, something indicated by the school's law review publishing his study on the ratification of the federal Constitution's amendments.[11] Two years after that, in 1936, when he was thirty-one, he finally married. He then settled in at the Patent Office, rose in its ranks, became a well-known man in Washington's bureaucratic circles, and became involved with organizations such as politically important Department of Commerce's National Inventors Council that was charged with finding inventions that would help the nation prepare for World War II. That council was run by John Green, another bureaucrat important to the history of science information and to the political battles over "Socialistic" science information during the 1940s.

Norman made additional connections, including membership in a wide range of professional organizations such as the American Institute of Electrical Engineers (later known as the IEEE) and the American Association for the Advancement of Science. Norman also devoted much time to creating solutions to the increasing intellectual challenges at the Patent Office. It was becoming overwhelmed by a flood of patent applications, and better methods were needed to allow timely and thorough reviews. Much was at stake. A delay or an error in the search for prior claims could lead to the loss of millions of dollars. The patent problems were so significant they caught the attention of Vannevar Bush.

WILL NORMAN BECOME A NEW MELVIL DEWEY?

During the 1930s, Norman was asked to join a new group at the Patent Office to review its existing classification system (some three hundred major categories and forty thousand subcategories) and to make recommendations for revisions, perhaps radical ones. He began studying the history and methods of classification. Quite soon, he became knowledgeable about all the major systems, especially those used for science information. He was more than familiar with the cutting-edge classification work in England, S. R. Ranganathan's ideas, the systems at the United States' Library of Congress, and the accomplishments of the Universal Decimal Classification group and its allied European documentation movement.

He also taught himself about emerging information technologies, ranging from edge-notched cards and tabulators to Vannevar Bush's ideas for a microfilm Rapid Selector. As well, Norman became involved with prominent government and library leaders who were interested in information problems. At the same time, he was gaining a reputation as a philosopher on the need for new types of institutions to overcome science's information problems. Within a few years, he was interacting with a wide range of prominent information luminaries and was becoming an information "insider." Vernon Tate of the National Archives (soon to aid the OSS, then to head MIT's library) and Verner Clapp of the Library of Congress were just two of his many professional friends.[12]

Being called to active service in the Office of Naval Intelligence in 1940 did not end Norman's information interests. The navy's work intensified them and provided him with more contacts who helped determine his postwar career. He rose from the rank of lieutenant to that of commander and, later, reserve captain. During his years in the service he was assigned to study electronics at Harvard University and MIT; he met intelligence leaders such as Sherman Kent; he worked on advanced electronics and air navigation projects; he continued to advise the National Inventors Council; and, he developed more ideas for the redoing of science and patent information systems. By the war's end, Norman was back in Washington and active in a group of influentials attempting to resuscitate and revamp the American Documentation Institute (ADI). He also received a grant from the MIT-based, and the Vannevar

Bush–influenced, Scientific Aids to Learning project. It would underwrite his proposed seminal book on the organization of information.

Ball's relationship with the ADI was important to him and to the history of postwar science information. The institute was a mid-1930s outgrowth of the American Association for the Advancement of Science, the National Academy of Sciences, and the National Research Council–sponsored Science Service. The service had begun under Watson Davis in the 1920s to bolster the image of American science and scientists. By the 1930s, Davis became interested in the science information problem, contacted the European documentalists, formed the ADI, and focused it on the use of microfilm systems to overcome the problems American scientists had in obtaining articles. With private funding, and in cooperation with the Department of Agriculture that had long experience in providing copies of documents to farmers and farm organizations, Davis established the nonprofit Auxiliary Publication Service/Bibliofilm Service in 1936. It planned to microcopy individual science articles, then send the microfilmed copy to the scholars who had requested the items. The service was a primitive version of the later JSTOR. Davis and the ADI had greater visions. They hoped to create a great system of interlibrary loans, using microfilm copies rather than paper. They also hoped to microfilm several hundred thousand books, then sell them at low cost to America's smaller libraries, an idea that John Langan later explored. The ADI had an additional plan that predated a part of the later open access movement: Davis wanted to establish a preprint operation to speed the dissemination of scientific findings.

The ADI's microfilm service sent out several thousand items, but the onset of World War II led to its demise, and to the ADI languishing. Several other ambitious library microfilming projects also were halted by the war. [13]

THE COMMITTEE ON CLASSIFICATION AND THE BEST INFORMATION MEN (AND WOMEN), EVEN VANNEVAR BUSH

When World War II ended, Norman Ball returned to the Patent Office and joined a group of other Washington-based librarians and docu-

ONE SYSTEM FOR ALL INTELLIGENCE

ment-center administrators to explore new methods for "documentation"—the study of problems related to nontraditional materials and libraries. The group grew to include members from across the country and soon received formal recognition as the Committee on Classification of the American Documentation Institute. This brought Norman into interaction with more of the new information elite such as Eugene Scott and Alberto Thompson of the Atomic Energy Commission, Jesse Shera (who had moved from the OSS to the University of Chicago), James Perry of MIT and the American Chemical Society, and Maurice F. Tauber of Columbia University. The classification group also served as a nucleus for those advocating a reinvigorated and redefined ADI, a redefinition that eventually led to a focus on methods and technologies rather than microfilm services.

Meanwhile, Norman gained recognition as a science information leader. The prestigious journal *Science* published his article "Research or Available Knowledge: A Matter of Classification" in January 1947.[14] In it, Norman bemoaned the newest "serials crisis"—the high cost of and difficulties in obtaining science publications. He called for the development and application of new technologies (such as the tabulator), the creation of new classification systems that fit science and technology's special needs, and, perhaps, the creation of a national government-sponsored science information center at the Patent Office.

That article, his experiences at the Patent Office, his intelligence background, and his many professional contacts led to his being offered the important job as the executive director of the scientific information section of Vannevar Bush's Joint Research and Development Board.[15] There were few institutions in the nation that had more influence. While at the board, Norman would be helped by Helen L. Brownson. She had worked with Bush at the OSRD and the Carnegie Institution and later achieved fame and power in science information circles when she led the National Science Foundation's post-Sputnik response to the Soviet's apparent science information advantage—an advantage that some believed had helped it beat America into space exploration during the 1950s.

Among Norman's many duties while at the Development Board was directing critical studies on classification, abstracting, and indexing. He oversaw many panels, ones staffed with very influential high-science advisors. Norman's contacts with them and with the powerful military officers on the board[16] gave him additional stature in Washington. He also continued his association with the Patent Office and was aware of its attempts to mechanize, and, with the guidance of Vannevar Bush, to once again try to redo its systems. As well, Norman soon became a major figure in the ADI and represented it in Europe, sadly concluding that Paul Otlet's dream of a universal information system was fading due to lack of financial support and the inherent problems in attempting to build one universal classification system. However, he called for more American aid for all the United Nations' science information initiatives.

Norman left the Department of Defense's science information group in 1950, but he did not forsake the cause of science information. He was sent to England to be the science information advisor for the new version of the Marshall Plan. Then, the government called on his patent and aeronautical expertise. He was asked to serve as the executive secretary for the influential Committee on the Application of Machines to Patent Office Operations and he spent a year at Stanford University advising on electronics projects. That was followed by a stint as an influential information program director at the National Science Foundation and several years as the director of a high-level interdepartmental committee on science and research. He also served as an American representative to the European organization for cooperative research, and as a consul for the National Patent Association.

BUSH DEMANDS BUT DOES NOT RECEIVE

Before then, in 1947, one of Norman Ball's first assignments at the Bush-led Joint Research and Development Board was to steer a committee tackling the board's own science information problems. With Helen Brownson's help he began to devise a classification system for the board's document collection. He was in the process of developing that when he was ordered to create the science and technology section of the Addicott-led CIG's Intelligence Subject Code (ISC). By then, Vannevar Bush's deep annoyance with traditional classification schemes (and their hierarchies) was well known and it might have been expected that Addicott, Norman, and Helen Brownson would create a truly revolutionary system for the CIG's science classifications.

ONE SYSTEM FOR ALL INTELLIGENCE

Kenneth Addicott had decided, however, on having a Dewey-like decimal system and Norman delivered quite a traditional hierarchical, but sparse, scheme for the science section. Ironically, Norman's was based on a classification system that Adolph Voge, a librarian with a less than glorious career, had created during the last years of his working life at the Library of Congress. Voge had always alienated his coworkers and employers, even his relative Herbert Haviland Field, and had barely escaped being fired while working on the library's science project at the end of World War II.[17]

Norman had explored the possibility of relying, as had Wilmarth Lewis, on subject headings (chemistry-organic, for example) but found that heading systems usually led to chaotic lists of thousands of disconnected terms. Important to him, they lacked a feature he believed was essential to any organization of knowledge—hierarchies that facilitated generic searching. Despite the rather conservative nature of his science section of the ISC, Norman's energy, quick mind, and sensitivity to the needs of intelligence analysis led to his being asked to take a permanent position with the CIA's information group. He did not accept the generous offer, however.

NOTES

1. David Alvarez, "American Clandestine Intelligence in Early Postwar Europe," *Journal of Intelligence History* 4, no. 1 (2004): 7–24.

2. Woodrow Kuhns, "The Beginnings of Intelligence Analysis in CIA: The Office of Reports and Estimates; CIA's First Center for Analysis," *Studies in Intelligence* 51, no. 2 (2008), https://www.cia.gov/library/center-for-the-study-of-intelligence/csi-publications/csi-studies/studies/vol51no2, accessed April 2017.

3. NARA RG226 146 b004; State Department Registers; Ludwell Lee Montague, *General Walter Bedell Smith as Director of Central Intelligence: October 1950–February 1953* (University Park: Pennsylvania State University Press, 1992); Kenneth K. Addicott, "Museums for the Army," Ph.D. diss., Teachers College, Columbia University, 1944. CREST, History of the Central Reference Branch .

4. Ironic, in later years Poly became the school for many of San Francisco's leading leftists (such as David Jenkins's family) because it served the Upper

Height/Cole Valley Districts where Harry Bridges and many of his friends lived.

5. The CIG and the CIA had repeated bureaucratic realignments, so many that specifying the exact department for any individual or activity would be a confusing exercise.

6. Robert M. Hayes, "Joseph Becker: A Lifetime of Service to the Profession of Library and Information Science," *Bulletin of the American Society for Information Science and Technology* 22, no. 1 (October–November 1995): 24–26; Lee Ash, ed., *Who's Who in Library Service* (4th ed.) (n.p.: Shoe String Press, 1966); Joseph Becker and Robert M. Hayes, *Information Storage and Retrieval* (New York: Wiley, 1967).

7. Crest, *A History of the Foreign Documents Division 1946–1952*.

8. Very useful on scientific acquisition programs during the war years are the numerous works by Pamela Spence Richards. For example, "Gathering Enemy Scientific Information in Wartime: The OSS and the Periodical Reproduction Program," *Journal of Library History* 16, no. 2 (1981): 253–64. See also Christopher Hollings, *Scientific Communication across the Iron Curtain* (New York: Springer, 2016); Ksenia Tatarchenko, "Cold War Origins of the International Federation for Information Processing," *IEEE Annals of the History of Computing* 32, no. 2 (April–June 2010): 46–57.

9. Others were trying to eliminate redundancy in the translation effort. The Library of Congress, professional organizations, the Special Libraries Association, and the John Crerar Library had coordination efforts.

10. *Who Was Who*, vol. 5, 1969–1973 (New Providence, NJ: Marquis-Who's Who, 1973).

11. Norman T . Ball, "Ratification of Constitutional Amendment by State Conventions," *George Washington Law Review* 2 (1934): 216–17.

12. Norman T. Ball, "Making a Classification System," in *Punched Cards: Their Applications to Science and Industry*, ed. Robert S. Casey and James W. Perry (New York: Reinhold, 1951), 379–92.

13. Robert Binkley of Case Western University had a similar set of ideas for microfilm's use for social sciences and humanities, ones sponsored by the Social Science Research Council and ACLS.

14. Norman T. Ball, "Research or Available Knowledge: A Matter of Classification," *Science*, n.s., 105, no. 2715 (January 10, 1947): 34–36; Norman T. Ball, *The Special Committee on Technical Information* [Booklet]. Washington, DC: The National Military Establishment Research and Development Board, 1949.

15. Ball's unit underwent several name changes. One name was Special Committee on Technical Information (SCTI).

16. The civilian advisors were of high rank, such as Detlev Bronk.

17. Colin B. Burke, *Information and Intrigue* (Cambridge, MA: MIT Press, 2014), 241.

6

CIA'S CLASSIFICATION AND AUTOMATION BATTLES

By summer 1947, a stalemate had developed over Kenneth Addicott's proposed Intelligence Subject Code (ISC). His hope that it would be the classification system for all the American intelligence agencies was fading. There was wrangling over many sections of the ISC and Addicott could not overcome the objections of the military and other agencies. He did not have the needed status or political savvy to end what seemed to be a never-ending cycle of responses and rejections. By the year's end, as the Central Intelligence Group (CIG) was becoming the Central Intelligence Agency (CIA), Addicott was tired and pessimistic about uniting the intelligence community. He was also frustrated by the lack of progress by those leading the project to mechanize the CIA's library and its data files.[1]

Kenneth did not, however, abandon the classification or automation efforts, nor did four other people who became critical to the history of intelligence as well as science information. Three of them became creators of the new "information science" of the 1950s and 1960s. Hans Peter Luhn, Norman T. Ball, and Joseph Becker were founding fathers of intelligence information systems and of America's new version of documentation, information science. The fourth major player on Addicott's intelligence information and automation teams was the dynamic James Madison Andrews, a man who would spend his entire career in the CIA.

AN INFORMATION TECHNO-REVOLUTION TOO SOON, DESPITE LUHN'S GENIUS

Although Addicott's classification group was dynamic, winning over the other intelligence agencies would take more years and required new leader. The other part of the automation mandate was also frustrating Kenneth. As 1948 began, the CIA's team was discovering that the order to immediately mechanize was as much a fantasy as a realistic goal. Kenneth Addicott had begun his 1946 search for an automated system by asking his customers what they wanted from a research service. They responded with requests for individually tailored, complete, and fast searches of data files, and for integrated bibliographies that minimized the time they would need to decide what full-text documents they might need to examine.

After his initial surveys Kenneth consulted with IBM's technical men on how to turn functions into machines and how to have a system in place as soon as possible. After somewhat of a false start, the IBM contact led to a long-term relationship with Hans Peter Luhn.

Luhn, a lead IBM consultant, was a man of action, a very creative one who had always thought outside the box and who was intrigued by the CIG's challenge. It was his first encounter with information problems, but his 1947 work launched him on a new phase in his career. He soon became one of the world's leaders in bringing a new kind of efficiency to science information and famous for his attempts to automate information retrieval, indexing, and abstracting.[2]

Luhn was born into a family of renowned German printers at the turn of the century. He attended the rigorous local schools where he mastered several languages, then went to Switzerland for an apprenticeship. Unfortunately, it was interrupted by his having to serve in the German army during World War I. He returned to Switzerland to study at a technological institute and then was employed as technician in Italy's textile (not printing) industry. He immediately gained a reputation as an inventor and capable executive, and he became an independent consulting engineer. That led to a German textile firm asking him to be its special representative in the United States.

That 1924 assignment proved to be a near disaster. Just as Hans arrived in New York City his employer went bankrupt. Hans was stranded. Resourceful, instead of borrowing money from his family for a return to Europe, he found work as a translator for an international bank, soon becoming a rather successful financier and Wall Street stock market investor. But technology remained his love. In 1927, he accepted a position as a technical expert for textile firms in Pennsylvania, began accumulating a large portfolio of patents, and married into high society in New York City. He felt confident enough by 1933 to become an independent consulting engineer and expanded the reach of his patents. By the onset of World War II he had invented a gas pump meter, a critical meter for textile manufactures, and a folding raincoat. He would soon become famous for his MOD-10 checksum algorithm that is still used to verify identification numbers.

His obvious genius led to a great honor: Tom Watson, the head of the huge IBM, asked Luhn to be a corporate equivalent of an academic professor. In 1941, Luhn became an "inventor" at the IBM headquarters in Armonk, New York. His only assignment was to pursue his ideas and apply his innovative mind to interesting projects that Watson might present to him. In 1946, Watson turned to him in response to the CIG's request for help. After a few weeks on the CIG project, and appreciating the time limit imposed on Addicott, Luhn and his IBM group decided it was best to use available, affordable, and reliable technologies. Luhn and his colleagues knew of proposed ultra-high-speed microfilm data retrieval machines, such as Vannevar Bush's Rapid Selector, but they were only in development stages. Paper tape systems were also well known, but slow and were serial.

So, Luhn recommended replacing Wilmarth's hand-searched index card system with IBM's tabulators, and with all indexing items' codes punched into the IBM cards. As had Langan's tabulator aperture cards for the OSS's graphics and maps, tab-cards would allow machines to select out desired items rather than having clerks laboriously search through Wilmarth's paper card files for the relevant documents. Addicott was not worried that using tab-cards meant a thoroughly machine-dependent system—tabulator files could not be easily searched by hand. Of importance to Kenneth, tab-cards were a well-tested technology and they were "unit record," allowing much flexibility in data manipulation.

It appeared certain to Addicott, because of IBM's history of serving large bureaucracies that processed millions of records at recognized organizations such as the Census Bureau, the Social Security Administration, and large insurance companies, that Luhn's recommendations were trustworthy. Addicott also accepted his own staff's estimates that the probable savings in labor justified the high rental or purchase prices of any tabulating equipment. He also believed Luhn was not being self-serving when he recommended using IBM's products. The Remington Rand Corporation had a line of tabulators and sorters and their own cards, but IBM had already triumphed over Remington to become the major supplier for the government.

Addicott's next step was selecting the specific hardware. IBM had developed advanced versions of their standard sorting/tabulating/collating machines for statisticians, such as those for Benjamin J. Wood and Wallace J. Eckert at Columbia University, and for World War II's code-breakers—some using electronic tubes. As well, Hans Peter Luhn and other IBM engineers were beginning to explore even greater advances, ones specifically tailored to information processing. But Luhn and the other consultants advised Kenneth against waiting for any great technological leaps, even from IBM, because the first prototypes of its new devices, such as Luhn's "Scanner," were at least five years away. Certainly, in 1946 and 1947, no one was sure when, or if, the newly born electronic computer would ever become more than a cranky, and very expensive, calculating machine.

Luhn and the other IBM experts advised Addicott to adopt the company's existing card-punches for data entry, its trusted electromechanical basic sorting machines with a few modifications[3] for the selection of items, and its standard collators to maintain card file order. Although using the off-the-shelf devices meant limiting the searching of a card to one column (letter or number) at a time, and requiring time-consuming multiple passes of cards through the machines to find items, IBM's recommendations seemed acceptable to Kenneth. Because of his experience at the Museum of Natural History, the CIA trusted his judgment and accepted having only one subject code on a card although that meant requiring multiple cards for documents related to several subjects or countries.

Of significance, IBM's consultants did not recommend the application of John Langan's ideas to the CIA's document collection. They did not suggest filming the full text of incoming documents and storing them on aperture cards, then retrieving full documents with the tabulating equipment. They and Addicott had more limited visions for data

TOWARD AN INFORMATION REVOLUTION: INTELLOFAX

storage and retrieval, partly because of the demand to immediately create a system.

TOWARD AN INFORMATION REVOLUTION: INTELLOFAX

Kenneth's next assignment was more challenging because it could not be fulfilled with any readily available technology. Finding that his customers liked Wilmarth's idea of having an abstract of a document typed on the same index card as its classification and identification data, Kenneth decided to have his tabulator cards also hold an abstract. He reasoned that even if his new system had much deeper indexing/classification than Wilmarth's, the abstracts were an essential substitute to having to pull a full document from the files and making an analyst read through the text to see if the indexing had pointed to a useful item. Having the abstracts on the same card as the identifiers would also avoid a time-consuming step for the system's personnel.

Once again, the consultants did not look to an aperture card solution. They recommended typing the abstract directly on the tab-card because punching the abstracts into the cards was impossible. However, typed abstracts presented another fundamental challenge to the designers: There was no easy way to reproduce an abstract typed on a tab-card. IBM machines could print the information punched into cards, but not typed or written text. Kenneth was disappointed and a bit upset with the consultants.

Kenneth could not accept defeat. He thought it was vital that a solution be found, one that would also avoid a difficulty that had frustrated the users of Wilmarth's system. If a card had been selected from Wilmarth's index card files and was being read by a user, the card would not be available to others. Kenneth was willing to spend much time on finding a way of minimizing the amount of time a card was out of its file. He wanted to have the text on his cards printed out as soon as one had been selected and to have the original card immediately returned to the active main file. He also wanted to have the abstracts printed in a continuous manner so that he could present his users with a complete report, one almost as pleasing as a book.

Those goals were challenging. It took much of 1946 and 1947 in searching for a satisfying technology. The possibility of microfilming the cards was investigated but ruled out because microfilm, the CIG's users said, was too difficult to read and could not be marked up. Addicott continued his quest. It wasn't until 1948 that the first exploratory development contract for a reproduction system was awarded. Exploration had been needed. No company then made a machine that could quickly transfer the text on a tab-card to another card or a sheet of paper. Fast and inexpensive photocopying was in the future, and practical Xeroxing was a decade away.

After many months, Luhn and the other consultants thought there was a possible solution. They decided that a variation of facsimile equipment would be the answer, at least the best answer. Facsimile equipment scanned a document, sensing light and dark shades, then converted the results into a continuous analog signal that was sent to a receiving fax machine that changed the tones it was receiving into a printed paper copy of text and images. The signals could be sent by telephone or radio. Newspapers and police departments had been among fax systems' early users.

Kenneth's team learned of the promises and pitfalls of facsimile when they contacted the major manufacturers, such as the Radio Corporation of America and General Electric, thinking that such big corporations would gladly provide special help to an intelligence agency. The larger firms did not seem willing to spend time on a small contract, however. Finally, Addicott's consultants located Finch Telefax, a New York City manufacturer of facsimile equipment. It seemed willing to work with the CIA in devising a solution.

ANOTHER LUHN

William G. H. Finch was a version of Hans Peter Luhn.[4] An immigrant genius inventor with a long list of patents and a lifelong urge to innovate, Finch came to America from England as a youth, attended high school in the Midwest, then took classes in electrical engineering—but never earned a college degree. He worked for the Hearst newspapers, setting up teletype transmission networks in the United States and abroad, and then decided to form his own company, one focused on improving facsimile systems. He led the development of radio transmission of images and text, even in color. He had a workable plan for a radio facsimile system for homes, and after World War II he created a system for the transmission of weather maps generated by radar. He also had a way to turn facsimiles into sound. By the 1930s, he was highly respected in his field and was frequently called on by the government. But his company never approached the size of the great electrical corporations of the era. Perhaps it was the small size of his firm and his near compulsion to innovate that led him to accept Addicott's challenge.

Finch believed fax technology had improved enough to meet the CIA's needs. The technology had been advancing quite rapidly in the 1940s. During World War II fax became very sophisticated as the military services used it to transmit from ship to shore and over vast land distances. At the war's end, several companies, including William G. H. Finch's, had plans to extend fax to create a system to send newspapers by facsimile directly to consumers. The Radio Corporation of America, Eastman Kodak, and the National Broadcasting Company had grander plans in development. In 1948, they gave the public a peek at the future by sending over a thousand pages of *Gone with the Wind* over their Ultrafax system at the Library of Congress—in just two minutes and twenty seconds.

INTELLOFAX, PERHAPS

Addicott's 1947 challenge for William Finch wasn't that adventurous, but it proved difficult for Finch to develop the text duplication and unified reports' printing system for Addicott. Much trial and error work went into coaxing Finch's devices into handling the IBM cards and reproducing the abstracts. Kenneth, fortunately, convinced the 3M Company to produce a special paper needed to turn the fax scans into a four-inch continuous bibliographic tape containing readable images of all the cards a machine search had selected. With redesigned Finch technology, the selected cards were fed into the fax scanner and then their typed data was transmitted to the receiver-printer with its chemically treated and heat-dried paper tape.

The new fax-tabulator combination was exciting and innovative. It seemed to be the first ever end-to-end automated information system. Kenneth and his advisors, however, almost abandoned it. They feared the cost of the soon to be called Intellofax would be too great. Addicott and this team calculated that Intellofax would need a larger support staff of reference librarians, data entry personnel, and machine operators than they had imagined.

Then, at the last moment Addicott's group reversed itself, deciding there was a compensating factor, although not a quantifiable one. They believed the price of the operation would be offset by the time saved by the analysts. As well, there was that mandate from their superiors, and Vannevar Bush, to create an automated system, now! They also believed they could soon go far in decentralizing Intellofax, thereby reducing labor cost and time. The Finch-IBM contract included the purchase of six transmitting and receiving fax stations that would electronically send distant users a fast response to their requests.[5] Addicott argued the cost of travel to and from the central office would be eliminated, thus justifying the need for more development funds.

OVER BUDGET, BEHIND SCHEDULE

Intellofax's development and initial testing took more time and money than anticipated. The first contract for production was signed in January 1948, the prototype was delivered in July (just as the war-threatening Berlin Blockade began), and it took a year of shakedowns and testing before Intellofax became operational. It was another year before an updated version was delivered. By that time, 1950, the cost of the system's development had doubled from some $1 million to $2 million and it was soon discovered that the plan for remote stations was unworkable. One reason was that even with the technical advice of the National Security Agency, there were problems in making Intellofax's transmissions safe. Encryption devices were added and the cable links to the microwave transmission tower were shielded, but the fax machines continued to radiate, making it possible for the transmissions to be tapped.[6] The transmitters and receivers had to be abandoned, much to the CIA's embarrassment.

CIA'S CLASSIFICATION AND AUTOMATION BATTLES   105

During the many years of Intellofax's development there were other frustrations for Addicott's vision of a mechanized central intelligence information system. The military and the State Department showed no interest in sharing the costs of Intellofax and it seemed it would become a costly one-off experiment if it was used only for the CIA's classified document-form reports. There was a greater disappointment: later calculations of the cost of composing the abstracts, and of indexing and data entry for Intellofax, led to a decision by management to use Intellofax only for critical materials.

SORRY GENERAL STRONG, BUT . . .

The Intelligence Subject Code also suffered. It had not become a universal system, even within the CIA. It became a "reports" system. The most secret (Special) file did use a modified version of the numeric ISC but was allowed some special privileges such as using alphabetic acronyms for people and places. As had been the case in the OSS's system, the data for industrial/military targets, biographies, scientific conferences, pictures and films, and the most secret documents were kept in separate files and used their own retrieval teams and systems. As well, open source research would rely on traditional library methods and technologies. Perhaps as much of a disappointment, the agency's scientists saved time and money by using Paul Otlet's Universal Decimal Classification (UDC) rather than the Intelligence Subject Code for much of the open literature. The reason was simple: the Soviets had required the UDC's use on all scientific articles, so time and effort were saved by adopting it.[7] Reliance on another special classification system, the Outline of Cultural Materials, was found necessary. It was for in-depth files on the cultures and politics of foreign nations. The file was an import from the CIA-funded Human Relations Area Files effort. That project began in World War II under George P. Murdock, the Yale anthropologist the U.S. Navy commissioned to gather academics' information on Japanese-held islands in the Pacific. The information was used by the OSS as well. After the war, the project was continued, with funding from the military, the CIA, and private foundations.[8]

It appeared the CIA failed to create a unified information system—something that would lead to severe criticism of the agency by the 1950s.

ENTER JAMES MADISON ANDREWS, HARVARD, AND A PROFESSIONAL STUDENT

In 1947, while Addicott and his staff were dealing with the first stages of the machine and classification projects, some political and institutional developments altered their playing field, making their job more difficult. When the CIG was replaced by the CIA, additional bureaucratic problems arose. The CIA was in a rush and although it had gained increased powers and funding, and was recruiting people for an aggressive approach to intelligence gathering to meet the Soviet challenge, the agency did not have the power to dictate to other agencies. The new men brought into the expanding CIA were, however, told to act as if it was already the king of the American intelligence community.

The recruits were typically not strangers to intelligence work. Important, among those called back to service were some men who had led the OSS's Research and Analysis and covert operations groups. Many of them were schooled in elite universities and were from high-status families. That kind of background helped the CIA to soon create its own independent intelligence identity and put to rest any remnants of the idea that its primary purpose was to serve the military or the State Department's information needs.

James Madison Andrews IV, one of the new recruits, hadn't been an OSS man but he had some intelligence background and, significantly, the social status needed to overcome many of the stumbling blocks that had frustrated Kenneth Addicott throughout 1946 and 1947. Andrews arrived at the new CIA in January 1948, beginning as the head of the reference section of the information group just as the agency began facing the Cold War head-on, and as its information initiatives (especially the classification project) were at critical junctures. It wasn't long before the forty-five-year-old Andrews was promoted to lead the near all-encompassing Collection and Dissemination group (and, later, the Office of Central Reference) that handled the delicate political relations with outside agencies. He was soon given more responsibilities, oversight over all the CIA's library and information groups.

Andrews was much like the nineteenth century's gentleman scholars. His family was wealthy and had colonial origins. He was a member of the Society of the Cincinnati due to his ancestors' roles in the War of Independence. Military leadership had been a family tradition. James's grandfather, for example, had been an aide to Teddy Roosevelt during the Spanish-American War. The Andrews families had also done well in the business and social worlds. The later generations became quite wealthy through their associations with the giant General Electric Corporation and through wise financial investments. The Andrews families had fashionable New York homes in New York City, Schenectady, and Saratoga Springs and they socialized with the likes of the railroad-fortune Harrimans. When in Washington, James remained part of that social world, even being asked to join the famed Cosmos Club.

James had grown up in an affluent Schenectady neighborhood and did well at its better schools, but he delayed entering college. When he finally enrolled at Harvard University he found his niche. He became committed to a new version of Franz Boas's type of modern-age anthropology (somatology/anthropometrics) as practiced by his mentor, Earnest Albert Hooton. Hooton, who knew and worked with the famed Harvard biologist/eugenicist Charles Davenport, gathered body measurements to try to gauge the roles of heredity and environment in human development. His work had peripheral relation to the troubled eugenics debates of the 1920s and 1930s.

Hooton and his colleagues and students, including Carleton S. Coon, the World War II OSS operative in North Africa (who became famous for inventing and using explosives disguised as camel dung) benefited from generous financial help from major foundations. Hooton's students spread across the world, almost as romantically as Indiana Jones, as they explored the race question as well as more general heredity issues. Their conclusions, unlike Davenport's, usually supported the liberal side of the race and eugenics debates. The samples they gathered in Asia and the Middle East, and from such groups as native American Armenians, and their sophisticated statistical analyses, usually showed that similar environments changed the bodies of various groups in the same way.

In 1933, after earning his Harvard undergraduate degree, and then a master's in anthropology and museum studies at age twenty-eight, Andrews seems to have decided to become a perpetual student. Although married, James spent years as a lowly paid research assistant on anthropometric and sociological projects in Canada and Siam, not receiving his Harvard Ph.D. until he was thirty-four years old. By then, he had become an anthropometric expert and had necessarily become somewhat of a skilled statistician and tabulating machine operator. That did not mean riches or even a sure pathway to academic success, however. Nearly thirty-five, he accepted a position as only an assistant curator of somatology at Harvard's Peabody Museum for anthropology. His friend Carleton Coon, in contrast, had received a professorship. James oversaw the Peabody's tabulator operations but found time to participate in a few additional anthropological expeditions. Despite all that, and his social background, he remained an assistant until 1942 when he joined the navy and began to work in the Office of Naval Intelligence where he did very well. He supervised statistical/tabulating projects and rose, in just two years, to the rank of commander. He made a very great impression on Captain A. H. McCullum, the old-line influential navy intelligence man and expert on Asia. Demobilization led to James's return to Harvard and the museum. Although Earnest Hooton turned the responsibility for the completion of his large government-sponsored study of the physical characteristics of World War II's soldiers over to him, James remained an assistant curator, and one without the kind of prestigious publication record that predicted a professorship.

Perhaps feeling he had reached a dead end, when Captain McCullum, who had been detailed to the CIG by the navy, heard of the need for someone to help with the information projects, he recommended Andrews. James did not hesitate and quickly settled in Washington, D.C. He arrived just as the new CIA was asserting its independence.

With his social and educational background, his economic security, and his past military rank, James was suited to aid the CIA's drive for autonomy. He was quickly promoted to be an assistant director and he asserted his authority within and without the agency. Kenneth Addicott, perhaps to his embarrassment and resentment, soon became James's executive assistant, focusing on the technicalities of the classification and Intellofax problems. That allowed Andrews to concentrate on the bureaucratic/political issues related to the completion of the long-de-

CIA'S CLASSIFICATION AND AUTOMATION BATTLES 109

layed intelligence classification system, the Intelligence Subject Code (ISC). He quickly made some decisions, ones he thought could force cooperation by the other intelligence agencies.

WE WILL BE "THE" INFORMATION SOURCE, ANDREWS DECLARES

As a first step, and with support from the CIA's top leaders, Andrews declared that the needs and wants of the CIA's own analysts would receive top priority—the wishes of the services would be secondary. That was reflected by the agency's standing its ground on its latest preliminary version of the ISC. No longer would it accept the seemingly endless revisions demanded by the State Department and the military services. Andrews believed that once the ISC was in place at his agency the others would have to adopt it. In March 1948, the confident Andrews stated the ISC's essential framework was set and that any revisions had to be reviewed and approved by his team. His goals were to ensure intellectual coherence and ease of use for indexers. Andrews also stated the agency's staff would have priority in determining what documents were to be collected and how they were to be processed. He also gained assurances from the CIA's leaders that his division would be allowed to continue to experiment with new information techniques.

But he had to promise that he would do everything possible to have all intelligence agencies adopt the ISC. He offered an enticement to those "outsiders." The other agencies would be allowed to add as many digits as they wished to the ISC's Dewey-like numbers if and when they desired more precision, if that did not undermine the coherence of the hierarchical system. Although many compromises were accepted, the refinement and testing of the ISC required an additional year's technical and political efforts.

The first operating edition reflected the CIA's and Andrews's growing power but, significantly, it also revealed that Andrews and the CIA had not achieved all their political goals. The CIA was still being treated as a provider to its customers and subordinate to the president's National Security Council rather than being a fully self-determining source of long-term strategic intelligence. The 1948 ISC also showed that immediate concerns and influences, rather than an abstract concept of intelligence information, were still at work.

NOT QUITE AS ALL MAY THINK, THE ISC UNDER FIRE

Despite the influential Vannevar Bush's condemnation of all traditional library systems, the Addicott-Andrews 1948 ISC kept the initial commitments of the original CIG's team to a Dewey-like subject-based, hierarchical decimal system—and to one with numeric indicators. Addicott's men had resisted pleas for the kind of long and sometime alphanumeric indicators the military services and the State Department used and had rejected Wilmarth Lewis's subject terms. Under Andrews there had also been no serious reconsideration of using any radical alternatives to a basic decimal approach such as the Universal Decimal Classification, S. R. Ranganathan's "colons," or Vannevar Bush's ill-defined "associations."

However, as the CIA's group was crafting a classification system that could be efficiently used on the tabulating machines, that would be easy to understand, and that would minimize the cost of indexing and searching, they realized that Lewis's two- or three-digit OSS indexing had imposed too much on researchers and users. There had been complaints that such shallow indexing wasted precious time because it forced users to search through huge stacks of items of possible interest. The classification team agreed to a compromise concerning length of the indicators. They had decided on what they called a "medium level of indexing," one using six digits. They hoped that all the 999,999 categories would never be used because they wanted a sparse as well as useful system.

The CIA's group had also fought to keep the ISC a logical and hierarchical system like Dewey's so that generic searches could be done and so that tabulator runs would be minimal. But they were not always victorious. Classification systems cannot be made in an intellectual bubble. Gaining the cooperation of the other departments and agencies necessitated more compromising. For example, the influential Norman Ball had agreed with Addicott's philosophy and recommended the use of the ISC's six-digit decimal system for his science section, but he had to acknowledge the importance of the military's interests by accepting

CIA'S CLASSIFICATION AND AUTOMATION BATTLES   111

up to 82 nonhierarchical science subcategories in the first (1948) edition of the ISC—the four major military categories had a total of 308.

Ball soon had to bow to additional pressures from the Joint Board and the new science analysts the CIA hired to fulfill the agency's mandate to be the nation's watchdog of Soviet science and technology. Their demands led to a vast expansion of the Science (600) category's subdivisions. One analyst demanded and was accorded sixty-eight categories for his narrow specialty, few of which could be aligned in a sensible hierarchy.[9] Another example of the results of having to please others, even from within the agency, soon appeared. In 1949, a consulting agriculture expert demanded eighty-eight subcategories for just diseases of plants. They were included, but never used. Another example was that as the Cold War deepened, the ISC's managers had to yield to pressures to add many subcategories for Communism. Within a few years, they grew from eight to almost one hundred.[10]

The 1948 edition did, however, hold the total number of subcategories below one thousand. But James Andrews realized that even with his military background and social influence the CIA was unlikely to be able to limit the number of categories in the future, or to keep the system a logical hierarchy. Perhaps expecting such problems, Addicott's team had wisely invested in creating their own version of a "relativ index" (a word-based explanatory index to the numeric identifiers) to help overcome difficulties with less than obvious classifications.

There were more complicating demands. The ISC's designers had agreed in 1948 that a geographic identifier might be used in addition to the subject decimals and that employing a seven-digit identifier of the source of a document, such as an army attaché in Tokyo (05a0601) was acceptable. The pressures for precise retrieval soon led to more additions to the ISC. Action codes (modifiers) began to be included. At first, there were only a few semantic clarifiers, such as, "import from" or "export to" for the economics section. Within a few years there were dozens for each of the major classifications. Fields for date of activity and security classification were soon included. Other types of modifications to the original ISC appeared in response to unanticipated user demands. In the early 1950s, compound categories, such as 115.773 for Greek Monetary Reform or 876.119 for Italian Language, were created to speed responses to frequent requests.

Other unforeseen challenges led to irksome logistical burdens. Two versions of the central Intellofax file were soon created, one organized by subject-area, another by area-subject. That speeded searching but imposed a high maintenance cost. As well, having only one subject code per card meant that four to eight cards per item usually had to be created and filed. With each addition of such things as action codes, additional labor-intensive tabulator/sorter runs were required.

GENERIC SEARCHES AND INTELLECTUAL ELEGANCE CONFRONT INTELLIGENCE REALITIES

A major goal of the ISC's creators had been to facilitate generic searching. The ability to directly go from the more general to the particular (and the reverse) within a commonly defined subject area had trumped suggestions that a Library of Congress–like subject-heading system be adopted, although such word-based headings were tempting. Using them did not call for the sometimes agonizing construction of hierarchies in subject areas that were not, unlike those that Dewey and Otlet had focused on, inherently hierarchical. Heading systems, however, tended to become chaotic, without intellectual structure, and puzzling to users.

Addicott's team had struggled to build a system that would allow a searcher to avoid, for example, naming all makes of rifles, handguns, and artillery when seeking information on modern armaments. Despite Addicott's and Andrews's influence, and their continued efforts to maintain a logically structured and consistent system, the 1948 ISC evolved into a not quite fully integrated scheme, even at its highest levels. The nine major categories (chapters) of the original ISC reflected outside demands as much as than the intellectual visions of "librarians of intelligence":

000.000 International Situation
100.000 National Information
200.000 Army
300.000 Navy
400.000 Airforce
500.000 Weapons and Scientific Warfare
600.000 Science and Technology
700.000 Geography and Economics

800.000 Social and Cultural
(and later) 900.000 Library Books

NOTES

1. The ISC group began in August 1947; the first draft was issued in January 1948. The next CIA version came in March 1948; the full version appeared in March 1949 but was subject to many changes; CREST, "ISC," passim.

2. Claire K. Schultz, *H. P. Luhn: Pioneer of Information Science* (New York: Spartan Books, 1968).

3. CREST "Intellofax," passim; CREST, "The Intellofax System."

4. *New York Times*, William G. H. Finch obituary, January 17, 1990; Jennifer S. Light, "Facsimile: A Forgotten 'New Medium' from the 20th Century," *New Media and Society* 8, no. 3 (2006): 355–78.

5. CREST, "The Intellofax System"; years later the fax machines were replaced by Card List Cameras, the Photo-Expediters.

6. CREST, "Facsimile Copying Equipment," April 19, 1952.

7. CREST, Paul A. Borel, "On Processing Intelligence Information."

8. Clellan S. Ford, *Human Relations Area Files, 1949–1969: A Twenty-Year Report* (New Haven, CT: Human Relations Area Files, 1970).

9. CREST, "ISC," passim.

10. CREST, John K. Vance, "Philosophy of Classification," 1959; by the mid-1950s the ISC had some five thousand subcategories, with many not integrated into the hierarchy.

Part II

Cold War Information Politics and Lives

7

IDEOLOGY AND SCIENCE INFORMATION POLICY

While Kenneth Addicott and James Madison Andrews were dealing with the problems of organizing intelligence systems, broader information struggles were emerging. They were over science, science information, and higher education's futures. They were more intense, public, and political than those over the roles of the CIG or CIA. One of the earliest examples of the intermixing of science information policy and the postwar political climate is linked to the history of FIAT, the Field Information Agency Technical effort. FIAT was the second of the two major nonsecret information-gathering initiatives Britain and the United States launched as they liberated Europe. FIAT's assignment was to collect "intellectual reparations" in addition to the documents being gathered by the intelligence and military agencies. While FIAT had been created with the goal of eventually releasing its holdings to the public, the results of other projects to collect enemy cryptologic documents (TICOM, Target Intelligence Committee) and those to capture Axis maps, photos, and industrial data on Russia were always to be top secret.[1]

FIAT targeted information that might help America's economy. Industrial and nonsecurity classified science and technological information, including patents, were FIAT's primary targets. Before any librarians began what became the Farmington Plan's efforts (led by Wilmarth Lewis) to obtain traditional science and humanities publications from the liberated areas, American industrialists and their university allies

117

were called on to aid in collecting sci-tech information. As the military forces began to seize Germany's, and then Japan's, industrial and university research centers, American trade associations provided the occupation forces with lists of what they desired.

In 1945, the civilian United States Department of Commerce was ordered to coordinate the FIAT operations and to prepare to publicize and disseminate the seized documents. To expedite the process, large industrial corporations and scientific societies were soon called upon to send representatives to Europe and Asia. They accompanied the military forces as they seized likely targets. The civilian experts picked out the documents they thought valuable and the military sent them to their copying and declassification centers, and then to the United States.[2] FIAT accumulated tons of science, technology, and applied-science documents, calling for the establishment of additional processing centers in Europe and Asia. Several young men who worked at those sites, such as Allen Kent (later of Western Reserve University), became extremely influential in postwar science information initiatives and policy debates—and in information and computer science circles.[3]

The American government advertised the FIAT information as an invaluable source for democracy and "the people," but the possibility of inequities was worrisome. As FIAT sent its first civilian operatives overseas, its administrators remembered the complaints about the inequality of access to patents and other information seized after World War I. Would World War II's documents to be of equal access to all, not, as before, to only the large corporations whose representatives helped gather them? Although some precautions, such as having FIAT experts on any project come from a minimum of two different companies, seemed to help, the equity issue remained a sensitive one as the war was ending. Complicating the situation, the FIAT problem was a part of a politicized debate about access to all types of government science and technology information that surfaced just as the Department of Commerce's Office of Technical Services (OTS) began processing and disseminating the FIAT materials.

INFORMATION FOR . . . ?

A central issue was what powers the OTS was to have. The office had been hastily created in 1940 with a mandate to encourage inventors to contribute ideas that might help the nation prepare for war and, perhaps, to aid the civilian economy. The OTS had the spirit of Thomas Edison's World War I Inventors Council's attempt to muster the talents of the common man, something not well regarded by the academics of the National Research Council and Vannevar Bush's Office of Scientific Research and Development. As well as having a reputation of being by and for amateurs, the OTS began with significant ideological baggage. The influence of the New Deal's spirit of trust-busting and egalitarianism was evident at its birth. Thus, although the OTS's wartime achievements were not great, it seemed politically wise to continue it and to give it the responsibility for transferring wartime technology-related information to the peacetime economy.

At first, the OTS thought it would be dealing only with the documents it had received from American inventors during the war years, but the government charged OTS's library division with distributing many of America's own war-related research publications, as well as those unclassified FIAT materials. OTS was given a heavier burden: create the solution to the politically sensitive task of creating rules and procedures for democratic access to all of them.[4]

The OTS's administrators soon made some sensitive ideologically driven decisions. They went beyond their original powers, expanding the organization's reach. First, the OTS's leaders argued their service should be made "the" disseminator of all secret German and Japanese documents held by the military agencies once they were declassified. And, they lobbied quite strenuously for the immediate declassification of all documents. They next tried to build a central and permanent sci-tech information center for the United States' civilian economy. In addition to the World War II declassified Axis and American documents, they sought ongoing access to all nonsecret sci-tech reports produced by American companies and universities working under government contracts—although those documents might contain proprietary information. They also wanted all civilian federal agencies to deposit their unclassified documents related to science or technology as soon as they produced them. Even the thousands of reports that had been generated by Vannevar Bush's wartime substitute for the National Research Council, the Office of Scientific Research and Development, were to be sent to the anticipated great civilian information center in Washington.

The OTS's proposals had the flavor of the more radical open access agenda of fifty years later and, expectedly, its demands immediately met opposition. Bureaucratic scuffles erupted and the OTS had to agree that other depositories, such as the Department of Agriculture and the Army Medical Library, could hold and distribute items in their special fields. Practical questions arose as well. The OTS's grand plans seemed infeasible to many experts. How could a new and low-budget agency with few employees (and even without its own building) store the materials and devise and implement indexing and library techniques that could allow all Americans to know of and have access to millions of documents?

INFORMATION FOR THE SOCIAL GOOD

More than practical and bureaucratic issues were behind the negative reactions. The OTS and the leaders of its parent organization, the Department of Commerce, had a broad and idealistic political agenda that went beyond document distribution. They were ideological New Dealers (the Commerce Department's director was ex–vice president Henry Wallace) and they hoped the department would become a center for stimulating the welfare of America's small businesses. The department's special favorite was the New Dealers' 1940s version of Thomas Jefferson's yeoman farmer, the independent entrepreneur who could, with the OTS's help, challenge monopolistic corporations. The Department of Commerce's and OTS's leaders of 1945 were not oriented, as Herbert Hoover had been, to the fostering of large-scale efficient enterprises that could compete in world markets. They were not believers in Bush's scientific frontier. For them, equality outranked efficiency and abstract knowledge. The businessman with a small-scale company was the OTS's true American hero, not the great captains of industry such as Andrew Carnegie or John D. Rockefeller.[5]

Following from those beliefs, the OTS sought to establish policies and institutions to counterbalance what they felt was an unfair informa-

IDEOLOGY AND SCIENCE INFORMATION POLICY

tion advantage held by large corporations, their special libraries, and their allied research and technical universities, such as MIT. The OTS wanted to transfer the results of all government-sponsored research at prices the small businessman could afford—even if that meant government subsidization.

YOU CAN'T DO THAT BECAUSE INFORMATION IS FOR . . .

For many in the business and academic communities the OTS appeared to be on a road to information communism, especially when OTS's supporters demanded that all patents related to government contract work by a corporation or a university be made part of the public domain. As a result, Henry Wallace's Commerce Department/OTS's idealism ran into strong opposition from influentials such as Vannevar Bush and plunged information issues into the heated broader postwar-era battles over "creeping Socialism" in America.

The opposition and its anti-Socialism arguments were successful. Despite much lobbying, Congress refused to fund much of what the OTS desired. The White House was also wary of Henry Wallace and his other plans. The Truman administration did not grant the OTS the power to be the sole repository for nonsecret government sci-tech materials, nor was it given the funds to adequately process the millions of documents that were put in its charge. Then, within a few years, the department saw its already skimpy operating budget slashed.[6] Bureaucratic infighting also continued to play a part in the struggle over the OTS's information universalism throughout the 1940s. Many agencies retained their own documents; sometimes because of reasons of national security, sometimes just to avoid the cost of transferring them.

There was a greater challenge. It was an initiative to create a competing great science information center within the government, one that was to have a different political orientation than Wallace's left-leaning departments. As a first step, the Library of Congress, not the OTS, became the custodian of the huge numbers of reports and publications of Vannevar Bush's Office of Scientific Research and Development (OSRD). Some of those who mistrusted the Department of Commerce's ambitions also hoped the U.S. Navy's science information project at the library would be turned into a permanent effort for science research needs, especially those of traditional academics.[7]

SCIENCE BY AND FOR THE "PEOPLE," NOT FOR ACADEMICS

The challenges to the OTS took place as intensified political and ideological battles over broader science policies were surfacing. The conflicts centered on another crusade by Wallace and involved emotion-filled concerns about Socialism in general and Soviet-American relations. Wallace's personality exacerbated the situation.

Wallace was determined to turn the entire Commerce Department into more than a resource for the independent businessman. He also thought a powerful department could free consumers from the dictates of the large corporations. Wallace's goal was to meet corporate domination with counterbalancing forces and for that he had his own version of Vannevar Bush's "endless frontier" of science. For example, Wallace wanted the Commerce Department's National Bureau of Standards and the OTS to be small-business-oriented versions of the Department of Agriculture's near century-old research and information system for the farmer. Equal access to information was central to his new hopes, as was his plan to establish a vastly expanded nationwide network of independent government engineering research and development centers.[8]

Wallace was not a narrow populist technocrat, however. His sci-tech plans were part of his sweeping vision of a future America. He was as much of a Socialist and pacifist as any mainstream American politician had ever been and his policies were not too far away from those of Eugene Debs, the early twentieth century's nominal Socialist leader. Wallace was also the national spokesman for a host of other broad Progressive policies. He argued for a continued battle against the "predatory corporation," for immediate racial desegregation; for a national health system; for world peace; for universities that performed socially useful, not abstract, research; and, significantly, for close cooperation between the Soviet Union and the United States. His position on those issues matched those of America's leftists. He also had a soft-spoken manner that was attractive to liberal idealists.

IDEOLOGY AND SCIENCE INFORMATION POLICY   123

Wallace was a romantic and had an uncommon individuality. Few doubted that he was one of the most unusual men ever in American public life. He was a curious mixture of scientist, ideologue, and mystic. Given his upbringing, that was an unexpected jumble. Wallace was born in 1888 to a very prosperous midwestern family of liberal Progressive Republican newspaper editors. Their papers were devoted to the cause of modernizing agriculture and to turning the state universities and the Department of Agriculture into dynamic centers for the creation and dissemination of helpful knowledge. The Wallaces and their publications had quickly become influential. *Wallace's Farmer* grew to be a political force, as well as a source of the latest scientific and economic information for agriculturists. The newspaper's success led President Harding to appoint Henry's father as the United States' secretary of agriculture in the 1920s. While holding the post, the elder Wallace increased the role of the department's research stations and expanded the department's central library and information services. The department had the first federal library to serve the public and it devised innovative ways to provide information to agricultural stations and farmers throughout the nation. The senior Wallace turned the department's library into a more effective tool. It became the most sophisticated agricultural information service in the world as its relatively generous budgets and its populist mission allowed it to use, for example, punch-card and microfilm technologies before many other government agencies. The librarians chosen to head the library, such as 1940's new chief librarian, Ralph Shaw, were usually among the most forward looking in the nation.[9]

SCIENCE AND SPIRITUALISM, TOO

The Wallace family's economic and political assent had not led to its abandoning its midwestern agricultural heritage. So, despite the family's wealth, young Henry attended one of those rural colleges, Iowa State University, rather than one of the elite eastern institutions. While at Iowa State he wedded scientific expertise with his family's passion for agricultural modernization. He loved the new biological sciences and became an applied geneticist. He bred new seeds that soon revolutionized agricultural production in many nations. He used new mathematical/statistical tools to help develop another field of study, the economics of agriculture. He also became an editor, a successful businessman, and a political spokesman for agriculture. At the same time, he was becoming a bit otherworldly.[10] Soon after his graduation from college Henry assumed the editorship of *Wallace's Farmer*, founded a major seed company, and wrote several books on agricultural policy. At the same time, he penned rather cryptic works based on his increasingly esoteric views on religion and democracy.

He was becoming a spiritualist. Although he held to his agricultural version of a calling, Wallace became a philosophical nomad, trying to find ways of "bringing the inner light to outward manifestations." He was also going beyond his family's old populism, liberal Progressivism, and traditional religion. Wallace abandoned his family's Presbyterianism. A first step was when he read the works of those liberal Harvard philosophers, Ralph Waldo Emerson and William James. Their writings cast doubts on any absolutes but Wallace went further. He began excursions into spiritualism and Masonic premises and he established ties with a Russian émigré's theosophist church/fund-raising operation. At the same time, surprisingly, Wallace was developing a greater faith in the power of modern knowledge, and in forward-looking governments, to fulfill his now almost messianic social visions.[11]

TO THE LEFT, TOO FAR

Wallace also abandoned the Republican Party and became a left-of-center Democrat. As a result, Franklin Roosevelt made him his secretary of agriculture and then, in 1940, his vice president. Wallace's policies quickly gained him a reputation as one of the most radical senior members of the administration. The economic policies he advocated went far beyond trust-busting and mild economic regulation. As a result, it became difficult for many to distinguish him from England's worrisome Socialists. He even seemed to be going beyond the economic policy ideas of John Maynard Keynes.

Concerns about Wallace's political policies increased as he became associated with several Washingtonians who were later accused of having ties to the American Communist Party, and during and after World War II he was a vocal and enthusiastic supporter of the Soviet Union.

IDEOLOGY AND SCIENCE INFORMATION POLICY

After a 1944 trip to Asia and Russia on President Roosevelt's behalf, Wallace let it be known that he had become an admirer of Stalin and his social and economic programs and methods. Unfortunately, the idealistic and naïve Wallace had seen only what the Soviets wanted him (and perhaps he wanted) to see on that trip. The Siberian workers' "paradise" he toured was a disguised gulag. As well, the Soviets found it easy to hide their aid to the Chinese Communists from him.

Well before the Russian trip Wallace's views and actions had become intolerable to President Roosevelt's advisors. Roosevelt did not ask Wallace to run for vice president a second time. In 1944, the Democrats chose Harry Truman, a practiced, commonsense politician. But Roosevelt did not cast Wallace out of Washington. He offered him the post of Secretary of Commerce. Assigning Wallace to Commerce was unusual. Most of the men who previously held the post were political conservatives, although, some, like Herbert Hoover, were very enlightened. Unfortunately, Wallace's tenure at Commerce was short. Roosevelt's successor, Harry Truman, could not tolerate Wallace's criticism of his administration's emerging Soviet policies. He dismissed Wallace from his cabinet in September 1946. But Wallace had been in charge of Commerce long enough to stimulate heated debates over science and information policies.

ENEMIES AT OUR INFORMATION GATES?

When Wallace, along with legislators such as Maury Maverick, proposed the idea of creating those engineering-industrial versions of the elder Wallace's agricultural development and information programs, cries of science information and educational collectivism quickly arose. But Wallace was not seeking to make the OTS what some in England, such as the Communist J. D. Bernal, were advocating, a centralized system for socialized research. Wallace's focus was on making research in all types of institutions, including universities, produce useful knowledge, not abstractions. [12] His version of science was not that of theory, but of practical applications. Energetic young legislators who soon joined Wallace and Maverick's crusade, such as Hubert Humphrey and J. William Fulbright, became, like Wallace, objects of conservatives' ire.

So did the men Wallace had picked to lead the Department of Commerce's efforts.[13] To spearhead his 1945 initiatives, Wallace relied upon Edward U. Condon. He was a noted nuclear physicist with a very liberal political orientation who had already had battles with conservatives such as General Leslie Groves of the atomic bomb's Manhattan Project. Condon was also a worry to those anxious about organizations he approved of, such as the American-Soviet Science Society that urged international control of atomic energy. Despite those issues, Wallace made Condon the head of the National Bureau of Standards. The man Wallace then selected to lead the postwar's Office of Technical Services, John C. Green, had a similar but deeper information philosophy than Wallace's or Condon's.[14] Green had led the OTS during World War II and had a longtime commitment to the needs of the lone inventor.

Condon's and Green's policies generated heated opposition because they went even further than Wallace's plans for distributing government sci-tech information. In doing so they antagonized publishers in the fields of science and technology, including academia's nonprofit providers. When Green proposed creating large government information centers that were to provide low- or no-cost bibliographies and other types of publications in all science and technical fields, there were public denunciations. No wonder. He announced he wanted to provide bibliographies and abstracts for all the academic sciences, not just for sci-tech's needs. Green seemed insensitive to the threat to established services, whether for-profit or nonprofit, under such tax-subsidized competition.

In 1945, as a first step toward his goals, Green began to seek ways to ensure that large corporations could not monopolize the flow of documents from the Axis countries.[15] Practicalities soon frustrated him. The lack of manpower and technology at the OTS blocked progress. Green turned to library innovators such as Ralph Shaw for advice. Shaw responded with estimates that made Green realize how daunting his task would be if there was to be democratic access to just the captured FIAT documents. Green knew that unless the OTS could quickly translate and then describe items with many index terms, only those customers with prior knowledge could benefit from any collection. Meeting such dissemination goals demanded the near impossible, including finding enough scarce subject-matter specialists with foreign language skills in

IDEOLOGY AND SCIENCE INFORMATION POLICY

the United States willing to work at low salaries. Green became desperate. Consequently, he was a bit too forceful as he searched for allies and money. He began demanding much additional funding and launched an aggressive search for labor-saving classification-indexing methods and technologies. He did it all with a messianic ardor nearing Wallace's. As Green was attempting to raise funds, and while he was exploring cost-saving methodological and technological alternatives (including the development of Vannevar Bush's automatic microfilm machine for retrieval), he, Wallace, and E. U. Condon encountered hostility from many sources—even from some they thought were friends.

DIFFERENT SYSTEMS FOR DIFFERENT PEOPLE

Opposition initially came from representatives, such as Vannevar Bush, of traditional academics and their elite institutions. The academics desired funding for their own journals and indexing services.[16] They demanded their publications be protected and their publishers be the first to be given the funds needed to handle the latest "serials crisis." There was more involved. The academics saw Green's proposals as part of a wide-ranging initiative that would lead to politicians and bureaucrats determining research priorities. Leaders like Bush wanted federal dollars for research within universities (not government agencies) and to have projects initiated and directed by academics, not bureaucrats with politicized definitions of what scientists should do. Allied with the academics were those responsible for older nonprofit bibliographic services. They feared government-subsidized agencies might crowd them out and worried that if government played a major role, science publication might be dominated by the likes of what would later be called political correctness.[17] The next interest group working against the Wallace-Green visions was composed of corporate and business representatives who were against any type of information and research Socialism. Others, who thought that nongovernmental, especially for-profit publishers would be more effective disseminators of all types of sci-tech information, joined them.

However, it was a more pervasive force that was the most important block to the realization of Green's government-sponsored sci-tech information systems "for the people."

WORSE THAN SOCIALISM, IT MIGHT BE COMMUNISTIC

The information policy issue became tangled in the general debates over Communism in America. John C. Green's and Edward U. Condon's association with groups that demanded internationalization of atomic science and technology, and Wallace's urging of cooperation with the Soviet Union, were two of the reasons. Less than wise political behavior was another. Green went so far in pursuit of information democracy that he alienated the White House. Green raised Truman's anger when he publicly objected to the American government's termination of scientific and industrial document gathering and other intellectual reparations operations in Germany. As part of the Marshall Plan's program to rebuild Europe's (and necessarily Germany's) economy to prevent the spread of Communism, the Truman administration felt the continued mining of German industrial secrets would discourage investments, innovation, and recovery. Condon's constant vocal criticisms of the White House's demands to keep atomic science secret, and of its refusal to support the movement for international control of atomic capabilities, also angered the administration—and many others.

In addition, the heated reactions to Henry Wallace's 1948 run for the presidency on a near-Socialistic, Communist-influenced, and clearly Soviet-friendly platform spilled over into the information struggle. As a result, both Condon and Green became targets of anti-Communist activists, including the young Richard Nixon, a future American president.

A MANDATE, BUT NO MONEY

Like Henry Wallace, the information crusaders were defeated. Although Congress gave the OTS a nod of approval as a permanent information service for both private industry and government agencies, it was always starved of funds. The OTS's leaders were not able to implement any significant programs to make sci-tech or other academic science information available to the public. To survive, it became a for-fee operation, and its usefulness declined when many government agencies were allowed to withhold important documents.[18] As important, when the OTS did supply government documents, they suffered from hasty and gross classifications and little indexing. Even the short book-form

IDEOLOGY AND SCIENCE INFORMATION POLICY

bibliographies the OTS rushed into print every few weeks were poorly organized. There were soon complaints that once again only the large corporations were requesting materials from the center because only they had knowledge of its holdings. The OTS was not the only information institution to suffer in the immediate postwar years. General reductions in federal budget lines for the civilian sector affected other science information programs. Although the Library of Congress was not associated with any leftist causes, its science information service for nonmilitary users endured very hard times.[19]

SOME TYPE OF INFORMATION SOCIALISM WAS OKAY

In contrast, as the nation focused on the newest threats in Europe and Asia, the government vastly increased its funding of defense, intelligence, and atomic energy information projects. However, partly because they were not tagged (somewhat inexplicably) as Socialistic, two older government information services received rather generous funding. One was favored because its work helped to fulfill some defense needs, the other because of its ties to politically powerful interests.

With new funding, the Surgeon General's Library launched an impressive medical information effort at Johns Hopkins University's Welch Medical Library. The project developed new indexing ideas and punch-card/tabulator machine techniques. Although driven by the needs of the military, those developments quickly spilled over into the private sector—partly because budding information scientists, such as Eugene Garfield, learned their trade while working on the Baltimore-based venture.[20] The Department of Agriculture, which was miraculously spared of being harmed by Henry Wallace's reputation as a Socialist, had enough in its budgets to be able to explore a few radical solutions to information retrieval and delivery problems. For example, it investigated the potentials of Vannevar Bush's huge information machine, the microfilm-based Rapid Selector.[21]

There was another but partial exception to the defense-only rule for government sponsorship of science information during the initial Cold War years. In the early 1950s, the government turned some minimal funds over to a new civilian science organization, Vannevar Bush's creation, the National Science Foundation (NSF). The foundation gave government grants to individual faculty members at prestigious research universities and to the old academic nonprofit indexing and abstracting organizations that served them.[22] Unfortunately, for close to a decade the foundation had little money for any purpose. As well, the foundation soon refocused and moved closer to the National Research Council's policy of supporting coordinated programmatic research. That meant it could do even less to aid the traditional academic science information providers that served individual scholars.

In fact, traditional academic science information in America had fewer important friends in the decade after World War II than after World War I.

WHERE ARE THE OLD FRIENDS OF ACADEMIC SCIENCE INFORMATION?

The American government began spending unprecedented amounts on information projects in the late 1940s and early 1950s, but for defense—certainly not for pure or abstract science. The intelligence agencies, the army, the navy, and the new air force[23] needed all types of information, and organizations such as the Atomic Energy Commission were developing and supporting huge and advanced analysis and distribution centers. But none of those projects were aimed at the academics' science information problem.

During the late 1940s there was little reason to hope for a bright future for academic science information. The institutions that tried to do so much for American and international science bibliography in the 1920s, such as the Rockefeller and Carnegie Foundations, had lost interest. As a result, there were no noteworthy private philanthropic initiatives during the early postwar period, and the few information programs that were funded did not do well. The National Academy's Carnegie-funded Scientific Aids to Learning project at Vannevar Bush's MIT lost its energy after a promising start. It was producing few results and caused disappointments. Thereafter, the Carnegie organizations made only grants to support Documentation Society meetings and to keep barely alive Watson Davis's American Documentation Institute. The Rockefeller's men also retreated.[24]

IDEOLOGY AND SCIENCE INFORMATION POLICY

The National Research Council (NRC) did not abandon the science information cause completely, but it did not attempt to assume the central role it had taken on after World War I. One reason for its diminished information presence was that during World War II it had been upstaged by Vannevar Bush's OSRD, the applied-science organization. The NRC never regained its dominance. There had been some activity at its impressive Washington, D.C., Foggy Bottom headquarters, however. During World War II, the council managed a few information projects and continued some of them after the war. The council's most interesting postwar venture was a path-breaking extension of a wartime exploration of the relations between chemistry and biology—and perhaps biological-chemical warfare. The NRC Coordination Center's imaginative information project, which was ahead of its time in the use of tabulating equipment, employed Karl F. Heumann, a soon-to-be leader in the American and international documentation movements.[25]

The NRC did send representatives to United Nations meetings on international science information, but those gatherings could do little to create and sustain meaningful international cooperation without massive financing. The NRC also assumed the responsibility for representing the United States at the Paul Otlet–inspired International Federation for Information and Documentation (FID) meetings that coordinated library standards, but the FID's information glory days had passed. The NRC made a few other attempts to be a more direct force in science information, but it could do little because it did not have its own funds and its old philanthropic information partners had withdrawn. The council eventually established a one-man documentation office, but it came late, in 1959.

Unexpectedly, businessmen's organizations contributed as much or more to information standardization. Beginning in the 1960s, a consortium of booksellers established the now familiar International Standard Book Number.[26] That ISBN was not a classification or indexing tool, however.

EVEN THE CAS WAS ALONE

No one stepped forward in the 1940s to take the NRC's old place in subject-field science bibliography, although the information problems of the academic disciplines were grave. The academics' information system had a strange life in the 1940s. During World War II, the traditional American journals and indexing-abstracting services had experienced a temporary resurgence. Although they had lost access to many foreign publications and had lost almost all their subscribers in Europe and Asia, the government's stimulation of research, as well as a short burst of philanthropic patriotism, rescued them from their despair of the dark years of the 1930s. *Biological Abstracts*, for example, was cut off from one-half of its subscribers during the war but help from the Rockefellers and government-induced subscriptions allowed it to end the war in better shape than in 1941.

In contrast, World War II's years had been exceptionally bad ones for most other bibliographic services, as well as for the profession-aligned journals. Indexing and abstracting operations barely limped through the postwar era. For example, one of the largest and richest nonprofit publishers in America, the Chemical Abstracts Service, was so far in debt by 1950 there was fear it might go bankrupt. Only its rather undignified hat-in-hand trip to the wealthiest chemical corporations saved it from oblivion. In return for their aid, *Chemical Abstracts'* leaders had to make a promise to become self-supporting and stop asking for any type of subsidies. Then, the *Abstracts'* attempt to fulfill users' demands for cumulative indexes nearly drove it under again. It was not until 1955 that the *Abstracts* became self-supporting—but even then, a significant portion of its income came from direct government funding because of its links to defense problems, especially atomic energy. Even with the governmental income, some major policy changes became necessary if *Chemical Abstracts* was to keep its promise to run at least a break-even operation. It had to raise its subscription rates more than twenty-five-fold between 1951 and 1965 to stay in the financial black. Such subscription charges hardly met early promises of providing abstracts to the poor and isolated professors who worked in small colleges rather than in cash-rich research centers. And, breakeven meant there was little or nothing for improvement. Although the chemical industry was doing well financially, there was no money for the *Abstracts* to do significant research into the special techniques needed for chemical information.[27] The *Abstracts* was not suffering alone. Almost all other major nonmilitary science information services in America experienced pain for a decade after World War II. *Biological Abstracts* suffered after

IDEOLOGY AND SCIENCE INFORMATION POLICY

the war and stumbled through the later 1940s and early 1950s, saved only by contracts with government agencies such as the Office of Naval Research.[28]

Fortunately, a tiny bit of relief for the traditional academic journals and indexing–abstracting services began to appear. The ill-funded National Science Foundation could provide a few small direct grants to indexing services, but those and the subsidies for article publication (dissemination) that it packed into its research grants did little more than help cover part of the mounting yearly deficits of such important journals as the *Physical Review*. At the same time, the escalating number of academic publications was besieging the indexing and abstracting services. The old problem of overly long time lags between publication and abstracting was growing worse. And, the services were falling far behind in producing useful indexes. The oversupply challenge was becoming too great. *Biological Abstracts'* index of 1950, for example, called for the equivalent of five miles of teletype tape. *Chemical Abstracts* had to try to manage some forty thousand different subject headings.[29]

NOTES

1. Lynda Hunt, *Secret Agenda: The United States Government, Nazi Scientists, and Project Paperclip, 1945 to 1990* (New York: St. Martin's, 1991).

2. John Gimbel, *Science, Technology and Reparations: Exploitation and Plunder in Postwar Germany* (Stanford, CA: Stanford University Press, 1990). Jerrold Orne, "Library Division of the Office of the Publication Board," *Special Libraries*, September 1946, 203–9.

3. National Council of Jewish Women, Interview with Allen Kent, May 12, 1993, http://images.library.pitt.edu/cgi-bin/i/image/image-idx?view=entry;cc=ncjw;entryid=x-ais196440.233.

4. Vera Gadberry Hunter, "Survey of the Office of Technical Services U.S. Dept. of Commerce, June 1945–August 1952" (M.A. thesis, Catholic University, June 1953).

5. Walter L. Reynolds, "The Senate Committee on Government Operations and Documentation," *American Documentation* 12, no. 2 (April 1961): 93–97.

6. Burton W. Adkinson, *Two Centuries of Federal Information* (Stroudsburg, PA: Dowden, Hutchinson & Ross, 1978).

134 CHAPTER 7

7. Elliott Committee Report, Select Committee on Government Research 88th Congress, 1964.

8. Thomas E. Pinelli, *NASA DOD Aerospace Knowledge Diffusion Research Project Report # 11, Chronology of Selected Literature Reports, Policy Instruments, and Significant Events Affecting Federal Scientific and Technical Information (STI) in the United States*, DOD, Indiana University, January 1992.

9. Alfred Charles True, *A History of Agricultural Experimentation and Research in the United States, 1607–1925* (Washington, DC: U.S. Department of Agriculture, 1937); Jana Varlejs, "The Technical Report and Its Impact on the Post–World War II Information Systems," in *History and Heritage of Scientific and Technical Information Systems*, ed. W. Boyd Rayward and Mary Ellen Bowden (Medford, NJ: Information Today, 2004), 89–99. On Ralph Shaw: http://en.wikipedia.org/wiki/Ralph_R._Shaw#Scarecrow_Press.

10. John Morton Blum, ed., *The Price of Vision: The Diary of Henry A. Wallace 1942–1946* (Boston: Houghton-Mifflin, 1973).

11. John C. Culver and John Hyde, *American Dreamer: The Life and Times of Henry A. Wallace* (New York: Norton, 2000).

12. Alastair Black, Dave Muddiman, and Helen Plant, *The Early Information Society: Information Management in Britain before the Computer* (Hampshire, UK: Ashgate, 2007), 77; W. Boyd Rayward, ed., *European Modernism and the Information Society: Informing the Present, Understanding the Past* (Burlington, VT: Ashgate, 2008), 201–22.

13. Jessica Wang, "Science, Security and the Cold War: The Case of E. U. Condon," *ISIS* 83 (1992): 238–69.

14. Robert K. Stewart, "The Office of Technical Services: A New Deal in the Cold War," *Knowledge Creation Utilization and Diffusion* 15, no. 1 (September 1993): 46–77.

15. David M. Hart, *Forged Consensus: Science, Technology, and Economic Policy in the United States 1921–1953* (Princeton, NJ: Princeton University Press, ca. 1998).

16. Zachary G. Pascal, *Endless Frontier: Vannevar Bush, Engineer of the American Century* (Cambridge, MA: MIT Press, 1999).

17. Bruce L. Smith, *American Science Policy since World War II* (Washington, DC: Brookings Institution, 1989, 1990).

18. Pinelli, *NASA DOD*.

19. Crawford Report, Task Force of the President's Special Assistant for Science and Technology, "Scientific and Technological Communication in the Government," April 1962, 43–45.

20. Anthony Thomas Kruzas, "The Development of Special Libraries for American Business and Industry" (Ph.D. diss., University of Michigan, 1960),

90; B. Cronin and H. B Atkins, *The Web of Knowledge: A Festschrift in Honor of Eugene Garfield* (Medford, NJ: Information Today, 2000).

21. Jana Varlejs, "Ralph Shaw and the Rapid Selector," in *Proceeding of the 1998 Conference on the History and Heritage of Science Information Systems, ASIS -CHF*, ed. Mary Ellen Bowden, Trudi Bellardo Hahn, and Robert V. Williams (Medford, NJ: Information Today, 1999), 148–55.

22. Vannevar Bush, Erich Bloch, and Daniel J. Kevles, eds., *Science, The Endless Frontier: A Report to the President on a Program for Postwar Scientific Research* (Washington, DC: National Science Foundation, 1990), esp. Bloch's introductory essay; J. Merton England, *A Patron for Pure Science: The National Science Foundation's Formative Years 1945–57* (Washington, DC, 1983); Jessica Wang, "Liberals, the Progressive Left, and the Political Economy of Postwar American Science: The National Science Debate Revisited," *Historical Studies in the Physical and Biological Sciences* 26, no. 1 (1995): 139–66; Madeline M. Henderson, John S. Moats, and Mary Elizabeth Stevens, *Cooperation, Convertibility, and Compatibility among Information Systems: A Literature Review* (Washington, DC: National Bureau of Standards, GPO, June 1966).

23. Thomas Thompson, "The Fifty-Year Role of the US Air Force in Advancing Information Technology: A History of the Rome, New York Ground Electronics Laboratory" (n.p.: n.p., n.d.).

24. *The Center for Scientific Aids to Learning: An Interim Report to the Carnegie Corporation of New York* (Cambridge: Massachusetts Institute of Technology, February 1, 1951); Jesse H. Shera, "Documentation: Its Scope and Limitations," *Library Quarterly* 21 (January 1951): 13–26.

25. R. L. Beard and Karl F. Heumann, "The Chemical-Biological Coordination Center: An Experiment in Documentation," *Science*, n.s., 116, no. 3021 (November 21, 1952): 553–54.

26. Adkinson, *Two Centuries of Federal Information*; William V. Consolazio and Margaret C. Green, "Federal Support of Research in the Life Sciences," *Science*, n.s., 124, no. 3221 (September 21, 1956): 522–26.

27. Ivan Amato, "A Century of CAS," *Chemical and Engineering News* 85, no. 24 (June 11, 2007): 38–39; Hedda Schulz and Ursula Gregory, *From CA to CAS Online* (Berlin: Springer-Verlag, 1988).

28. Richard T. Kaser and Victoria Coz Kaser, *BIOSIS Championing the Cause: The First 75 Years* (Philadelphia: nfais, 2001); Anonymous, "Technical Information Activities of the Department of Defense," *Science*, n.s., 114, no. 2973 (December 21, 1951): 653–61.

29. H. E. Pietsch, "Future Possibilities of Applying Mechanized Methods to Scientific and Technical Literature," in *Punched Cards: Their Applications to*

Science and Industry, ed. Robert S. Casey and James M. Perry (New York: Reinhold, 1951), 437–55.

8

THE CIA'S LIBRARIANS UNDER FIRE

The Central Intelligence Agency (CIA), the United States' foreign intelligence organization, came under extreme pressure in 1949, and so did its information division. Just as James Madison Andrews and Norman Ball's CIG/CIA team had finalized their innovative hierarchical Dewey-like Intelligence Subject Code (ISC), when the Intellofax system began operating, and when Henry Wallace's supporters were licking their "Socialistic" information system wounds, Andrews came under intense criticisms from the CIA's group charged with monitoring Soviet science and technology. The agency's science watchers demanded more than the ISC and Intellofax could provide.

The CIA's recently expanded Office of Scientific Intelligence (OSI) was responsible for fulfilling the information needs of the successor to Vannevar Bush's Research and Development Board. That new "Bush board" was charged with gaining the information needed to provide the president with timely and accurate forecasts of Soviet strategic capabilities. That was a formidable challenge, one not being met. The board's frustrations were passed on and led the OSI to demand that Andrews immediately introduce newer information technologies and new classification methods. Threatening, the board was also signaling that it did not trust Andrews's crew to do any better than the inadequate hierarchical ISC and Intellofax systems. OSI's men responded with a recommendation that a new group of outside experts be called upon to create better classification methods and information machines.[1]

138   CHAPTER 8

That was a serious concern to Andrews and Ball as the OSI had influential connections. Its wishes could not be ignored. As well, complaints about the CIA's performance in general had reached the highest levels of government. In 1949, two powerful committees reported to congress and to President Truman, Ferdinand Eberstadt's and Allen Dulles's. The reports contained very unpleasant things about the agency's overall performance and about its science monitoring capabilities— prompted in part by Vannevar Bush's testimony. The CIA's failure to warn of Russia's detonation of an atomic bomb, Joe-1, in August 1949 added weight and urgency to the criticisms. There were more problems for the CIA. The condemnations by the boards and the OSI's demand for a new science information retrieval system came in the context of the Berlin Blockade, America and its allies' inability to deploy human agents inside Russia, and a loss of the ability to decode any high-level Soviet radio transmissions after a Soviet agent inside America's code-breaking agency revealed the few British and American successes against Russian targets.[2]

WE ARE INTELLIGENCE BLIND

The criticisms were justified. Sadly, by the late 1940s the United States was science-intelligence blind. It was left with a dependency on open source information while the Soviets were diligent in their efforts to protect their secrets. America had to rely on teasing out hints from science journals and newspapers obtained by its Foreign Documents Division, from the CIA's special group that monitored scientific meetings, from a few defectors, from monitoring air samples, and from some very risky and expensive clandestine adventures.

The need to pluck any type of information out of unlikely sources was so great that America's leaders were willing to invest in chancy operations such as the Berlin Tunnel to tap Soviet phone lines, perilous flights near Russia's borders, and the special U2 aircraft to fly high over Soviet territory. The situation was desperate enough that the intelligence agencies financed a project that traced Soviet scientists through purloined Moscow and Leningrad phone books, hoping to determine what major research and development projects were under way. So, in the context of such actions, and the beginning of enormous investments

THE CIA'S LIBRARIANS UNDER FIRE 139

in what became the spy-in-the-sky Corona satellites, the OSI's asking for perhaps one or two million dollars for more advanced information machines and revolutionary classification systems for the science information challenges seemed acceptable.

THE POSSIBLE ALTERNATIVES TO THE ISC AND SUBJECT HEADINGS

Andrews had no ready answer to the demand for replacements for the ISC and Intellofax, but he wanted to keep control over any development projects. His first response was to ask his own librarians to begin exploring alternative methods and hardware. He created a special in-house team to survey the newest classification systems, ranging from "aspect" and "colon" systems to "terms," and an ill-defined but enticing semantic factors.[3] The term methods seemed a good possibility although they were new, revolutionary, and controversial. There were several variations and all broke the rules of traditional classification.

The most influential was Mortimer Taube's. He had been developing it since shortly after World War II. Taube had worked on military- and science-related projects at the Library of Congress since the mid-1940s and found the library's classification and subject-heading systems did not fit well with the types of technical reports he and his team were processing. Using the older methods had required expensive specialists and unacceptable amounts of time. Worse, they did not meet the needs of users who complained that materials were difficult to find.

In response, Taube explored a method that had been suggested by British sci-tech librarians during the 1930s.[4] Taube went far beyond their approach of merely splitting up of the terms in existing subject headings to allow flexibility in document retrieval. His Uniterm system avoided the intellectual demands of devising subject headings and hierarchical systems. To save time and money, his term system shunned what all previous classifiers and indexers had thought necessary: expertise, deep thought, and a universal system of concepts and identifiers that could transcend language and cultural differences. Taube's Uniterms avoided the use of anything outside of a document. As had Vannevar Bush, he thought hierarchies and how "others may think" seemed unnecessary.

THE GENERIC PROBLEM AND LUHN, ONCE AGAIN

Taube asked his workers to use just the major terms within a document. To library professionals that was an insult, a heresy. There were objections to his Uniterms. A frequent complaint was the systems being unable to support generic searching. Because Uniterms relied on individual words, and the special vocabulary in a document, a researcher could not just ask for items on biology. He would have to specify each of the component terms found in the concept "biology." Critics also pointed to Taube's system being bound to the technical or national language within a document.

Most critics failed to appreciate something of great importance: only a few others besides Taube came to realize the potentials of term methods for reducing labor cost to near zero for indexing and retrieval if the method was combined with appropriate technology. IBM's Hans Peter Luhn did. He was among the first to use the full text of documents when coded for a computer to replace human retrieval efforts with, for example, counts of the frequency of words in a document. Others would soon take automatic computer-based retrieval into the realm of sophisticated mathematics when electronic computers became more than advanced calculating machines. By the end of the 1950s, there were reports of computerized term systems under development at the National Security Agency, several aero corporations on the West Coast, in England, and at IBM itself.[5]

Andrews's team was, however, not convinced that terms would ever become the answer to the OSI's demands.

BUSH'S SELECTOR AND THE LUHN SCANNER

In addition to his survey of alternative classification and indexing methods Andrews searched for retrieval machines better than Intellofax's electromechanical IBM tabulators. His first commitment was a gamble. Realizing that it would be a lengthy and rather speculative investment (but one that would please Vannevar Bush), Andrews awarded a contract to Richard Ruggles, an ex-OSS economist who had returned to Wilmarth Lewis's Yale University, to develop a new version of Bush's microfilm Rapid Selector. Although Yale did not usually house techni-

THE CIA'S LIBRARIANS UNDER FIRE

cal projects, and while others had Selector development efforts under way, including Ralph Shaw's at the Agriculture Department and Jacob Rabinow's at the National Bureau of Standards, Ruggles hired a team of student engineers and began to experiment. Working within Yale's electrical engineering department, the young engineers began a long period of attempting to make the hoped-for special CIA Selector function properly and, importantly, to improve Bush's original design so the Selector could test for long codes and be able to perform "and/or" Boolean testing.[6]

Andrews had also begun contacting consultants outside the agency. They advised him to consider the use of one of the new devices the agency had known about for some time because of its earlier connections to Luhn. Since working on the first stage of the Intellofax project in 1947 Luhn had been contemplating a much more powerful version of IBM's tabulating/sorting machines. His primary goal was to create a device that could allow selection of items by more than one indexing criteria on each pass of a data card through a machine, the kind of "and" combinations that became familiar to those later using computerized search programs. Although his colleagues at IBM were, with his guidance, designing an advanced 101 electromechanical and electric relay statistical tabulator with "and" capabilities for the Census Bureau,[7] Luhn was already sketching ideas for his unique machine, the Scanner.[8]

Although the Scanner was to be based on IBM's standard card and electromechanical technologies, rather than electronics, microfilm, or magnetic memory, it was innovative. The central idea was to use optical coincidence testing rather than electrical sensing. With electrical sensing, wire brushes completed a circuit when a hole in an IBM card allowed contact between the brush and a metal plate. Such relatively slow and error-prone mechanics were not required in optical testing. Rather than electric current, the presence or absence of light sensed by photoelectric cells would determine if an item fit selection criteria, and without requiring the large number of mechanical parts and circuits a wire-brush tabulator would need when "and" selection was desired. Optical coincidence testing was not original to Luhn, but his use of it in tabulator/sorters was creative. IBM and Eastman Kodak had built optical coincidence testing into special devices it constructed for America's codebreakers during World War II, as had Vannevar Bush's students while working for naval intelligence. As well, optical testing had been the basis for microfilm selection machines such as Bush's Rapid Selector. But basing a tab-machine on optics was innovative.

The Scanner used photoelectric cells to see if the punched code-holes in the item cards matched a master card's codes. The item cards were automatically moved over the master card and if the code patterns coincided, an item card was selected as relevant. The master card technique allowed the optical coincidence method to instantly test on many lengthy codes, unlike the usual tabulator/sorter that searched one card column at a time. The light test allowed simultaneous examination of complex patterns of holes in all a card's columns. The Scanner was also designed to test for codes continuing onto following cards.

Optics would also avoid the information-limited nature of the traditional IBM fixed-field coding. With fixed fields an indexing component could have one and only one location on a card. A four-digit code for item number (say, 1222), would be, for example, restricted to just columns 8–11 on the card. With Luhn's optical testing (he used the blackout version that was simpler than measuring the intensity of light), if the master card held the code "1222," if that code was anywhere on a data card, that card would be selected.

Luhn was also searching for solutions to a problem that was becoming very important. The constraints on information retrieval caused by the limited number of items that could be coded on IBM tabulator cards, or on the handheld edge-notched cards that were becoming popular in the business world, were frustrating everyone. One of his remedies was to have his Scanner read the IBM cards vertically rather than horizontally as was usual for IBM's machines. That allowed longer codes and facilitated the free-field optical scanning. Another solution was to devise a new coding scheme that minimized the space needed for an indexing entry. His "5 of 12" design needed a special keypunch machine and it allowed more information on a card, but it meant that older cards punched on typical machines could not be readily used on his Scanner.

In addition, Luhn devised his own version of superimposed coding. Superimposition had many variations, but each type combined several codes into one, thus saving much space on a card. An example that uses binary codes is: adding together the codes for "magnetic digital computer" (five digits each for each term) to produce a single five-digit code (Magnetic 01000 + Digital 10000 + Computer 00001 = 11001). Super-

THE CIA'S LIBRARIANS UNDER FIRE 143

imposed coding had a significant weakness, however. The resulting superimposed code might not be unique, so the code could lead to incorrect items being selected. However, the savings in coding space seemed worth the chance of what were called "false drops."

Luhn explored solutions to other information problems. As a result, his planned Scanner became a system of four large components: the optical scanner, the special cardpunch, and two other machines. One of them was a new type of sorter to arrange the selected cards in ways a typical sorter could not. The other was, to a degree, a competitor to Intellofax. It printed out a listing of the punched codes on the selected cards.

WAITING FOR LUHN, THE 101, THE MIT CONNECTION

In 1949, Luhn's new system was only an idea. In contrast, IBM's 101 statistical tabulator project was advancing to the final design stages and was expected to be in operation for the processing of the 1950 census and to be in use by large corporate information centers by 1951. There were great hopes the 101 would revolutionize all types of information processing. A 101 was obtained for the Army Medical Library's far-reaching explorations of medical classification methods being conducted at Johns Hopkins University's Welch Medical Library under Stanford V. Larkey. The Welch 101 was the machine that led Eugene Garfield, a future information innovator, on his path to developing the system that came closest to matching Vannevar Bush's goal of indexing and retrieving "as we may think" and, eventually, to algorithms that predated those used to rank Internet web pages.[9]

Luhn, however, had decided not to wait to see the final results of the 101 project before building his Scanner, partly because Tom Watson, IBM's forceful leader, decided in 1948 to aid a chemistry information project at the Massachusetts Institute of Technology. Watson assigned Luhn to help a very unusual man who became one of the first of a new breed of academics, a type never envisioned by the university builders of the late nineteenth and early twentieth centuries: the "soft-money" professor.

JAMES PERRY, A SOFT-MONEY PROFESSOR WITH INCREASINGLY GRAND INFORMATION VISIONS

James Whitney Perry was one of the first documentalist/information scientists of the postwar era. He was among the new field's most prolific publishers and he became one of its most well-known figures. Yet he left few traces of his early life and little about his activities after the late 1950s. As well, there are gaps in his life story during the 1940s and 1950s.

James was from Raleigh, North Carolina, born to a family that seems to have been middle class but not prominent or rich. The family's financial status is indicated by James attending high school and finishing college—but not at a famous or high-status university. He was bright enough to qualify for admission to the nation's best schools but chose to attend a struggling small land-grant college in his hometown. It had recently changed its name from the North Carolina College of Agriculture and Mechanic Arts to North Carolina State College of Agriculture and Engineering. The school had begun in 1889 with a mandate to improve the state's economy, especially its paper and ceramics industries. As a result, it had devoted scarce resources to develop a small program in chemical engineering.

Although James was noted for his mathematical skills and sociability, instead of preparing for a position as a mathematics teacher or professor, he completed a chemical engineering major. He was awarded his bachelor of science degree in 1927 at just twenty years old. Somehow, he could afford to continue his education. He obtained his department's first master's degree in 1928. Reflecting the school's commitment to applying knowledge to practical problems, Perry's thesis was titled "Determination of the Iodine Content of the Public Water Supplies of North Carolina as a Possible Explanation of the Lack of Goiter among the Inhabitants."[10]

James then began to behave like a perpetual student. In 1929, although already having a master's degree, he enrolled at the Massachusetts Institute of Technology (MIT), receiving a second master's in 1931 after four, not two, semesters—although he already had a degree. He stayed on for another year as an assistant instructor.[11] His MIT thesis was on the oxidation of linseed oil, a topic linked to practical industrial applications.[12] Perhaps having ambitions of becoming a professor,

James found a way to pay for some two years of study in Germany's advanced technical schools. That did not lead to a doctorate, however. That is surprising as the German universities often granted doctorates after one year of residency and the completion of a short dissertation.

When James returned to the United States in 1934 the nation's economy was still reeling, universities were not hiring, and if they did they usually sought candidates with advanced degrees. James was fortunate, however. Although not finding an academic position, he secured a job as a junior research chemist. He was hired at Allied Chemical Company's aniline division in Buffalo, New York. While there for almost seven years he worked on the development of synthetic detergents, and he married. He soon built somewhat of a reputation as an expert in the field of detergents and in the chemistry of all such "surface agents." He was also active in professional organizations, including the American Chemical Society. Of significance for his later career, he never failed to tell his colleagues that he had become frustrated after having been assigned to find all the relevant scientific literature for his team's projects.

At the beginning of World War II, although he might have obtained a deferment to continue his work in Buffalo, Perry moved to the army's ballistics research center in Aberdeen, Maryland, where he worked as a civilian researcher on the chemistry of rocket propellants and high explosives. As part of his job he had to explore Russia's technological literature. That led to more information retrieval frustrations and to his teaching himself the Russian language, at least scientific Russian. He also seems to have launched into self-study of the latest alternative classification schemes, general linguistics, and emerging information technologies such as the handheld edge-notched cards. While at the Aberdeen Proving Ground, he became familiar with the potential of the constantly improving tabulating equipment (Aberdeen had some of the most advanced models in the world) [13] and he let his fellow members of the American Chemical Society know that he had ideas for the use of tabulators and edge-cards in information retrieval. [14] His hints soon motivated the society to form a committee on science information and one on the use of all types of punch-cards.

As the war was ending, Perry's information retrieval frustrations led him to make a critical life decision. At age thirty-eight, and with family responsibilities, he decided to change careers and to bet his future on a

146   CHAPTER 8

yet-to-be profession that had only a tentative name, documentation. He may have felt he was not taking too much of a risk because the American Chemical Society was giving hints that it might support research programs in information (documentation), especially in the worth of new chemical notation schemes and in the application of new technologies. James also hoped he would be successful in writing instructional texts on scientific Russian and he believed he would be able to gain some income by publishing a survey of all modern information technologies. [15] As well, he had kept in touch with his mentor in Buffalo who was planning to publish, along with his collaborators, the definitive work on the chemistry and technology of surface agents. Beyond those immediate hopes, Perry seems to have had visions of at last becoming a university professor. Although he did not have a Ph.D., a professorship seemed a possibility because he now envisioned that engineering, not chemistry, would be his academic destination. He knew that engineering departments had a record of hiring non-Ph.D.s who were recognized innovators. As well, there were indications that American higher education was on the verge of a great expansion and an across-the-board need for new faculty.

A RETURN TO CAMBRIDGE

James's faith in himself and the future of information led him to make a great gamble: he accepted a temporary position at MIT, but not as a regular member of the chemistry or engineering departments. It was a strange choice because being a fellow did not mean he was on a track toward a faculty position or long-term employment. His fellowship had just been established by the university with funds coming from professional societies and industry, not from the university's regular budget. Fellowships were to be for no more than two years, with their holders assigned to both the library and a subject-area department. Recipients were expected to pursue interests that aided the library, the school, and industry. Perry, the Diamond Alkali Fellow, was assigned to the library and the Department of Chemical Engineering and his salary came from that chemical company's fund as supervised by the American Chemical Society. [16] Despite the society's prestige, James and the other fellows received very little in salary. [17] James, however, had visions that the

THE CIA'S LIBRARIANS UNDER FIRE

fellowship would be a first step toward a regular position at the institute.

Neither Perry nor MIT explained why he was selected for the fellowship or why it would untypically be renewed for another two years. But there are some hints. His previous work with the chemical society on information problems was a key factor. Also, it appeared that larger grants from the American Chemical Society and the chemical industry were imminent if Perry was retained. Another hint is that his interests coincided with a new and grand library-based Scientific Aids to Learning project at the institute—and with the institute's hope it would become a leader in new information theories, technologies, and library architecture.

TWO INFORMATION CULTURES AT THE INSTITUTE, SHANNON AND WEAVER VERSUS BURCHARD AND TATE

There were two approaches and two separate groups involved in the institute's newest information ambitions, and there was a bit of a technologist versus humanist division between them. Some of MIT's faculty and their friends had already begun to create radically new definitions of what "information" was. Hopefully, they would be the ones to provide the field of information with the kind of theory that could make it a true science and academically respectable. In the mid-1940s, Norbert Wiener, an MIT mathematics genius, and his colleagues who had been working on the automation of aiming antiaircraft guns announced their grand theory of "cybernetics," a combination of biology-linked homeostasis ideas and statistical theory. In their theory of feedback and control, information was central, just as gravity had been vital to traditional physics. Cybernetics was not all that was vying for a place at the institute. There were more theoretical information conceptualizations arising from the work of alumni and friends of the institute. Claude Shannon, an ex-student of Vannevar Bush, had developed a cutting-edge statistical view and definition of information that was based on physical science concepts such as entropy while at the fabled Bell Laboratories. His years of work on telephone networking problems and cryptanalysis led him to fashion what many regarded as the basis of an all-encompassing information science (albeit one not concerned with meaning), a theory that might also provide a pure-science basis for new social sciences and a new linguistics.[18]

Shannon's type of engineer's information science soon received a boost from Warren Weaver, the mathematician and Rockefeller Foundation executive. He had supported many of his friend Vannevar Bush's expensive computer projects of the 1930s and had guided the development and use of other tools for mathematicians while he was with World War II's Office of Scientific Research and Development (OSRD). At the war's end, Weaver let it be known that he believed Shannon-like techniques that were being used in cryptanalysis, and the kind of work done on the statistical distributions of words by George Kingsley Zipf and Alfred James Lotka,[19] would soon allow the automatic machine translation of foreign languages, thus overcoming one of the great obstacles in scientific communication.

Wiener, Shannon, and Weaver quickly became very public and iconic academic stars, but others at the institute, such as James Perry, did yeoman information work without receiving such international attention. Perhaps that was because, while not a humanist like Wilmarth Lewis, Perry never associated himself with the thrilling and attention-grabbing statistical view of the nature of information.

When Perry arrived in Cambridge in late 1945 there were other less theoretical but still far-reaching information ambitions at MIT. Vannevar Bush was in Washington leading the Carnegie Institution, but he was a force behind the institute's group pushing for a vast expansion of MIT's library system, and for making the institute the national leader in new library architecture, technology, and methods. Initially, Bush applauded the appointment of John E. Burchard, an MIT master's graduate in architectural engineering who had moved to the architecture department, as the head of MIT's project for an innovative new library. Burchard, soon to be made the institute's dean of humanities, already had experience as a fund-raiser and administrator and later became a consultant to the president of the United States' Science Advisory Committee. He also seemed, at least to Bush, to be a man who would welcome new library ideas and experiments. A plus in Bush's eyes was that Burchard was not a librarian, one of those people Bush thought were and would always be conservatives who hated change and originality.

THE CIA'S LIBRARIANS UNDER FIRE

As Burchard and MIT's administrators searched for construction funds, Burchard sketched his plans for the new library building and the innovations it would house. As might be expected, he focused on the physical plant and technology. The technology emphasis is indicated by Burchard's choice of a chief librarian who was expected to define and supervise the future library's inner workings. The man selected was not an experienced library administrator. Yet, he was not a Shannon-like engineer. After long negotiations, in 1947 Vernon Tate, the microfilm technology expert, moved to Cambridge. He had provided vital help to Wilmarth Lewis and John Langan of the Office of Strategic Services during the war and had become the new leader of the American documentalists. In contrast to James Perry, Tate was a "hard-money" academic. He was appointed to a regular faculty position at the institute. However, he and Burchard knew his research and development efforts would have to be supported by outside grants.

OUTSIDERS TO THE RESCUE

MIT's leaders had been able to convince the Charles Hayden Foundation to deviate from its new guidelines to limit its financing to programs for children and youth. The foundation made a multimillion-dollar grant for the design and construction for the new library building and, due to Bush's influence, a large grant for allied information research seemed likely to be approved by the Carnegie Corporation, that branch of the Carnegie Foundations that focused on general education problems. Unfortunately, there were delays. The funds from the Carnegie grant for that reborn Scientific Aids to Learning (SAL) project were not received until the end of 1947. As well, the new Hayden Library building's construction fell behind schedule. It wasn't dedicated until May 1950, much later than expected. Burchard was embarrassed and under constant pressure from Bush and his institute allies.

NOTES

1. CREST, "History of the Reference Branch"; Office of Scientific Intelligence, *The Original Wizards of Langley: A Symposium Commemorating 60 Years of S&T Intelligence Analysis* (Washington, DC: CIA, ca. 2008).

2. David Alvarez, "Behind Venona: American Signal Intelligence in Early Cold War," *International and National Security* 4, no. 2 (Summer 1999): 179–86; Oleg A. Bukharin, "The Cold War Atomic Intelligence Game, 1945–70: From the Russian Perspective," *Studies in Intelligence* 48, no. 2 (2004).

3. CREST, passim, 1950–1951; Central Intelligence Agency Office of Central Reference, *Document Classification: Papers Presented at the Conference on Philosophy of Document Classification in OCR* (n.p.: Office of Central Reference, January 1960).

4. J. C. Costello, "Uniterm Indexing: Principles, Problems and Solutions," *American Documentation* 12, no. 1 (1961): 20–26; Andrew D. Osborn, "From Cutter to Dewey to Mortimer Taube and Beyond: A Complete Century of Change in Cataloging and Classification," *Cataloging and Classification Quarterly* 12, no. 3/4 (1995): 35–50; Mortimer Taube and Harold Wooster, eds., *Information Storage and Retrieval: Theory, Systems, and Devices* (New York: Columbia University Press, 1958).

5. H. P. Edmundson, V. A. Oswald, and R. E. Wyikys, *Automatic Indexing and Abstracting of the Contents of Documents* (Los Angeles: Planning Research Corporation, October 31, 1959); Lauren B. Doyle, "Indexing and Abstracting by Association," *American Documentation* 134 (1962): 378–90; Melvin Earl (Bill) Maron and John L. Kuhns, "On Relevance, Probabilistic Indexing, and Information Retrieval," *Journal of the ACM* 7, no. 3 (July 1960): 216–44; Harold Borko, "Measuring the Reliability of Subject Classification by Men and Machine," *American Documentation* 15, no. 4 (1964): 268–73.

6. CREST, "Interim Report on the Development of the Rapid Selector," 5-1953.

7. Williamina A. Himwich et al., *Final Report on Machine Methods for Information Searching* (Baltimore: Johns Hopkins University, 1955) at http://garfield.library.upenn.edu/papers/26.html.

8. CREST, "Scanner," passim, 1950–.

9. Eugene Garfield, "Preliminary Report on the Mechanical Analysis of Information by Use of the 101 Statistical Punched Card Machine," *American Documentation* 5, no. 1 (January 1954): 7–12.

10. James W. Perry, "Determination of the Iodine Content of the Public Water Supplies of North Carolina as a Possible Explanation of the Lack of Goiter among the Inhabitants" (M.A. thesis, North Carolina State College of

Agriculture and Engineering, 1928); David A. Lockmiller, *History of the North Carolina State College of Agriculture and Engineering* (Raleigh, NC: Edwards & Broughton, 1939).

11. MIT, Course Catalogs and Reports of the President, 1931–.

12. MIT, Course Catalogs; James W. Perry, "The Mechanism of Oxidation of Linseed Oil" (M.A. thesis, Massachusetts Institute of Technology, 1931).

13. Herman H. Goldstine, *The Computer from Pascal to von Neumann* (Princeton, NJ: Princeton University Press, 1980).

14. Gerald J. Cox, C. F. Bailey, and R. S. Casey, "Punch Cards for a Chemical Bibliography," *Chemical and Engineering News* 23, no. 18 (September 25, 1945): 1623–26.

15. Perry wrote one of the most elegant texts on scientific Russian: *Scientific Russian: A Textbook for Classes and Self-Study* (New York: Interscience, 1950).

16. MIT, Course Catalogs.

17. Madeline Henderson, CHF Oral History. The best estimate is that James received a 1945–1946 budget-year salary of between $3,666 and $5,090, or $36,000 to $50,000 in 2006 dollars, well below academic salaries of the period.

18. Claude Elwood Shannon and Warren Weaver, *The Mathematical Theory of Communication* (Urbana: University of Illinois Press, 1949); Norbert Wiener, *Cybernetics; or, Control and Communication in the Animal and the Machine* (Cambridge, MA: MIT Press, 1948); David A. Mindell, *Between Human and Machine: Feedback, Control, and Computing before Cybernetics* (Baltimore: Johns Hopkins University Press, 2002).

19. Alan M. Turing, *Mechanical Intelligence* (New York: Elsevier Science, ca. 1992); A. J. Meadows, ed., *The Origins of Information Science* (London: Taylor-Graham, 1987); W. John Hutchins, ed., *Early Years in Machine Translation: Memoirs and Biographies of Pioneers* (Philadelphia: John Benjamin, 2000).

9

LIBRARY AND CLASSIFICATION REVOLUTIONS?

SAL, Semantic Factors, the Luhn Scanner

Although the Massachusetts Institute of Technology's (MIT) library initiatives had stalled, James Perry was fortunate. He could begin work on his information projects as soon as he arrived in Cambridge in 1945 and could continue them because of new grants from the American Chemical Society and some industrial contributors. Then, as those grants ended, he faced unemployment. His was saved, but only because of the strange history of the new Scientific Aids to Learning (SAL) project and by James Madison Andrews's search for new classification methods as demanded by the Central Intelligence Agency's scientists.

Perry had taken on many responsibilities while in Cambridge—and without much help. As soon as he arrived he aided the MIT chemistry department in obtaining captured German documents being held by U.S. government's Publications Board. He ran a crash course in reading scientific Russian, worked on possibilities for exchanges with Russian scientists, and organized an American Chemical Society symposium on his ideas for information retrieval by punch-card and "rapid selectors." Although still a lowly fellow, he also began publishing a continuous stream of academic articles on his information work. They appeared in chemical journals, American and British documentation publications, and those with a broader audience, such as *Scientific Monthly*. Four or more publications per year were not unusual for Perry.[1]

153

In 1950, he could afford to hire a young chemist, Madeline Berry (Henderson), who later became a National Science Foundation administrator, as an assistant. She aided him in fulfilling his first and central obligation to the American Chemical Society, to evaluate two new and competing chemical notation systems. Such systems were needed to allow economical descriptions and efficient, perhaps machine searching, of the literature on organic compounds. James and Madeline gathered comments and analyses of the systems of William J. Wiswesser of the United States and G. Malcolm Dyson of England. The chemical society, the National Research Council, and the International Union of Pure and Applied Chemistry needed to make a judgment as to which one of them should be the international standard. So, Perry's reports about the two systems were carefully read.[2]

Of necessity, both systems led to complex codes, such as "B6.C.X,7.C4,7,Q,3,4,5, C2" or "L66J BMR& DSWQ IN1&1," but compared to long written descriptions or diagrams, they were parsimonious. Perry's other task for the chemists was to find new methods for searching the chemical literature using such complex notation codes. With a focus on Dyson's, when it seemed his would be selected as the standard, Perry first attempted to expand his previous use of edge-notched cards with multiple codes punched along their sides. To make the cards useful, Perry and his collaborators had created their own versions of the "postcoordination" of subject headings and concepts. That approach was another variation on "terms." It separated out each of the words describing an item and gave each an individual code on a card. When a user wanted information on, say, Starch and Applied Chemical and Dye Co., a search was made to determine which indexing cards held the codes (e.g., STAR and ACCO) for both items.

THE LUHN FACTOR, ONCE AGAIN, AGAIN

Perry had enough experience to know that regular tabulator/sorters would be little better than the edge-cards for such compound code combinations as Dyson's. That was what led him and Malcolm Dyson to ask IBM's Tom Watson and Hans Peter Luhn for help. Luhn responded with his Scanner design. While waiting for the Scanner's appearance (it took over two years to build) Perry began to think the

LIBRARY AND CLASSIFICATION REVOLUTIONS? 155

device might become a universal information machine, one able to deal with all types of coded information, not just chemistry's. That led him to expand his research and to investigate classification systems for all types of information.

But other projects competed for his attention as he awaited the arrival of Luhn's device. There were his books and articles on Russian for scientists and chemists; the revision and editing of the volume on surface agents; more explorations of superimposed coding (even for Bush's microfilm Rapid Selector); projects to code enough articles to allow a full test of Bush's Selector; investigations of automatic translation, even for Russian;[3] and, joint editorship of a seminal book surveying all punch-card technologies and methods. James also found time to motivate several of the institute's electrical engineering graduate students to work on coding possibilities in medical and legal subjects for the Rapid Selector, and he persuaded one to design a literature searching program for the institute's yet-be-completed Whirlwind electronic computer.

TOWARD AN ABSTRACTS AND CLASSIFICATION REVOLUTION

Perry was not a closet academic. Important to his career, he devoted much time to attending Chemical and Documentation Association meetings. He also helped Vernon Tate and Norman Ball with the journal *American Documentation.* Despite such a workload, Perry revisited the literature on alternatives to traditional classification and indexing methods. He concluded all had weaknesses that had to be remedied if he could fulfill his and Bush's goals of a system that was easy to use, affordable, and understandable. He decided to begin creating his own grand and unique classification scheme. The ambitious Perry assigned himself another chore, to solve the "abstracts problem." Since the 1920s there had been international meetings attempting to create international standards for the summaries (abstracts) of scientific papers but all had failed to attain their goals. Perry's intention was to create a universal language for abstracts, one that allowed each to be compared to others and that facilitated mechanized searching.

James knew the Shannon-like statistical approaches were not, at least not yet, ready for use in classification and information retrieval. So, he started with an approach that had long been used in business systems, but in ad hoc ways. In the 1930s the "facet" approach was made applicable to all knowledge by Dr. Shiyali Ramamrita Ranganathan, the British-trained Indian librarian and information theorist. His "colon" system classified an item by linking together different aspects or factors of the item, rather than by placing it in a hierarchy, or by using multiple subject terms. For logistical reasons Ranganathan favored numeric codes, something that made his identifiers rather forbidding. For example, his "colon" (combined code) for a document concerned with the x-ray treatment of tuberculosis in India in 1950 (Medicine; Lungs; Tuberculosis: Treatment; X-ray: Research. India. 1950) became the code number L,45;421:6;253:f.44'N5. That did not deter his admirers, however. After World War II, Ranganathan's methods were being deepened and revised by a group of theoretically minded librarians in England. Members of their Classification Research Group were creating new facet systems for specialized fields and seeking ways to use them in mechanized settings.[4] Perry found Ranganathan's sometimes very abstract terminology worrisome and he soon concluded that the Indian's system was ill suited for generic searches. Generic searches were one of the benefits of older hierarchical systems.

Perry began his own great exploration for ways to avoid the rigidities of hierarchies while allowing a search for, say, all items related to explosives, without listing each one. Perry also felt that Ranganathan's and other systems failed to deal with the "meaning" and the "specificity" problems. In most systems, one could not be sure that when seeking information on, for example, "dogs biting men," that items on "men biting dogs" would not be retrieved, or that a user could avoid looking through all items on China–United States–Cotton, when the specific goal was information on exports of cotton from the United States to China. Perry may have learned that the OSS had tried to solve that problem by its action codes.

PERHAPS THE BEGINNING OF ACADEMIC STARDOM, SEMANTIC FACTORS

Perry was certainly not convinced that England's researchers were ever going to overcome the shortcomings of facet classifications. Although he had no ready answers, and while his information research remained dependent on rather primitive technologies (such as the edge-card) and while he was busy with his many other projects, he began to design his own ideal system. It would be first called "abstraction ladders"[5] and, finally, semantic factors and telegraphic abstracts. The system would take years to complete. In the meantime, Perry had to endure some worrisome career uncertainties.

The first threat was the termination of his MIT chemical project's funding. The next were a series of shifts in his status at the institute. The signals he began receiving were ambiguous. Some indicated that he was highly respected and was a candidate for permanent status. Others suggested that he was only a lowly, barely tolerated soft-money associate whose position was dependent on his securing outside funding for his work. Certainly, the institute was not treating him as a star like Norbert Wiener or Claude Shannon.

Fortunately, in 1948 Vannevar Bush and the institute's leaders were interested enough in Perry's work to provide him with new support, but not from the institute's own budget and not because of any long-term plan for his career at the institute. James was saved because of the failure of the planning for the new version of the Scientific Aids to Leaning (SAL) project.

SAL IN TROUBLE, PERRY TO THE RESCUE?

Perhaps John E. Burchard's embarrassment over SAL led to Perry's good fortune. Burchard, the institute's SAL project administrator, had reason to fret. When the Carnegie SAL monies arrived in late 1947 there were few projects ready, and the few professors at the institute who seemed willing to use the funds had proposals with little relation to the goals of creating innovative educational and information technologies. As a result, and despite Vannevar Bush's connections to the new SAL, the project drifted and became an exercise of "money-chasing

CHAPTER 9

recipients." That wasn't all Burchard's fault. SAL had never had a good life. Its first incarnation began in the mid-1930s when the Carnegie Foundation decided to generously fund a National Research Council effort to apply academic science and technological expertise to education problems. Irwin Stewart directed the work, reporting to a prestigious board of directors that included Vannevar Bush. Stewart, who later worked for Bush's OSRD, oversaw some fifty-seven SAL projects at universities across the nation as well as at the National Archives and the Library of Congress. The early SAL-sponsored research ranged from very general investigations of eye fatigue and the quality of sound and film systems for schools to Vernon Tate's practical survey of the state of microfilm technology. Stewart also approved expenditures to aid the work of the American Documentation Institute. There were, however, few results that had a direct impact on education. The onset of World War II led to SAL's ending its first life with an embarrassing sale of its administrative office's furniture in early 1942.

Although the first SAL had not measured up to expectations, at the war's end the Carnegie leaders appeared willing to resume calling on academic science to advance education. Bush, MIT, and John Burchard knew of that and thought the institute's library project fit the Carnegie's visions. MIT began making inquiries about a new SAL, but one to only be at MIT, and with a focus on the new library's needs. Negotiations led to an agreement to deemphasize the MIT library's immediate goals and to an agreement that research would be on solutions to the newly declared crisis in science information. That satisfied the Carnegie administrators, but they decided to avoid committing to the $2.25 million for five years of work that Burchard and Tate requested. They agreed to give MIT one million over three years and then evaluate the progress at the institute before granting the next million dollars.

In December 1947, with Vernon Tate helping Burchard administer the first year's installment, a problem arose. Almost no one at the institute wanted the money! Vernon Tate received a large proportion of the grant for apparatus for his proposed great microfilm research laboratory, but because the new library's construction was behind schedule he did not have adequate space to use the equipment. A small portion of the grant was spent on the exploration of remedial English teaching using MIT's own language-needy students. The trip of an MIT administrator to the great Royal Society science information meeting, the microcopying of President Theodore Roosevelt's papers, Norman Ball's projected book on information, another attempt by Atherton Seidel to design a handheld microfilm reader, and the beginnings of a new version of the old ADI journal (renamed *American Documentation*) were financed. No one, however, appeared to fulfill one of SAL's stated goals, to research new printing and reproduction technologies. As well, the first SAL's interests in sound and visual displays were not followed through. The result was that at the end of the first year there was a great deal of money left unspent and little to brag about to Carnegie's administrators.

The later part of 1948 and early 1949 saw more activity, but not much. Most of the money continued to go for Tate's equipment. Then, a new participant appeared, William N. Locke, the chair of the institute's Department of Modern Languages. He began researching the visual presentation of speech, an early version of voice recognition. He had his graduate students studying graphs of phonemes, the basic parts of spoken language.[6] To his, Vannevar Bush's, and MIT's later frustration, that work was already being done in other research centers, including the Bell Telephone Laboratory. The Carnegie overseers and one of their advisors, J. C. R. Licklider, also had some worries about the relevance of Locke's phoneme work.

SAL's problems rescued James Perry. His classification and coding work were shifted to its budget, supplemented by a small amount from the U.S. Department of Agriculture to help with coding problems for its own experiments with Vannevar Bush's Rapid Selector. Perry would, however, not be able to save SAL.

There were no other significant additions to SAL's team. From 1948 to 1952 it had only three major participants: Tate, Locke, and the appreciative James Perry. Even after a displeased Vannevar Bush had the MIT project oversight committee revamped, SAL continued to drift. In 1950, a third of the Carnegie funds had yet to be expended and an extension of the first grant led only to two more years of attempting to put SAL on track. In 1952, the institute returned more than 10 percent of the original grant and did not ask for a renewal or the next million dollars. It would be a decade and a half before the institute launched another great SAL-like library initiative, the INTREX project that benefited from the Ford Foundation's drive to improve science and tech-

160   CHAPTER 9

nology education so the United States would not fall further behind the Soviets' supposed science and engineering achievements.[7]

SAL's woes had not immediately impacted James Perry. In 1948, he even had a glimmer of hope for a regular faculty appointment. While continuing to work on information problems, and although still only a faculty fellow supported by outside funding, he began being shunted between regular institute departments. He was assigned to the prestigious Research Laboratory for Electronics. Tate's microfilm center followed for a time, then he was assigned to the Modern Language Department, and then to the institute's new Center for International Studies that served as a high-level policy think tank for the Central Intelligence Agency (CIA).[8]

A DREAM COME TRUE?

The 1949 appointment to the Modern Language Department came with a hint that James was going to be a real university professor. MIT made an unusual move by giving James the title of associate professor, making him the second-highest-ranked man in the department. The MIT president's report of 1950 pictured him as a unique blend of chemist, linguist, and specialist in documentation and "rapid selection." James should not have been overly optimistic, however. The appointment did not come with the security of tenure, and he was still a soft-money employee. All his work was on SAL's budget and there already were indications that SAL was not to continue.[9]

Perry, however, was coming to be regarded as the major figure in and perhaps a savior of SAL. MIT's final report to the Carnegie's administrators featured James's accomplishments. It saluted his classification-coding work, including the exploration of systems for law and medicine, his contributions to mechanical language translation (a new MIT interest), his ambitious plans for a grand centralized information retrieval center, and his developmental work on a special "words and phrases" retrieval system linked to new electronic machines. Another hopeful sign for Perry was that during his years in the various departments he encountered men who were or who would become famous in computer science, linguistics, automatic translation, and international policy making. Perry Crawford, Robert Everett, J. C. R. Licklider, Max

LIBRARY AND CLASSIFICATION REVOLUTIONS?

Millikan, and Yehoshua Bar-Hillel were among the greats he met. Perry also learned more valuable lessons about the changed nature of academic life, especially the need to be a skilled grantsman and a constant publisher—even when one held a regular faculty position.

James had learned much about faculty life, but by the close of 1950, although he was planning major conferences at MIT on machine selection and translation (sponsored by the Rockefeller Foundation and perhaps with extra CIA support) Perry did not have the security of a regular appointment, he had not become an academic star, and he remained dependent on outside grants. With the indications that SAL would end, the middle-aged Perry, now forty-four, again worried about his career and his dream of a great new classification system.

THE CIA TO THE RESCUE?

Then, James Madison Andrews and the CIA's science watchers gave James some hope. Perhaps because of the connections between Vernon Tate, Norman Ball (of the military's Research and Development Panel), and Joseph Becker of the CIA, the agency awarded James Perry a significant grant for work on mechanical indexing, exploration of his proposed semantic factors to replace the Intelligence Subject Code (ISC), and, significantly, automatic language translation.[10] There were indications that this grant would be the first of many. With the monies in hand, Perry was transferred to the CIA's deeply funded Center for International Studies at MIT as a research associate. He may even have thought that he could establish a CIA-sponsored big information version of the many permanent income-producing centers for research and operations that Cold War funding was supporting in universities such as MIT, Johns Hopkins, and the California Institute of Technology.

The CIA grant did more than move James into a new department. It brought him into the world of lavish funding and income. The best estimates for the two years of the CIA project (that had few personnel) range from a low of $850,000 to a high of $1,009,000.[11] Perry's and his new associate Allen Kent's salaries reached the level of those of well-established university professors of the period. Kent, for example, had a separate contract for six months' work in Washington, D.C., for some $46,500, or, at level of almost $100,000 a year.

In 1950, as James Perry was negotiating the details of the CIA's grant for his efforts at MIT, he was being vetted for security approval. He and the CIA, and probably the predecessor to the National Security Agency,[12] awaited that and the arrival of the innovative Luhn Scanner so that Perry's explorations of alternatives to the Intelligence Subject Code (ISC) including the semantic code, automatic retrieval, and machine translation could go beyond the paper-and-pencil stages.

By the time Perry received his security clearance it was clear that the United States had entered the Cold War, at home as well as abroad. The Marshall Plan had helped avert a Communist takeover in Western Europe, but there was fear of Communism within the United States. By 1949, the coups in Hungary and Czechoslovakia indicated total Soviet control in Eastern Europe and the end of any hope that the "bloc" would ever be free. The Korean War that began in 1950 meant the Far East was in jeopardy. In America, ideological battles intensified as the Rosenbergs, the atomic spies, were discovered and as Alger Hiss faced a new trial and imprisonment for his supposed help to Russia. Joseph McCarthy's investigations deepened the older search for Communist influence, and major American Communists, including such leaders as Gus Hall, went into hiding while many others were jailed or deported.

Those taking contracts with the CIA in the early 1950s must have known they were involving themselves in international and national ideological struggles. They were not merely professional technicians and their information work was not purely academic.

PERRY'S UNLIKELY NEW HELPER, ALLEN KENT

After the CIA approved his funding, Perry had enough money to hire someone in addition to Madeline Berry (Henderson). That man would become one of the greatest grantsmen and program builders of information sciences' first generation. Given his background, one like a typical idealist young Communist of the era, Allen Kent was an unlikely candidate for a position at the now security-cautious CIA. He was born in 1921 to a Russian Jewish, Yiddish-speaking family that had immigrated to New York City's Harlem district to work in the garment industry. The Great Depression did not treat his father well and the family was stressed. Allen Kent (Abe Kaslofsky, before 1946), after a series of

LIBRARY AND CLASSIFICATION REVOLUTIONS?

rather demeaning but well-paying part-time jobs, attended the tuition-free City College of New York (CCNY). Kent's studies were subsidized by a National Youth Grant—until the government discovered he was making too much money and withdrew the fifteen-dollar-a-month support. Kent was at CCNY when the institution was a hotbed of radicalism but he seems to have ignored much of the ideological turmoil. He graduated in 1942 with a chemistry major and a minor in German. He then worked as a civilian quality control inspector for the military's armament groups. After that, although married, he was drafted. He was assigned to the air force. An illness kept him from combat but near the end of the war he was sent to the air force's document center in London where his chemical background and his ability to read German were put to work processing captured technical documents from Germany's missile program.[13]

After his return to the United States he should have become bitter. He was unable to launch into a successful career. A risky job as a chemist on a speculative project to manufacture saccharine ended in failure. He was saved by finding a position in 1947 as an associate science editor and supervisor of many copyeditors at the Interscience Publishing Company in New York City. His four years on that job, and the friends he made at the company such as Marcel Dekker, would play an important role in his and Perry's information careers. While at Interscience Kent learned about editing manuscripts, the economics of publishing, even how to index publications. His success at Interscience had not led to an executive position, however.[14]

In 1951 when Perry, whose book on surface agents had been edited by Kent, asked Allen to join him on the Scientific Aids to Learning project, Allen accepted—at first unaware of Perry's CIA connection. Then, Kent gladly went to work with Perry on the extension of the CIA project in Washington, D.C., where the classified part of the work could be conducted. Like James, he expected a return to MIT and a permanent position after the stint in Washington.

CURING ALL THE ILLS OF INFORMATION RETRIEVAL

As IBM was preparing to ship the Luhn Scanner to the CIA's tabulating machine center in Washington for Perry's use, James and Allen Kent

164   CHAPTER 9

began refining James's ideas for a revolutionary sci-tech classification system for machine searching. Perry thought his evolving abstraction ladders (semantic factors) system would overcome most of the long-endured problems of information retrieval.[15] He believed it would avoid the complexity and rigidity of hierarchical systems, reflect how scientists organized ideas, and be based on the words and concepts they used. He also let it be known the system could conquer the "meaning" problem and the difficulties caused by synonyms and homonyms. As well, he thought it would allow generic searching and the identification of items specifically desired while eliminating false drops (irrelevant materials) from search results. Perry also declared he could surmount the uncontrolled vocabulary problem. That problem arose out of classifiers creating their own words for items already covered by existing categories. The result was confusion and the need to search through long lists of terms to be sure a search query was adequately composed.

High on James's list of the advantages of his unique version of factors was its supposed ease of use and its ability to generate unlimited combinations of search terms. It allowed many entry points to be constructed by users with unique questions, unlike a Dewey system that posed severe restrictions on what could be asked because of the nature of hierarchies with fixed categories. The words "deep" and "shallow" do not well describe Perry's factor classification, but they give an indication of the range of its possibilities when classifying and searching.

To aid his classification effort Perry had been exploring the latest psychological and social science theories on concept formation as well as examining writings in philosophy and library science. However, the original motivations for his system were rather commonsensical. One of them seems to have followed Vannevar Bush's demands in his famous "As We May Think" article.

AS WE MAY TALK

Perry began by rejecting the type of categorizations made by "outsiders" (library professionals) such as those found in typical subject-term, Dewey, and Library of Congress classification systems. Not yet informed of all the details of the various terms systems, and not envisioning simply using the words within each document, or thinking of eliminating classification by professionals, he began creating his own version of classifications that could rely on the language and terms used in contemporary science and technology. He, Madeline Berry, and Allen Kent examined hundreds of encyclopedias, lists of subject terms, classification guides, academic papers, and reports in science and technology fields. Their goal was to eventually collect a list of all the important terms currently used by practitioners.

They did the same for James Andrews's CIA systems. After a further clearance for the CIA's task, Perry and Kent read through the Intelligence Subject Code and agency intelligence papers looking for the important contemporary terms used in the intelligence field. They eventually compiled a list of terms (thirty thousand for the sci-tech domain) they hoped would provide a complete coverage of all science and technology literature and, thus, a complete dictionary for the CIA's Office of Scientific Intelligence (OSI) and other science watchers. Perry believed he could forestall semantic chaos by limiting all indexing and classification to those terms only. A classifier or indexer would need special permission to use any new terms.

FROM TERMS TO THEIR SEPARATE FACTORS

When Perry and his two aides collected a term, it was checked against dictionaries and other sources for its meaning, and then its underlying factors (meaning components) were determined. An edged-notched card with all information was made for each term.[16] By the time Perry and Kent had finished their first round of work for the CIA they had collected six thousand terms, and determined the underlying semantic factors of each of them. For example, an indexer would consult Perry's "dictionary" and find that a "colorimeter" was composed of (defined by) the combination of the three underlying factors (facets): machine + analysis + color. Or, that " abattoir" was composed of three factors: factory + destroy + animals. Each of the factors was given a short alphabetic code (at different times three or four letters) arranged in such a way as to facilitate generic as well as particular item searching. For example, with "colorimeter" coded as machine + analysis + color (MACH, NALL, CALR in one version of Perry's dictionary) a searcher could easily know how to switch to a quest for all machines that "analyzed" by using just MACH + NALL). By 1960, the sci-tech terms in Perry's system could be generally identified by a total of some two hundred factors. The dictionary of terms, along with their semantic factor definitions, was punched onto tabulator cards, allowing automated searching and manipulation.

Perry believed the combinations of his factors would be sufficient for indexing and retrieval. He soon learned, however, that much more was needed to conquer the ills of classification, especially the goal of selecting only the items needed by a scientist making a request for a bibliography. The semantic factors system became increasingly complex as Perry attempted to solve all the retrieval problems. It evolved into perhaps the most complicated classification system ever devised and it certainly drifted further and further away from the engineering goal of simplicity and Bush's demand for an "as we may think" system. As a result, it would require the use of expensive, highly trained indexers and searchers. The system's 1958 manual, for example, was 972 pages long, something not to be mastered by the unskilled.[17]

Much had to be added to the rather simple initial semantic factors system to meet Perry's grandest objectives. For example, the factor codes were augmented by ones indicating different relationships between a term and a concept represented by the factors. The second letter in a factor became an "alphabetic infix," with different letters indicating different relationships. There were ten of the alphabetic infixes. An A, for example, indicated the term was a member of the factor's class, U indicated the term helped to produce the factor, and Y indicated the term was characterized by the factor. W was used when the term was produced by, acted on, or was influenced by the factor. An absence of an alphabetic infix indicated the generic version of the factor. For example, using the infix W, B_PD (Digestive System) became the code BWPD. When BWPD was used for retrieval it recovered all items related to something that acts on the digestive system. When just B_PD was utilized, all items related to the digestive system were retrieved. The code B_FL retrieved all items concerning body fluids, but when BAFL was used, a species of body fluids were selected.[18]

Perry soon concluded that even more was required. A numeric infix was added to the factor code because there might be many items defined by any alphabetic-infixed code. In many instances, a numeric identifier was required to select an item. For example, to find items

LIBRARY AND CLASSIFICATION REVOLUTIONS?

related to "bile," the complete code BAFL. BWPD. 002 was needed.[19] Another example taken from the 1958 semantic factors' manual dealt with the codes needed for the retrieval of information on telephones: DWCM. TURN. LQCT. MACH. 001.[20] M_CH was the code for machine or device with A added to indicate the "species" relation. T_RN was for transmission and the infix U indicated the concept (telephone) produces something. D_CM indicated communication and W was for acting upon whatever was indicated by the factor. L_CT was for electricity with Q indicating the concept makes use of electricity. Combined, those factors pointed to any device used to transmit information by means of electricity, so an additional infix was required to select just telephones. In the case of telephones, it was 001, and for telegraphs it was 002. During the 1960s, when semantic factors was used in the education field, more numeric infixes were required to find a specific item. A numeric suffix was also called into play to further specify meaning. The code necessary to select documents concerned with the Minnesota Multiphasic Personality Inventory was DACM. MUSR. MYMT. 1017 3102.

Adding to the complexity of Perry's factors system, the search codes (and the related special summary Telegraphic abstracts) were not always confined to the factors for one term. The complete code could become very long, with terms divided by symbols for subphrases, phrases, sentences, and paragraphs. Other features that Perry added increased the system's power—and its intricacy. In addition to the codes, alpha infixes, and number infixes/suffixes, Perry employed "role indicators," many special term codes, codes to indicate a numeric value followed, codes for lower and highest values, a unique system to identify geographic locations (New York City was ASNANEN1), and codes indicating that a personal name would follow. There were also special codes for material such as metals and ores. "Material processed hematite, center" became KEJ. MANR.117./ FQE2/03.

Role indicators were important because they helped with the "meaning" problem and with composing the telegraphic abstracts. During the early years of his system, depending on what organization Perry was working for, the role indicators, as well as the factored terms, might be relatively simple. An early form of an abstract had just a list of major terms from an article with a few simple general role indicators. By the end of the 1950s, however, they were usually quite involved. The role indictors, some twenty of them, were three-letter codes that began with a K. For example, KQV stood for "property given for," KWV was for "property given," KAP stood for "property influenced," and KAL was for "influenced by."

NOT FOR THE WIRES, BUT STILL TELEGRAPHIC ABSTRACTS AND UNIVERSAL ONES

When combined with the factored terms the role indicators created an advanced telegraphic abstract. One example of such an expanded "telegraphic" is from the written abstract of "The Possibility of Changing the Brittleness of Cermet Materials by Modifying their Microstructure." Encoded (translated) with the role indicators and factors, the original sentence became the telegraphic abstract (with the comma in this case indicating a subphrase) KOV. CERM. 2x. METL. O01, KWV. KAP. PAPR. 010, KAL. CIRS. MYTL. RANG. 13x. 001. Another example of complexity when using role indicators was the search code compiled in the late 1950s in response to a request by a user for "articles available on the vacuum melting of nickel-containing materials, as well as the use of nickel in the apparatus and equipment used in vacuum melting." The telegraphic code (program) used for searching was: &-. KEJ.+KOV.+(,KAD.+,KAG, KUJ.). NQI.-KAM.+KAL. (C-NG.+P_ SS.) R-HT..T_MS.0044. &+&-KAM. (CUNG.+PASS) R-HT. T-MS.004., KIJ. MQ1.,-&.[21]

What a user received after a search was completed was a copy of the initial, but short, traditional abstract that had been used to build the search codes. Copies of the preliminary abstracts were microfilmed and filed by a document's number then retrieved, copied, and sent to the customer. Perry regarded providing the full text of articles as impractical.[22]

Important to Perry and Kent, they hoped their telegraphic abstracts would become "translations" that would allow diverse types of abstracts to be reduced to a uniform, minimalist structure with a universal vocabulary while retraining original meanings. With such basic telegraphic abstracts, a document's codes could easily be constructed for retrieval. Madeline Berry, who did so much traveling to collect and factor the terms, was proud that attaching the telegraphic abstract worksheet to a document, or publishing it separately, allowed a trained user to know the contents of a document at a glance. Perry also had visions of his semantic factors becoming a universal system that would allow a national, hopefully international, network of bibliographic services to share with each other and establish a universal searchable database.

DISAPPOINTMENTS AT THE CIA, IBM, AND MIT— ANDREWS TRIUMPHS, LUHN CAST ADRIFT

Only fragments of Perry's 1950–1952 preparatory coding work for the CIA have been discovered, but his long reports containing philosophical wanderings on the future of information and the need for the CIA to finance more of his research have been found in the CIA's CREST files. The coding fragments indicate that Perry had not completed his semantic factors system and, despite Andrews's desire for great depth of classification, Perry was somewhat of a traditionalist and a minimalist during his CIA years. The one classification worksheet that has been discovered was in a 1952 progress report that has notations different from those in the later semantic factors system.[23]

While Perry and Kent were working on the classifications, the CIA's tabulator machine department had been testing the Luhn Scanner. It had become publicly renowned through newspaper coverage of presentations about it at the meeting of the American Chemical Society in 1951, and at a 1952 symposium at MIT.

Despite the machine's fame, the CIA's tabulator team rejected the Scanner. They could not cure problems with the card feeder and they were frustrated by the difficulties of the optical system. Andrews agreed with his men and decided that although the Intellofax's regular IBM machines did not have any "and" capabilities, they could be coaxed to do all the work the CIA needed. He decided they would not be replaced until there was technological revolution well beyond Luhn's offering.

The Luhn Scanner faced another rejection—even before the final results of the machine's engineering tests were revealed to Andrews and Perry. Perry had changed his mind about the Scanner! He declared that even if it worked perfectly, the Scanner's powers were not up to the needs of advanced information retrieval. He reported that the Scanner's "and" logic was not enough. He wanted a machine that could do all the variations and combinations of Boolean logic. In 1952, he also recommended abandoning the optics of the Scanner. He wanted a more advanced version of the electromechanical IBM 101 with wire-brush sensors for each column of a card and the plugboards that allowed the programming (rewiring) of the machine to perform any of the possible combinations of "and," "or," "not." Perry asked IBM to design and build such a new (and expensive) machine.

NOTES

1. MIT, President's Reports 1947–1948.
2. Madeline Henderson, CHF Oral History.
3. CREST, James W. Perry, "Machine Translation of Russian Technical Literature: Notes on Preliminary Experiments," 1952.
4. M. J. Satija, *Manual of Practical Colon Classification* (New Delhi: Sterling, 1984); B. C. Vickery, "The Structure of Semantic Coding: A Review," *American Documentation* 10 (July, 1959): 234–41; B. C. Vickery, *Faceted Classification Schemes* (New Brunswick, NJ: Graduate School of Library Service, Rutgers, the State University, 1966); D. J. Foskett, "The Construction of a Faceted Classification for a Special Subject," *Proceedings of the International Conference on Scientific Information, 1958* (Washington, DC: NSF-NAS, ca. 1958).
5. CREST, "Machine Techniques for Information Selection," 6 10 and 12 1954.
6. MIT, President's Report, 1950.
7. Columbia University Archives, Collection on the Second Scientific Aids to Learning Project and Carnegie Foundation.
8. Christopher Simpson, ed., *Universities and Empire: Money and Politics in the Social Sciences During the Cold War* (New York: Free Press, 1998).
9. MIT, President's Report, October 1949–1951 and MIT catalog 1950.
10. CREST, "Machine Indexing and Translation," 1951.
11. CREST, "Perry Grant," September 1950, Office of Scientific Intelligence, "Machine Indexing Project," May 1953.
12. NSA FOIA req. 78011a.
13. National Council of Jewish Women, Interview with Allen Kent, May 12, 1993, http://images.library.pitt.edu/cgi-bin/i/image/image-idx?view=entry;cc=ncjw;entryid=x-ais196440.233.

14. Cornelis D. Andriesse, *Dutch Messengers: A History of Science Publishing, 1930–1980* (Leiden, Netherlands: Brill, 2008).

15. Shawne D. Miksa, "Pigeonholes and Punchcards: Identifying the Divisions between Library Classification Research and Information Retrieval" (Ph.D. diss., Florida State University, 2002); Francis L. Miksa, *The Development of Classification at the Library of Congress* (Champaign: University of Illinois, Graduate School of Library and Information Science, ca. 1984).

16. Allen Kent, J. W. Perry, and M. M. Berry, "Machine Literature Searching V: Definition and Systemization of Terminology for Code Development," *American Documentation* 5, no. 3 (August 1954): 166–72.

17. James W. Perry and Allen Kent, *Tools for Machine Literature Searching: Semantic Code Dictionary, Equipment, Procedures* (New York: Interscience, 1958).

18. Gordon C. Barhydt, *Western Reserve University Index of Educational Resources* (Cleveland, OH: Western Reserve, 1964); B. C. Vickery, "The Structure of Semantic Coding: A Review," *American Documentation* 10 (July 1959): 234–41; John L. Melton, "The Semantic Code Today," *American Documentation* 1, no. 2 (April 1962): 176–81.

19. Vickery, "Structure of Semantic Coding."

20. Perry and Kent, *Tools.*

21. Allen Kent, "Exploitation of Recorded Information. I. Development of an Operational Machine Searching Service for the Literature of Metallurgy and Allied Subjects," *American Documentation* 11, no. 2 (April 1960): 186.

22. Kent, "Exploitation," 181.

23. CREST, "Machine Indexing," 1952–1953.

10

AUTOMATION DREAMS, MINICARD

The CIA's rejection of Luhn's widely acclaimed Scanner was just one of James Perry's problems in 1952. His hopes of a career as a professor had been shattered when the Massachusetts Institute of Technology (MIT) gave indications it would never grant him a regular full-time faculty position. His dreams of becoming the creator of a revolutionary new classification system and a founder of a new information science seemed doomed when he received more bad news from Washington. James Madison Andrews had rejected Perry's request for a renewal of his classification contract, although the CIA indicated it would continue to monitor the development of Perry and Bar-Hillel's machine translation ideas. Semantic factors seemed dead because Andrews had somehow convinced the agency's science watchers that the older classification systems would suffice, at least until one besides Perry's was discovered. Andrews did not feel secure, however. He immediately assigned his librarians to a continuous survey of emerging methods and technologies to prove to his superiors that he was open to innovation.

As bad as Andrews's rejection was for Perry, MIT decided to end the SAL project. With that, for the first time in years there was not even soft money for James Perry. Then, MIT went further, giving him more than a hint that it no longer had any type of position for him, even a soft-money one—despite all his research and publications. There were no indications the institute would find places for Kent and Berry.

THE WORST OF TIMES FOR PERRY, A NEW INFORMATION WORLD'S OPPORTUNITIES

Perry, Kent, and Madeline Berry might have gone their own ways, even abandoning the library world, but they sensed that a new information era was emerging, one with great opportunities. Although dismissed from MIT and the CIA, they decided to bet their futures on an undefined profession, information science. They felt the Cold War–related increase of science-technology publications and the unprecedented expansion of American higher education would continue. They were prescient. The number of traditional scientific and technical periodicals began skyrocketing, as did the number of college faculty. The American government's investment in research was heading toward three times its early postwar level. There would also be a change in the orientation of America's colleges. As government financial support for sci-tech research multiplied, more universities emulated World War II's great applied-knowledge centers, such as those at MIT, Caltech, and Johns Hopkins. Traditional teaching colleges began restructuring to take advantage of the surge of funding and sought other ways to support increasingly expensive programs as they attempted to become recognized as universities. Many schools even became entrepreneurial, creating departments and centers whose focus was not on teaching or pure research but on providing income-producing services, sometimes in competition with private companies and nonprofit organizations.

At the same time, the phenomenal growth of all higher education was creating an ever-increasing demand for information products of all types, ranging from textbooks to those the traditional indexing and abstracting services had provided. Unfortunately, those old indexing services were finding it difficult to deal with the increase in traditional academic publication—the flood of technical and scientific reports was overwhelming them. That deluge of science and technology information called for new institutions, methods, and machines—at more than a few elite universities and research centers.

Perry gambled that his and his colleagues' careers could be based on servicing a huge market for the retrieval of sci-tech documents. He was correct about the level of demand. Some scientists estimated its value would be in the range of $20 billion a year by the 1960s because, they believed, information searching typically ran at least 10 percent of any

AUTOMATION DREAMS, MINICARD

research project's budget. However, the true value of efficient information retrieval remains immeasurable.

UNEXPECTED COMPLICATIONS

During the 1950s and 1960s much of the demand was tied to Cold War needs, and government monies. That meant unexpected complications for those like Perry who based their livelihoods on information retrieval. Although hesitant to see themselves as part of an industry, or as being ideologically engaged during the era of what historians have called the age of consensus (or the era of the end of ideology), during the 1950s and early 1960s new information professionals like Kent and Perry became inescapably involved in a serious political and ideological dispute over the fundamentals of the organization of America's sci-tech information systems. Perry and Kent even became public figures in a new round of debates over private versus government roles in science information in the 1950s and, as had been the case in the Henry Wallace years, over the underlying ideological premises.

While the political struggles Andrews faced at the CIA during the 1950s would not be known to the public, they were as or more intense than Perry's would be, making the goal of a unified intelligence information system seem an impossibility. There were struggles over budgets, methods, and technologies, all in the context of increasing pressures on the intelligence community to penetrate the Soviet bloc.

OVERLOAD AT THE CIA

In 1952, as James Perry searched for work, James Madison Andrews faced more troubles at the CIA's information center. His immediate problem was an overwhelming workload. The intensified Cold War had led to a data explosion at the agency. Between 1950 and 1954 its work increased 100 percent, and, despite Andrews doubling his workforce,[1] the tasks of indexing, storing, and retrieving documents (and notifying analysts of their existence) became overpowering just as Andrews was fending off attempts by oversight committees to tear apart his Office of Central Reference (OCR).

176 CHAPTER 10

The CIA's library old-timers, and a new crew of professionally trained librarian-classifiers, made some progress, but they were always frustrated. Demand exceeded budgets as well as the abilities of CIA's pool of skilled indexers. By the late 1950s, the agency was so desperate for proficient indexers it thought of establishing a technical school to train recent high school graduates.[2] In addition, there were unrelenting demands from national leaders like Norman Ball and Vannevar Bush for the adoption of technological innovations that Andrews and Joe Becker considered unnecessary and speculative. But they had to continue investing in the development of such adventures as automatic indexing and abstracting.

INTELLOFAX FACES NEW CHALLENGERS

Although Intellofax remained the pride of the OCR, Andrews knew that information technologies were rapidly changing and he had to contend with relentless demands to replace Intellofax with new systems. Some of those pressures resulted from the autonomy of other divisions in the CIA, ones that independently sought solutions to their information challenges. Andrews, for example, had been unable to refuse the agency's science group's demand to launch the James Perry–Hans Peter Luhn rather unproductive machine and classification project at MIT. Later, other branches of the agency began initiatives on their own, including a very secret and expensive one at IBM for the giant Walnut microfilm machine. The military's intelligence agencies also had information-technology projects that threatened to make Intellofax appear to be a techno-dinosaur.

Greater demands on Andrews came from very high-level groups, ones within and without the agency. The deep criticisms and recommendations in the Eberstadt and Dulles reports of 1949, which called on the CIA to overcome any obstacles and act as the nation's central information organization, had a continuing influence. At the same time, groups such as the United States Intelligence Board constantly pushed the CIA's divisions to change their methods, although many of the machines they proposed adopting were merely conjectures. Andrews was able to avoid accepting many machines and procedures, but he

ANDREWS CUTS BACK TO MOVE FORWARD

Before then, without an ever-increasing budget, Andrews had to turn to some rather professionally distasteful quick fixes during the 1950s as he tried to meet the data overload challenge. Intellofax alone was dealing with a thousand new items (with as many as fifteen copies of each) every workday and was so inundated that Andrews initiated a policy that went against the grain of his users' preferences and his staff's information professionalism. As each report was received, it was evaluated as to its long-term value. Only those judged to contain more than fleeting information were indexed. That NODEX system saved much effort, but because even the best indexers could handle no more than thirty items a day, there continued to be major delays in posting reports to the center's files.[3]

That had led to protests from intelligence analysts and the subject-area specialists. In reaction, Andrews broke other established indexing rules. He began allowing the analysts to do the abstracting for Intellofax. He soon regretted that decision. The results of an examination revealed a long-known problem with indexes and abstracts done by nonprofessionals. Specialists focused on their limited interests and produced abstracts that neglected all other content. Andrews had to endure a serious in-house political struggle with his bureaucratic superiors to return the abstracting and indexing responsibilities to his staff who, he believed, would be sensitive to all subject areas.

Andrews may have won that battle because he had been willing to abandon his Office of Central Reference's newspaper clipping service and to replace a daily printed summary notice of incoming reports and other materials with a less frequent and labor-saving QUICK system. That 1952 version of Hans Peter Luhn's 1958 KWIC (keyword in context) service was another deviation from best information practices— but a very useful one. QUICK and KWIC used only the substantive words in the titles of documents to quickly produce a tabulator-generated index printout, with each of the substantive words permuted so that each became the first in a printed line, with that line sorted to be grouped with lines with similar "first words." The printouts were often enormous but they allowed users to find items by browsing through the grouped title words. The weaknesses of the system, such as lack of generic searching and the absence of a standardized and controlled vocabulary, were evident even then—but speed of production and cost savings outweighed those defects.[4]

Andrews had to confront more mundane challenges to the OCR's reports system, and to the other sections he supervised. Space was a serious and immediate issue. The OCR, housed in a crowded and leaky old ice rink, discovered that the size of its accumulating paper files was becoming a nuisance. Andrews decided to replace the paper files with microfilm copies. That angered the analysts, who demanded instant access to the full text of any report. Andrews was soon able to reach what he thought was a satisfying compromise. The most valuable previously microfilmed items were put into Langan-like aperture cards, with paper copies of only the most recently received documents kept in readily accessible files. All others were archived. The use of Langan cards meant a fourfold reduction of the physical size of the OCR's local storage files, while allowing relatively quick retrieval. With its files building at a rate of more than three hundred thousand reports a year, the OCR soon held several million of John Langan's aperture cards.[5]

Microfilm and aperture cards were not a panacea. By 1966, with the agency handling 1,500 classified and 100,000 unclassified documents a day, Andrews's division had accumulated thirteen million regular reports' cards, four million aperture cards, thirteen thousand rolls of microfilm, three million hard-copy documents, and an amazing twenty million cards in its ultrasecret Special Register. That register appears to have held copies of the National Security Agency's radio intercepts and the CIA's reports from clandestine operations.[6]

MORE THAN INTELLOFAX PROBLEMS

Andrews had much more on his managerial plate than Intellofax and its reports system. They were only small parts of his OCR. They accounted for just 10 percent of the division's workforce. The OCR had a half dozen other organizations, most with their own tabulators, and each having a great degree of budgetary and policy independence. There was the library reference center, the domestic contacts and industrial (target) registers, the biographies group, the group tracking all international scientific meetings, the ultrasecret Special Register, and the photos (PIC) group. The PIC group was especially demanding and influential. It needed more and more resources, and special ones, as it prepared to process the films from the secret U2 planes and the Corona satellites that were the hoped-for ways for the CIA to get behind the Soviet Iron Curtain. There were also demands for resources by the branches that acquired foreign publications (the FDD) and the group monitoring foreign open source broadcasts (the FBIS).

There was another type of threat facing Intellofax and the reports group. The agency's information professionals in the other OCR divisions handled ten times the number of requests than did Intellofax's staff. The OCR's traditional librarians usually dealt with multiples of the number of inquiries to Intellofax, and the type of questions the librarians tackled were complex, so much so they frequently had to call on many outside contractors to handle larger research projects. For example, Ralph Shaw of the United States Department of Agriculture took a contract to survey all the veterinary literature to see if the Soviets were preparing for biological warfare. The Library of Congress, the John Crerar Library, and the Battelle Memorial Institute also performed many reference chores, including surveying thousands of sci-tech journals.

More problems arose when the CIA accepted the responsibility for producing the comprehensive Intelligence Publications Index (IPI), a printed monthly and cumulative yearly publication to be used by all organizations in the intelligence community.[7] That called for initially hiring six new librarians who launched a survey of existing digests including the Readers Guide and the New York Times Index. They also made a tour of all the major government indexing centers to determine the best set of subject headings (not ISC codes) for the IPI.[8]

THE NEVER-ENDING CLASSIFICATION CHALLENGE

Andrews also remained mired in the deeply frustrating classification conflict during the 1950s. He was caught between the mandate to convince all the intelligence agencies to adopt the ISC and the need to

180 CHAPTER 10

keep it a logical and hierarchical system. As well, the politics of classification was becoming more complex and frustrating. To gain allies (even among his own analysts) Andrews had to bend to more demands to include numerous additions that made the ISC less and less like the well-organized and parsimonious system created in the late 1940s. Despite such accommodations, the goal of a single uniform classification system for the entire intelligence community always seemed unattainable.

WAS THERE A TECHNOLOGICAL FIX? THE MAJOR MINICARD PROJECT

Andrews had no alternative but to continue to keep informed about all innovations and he became technologically proactive. He agreed to continue investing significant amounts in Richard Ruggles's secret project at Yale University. Ruggles's team of three technicians and some eight graduate students were aiming high. Their new ultra-high-speed five component version of Vannevar Bush's Rapid Selector was to have a superfast microfilm copier for putting abstracts on film with the index areas holding the equivalent of five full IBM cards of codes. The special "interrogator" component was to be able to scan all the codes simultaneously and to use advanced Boolean (and/or) testing.[9] Sadly, the project reached a dead end and was canceled in 1954—but it was one of the threads that led to the CIA's involvement in one of the greatest and most expensive attempts to conquer all the ills of microfilm as an information technology, Eastman Kodak's adventurous Minicard information system.

Predictably, Ruggles's engineers had gone to Eastman Kodak for advice.[10] The company was "the" microfilm organization in the world. It had helped Vannevar Bush's team with its Rapid Selector work in the 1930s and 1940s and, known only to members of the intelligence community, had built the most advanced automatic microfilm devices in the world during World War II.[11] Under Dr. A. W. Tyler, Eastman's principal technological researcher, the company provided the army's and navy's radio spies with a series of automated microfilm codebreaking devices, including the amazing 5202 machine and the HYPO. The 5202 was a microfilm version of Britain's electronic Colossus protocomputer.

AUTOMATION DREAMS, MINICARD

HYPO was designed for a special type of attack on the German Enigma machine and other similar devices. After the war, Tyler and his colleagues had continued their microfilm explorations and given advice about microfilm as input, output, and memory to early electronic computer designers.

Tyler and his coworkers, such as J. W. Kuipers, began to explore some extraordinary ideas. They also sought advice and potential customers. After they met with representatives of the air force's huge intelligence branch, they thought they had an economic incentive to begin developing a radically new machine. The air force and then the CIA's representatives indicated a desire for a microfilm selector device far more advanced than what Ruggles had been working on and indicated their agencies would likely provide subsidies for its development, as well as serving as an initial market for such an advanced "selector."

THE AIR FORCE TAKES THE INFO-TECH LEAD TO CONQUER THE MEMORY PROBLEMS

Although the air force's documents division in Dayton, Ohio, later known as CADO, had been at the forefront in the use of tabulating machines for document retrieval, it had need of more powerful information technologies because it had taken on additional critical information responsibilities. The threat of Soviet air attacks, especially ones that might employ atomic weapons, was so great that the American government wrote an almost blank check for the air force. As a result, it had more latitude than the CIA to invest in costly technological adventures. Billions were allocated for an early warning radar-computer system and more went to new airplanes and missiles. The service even had its large Foreign Technology Division in Dayton with hundreds of people, as well as contract employees at institutions such as the Battelle Memorial Institute, surveying the world's technical literature for hints about Soviet airpower. Meanwhile, the air force's Rome, New York, research center was becoming one of the most generous sponsors of information technology and systems.

The air force could afford to generously invest in the development of devices such as the microfilm machine Eastman's men were proposing—and much more. Later, the air force underwrote costly efforts such as Gilbert King's Photoscopic high-density glass disk memory that became part of an ambitious IBM–air force automatic language translation device, the AN/GSQ-16 (Mark I) computer.[12] Avco, the aero contractor, also shared in the air force's largesse. It was developing a total information system based on the Photoscopic store while other air force contractors were exploring more esoteric information/computer technologies.[13] A solution like King's to the memory problem was needed because at the time fast digital computer memories were very expensive and held little data. In 1956, IBM's best magnetic digital "random" disk system could store only twenty thousand bibliographic records with an average cost $7 per year for each character. In the mid-1950s, no one could predict that in a decade a digital disk could hold thirty-two million bibliographic records at a cost of a half cent per year per character.

In the 1950s, microfilm remained the most likely solution to the memory challenge.

THE CIA AND THE PICTURE PROBLEM

The CIA's initial involvement in Eastman's great selector project was less direct than the air force's. It had first come through Richard Ruggles seeking advice from Tyler about such things as the inability of Bush's Selector films to hold a significant number of indexing codes and about how to overcome the woes of serial processing. His inquiries were soon followed by two CIA men with more urgent needs.

They were not from Andrews's Intellofax office. Arthur C. Lundahl oversaw the CIA's PIC graphics "register" and was in search of a machine to handle the flood of expected photos from the CIA-directed U2 spy planes, as well as from reconnaissance satellites.[14] On the same quest was Henry S. Lowenhaupt, the chief of the atomic energy division of the CIA's Office of Scientific Intelligence (OSI). He badly needed the photo evidence Lundahl's organization was to process. Photographs taken from the high-flying U2s and satellites, aided by the information in the CIA's Industrial and Biographic Registers, became "the" means to monitor Russia's atomic, missile, and bomber capabilities.[15]

Because photographic evidence was critical, Lowenhaupt and Lundahl gained an influential supporter within the CIA. After learning of

Tyler's first technical responses to the air force's inquiries, Richard Bissel, one of the agency's most important leaders (and the head of the U2 project), came to believe that Eastman was the company that could devise the solution to the new photos problem—although some of Lundahl's technicians had informed him that Eastman's favored technology, microfilm, might never provide the picture quality that photoanalysts needed. To the great disappointment and embarrassment of all, some years later their predictions proved correct.[16]

Despite hesitations by some PIC analysts, Bissel pushed for the CIA's involvement in the Eastman–air force project while he awaited the arrival of the U2s and satellites. Lundahl then informed James Andrews, who was providing much help in organizing the expanded PIC, that Tyler's machine would be perfect for the OCR.

WHAT IS GOOD FOR PIC SHOULD BE GOOD FOR OCR

In 1952, Andrews and his men, who had remained loyal to Intellofax and were a bit upset about Perry's failed project, began to look at the sketches of Tyler's proposed machines that were soon to be called the Minicard system. They became skeptical. So, Andrews did not rush into a commitment to Tyler's project. It took three years before the OCR agreed to share in funding Minicard's development. Unfortunately for Andrews, the CIA's managers came to believe that he also agreed to replace Intellofax with a Minicard system.

Eastman's management was also evaluating Tyler's plans. It decided to make Minicard a business venture. In 1954, as the CIA's contract for Ruggles's selector work was canceled, Eastman issued public announcements that Minicard was to be a commercial product. The company advertised that Minicard would be a boon to information centers in business, law, and medicine. Within a year, Eastman gave a demonstration of a prototype and promoted the machine's information retrieval worth by reporting the positive results of tests that were using all the major indexing-classification systems, including Uniterms, semantic factors, and the Universal Decimal Classification, on large databases such as the CIA-financed metallurgical files that James Perry had worked on for the CIA since the late 1940s.

THE GRAND MINICARD, UNIT RECORDS PLUS A GREAT MEMORY AND COST

The Minicard design kept evolving but even in its early form it promised to be an impressive technological leap. It was an innovative combination of features that went far beyond the Frenchman Jacques Samain's 1952 Filmorex. Minicard combined the merits of unit records, the storage capacity of microfilm, and the flexibility of the most advanced tabulators. And, it was designed to require a minimum of human labor. [17]

The name, Minicard, was selected to emphasize that Eastman was casting aside the limitations of serial organization and processing in favor of the unit record. Instead of rolls of microfilm, Minicard employed small chips of microfilm, each about the size of two U.S. postage stamps. Being so tiny, the cards took up a fraction of the space needed for IBM cards. Two thousand Minicards fit on a small stick sixteen inches long. Each stick held the equivalent of four drawers' worth of documents. Like IBM's tabulator cards, Minicards could be rearranged in endless ways useful in data analysis. They could also be replaced and reproduced with ease and Minicard's files could be quickly updated.

Eastman's advertising always emphasized the combination of the flexibility of cards and the great data capacity of microfilm. The size of the Minicards was determined by a trade-off between the width of standard microfilm stock and the desired density of text, graphic, and code recording. The alpha or numeric codes for indexing were recorded as small digital white and dark spots that could be tested by a bank of forty-three tiny photocells, a cell for each segment (bit) of a Minicard's columns. Each column could hold seven characters plus a space for a data consistency, a parity check. Because a design goal had been to allow deep indexing, depending on how much data or graphics were on a Minicard, there could be perhaps twenty columns for the indexing codes. With the maximum number of pages of text on a card there would be a minimum of six code columns. Space-saving and information-rich "free-field" coding was also incorporated. That allowed the use of terms and phases as well as numeric codes. For long codes or terms, the system used "flags" to indicate their beginning and ending. "Fixed fields" were used to record standard bibliographic information such as author and date of publication and to facilitate sorting of cards.

AUTOMATION DREAMS, MINICARD

Another Minicard feature was keeping human intervention to a minimum, partially because it was realized the small cards would be difficult for humans to manipulate. To facilitate automation each card had a small slot punched out at its bottom edge. That allowed the cards to be automatically sent to and placed on the small metal storage sticks. The sticks could be inserted into the Minicard machines for processing in blocks of ten or one hundred. It was intended that each stick would hold subject-related (code-related) cards. That would make retrieval faster than if the cards were scattered over the other sticks. The outcome of Minicard searching would be another stick of microfilm cards, a disposable one approximately six inches long that held the reproduced copies of selected Minicards. A user could examine those cards on a special large viewer, or on a desk-sized one, or have them printed on a custom-made enlarger. With some configurations, intended for small businesses, the selected Minicard "chips" could be mounted on Langan-like aperture cards.

The Eastman system was as fast or faster than most of IBM's tabulating/sorting machines, and more powerful. It was also much, much more complex. Its selection device processed some 1,200 to 1,800 Minicards a minute while IBM's sorters ranged from 220 to 2,000 a minute. Minicard's discrimination power also matched or exceeded other selectors. A complex plugboard system (and, later a small computer) allowed full Boolean searching using as many as twenty "question" codes for comparison to a card's index entries on a single pass. There were also tests for greater than or less than and for the closeness of words in a series of index codes. A special test allowed weighting, such as scoring the number of index codes that matched the question codes. Generic searching and tests for role and action indicators were also features of Minicard. Additional tests, such as for date of publication, were possible.

Minicard's great selection power came with a huge price. A Minicard system was composed of a minimum of thirteen machines.[18] Minicard's two most important, complex, and costly machines were the sorter and the Selector. Using them, incoming microcards were examined to see if they contained more than one indexing code. If so, a new card was created for each of the codes, with one of the codes reproduced in each new card's special fixed-field area that was used for sorting. That card was then automatically sent to the appropriate data stick. Typically, there were six to ten new cards produced. Those new cards became part of the "working file." After all the new cards had been produced and sorted onto sticks with similar sorting codes, the master card was returned to its original stick. With appropriate sticks mounted on it, the Selector scanned all the codes on each card, picked those items meeting the search criteria, and returned the other cards to their original stick. The Eastman designers were especially proud that the original cards were out of the working file for only a short time and thus were available to all users. They emphasized that with the cards always sorted into homogeneous code categories, and with a smart classification system, selection runs would be on just a few cards and would take only moments.

None of those goals were easy to realize. It took ingenuity, time, and a great deal of money to make Minicard come to life. More than mechanical problems were involved in overcoming the challenges to its development. Eastman's chemists had to create a new film emulsion that yielded four times the resolution of standard microfilm and the company's optical specialists had to devise more powerful lenses. Such a costly high-resolution system, Eastman's technicians announced, allowed the 1 1/4 inch by 5/8 inch cards to hold up to twelve 8 inch by 14 inch documents as well as indexing codes. They asserted that with the sixty-to-one size reductions, a small file cabinet could hold 10.8 million pages of documents along with forty-four million index code characters.[19]

NOTES

1. Arthur B. Darling, *The Central Intelligence Agency: An Instrument of Government to 1950* (University Park: Pennsylvania State University Press, 1990).

2. CREST "CHIVE Indexers," 1963.

3. CREST, "Intellofax," passim, 1948–.

4. The American Chemical society also relied upon KWIC. Robert V. Williams, "Hans Peter Luhn and Herbert M. Ohlman: Their Roles in the Origin of Keyword-In Context/Permutation Automatic Indexing," *JASIST* 61, no. 4 (2010): 835–49.

5. George L. Fischer et al., eds., *Symposium on Optical Character Recognition* (Washington, DC: Spartan Books, 1962), 358.

6. CREST, "Intellofax CHIVE," ca. 1964.

7. CREST, "Library," December 1952.

8. CREST, "Library," 1951.

9. CREST, "Interim Report," May 1953, "PIC History," 1960.

10. CREST, "NPIC Historical Studies."

11. Colin B. Burke, *Information and Secrecy: Vannevar Bush, Ultra, and the Other Memex* (Metuchen, NJ: Scarecrow Press, 1994); Alan Marshall Meckler, *Micropublishing: A History of Scholarly Micropublishing in America, 1938–1980* (Westport, CT: Greenwood, 1982).

12. Anonymous, *Large Capacity Memory Techniques for Computing System* (n.p.: ACM, 1962).

13. Avco Corporation Electronics and Ordnance Division, Cincinnati 41, Ohio, *Technical Investigations of Addition of a Hardcopy Output to the Elements of a Mechanized Library: Final Report 20 Sept. 1961*; Harold Wooster, "Current Research and Development in Scientific Documentation," in *Encyclopedia of Library and Information Science*, ed. Allen Kent and Harold Lancour, vol. 16 (New York: Marcel. Decker, 1971): p. 336–365.

14. CREST, "NPIC Historical Studies."

15. Dino A. Brugioni, *Eyes in the Sky: Eisenhower, the CIA, and Cold War Aerial Espionage* (Annapolis, MD: Naval Institute Press, 2010).

16. CREST, "NPIC Historical Studies."

17. J. W. Kuipers, "Microcards and Microfilm for a Central Reference Service (of Eastman Kodak Co." (presented before the Micro Documentation Symposium, Division of Chemical Literature, at the 116th meeting of the American Chemical Society in Atlantic City, September 18–23, 1949); Martha Boaz, *Modern Trends in Documentation: Proceedings of a Symposium Held at the University of Southern California April 1958* (London: Pergamon, 1959).

18. CREST, "Minicard," passim, ca. 1952–.

19. Alan J. Rahm, "The Minicard System for High Speed Data Retrieval," (n.p.: Recordak Corporation, 1960).

11

THE CIA VERSUS THE LIBRARIANS

While Minicard was under development and facing James Madison Andrews's cautious consideration, the CIA's Office of Central Reference (OCR) had to obey orders from on high and endure humiliating rounds of evaluations by outside consultants. The first was led by one of the most influential librarians in the world.

Ralph Shaw knew and was known to everyone in the library field and had unique professional credentials. He had earned a bachelor's degree from Cleveland's Western Reserve's Adelbert College in 1928 when he was twenty-one, finished a Columbia Library School program in 1929, and two years later gained a master's from that famous school. He then worked at the highly regarded Engineering Society's Library in New York City. After that, he built a reputation as a library innovator when he directed the public library system in the working-class steel town of Gary, Indiana.

Shaw was ambitious and vigorous, attributes that helped him to be chosen in 1940 as the director of the United States' National Agricultural Library, an institution that had a well-deserved reputation as the most technologically advanced library in the nation. It had been a pioneer in the use of microfilm and a leader in developing techniques to serve distant users. The library sent tens of thousands of documents and reports to its patrons every year as it fulfilled the long-standing mandates set by the Wallace family that it should be a "people's" library and one that furthered the economic status of the average American farmer. Shaw became an international library figure and a frequent publisher.

189

He climbed professional ranks to become the president of the American Library Association (ALA) in 1956. He was also influential in the documentation movement. Before then, at the end of World War II, Shaw's experience in building systems to widely distribute information had led John Green, the director of the postwar Office of Technical Services, to ask for Shaw's help, including in the development and use of Bush's microfilm Rapid Selector.

Although busy with his own very frustrating Rapid Selector project, and with his regular library responsibilities, Shaw earned a Ph.D. from the University of Chicago's graduate library school in 1950 and, in the same year, founded Scarecrow Press, a publishing house devoted to low-cost production of scholarly books that regular publishers thought would not make a profit. That was not enough for Shaw. In 1954, at age forty-seven, he left the Agricultural Library to join, then lead, the Rutgers University graduate library school faculty. After seven years in New Jersey, he founded the library school at the University of Hawaii.

With that background Shaw was not a man to be taken lightly—but James Madison Andrews would unwisely do so after Shaw and other library influentials were called in to evaluate the OCR's systems and plans for its future.

RALPH SHAW'S VERY BAD NEWS

Shaw and the other consultants spent parts of fifteen weeks at the CIA's Office of Central Reference during early 1957.[1] They met with the staffs of most of the several registers (file systems) but not the supersecret Special Register. They talked with the files' users and even conducted tests to evaluate Intellofax's retrieval power. Their conclusions were clear and unwelcome.

To them, nothing about the OCR and Intellofax seemed acceptable. The first complaint was about the Intelligence Subject Code. They declared it a logical mess and demanded that it and the "intellectual level" of the Intellofax system be raised. As well, they demanded more than a purified classification hierarchy. They wanted much deeper indexing, the use of words within texts (terms), plain-language phrases, and more "action" codes.

THE CIA VERSUS THE LIBRARIANS   191

There was a frustrating and rather puzzling push-me-pull-me aspect to the consultants' report. Parts of it saluted the advanced microfilm retrieval device the CIA was considering (the Minicard), but Shaw made pointed comments against reliance on any microfilm-based systems. Worse for Andrews, Shaw recommended the OCR drop the Intellofax tapes and return to the use of paper volumes patterned on traditional subject-indexed bibliographies. Also included in Shaw's list of information enemies were the Langan aperture cards the OCR was now using to store documents to save floor space. He wanted all documents in paper form and stored in file cabinets so they could be immediately and directly retrieved by users.

Shaw then recommended something that was puzzling to anyone with knowledge of the workings of a "spy" agency. He decried the OCR's "closed" system, condemning anything that placed librarians or technicians between the user and information. He wanted weekly volumes, deeply subject indexed, that listed all new information openly available in the OCR offices so that any (underline, any) user could do his or her own searching. There were additional and more fundamental criticisms and recommendations. One of the most stinging was that the OCR had failed in unifying the nation's intelligence information system, at least in terms of a single classification scheme. Another jibe was a repeat of the demands that the OCR's own systems be unified so that it could be a one-stop indexing center.

The segments of the consultants' report that galled Andrews the most were those stemming from the quick evaluation of Intellofax as a search engine. The tests they conducted, the consultants claimed, revealed that Intellofax missed many important documents and delivered many irrelevant ones. Shaw's men also stated that Intellofax was too slow, too expensive, and even the coding and IBM sorting for it was "sloppy." Intellofax should be phased out as soon as possible, they concluded.[2]

ANDREWS VERSUS SHAW

Andrews was not the kind of man who thought he needed to bow to such criticisms, nor to demands that the OCR make radical changes. He quickly sent a thirty-page rejoinder to his superior, the deputy director of intelligence.[3] Andrews's July 11, 1957, memo reflected his anger. He dismissed all the criticisms and recommendations except the one aimed at the ISC. While not accepting Shaw's views on subject indexing, Andrews admitted the ISC had become cluttered because of the demands of specialists and he agreed it should be redone. Andrews wrote that all of Shaw's other recommendations were ill founded, even ill informed. He also attacked most of Shaw's demands for change. He stated there was no room to keep all the paper documents; a paper subject bibliography was impractical; OCR's unification was unwise, especially because of security concerns; pushing too hard for more centralization of the intelligence community would create a destructive political backlash; and, that Intellofax was an indispensable, irreplaceable tool.

Andrews's reaction to the Intellofax retrieval test was less tempered. The test, Andrews said, was handled "in a manner so unbelievably careless that it can only be described as irresponsible." Then, there was a scolding of Shaw's own book-form *Bibliography of Agriculture* and its utility as a retrieval aide. More intense were Andrews's comments about Shaw himself. Shaw's views on Intellofax and even Minicard, Andrews wrote, were irrational and due to the failure of Shaw's Rapid Selector project. Shaw's fury over the Selector's failure, Andrews wrote, "brought on so severe an emotional disturbance that he became incapable of telling black from white. I can think of nothing else which could account for the way he shuffled perfectly simple and straightforward data in such a way as produce false arguments in support of his prejudice."[4]

Andrews's social as well as professional status aided his protest. His superiors decided to accept his criticisms of Shaw's report and to retain Intellofax, at least until a better system such as Minicard arrived. But Shaw's report was not shelved and forgotten—he was too influential for that to happen. The agency decided to keep a watch on Andrews's OCR.

THE TROUBLE WITH CONSULTANTS II, WOULD THE CIA NOT BE CENTRAL

Another group of consults was soon hired to double-check Shaw's recommendations. Their conclusions mirrored Shaw's, but not as harshly.

THE CIA VERSUS THE LIBRARIANS

The new group submitted a tentative but positive report on Minicard but at the same time wrote a condemnation of Intellofax and the ISC. They stressed, however, that before Minicard's potential could be realized, the "intellectual level" of the CIA's ISC classification system had to be improved. Soon after that a team put together from within the CIA compared what was known about Eastman's offering, admittedly still in the development and debugging stage, with the seven-year-old Intellofax system. The group recommended that the OCR, at minimum, fulfill Andrews's earlier commitment to supporting the development of a basic Minicard system, one complete enough to begin acceptance testing and a critical comparative test of the Intellofax and Minicard machines and their allied classification systems.[5]

All the previous reports had made it clear that Intellofax was viewed as behind the times in technology and retrieval power but the latest added a telling bureaucratic-political point. It emphasized that if the OCR did not switch to a Minicard system, it would become a lonely intelligence dinosaur because, in addition to the air force, all the other intelligence services seemed poised to adopt Eastman's system, partly in response to being prodded from above. The report claimed the United States Intelligence Advisory Board, the Defense Intelligence Agency, and the Strategic Air Command (SAC) had already made commitments. (In a few years SAC had some three hundred thousand target photos on its "Mini.")

Worse for Andrews, all the evaluation reports gave the Minicard higher scores than Intellofax on many dimensions. They predicted it would allow the kind of data mining Intellofax could not do, even with the best of the newest IBM tab-card equipment. Important, they said Minicard would demand less than one-half the floor space than Intellofax (2,309 vs. 5,872 square feet) and that its need for personnel would be only two-thirds of Intellofax's. Its total cost per year would be 10 percent less.

Those predictions and estimates caused Andrews and others at the OCR great concern as their own explorations had shown that Minicard's space, cost, and power predictions had been shifting since the early 1950s. The first Eastman estimate about the critical space issue was that Minicard would need only one hundred square feet of floor space. Eastman's cost projections had also been rising, frequently doubling; its estimates of processing speeds had been lowered; and, its estimates of the manpower needed for the system had skyrocketed.

The OCR's worries about the cost of Minicard were well grounded. By 1960 a minimal system was publicly announced at $7 million. If a customer wanted all the possible features, including a small transistorized computer system to allow easier full Boolean selection and another that implemented Eastman's version of Hans Peter Luhn's automatic selective dissemination of information, the price could be over $20 million.

Given the many changes to Minicard's technology and cost during the 1950s, OCR's staff, despite the prodding from above, continued to resist making any hasty or permanent commitments to an Eastman-based system. But, responding to pressures from management, and from the influential Intelligence Advisory Board, Andrews had recommended in April 1955 that the OCR continue its involvements but contribute no more than $2.1 million for the ongoing development of Minicard's basic machines—and for testing at the agency when it was ready. Although it was known that there would a lag between the contract date and the delivery of a Minicard, there was a great disappointment when a system for the OCR was not in place until February 1959—seven years after the first commitment to Tyler's vision. As disconcerting, the basic hardware came at a price nearly twice what had been estimated in 1955.[6]

ANDREWS PASSES THE MINICARD AND TECHNO-POLITICAL HOT POTATOES TO PAUL BOREL

As the OCR was awaiting the arrival of the first components of its Minicard system, the CIA had other politically sensitive information issues to confront. Making the situation difficult, a very discontented James Madison Andrews left the CIA in early 1959, and in a huff. He retired at age fifty-two and led a life that fit his social and family background. Harvard University's yearbooks reported him alternating between his home in a posh Washington, D.C., neighborhood, winters abroad, and summers in Nantucket.

Paul Borel, a high-level manager in the agency, was assigned to Andrews's old slot. Borel had to oversee the OCR's long-term response

THE CIA VERSUS THE LIBRARIANS 195

to the consultants' negative reports and had to handle the increasingly strident demands from the high-level Intelligence Advisory Committee that the agency immediately shift to the Minicard system. He also had to oversee a complete revision of the ISC.

Trying to make a quick shift to Eastman's system proved to be a bureaucratic nightmare. The delays in delivery of the OCR's machines had frustrated the CIA's management, although a basic model had been sent to the PIC (graphics) division a year earlier, in March 1958. However, the CIA's leaders stood by the decision to have a Minicard in operation at the OCR and they looked forward to what they believed would be the positive results from the promised critical comparative test of Minicard versus Intellofax. One reason for management's faith in Minicard's powers was its ability to hold many codes on a single card. They thought that meant retrieval powers far beyond those of the limited-capacity Intellofax's IBM cards. Another important reason for the continued commitment to the long-delayed OCR Minicard was the decision to immediately revise and improve the Intelligence Subject Code (ISC) to meet the consultants' demands for a "higher intellectual level" and a truly common system for all the intelligence agencies. Management was convinced that Intellofax's limited room for codes meant that it would not be able to fully utilize the new version of the ISC the air force had already pledged to employ on its Minicard machines. With a major intelligence organization like that promising to use the new ISC, standing by Intellofax made little sense to the CIA's decision makers, and those in the Intelligence Advisory Committee (IAC).

BUT THE MINICARD IS NOT . . .

In contrast to the views of those in the IAC, the OCR's staff did not foresee a triumph for the Minicard system in the great comparative test, and they persisted in questioning the expense of Eastman's system.[7] They forwarded additional criticisms of Minicard to their superiors. They stressed that it would not allow hand processing in case of a machine breakdown. They warned that an expensive backup Minicard system would be needed because, for one thing, their Minicard version was not going to regularly produce Langan-like aperture cards that could always be retrieved by hand or by IBM machines if a Minicard system became disabled. The OCR's group also was unhappy that Tyler's system was abandoning the Intellofax's bibliographic tape that analysts had found so useful. All that users would get from a Minicard run would be those tiny microfilm cards or enlarged paper copies of them, they emphasized.

The OCR's personnel continued to fuss over the probable loss of data because of the small size of the Minicards and warned that the cards could be scratched and bent too easily. They went on to warn that even if all the Minicard's technologies worked, if the OCR implemented a Minicard system, it and Intellofax would have to be run in parallel for several years because the older Intellofax cards could not be converted to contain the new ISC codes. That parallel operation, they emphasized, would nearly double the yearly processing cost for as long as five to seven years. Moreover, they argued, the proposed full comparative test of the two systems might itself increase the total development investment in the first bare-bones Minicard system to almost $6 million.

The OCR's men underlined that having the code data and the full text on the same Minicard could lead to missed items during a search and they complained about the extreme difficulty of changing the codes on a card. The OCR also cautioned that coding for the Minicards, because of room for so many ISC and other codes, would lead to a great and unproductive rise in the cost of indexing. Deep indexing, they asserted, was not always productive.

The OCR's representatives then emphasized that computer technology was changing so fast that the expensive Minicard would likely be outdated in a few years. They also protested that it was not certain all the other intelligence services would, as the IAC believed, commit to Minicard because the army's and navy's branches had contracts with RCA, General Electric, and UNIVAC for the development of computerized total information systems that might not include Minicard. As well, the military services' ASTIA, the integrated organization for sharing technical documents, was well on the way to creating a system based on a UNIVAC electronic computer and magnetic tape system.[8] Another critique of Minicard, written by Mortimer Taube, the leading developer of term-based systems, reached the CIA's information experts and reinforced their negative views. Taube reported his uncertainties after Eastman had tested his own system on their machine at its Rochester headquarters. Although rambling, his report clearly was less than enthusiastic.[9]

With Taube's and their own criticisms in hand, the OCR's staff recommended the CIA wait before relying upon Minicard, at least until it was certain that it had a long-term future and that it could clearly outperform Intellofax.

That was not acceptable to CIA's managers because so much money had already been invested in Eastman's project. The OCR's representatives then suggested just a quick, short, and minimal test of an operating Minicard system. Management also rejected that proposed compromise. The CIA's managers ordered a renewed commitment to Andrews's earlier agreement for a full test, again anticipating a favorable result for Minicard.

The OCR and other CIA tabulator crews had no alternative but to prepare for what became a very expensive, delayed, and near yearlong comparative testing process.

1960, THE CLASSIFICATION STRUGGLE, THE ISC ONCE AGAIN, DEWEY AND HIERARCHIES RETURN

While Paul Borel and the OCR waited on Minicard's arrival, there had been progress on the revisions of the ISC. It had taken many years, and the efforts of librarians and documentalists in all of the intelligence-related services, to gain agreement on the long-sought thorough revision of the 1940s code. After consulting the nation's leading librarians, such as Verner Clapp, the United States Intelligence Board's Committee on Documentation (CODIB) gave its approval to the new ISC in 1960 and signaled it would work to ensure the acceptance of a single classification system for all of America's intelligence-related agencies.[10] Paul Borel, the CIA's new information leader, and now head of CODIB, was especially pleased because he thought the new system met all the criticisms of the hotheaded Ralph Shaw's review committee of 1957–1958 that had led to James Madison Andrews's angry resignation and early retirement.

Years of research and many negotiation sessions had gone into shaping the new 1960 classification. The long list of complaints about the original version, especially its loss of hierarchical coherence and its limited ability to allow generic searching, were addressed. It had soon been realized that a cure called for a fundamental intellectual reshaping. In turn, that meant the CIA had to ask all the intelligence groups to examine their own orientations and priorities. While the internal reexaminations and negotiations were in progress, the CIA launched another examination of the fundamentals of classification and information retrieval.

Central to the task was whether a hierarchical system should remain as the basis for the new version of the ISC. John K. Vance (who later blew the whistle on the CIA's MKULTRA LSD drug experiments),[11] was joined by other CIA library professionals, such as David C. Weeks, Robert Young, Josephine Brahn, and Mary Veilleux, in conducting another in-depth examination of all classification alternatives. They concluded that subject-term systems had always been chaotic and would not allow generic searching. Perry's semantic factors received little attention.

The librarians found the increasingly popular postcoordinate, single word within texts ("term") systems, such as that of Mortimer Taube, had three critical weaknesses. Using terms from within a document or a specialized field meant that a searcher could never quite know what search terms to use, something that was called an "unstable vocabulary" during the era. Terms, they found, were also unsuited to large files (something true until the appearance of powerful computers and their spectacular memories) and they did not allow generic searching. Another major fault with terms, the CIA's librarians reported, was that relevant documents were bypassed during a search. For example, an article on toxicity might be missed because the exact term "toxicity" did not appear in the text. So, despite the growing popularity of the approach, even at the National Security Agency, the CIA's librarians rejected Taube's method.

Vance and his colleagues concluded that any new ISC had to be based on categories created by professional classifiers because that was the only way that stability and universality of meaning could be achieved. They also declared that a hierarchical system was a necessity. They then examined the existing hierarchical alternatives to see if they could deal with intelligence information. Although tempted by the idea of incorporating intelligence into a universal classification, they determined the Universal Decimal Classification and the simpler Dewey classifications were unsuitable, as were existing Ranganathan-like colon systems. Although the CIA's library had adopted the Library of Congress's (LC) classification, the CIA's investigators found the LC unsuitable for the rest of the agency. Like the others, it did not have the correct vocabulary or concepts, they informed Paul Borel. One of the objections to all the established systems was that outsiders to the intelligence world had shaped their concepts.

Vance and his allies admitted the original ISC had many, many faults; so many that it might be worthwhile to face the political-bureaucratic challenges to creating a brand-new hierarchical system that was orderly and coherent. Vance's group knew demands by the various intelligence agencies for special features remained a barrier to creating a logical system. [12]

Much more than the CIA's team's drive for coherence would determine the nature of the new 1960 ISC. Before Vance and others began their work, America's intelligence system had been maturing. The CIA had been defining its new and more powerful role in long-term strategic intelligence while the military, soon coordinated by the Defense Intelligence Agency, had been honing its special capabilities. The new ISC would have to accommodate all those changes.

There were technical details as well as political challenges to overcome. After the decision to use a hierarchy there was a commitment to a numeric decimal system. Then, the more difficult issue of how detailed the system should be was addressed. It was decided to continue with a "medium system" using, as in 1948's ISC, a six-digit decimal organization. Compromises to a pure numeric decimal system were soon made, however. Because the designers wanted to allow as much specific description as practical, they agreed to permit users to add additional digits to their identifiers if they did not modify the original six. As before, there were special codes for dates and places. As well, it was decided to expand the use of the modifiers (facets) that had been applied to the early 1948 versions. Each major subdivision of the 1960 ISC had a list of three-digit numeric appendages that allowed more specific retrievals and that minimized the amount of time an analyst had to spend to determine if a retrieved item was relevant. The modifiers allowed greater classification depth without making the general classification scheme too long, complex, and unwieldy. The number 001 was for "biography" in any subdivision; 020 was for "exploration and prospecting" in the Resources category; 108, "plates, strips, and sheets," could be appended in Commodities; and 186, "enlisted personnel," could be used in parts of the Armed Forces section.

There were other deviations from decimal purity. A radical one was permitted despite the advice of some experts. Based on expectations of more room for codes in a document's index record, the designers allowed the use of some terms and alphabetic personal and geographic names. But to prevent chaos, a strict control on terms was imposed. An official dictionary was created and only those appearing in it could be used. In addition to single words, phrases could be included if they, too, were controlled by a dictionary. Combined words, such as "gun exports," served as another means of avoiding irrelevant documents, ones that might have both guns and exports in their index. Significant to the attempt to satisfy the demands for specificity was the vast increase in the number of categories included within the main six digits of any of the highest-level categories. The counts of the total number of categories vary, with some stating as many as fifteen thousand, but it is clear there were multiples of the some one thousand in the original ISC of the 1940s. Communism, for example, had three hundred, not eight. Science and Technology had a prominent place in the system. Of course, such detail led to a huge system's manual, some 493 pages long, that included the dictionary and a "relativ index."

AN INDEPENDENT AGENCY'S CLASSIFICATIONS

What was most impressive about the new ISC was its conceptual structure. It was much more of a system for central intelligence's use than the 1948 version that served the disparate interests of the armed services and the State Department. That difference came at a high logistical price, however. The 1960 and 1948 versions were not at all compatible. The nine million cards in the OCR's central file[13] that had been indexed under the old 1948 system could not be reindexed and had to be separately maintained for years. Costly duplicate searches had to be run with the cards indexed by the old and new systems. It would be years before the information pointed to by the old cards "decayed" and became outdated. The duplicate processing seemed acceptable in 1960 because of the improvements to the ISC's intellectual framework, its better fit with the needs of strategic intelligence, and because of its improvement of retrieval success rates.

The 1960 framework, with the number of the first "three-level" subcategories listed in parentheses, suggests the relative interest in topics:

100.000 Government, Politics, and International Activities and Institutes (31)
200.000 Social and Cultural Structure and Institutions (16)
300.000 Science and Technology, Engineering (32)
400.000 Commerce, Industry, Finance (39)
500.000 Transportation and Communications Systems (60)
600.000 Resources, Commodities, Weapons (68)
700.000 Armed Forces (66)

Most of the general "three-level" categories (chapters) had very detailed subdivisions. The list of the six-digit subcategories for the "100" chapter alone ran forty-five single-spaced pages. Under "Laws, International" (121.000), 121.251 was for patents, trademarks, and copyrights. Other chapters were as detailed. For example, 333.320 was for drainage systems and 355.435 was for pediatrics.

The designers of the new ISC admitted they found it difficult to maintain hierarchy at even the fourth- or fifth-digit level. The subject matter simply did not fit with an ideal hierarchy as did older academic fields such as zoology that had emerged during Western science's era of classification. However, they did their best to maintain a hierarchy allowing generic searching. They also provided guides for searchers, such as listing all the ISC numbers for general categories. An analyst interested in the general category of Security was told to request a search on all ISC umbers from 153.000 to 164.999. The new ISC also reflected an attempt to prevent scattering of topics over different chapters. That attempt at control usually succeeded.

The 1960 ISC was not perfect, but when tests of its retrieval power were made against the older version, it was shown to be much, much more powerful.

NOTES

1. CREST, "Consultants Report on OCR, Minicard" passim, 1957.

2. CREST, "Memorandum for Deputy Director" and other memos by Andrews, July 11, 1957.

3. CREST, "Andrews Memorandum," C5.

4. CREST, "Andrews Memorandum," C5.

5. CREST, "Minicard," passim, 1957–1960.

6. CREST, "Project Outline for Minicard," April 25, 1955.

7. CREST, "Minicard" and "OCR," August 16, 1956, 1958 passim, December 22, 1958.

8. Anonymous, *Automation of ASTIA* (Arlington, VA: ASTIA, 1960).

9. Mortimer Taube, *The Minicard System: A Case Study in the Application of Storage and Retrieval Theory* (n.p.: NITS AD137472, ca. 1957).

10. CREST, "ISC," September 1956.

11. CREST, John K. Vance, "Philosophy of Classification," 1959; David C. Weeks, Mildred Benton, and Mary Louise Thomas, *Universal Decimal Classification* (Washington, DC: U.S. Air Force Office of Scientific Research, 1971); *Washington Post*, John K. Vance obituary, June 16, 2005.

12. CREST, "Intellofax," passim, 1949, 1956, "Panel on ISC," November 29, 1959.

13. The supersecret Special Register had some twenty million cards under the old system. It is not known if they were converted.

12

FROM MICROFILM TO COMPUTERS

The politics of gaining acceptance of the new Intelligence Subject Code (ISC) proved less explosive than the frictions caused by the comparative test of Intellofax and Minicard at the Office of Central Reference (OCR). An initial frustration was the result of postponing the test until a workable Minicard system was in place and when it seemed sure the new version of the ISC would be implemented. In the meantime, preparatory steps were taken. The OCR's machine experts examined each of the Minicard devices as they arrived, and the reference center's staff began coding some twenty-five thousand incoming reports in both Intellofax and Minicard formats for a test database. Critical, the old ISC format was used for the Intellofax cards and the draft of ISC's new version for the Minicards. The details of the test came next. A systems evaluation team allied with a new all-CIA Automation Development Group was assembled from within the OCR. Its members worked on a test plan that included asking the same twenty retrieval questions per day to each system for two weeks.

All seemed ready, but the test was repeatedly postponed. It did not begin until February 1960. The reports for the CIA's management did not appear until April. The other special reports for the influential Committee on Documentation (CODIB) of the United States Intelligence Board that was trying to unify all intelligence processing did not appear until the end of June.

PAUL BOREL, THE MINI SLAYER

In both sets of reports, Paul Borel came to a surprising and politically sensitive conclusion. He declared that Minicard had no advantage over Intellofax. He bravely recommended that a Minicard system not be implemented and that the expensive machinery on hand be discarded—perhaps to be sent to PIC. With that, he committed to a bureaucratically dangerous policy: the agency should write off the millions it had already spent on the OCR's Minicard. In Borel's view, James Madison Andrews was vindicated.[1]

Fortunately for Borel, he was trusted by the CIA's top leaders. They were willing to help him face the reactions to his decision. He had earned that trust. He had been selected as Andrews's replacement because of his management experience and his bureaucratic-political skills. Borel had joined the CIA in 1947, had become a colleague of important men such as Sherman Kent, and was sent to the National War College to be groomed for executive positions in the agency. His background suited him to be a public spokesman for the CIA and to be the agency's representative on many interagency committees, including the one on automatic translation.[2]

The son of an immigrant Swiss watchmaker who had settled in Kansas City, Missouri, Paul worked his way through college, earning engineering, business, and law degrees at prestigious universities such as Columbia, Harvard, and George Washington University in the District of Columbia. While working for the CIA he was admitted to the Washington, D.C., bar and was certified at the Supreme Court. Before then, in the 1930s, he had gained practical engineering experience working as a mining consultant prior to joining the navy as World War II began. During the war he developed diplomatic-political skills as a navy representative at meetings such as the Potsdam peace conference of 1945. Asked to join the fledgling CIA, he quickly rose to its highest levels. He was remembered for his administrative wizardry (and his poetry) and was later saluted as one of the agency's fifty "trailblazers."

Although Borel's 1960 negative recommendations about Minicard angered the CIA's top-level decision makers, they were accepted by the deputy director of intelligence, Borel's immediate superior. Borel reported that the tests revealed no true advantage for Minicard, in any respect. He stated that although Minicard had done somewhat better in

FROM MICROFILM TO COMPUTERS

retrieving relevant documents, that result was only because the new ISC codes were better than the ones used on the Intellofax runs. He reported that Intellofax, with its now somewhat old-fashioned IBM electromechanical tabulating equipment, would be as good as or better than the revolutionary microfilm system for retrieval when it used the new ISC. He emphasized that Intellofax's operating costs were lower than Minicard's.

Furthermore, he argued that since the requests for Intellofax searches were declining, it was unwise to commit to such an expensive replacement as Minicard. Borel recommended investing in improvements to Intellofax and allied procedures. He then successfully proposed the creation of a new CHIVE team to continually pursue improvements to OCR's existing systems, to ensure coordination among users and the Intellofax staff, and to keep a watchful eye on developments in the computer industry.[3] As part of the CHIVE initiative, Borel detailed Joe Becker to a two-year residency at the cutting-edge national government computing center at the University of California at Los Angeles (UCLA).

JOE BECKER AND THE FUTURE OF COMPUTERS

Becker was told to learn all he could, meet innovators, and return to Washington to lead CHIVE, as well as any other new information-technology efforts at the agency. Becker had two highly productive years in Los Angeles. The UCLA center had a contract with IBM that ensured it had the latest in computer technology and programs and, of great significance, the center had established perhaps the first general-purpose remote computer network. UCLA was located amid the aero-missile-spaceflight industry that was hosting a new breed of information scientists, ones with mathematics and physics backgrounds who had access to the most powerful computers. They were forging surprising new approaches to information retrieval and language translation problems. Becker met such future luminaries as Don Swanson, David G. Hays, Robert Hayes, and Gilbert King. The area around UCLA was also home to several aero corporations that were in the process of developing computerized online information searching and bibliographic systems, such as the National Aeronautics and Space Administration's (NASA) RECON and Lockheed Aerospace Corporation's DIALOG.

Through his ties to professional organizations, Becker learned of other innovative methods and hardware under development around the nation. Explorations of new techniques, such as Mike Kessler's citation coupling at MIT's computerized online Technical Information Project, caught Joe's attention, as did the efforts by the nonprofit Council on Library Resources, funded by the Ford Foundation, to advance library technology.

POOR MINICARD, POOR BOREL, A WALNUT

Meanwhile, as Joe Becker was learning about advanced computer systems, Paul Borel had to deal with more political difficulties in Washington. In addition to furor over the OCR's rejection of Eastman's machine, another Minicard-related issue was causing problems. There was gossip circulating that was unpleasant for the CIA, for Eastman Kodak, and for ITEK (Information Technology Laboratory).

ITEK was the new for-profit company that began its life in 1957 based on marketing Minicards. It was also considering building a language translation machine to compete with IBM's, expecting that IBM would soon shift away from investing in mechanical translation (MT).[4] ITEK would eventually turn its focus onto manufacturing camera systems for the Corona satellite program, but in the early 1960s Minicard and its photo-storage capabilities were the new company's great hope.

When the latest rumors about Minicard and the CIA reached Eastman and ITEK, the two companies became furious. In addition to Borel's rejection, the CIA's PIC group had concluded that Minicard was unusable for its intended critical role in monitoring the Soviets. The division declared that Minicard's microfilms did not have the clarity needed by the analysts who were to work with U2 and satellite photos. Traditional photo-storage and reproduction methods would have to be relied upon. PIC's expensive Minicard(s) were to be used only for documents and lower-density "mosaic" graphics.[5]

There were additional blows to Eastman, ITEK, and those CIA upper-level managers who still had hopes for Minicard. Despite the earlier predictions, no other intelligence agency besides the air force

FROM MICROFILM TO COMPUTERS 207

had purchased a Minicard. But another microfilm system that had been rather secretly created for the CIA's Biographics (biography) group appeared. Under development since the mid-1950s, Biographics' multi-million-dollar IBM Walnut automated microfilm system was put into operation in 1962. It used a small computer to help it to avoid some of the Minicard's shortcomings (including having both codes and documents on the film) and it also was designed to readily produce aperture cards. Perhaps because of some of the very sensitive work the Biographics group was doing, its development and operations were compartmentalized so that even many high-level CIA personnel were not informed of the Walnut project. None of the documents on Minicard's development mentioned Walnut.

Also irritating to Eastman and ITEK, Andrews's OCR's evaluation teams were soon proven correct about the short life span of the era's technologies. Minicard had a brief and limited life, as did Walnut. It seems only six copies of Minicard and Walnut machines were built, all the dozen or so were sold to government agencies, and they were put into operation just as electronic computers were making such huge microfilm machines obsolescent. Perhaps ironic, when Minicard and Walnut appeared, the first workable versions of Vannevar Bush's serial microfilm tape-form Selector emerged. Benefiting from technological advances, the small but practical FMA Filesearch and the Benson-Lehner Flip sold for under a million dollars, outpricing huge the IBM and Eastman systems. The U.S. Army found the FMA machine especially useful for supporting field intelligence work.[6]

1960, DULLES, THE POLITICS OF COLD WAR TECHNOLOGY

However, Eastman and ITEK had not given in after Borel's 1960 report, or after receiving the news of PIC's decision to abandon Minicard. On hearing of Borel's conclusion, Eastman Kodak's lobbyists, ITEK's leader Richard Leghorn, and air force representatives rushed to the top. They contacted Allen Dulles who had been heading the CIA since 1953. The air force complained about being stranded as the only Minicard user; Eastman grumbled about an unfair evaluation and, of course, about the CIA's breaking an implicit promise to always support Minicard. Leghorn, with an option to make and market Minicard, protested about being left high and dry by what he had assumed would be his best customer.[7]

Minicard had become a threatening political issue. Dulles had to respond. Eastman was a huge company that was vital to the defense effort and the national economy. Leghorn also had political punch. He had been involved in the country's reconnaissance programs since World War II and ITEK was being financed by Rockefeller investments. The air force had its own powerful allies in Congress, as well as in the White House. Dulles knew all that and quickly turned the problem over to Lyman Kirkpatrick, the agency's inspector general and another powerful CIA old-timer. Although confined to a wheelchair because of contracting polio while on a 1952 foreign mission, and busy with such projects as planning the invasion of Cuba, Kirkpatrick was sensitive to the threat the Minicard issue posed to the agency and he was concerned about the welfare of the CIA's other information systems. He began a thorough and lengthy investigation.

His March 1961 report was scathing. Kirkpatrick condemned the OCR's test as being, at best, intellectually sloppy. He called it biased against Minicard from the beginning of its design. He declared that many of the most important questions the OCR had been told to answer had been ignored. He complained that there had been no contact with Eastman's engineers (who had volunteered their help and who already had security clearances), no contact with Intellofax's main users, and no consultations with the men running the other major CIA file systems. Important, he claimed the OCR had not interacted with two very important and powerful groups, the United States Intelligence Board and Intelligence Advisory Committee whose members' requests were one-third of all Intellofax's usage. He also complained that the late-arriving reports on Minicard that the OCR sent to those oversight groups were uninformative. Kirkpatrick and other CIA managers also argued that abandoning Minicard was tantamount to the CIA giving up its role as the organizer of a unified intelligence information system. They added that with the air force, and possibly the other services using the Minicard-ISC data format, the OCR would have to assume the expense of converting incoming air force Minicards to the Intellofax format.

BOREL DOES SLAY ONE GIANT—AND, AN OLD TECHNOLOGY IS THE BEST TECHNOLOGY

Perhaps because Kirkpatrick's investigation had taken so long, and because of Paul Borel's reputation at the agency, Dulles did not order Borel to redo his study nor did he demand the purchase of more Minicard systems. Kirkpatrick did, however, take an additional slap at the OCR. He demanded the creation of another new and stronger agency-wide group to monitor future information-technology innovations to ensure that any decisions would not be made in isolation by a small branch of the agency, as had been the case, he claimed, with Minicard.

Despite Kirkpatrick's status, Paul Borel's career was not seriously damaged by his report. Paul remained in charge of the OCR, oversaw the agency's computer developments, continued to head the CODIB, and became the leader of the reinvigorated Foreign Broadcast Intelligence System that monitored the world's open source airwaves.

But in 1960 and 1961 Borel's immediate and pressing chores were to ensure that Intellofax and the OCR would survive and that the new ISC would become the standard for the intelligence community. He structured the new technology committee, CHIVE, to include members of all the CIA branches, assigned Joe Becker to oversee attempts to make Intellofax and the other registers more efficient, and responded to the lingering criticisms by Shaw and CIA's own users.

Borel also ordered the revamping of Intellofax's IBM card so it could hold a term as well the older codes. Most important, he pushed a training program to answer the old complaints, especially those from the Office of Scientific Intelligence (OSI), about the inconsistencies in indexing. Courses in the new ISC were begun and a thoroughly revised training manual was developed. Although still dependent on the IBM tabulating equipment, Borel's and Joe Becker's teams brought some new copying and printing technologies into play to speed up Intellofax document processing and printing.[8] Most revolutionary was the development and testing of the DARE system. Put into operation in 1964, it reproduced the first page of a document and automatically copied it onto the Intellofax card. The OCR's tests had revealed that initial pages of a report usually summarized its content and were a good substitute for Wilmarth Lewis's beloved abstracts.

210   CHAPTER 12

Such "fixes" to Intellofax worked. The system was in operation until 1967. Intellofax's long eight-year operating life span during an era of rapid technological change remains impressive.

GIANTS BOREL COULD NOT SLAY, STRUGGLING TOWARD A COMPUTER FUTURE

Fixing Intellofax was not enough to end the complaints about the OCR. In 1960, after rejecting the costly Minicard system, Paul Borel remained under pressure to prove the OCR was not technically backward. He had to show it was willing to accept new technologies and methods. Luckily, Joe Becker had become a noted figure in the computer and network field and could help the OCR learn of and evaluate new systems. As well, many of the OCR's staff, including Borel, attended major information science meetings, even the International Federation for Information Processing's conclaves in Europe.

Although tempted by vendors' offerings, Borel was determined to avoid more techno-political disasters such as the Minicard debacle. He also was determined that the OCR's technological fate would never be shaped by outside contractors. So, in 1960 he announced he wanted to create a large in-house "computer laboratory" group with its own stock of computers to independently evaluate technologies and, hopefully, to develop any new CIA systems. The laboratory, he said, would let the OCR join the ranks of other government branches, such as the National Security Agency (NSA) and the National Aeronautics and Space Administration (NASA) that were leaders in creating advanced computer and information systems. NSA was sponsoring the supercomputers of the era and NASA had a multimillion-dollar project under Mortimer Taube for indexing all its information using his innovative "term" methods.[9]

OUTSIDERS, ONCE AGAIN

But Paul Borel proved unable to ensure the OCR could shape its own techno-future. His vision of an independent CIA laboratory was not

FROM MICROFILM TO COMPUTERS

realized, and he would later admit the CIA remained behind the technology curve during the first half of the 1960s.

Although the well-informed Joe Becker was leading the CHIVE program that was remedying the ills of the existing OCR systems, two nationally recognized consulting firms were called in to advise on the possibility of shifting all the OCR's operations to electronic computer systems. The CIA had teams from IBM and the Systems Development Corporation (SDC), the nation's first large-scale independent programming/systems organization, security cleared and then had them survey all the OCR's processes and machines—except those in the sensitive Special Register.

The consultants' reports were devastating—and they had the abrasiveness of Ralph Shaw's. Nothing at the OCR received a passing grade. The consultants repeated the criticisms of Shaw's 1957 committee— with additional emphases on the need to create a fully integrated one-stop CIA information system and on the necessity for much deeper indexing than Intellofax or the other registers used. But there was a great difference between the 1957 and 1961 reports. While the Luddite-like Shaw had recommended a return to traditional library methods and technologies, IBM's and the SDC's men demanded a shift to the most advanced electronic computer systems. IBM soon announced it would submit a grand multimillion-dollar futuristic proposal, one that would shift CHIVE to a focus on computers and the development of the software needed to integrate and automate all OCR systems. That large-scale centralization, computerization, and programming project later became known as CAPRI (the Centralized Automatic Processing and Retrieval of Intelligence).

JOE BECKER, YET AGAIN

While IBM's teams worked on their grandiose plans, Joe Becker tried to persuade the agency to focus on gradual and practical technological adjustments. He was trying to do so without interfering with the OCR's independent components. At the same time, Becker was very busy with outside interests. At the request of the American Library Association, he designed the Library of the Future demonstrations for the Seattle and New York City World's Fairs, and he and his UCLA contact, Robert Hayes, published *Information Storage and Retrieval: Tools, Elements Theories*, one of the foundational texts of information science. Such outside interests may have been one of the reasons why some friction developed between Becker and Borel after the agency accepted IBM's plan for the great new CAPRI system in 1964.

Becker had not put aside his other CIA projects while IBM was organizing its team for CAPRI. One of Joe's first CHIVE gradual changes was intended to replace many of the OCR's older tabulating machines with newer models. Then, those tabulators were swapped for IBM's computerized version of them, the small-scale 1401. The company had introduced the 1401 some five years before. By 1963, a much more expensive machine was purchased in response to the Office of Scientific Intelligence's (OSI) demands. The OSI wanted it so its staff could do most of its own data analysis. Although not the first to acquire one, the OSI spent a handsome sum on an IBM 7090, an advanced electronic machine designed for scientific calculations that some researchers would coax into being a translation machine.[10] Soon after that, OCR's central group was allowed to purchase a special-purpose electronic computer to experiment with methods of document retrieval. That General Electric Rapid Selection Machine, a descendant of the James Perry project's hope for a super IBM 101, had more Boolean power than Minicard and allowed the researchers in the reports group to explore methods such as term and full-text searching. Somewhat later, the Special Register's team purchased one of IBM's truly modern computers. That IBM 360/30 was one of the smallest of the 360 series but was more powerful than any machine the group had used. The OCR's research group was also allowed to bring in two of the other smaller 360s so that it could evaluate new methods proposals and to begin exploring how the Intellofax processes might be turned into computer programs. Reflecting the independence of the OCR's components, the PIC group began to rely upon machines built by IBM's greatest competitor, UNIVAC.

THE GIANT'S GRAND PROPOSAL

In 1963, as Joe Becker was dealing with the needs and politics of the OCR's departments, IBM submitted the details of its own visionary

FROM MICROFILM TO COMPUTERS

multimillion-dollar plan for a one-stop and fully centralized system, one that would erase the boundaries between the separate registers and that would include computerized language translation, auto-indexing, and automatic inference–making (AI) software. CAPRI was to rely on the company's most powerful version of its 360 line, a machine that could support remote users and networking. IBM claimed its new machines and software would remain cutting edge for a decade. Significant, under the company plan the programming for the system (an obviously great challenge) was to be done by IBM's team, not by Joe Becker's staff.

The proposal was so far reaching that it took almost a year before the CIA was willing to sign an initial contract. But IBM's system and programming teams had begun exploratory work before then, confident that the CIA would decide in their favor. No wonder, as IBM had a special advantage in the computer market: its 360 series had been designed so that programs written for one computer could be used on another with little or no modification. The company could assure customers that investments in software would not be lost as they migrated to new versions of the 360s. While that did not mean IBM's group had an easy time turning the many complex processes and methods the various OCR registers were using into a viable unified software package, the company had gained another special advantage. Although Paul Borel had warned that all such extravagant projects had less than enviable development histories, he had become an active admirer of the one-stop concept and a generous and always patient supporter of the IBM project.

Despite that help, the IBM effort faltered.[11] A major reason for the problems was the inability of the IBM team to communicate with the OCR's information specialists, or with the analysts they served. As a result, the CIA's men thought they were being dictated to, rather than being regarded as experts. In turn, it seems that by 1965 IBM's group had decided to make its own design decisions, ignoring the OCR's staff. The differences that arose between the groups were about more than how to automate procedures. IBM appeared determined to dictate intelligence information methods, even the depth of indexing, and appeared to be forcing fundamental data reorganizations so that all information would be grouped by geographic regions.

CHAPTER 12

ANOTHER COSTLY INFORMATION WAR CASUALTY, CAPRI WAS NOT FREE

Although Paul Borel continued to support the one-stop automation goals, and remained tolerant of the mistakes that were common to all large-scale computerization projects of the era, he could not prevent the CAPRI project from becoming part of what a CIA computer consultant said were the 40 percent of twenty-seven thousand computer systems in the United States that were behind schedule, over budget, and, most important, unsuccessful in achieving their design goals. By 1966, Borel had to lower his expectations, publicly stating, "My own rule of thumb in the application of machines to nonnumeric problems is this: expect half as much in twice the time at twice the cost. If you get it you can count yourself lucky."[12] Helen Brownson, Norman Ball's co-worker at Bush's science committee, then of the National Science Foundation's information science office, and who had moved to the CIA in 1966 to help with its systems problems, would have agreed.[13]

In 1967, Borel had to confront more than system delays and cost overruns. Although the OCR had already contracted for the delivery of a powerful and costly IBM 360/67, it decided to dismiss the IBM programmers and to abandon the goal of a single, totally integrated software package. Borel brought in a new contractor who pledged to listen to the CIA's staff. Some of the programs the OCR's group had developed in house were incorporated into the resulting workable but less adventurous Already Existing General Information System (AEGIS) software package used for the main registry.

With that, Intellofax was finally retired, replaced by AEGIS. That was an achievement, but the software developments had taken so much precious time that the CIA's information centers were unable to get and keep ahead of the curve of computer system development.

FAREWELL, OUR BELOVED ISC, FAREWELL OUR BELOVED JOE BECKER

The adoption of AEGIS was accompanied by something more basic than a shift in software orientation. The indexing studies the OCR had been conducting interacted with CIA budget cuts to lead to the deci-

FROM MICROFILM TO COMPUTERS

sion to do only shallow indexing. The OCR's efficiency studies had revealed that only a few requests from the military needed much indexing. As a result, the CIA turned away from the ISC and began using a very short version, the Subject Intelligence Code (SIC), for its own indexing. The military's new umbrella intelligence organization, the Defense Intelligence Agency, was given the responsibility of maintaining the ISC.

Meanwhile, Paul Borel had survived the 1960s turmoil and stayed on at the agency until 1972 when he was sixty years old. But the problems and conflicts of the mid-1960s may have been a major reason for Joe Becker retiring at age forty-five. He left the agency with honors and went on to gain more. He established a consulting firm and became a highly respected advisor on computer and network projects. His work with EDUCOM, the organization formed to encourage computer use in higher education, was aided by his growing skill in raising funds from America's largest philanthropic organizations. He was frequently called on to help design library systems and was an advisor to American and foreign agencies. He also became the president of the new version of the American Documentation Institute, the American Society for Information Science, and was a longtime member of the National Commission on Library and Information Science that advised the president. He also gained a well-deserved reputation as a liberal through his unpaid work developing library networks around the world, always with hopes of equalizing access to information.

NOTES

1. CREST, "Minicard," 1958–1960.

2. Paul Arnold Borel, *Along the Way: Fragments from My Three Score Years* (Great Falls, VA: River Bend House, 1986); CREST, "History of FBIS," "On Processing Intelligence"; autobiographical materials at http://www.rhymeandreasonsite.xbuild.com/#/memoirs/4523108098.

3. CREST, "Minicard," ca. 1960, "CHIVE," 1960–1963.

4. Jonathan E. Lewis, *Spy Capitalism: ITEK and the CIA* (New Haven, CT: Yale University Press, 2002).

5. CREST, "NPIC Historical Studies."

6. Richard A. Condon, "Mechanized Image Systems," in *Data Acquisition and Processing in Biology and Medicine, vol. 4, Proceedings of the Rochester*

Conference, ed. Kurt Enslein with John F. Kinslow (Oxford, UK: Pergamon, 1966), 179–88; Charles P. Bourne and Trudi Bellardo Hahn, *A History of Online Information Services 1963–1976* (Cambridge, MA: MIT Press, 2003).

7. CREST, "From Kirkpatrick," March 27, 1961.

8. CREST, "Intellofax," 1960–1965.

9. CREST, "CHIVE," 1962–1966, "Controlling Intelligence Information."

10. George L. Fischer et al., eds., *Symposium on Optical Character Recognition* (Washington, DC: Spartan Books, 1962), 349.

11. CREST, "Intellofax-IBM-SDC," passim, 1961–1965.

12. CREST, "CAPRI," 1964–1970. One report said CAPRI remained somewhat behind technology and was still a batch system in 1970.

13. Tina J. Jayroe, "A Humble Servant: The Work of Helen L. Brownson and the Early Years of Information Science Research," *Journal of the American Society for Information Science and Technology* 63, no. 10 (2012): 2052–61. In 1966, Brownson went to the CIA to work on their information problems.

13

AUTOMATIC TRANSLATION'S WOES

Paul Borel always had a full plate of contentious technology issues at the Central Intelligence Agency (CIA). Besides dealing with the politically sensitive complexities of the Minicard and computer projects, he became involved with another tangled high-tech issue, mechanical language translation (MT). Since the end of World War II, influential advocates for automatic translation, such as Warren Weaver, had urged government agencies to invest in developing language translation systems for science. The CIA responded and began an involvement with machine-based translation that stretched over a decade and a half and cost millions of dollars. Fortunately for Borel, he had two smart and politically adept helpers: John Bagnall, who was leading its important Foreign Documents Division (FDD), and then Paul Howerton, a more recent arrival who became a jack-of-all-trades in the agency.

John J. Bagnall had been in military intelligence during World War II, learning Japanese to help in the postwar occupation. He had joined the Central Intelligence Group (CIG) when it acquired the huge collection of Japanese documents from the military's Washington Document Center. That collection contained much about the Soviet Union, Japan's decades-long enemy. Bagnall eventually replaced Joe Becker and Paul Borel as the head of the CIA's FDD that was charged with acquiring and processing foreign publications. That work included supervising the translation of foreign documents by large in-house and contract staffs. With the CIA tasked with the primary role in monitoring Soviet science there was much pressure on the FDD to quickly provide the

THE CIA'S WHITE WHALE AND A MATCH MADE IN DENVER, IF NOT IN INFORMATION SCIENCE HEAVEN

The CIA's translators had always been overworked and, they complained, underpaid. There certainly always was a critical backlog.[1] The agency needed a solution, so much so that it grasped at techno-straws, hoping that translating could easily be mechanized. But it was a hope based as much on need as on realities. As a result, automatic translation became the CIA's and other intelligence agencies' version of Ahab's white whale.

As the CIA became involved with adventurous and expensive machine translation efforts in the early 1950s, it needed someone with a unique combination of skills to evaluate, guide, and monitor the work. Joe Becker and James Madison Andrews, then Borel and Bagnall, soon realized that a man with near-perfect credentials was already on board. Paul William Howerton, a unique combination of chemist, special-librarian analyst, linguist, and information scientist, had been hired by the chemistry branch of the CIA's Office of Scientific Intelligence (OSI) in 1951 when he was thirty-five years old.[2] Within a year, he became a deputy assistant director, a position he held for a decade. He was an important part of all the agency's information work and was a trusted spokesman for the agency on topics ranging from mechanical translation to methods of estimating the state of the Soviet economy. After a decade at the agency, he left for the private sector, became a central figure in the science information field, and a prolific publisher on science information and management topics.

Howerton was the son of a college-educated pharmacist who had a business in a small Indiana town. The family was well off, but not rich. It had enough to help two sons enter college. Paul, the older of the two, entered the University of Indiana but left and chose to begin a career as a chemist at the Carbide and Carbon Company of Indiana when he was just nineteen. He married in 1938 when he was twenty-two and began a family. He stayed at the Indiana firm until he entered the army air force in 1942. His assignment to the China-Burma theater, to supervise the

AUTOMATIC TRANSLATION'S WOES

production of oxygen, allowed him time to pursue three of his life's great interests: foreign languages, mathematics, and chemistry. He studied at the University of Calcutta and the American University in Lebanon. Besides deepening his general education, he learned Hindi. After his return to his family and his old company he continued his education and his study of languages.

Although working, he obtained a rather special college degree with honors in mathematics, chemistry, and languages from nearby Northwestern University in Evanston, Illinois, an institution linked to a later information open access leader, Peter Suber. Howerton's Ph.B. (not Ph.D.) degree was awarded for his work in a program tailored to the backgrounds, needs, and goals of students who wanted a special combination of courses and credit for performing research. Paul had a specific career goal, to mine the literature of science, in all languages, for new knowledge. He sought to become a "literature scientist." By 1949, after he graduated, he could claim facility in at least three scientific subfields and in all the Slavic (including Russian) Teutonic and Latin languages.

He never claimed to be a traditional linguist with deep knowledge of any of those languages. Rather, he, as had James Perry, claimed just a working knowledge of each of them. Shortly after graduation he began to contribute analytical articles on scientific publications in Russia and its satellite nations. They were early and innovative examples of what became known as "bibliometrics." Paul had also become a regular contributor to *Chemical Abstracts*, the leading source of chemical information in America. He composed abstracts of articles written in many languages. He also became a frequent participant at chemical society meetings, but he, also like Perry, did not establish a publishing record in the science of chemistry itself.

A NEW, VERY SPECIAL, SPECIAL LIBRARIAN

After his graduation Paul made a career change, one that fit with his bibliographic goals. In 1949, he moved to Denver to become a member of the research team at Julius Hyman's new company at the army's Rocky Mountain Arsenal. The arsenal had been the nation's major producer of poison gases and toxic agents during World War II, as well as a major site for their disposal. After the war, the government decided to lease parts of the site to private companies that needed to be isolated from the general population. Having safe disposal facilities for poisonous chemicals was critical for Julius Hyman so he took up the government's offer, leased a facility, and began manufacturing new and very powerful agricultural pesticides. Within a few years the world-famous Shell Corporation bought the very successful operation.[3]

Paul Howerton played many roles at Hyman's company; the major one was as a research bibliographer who searched the scientific literature and patents for new ideas, as well as possible infringements. He had time to do much more. Along with Robert, his younger brother who had earned a master's degree in mathematics at Northwestern University two years before Paul and then taken a position as an assistant professor at Denver's Jesuit Regis College, Paul began to publish a series of major analytical articles on chemical and mathematical publications in history and, especially, on chemical publication behind the Iron Curtain since World War II.

His quantitatively oriented articles were well regarded because they were methodologically path breaking. They appeared in mathematical and chemical journals and, most significantly, in *Science*, the prestigious journal that covered all scientific fields. Paul also served as the science information consultant for the Denver region's bibliographical center, a consortium of some fifty libraries. He then founded Howman Research Associates to put his language and bibliographic skills to work for commercial firms.

Paul's efforts on Soviet science and his language skills attracted the attention of the CIA. The CIA made him an attractive offer, so he and his family moved to Washington in the summer of 1951. Meanwhile, his brother Robert stayed at the Jesuit college for a few more years while he honed his skills in scientific data analysis. He became good enough as a nuclear engineer and data analyst to take a position in private industry and then as a director of research-data collection and analysis at the famed Lawrence Livermore nuclear research center of the University of California. While there, he gained a solid reputation, despite having only a master's degree, as one of the leading men in his field. His reputation also led him into intelligence work: he became a valued consultant to the CIA.

Before then, Paul had arrived at the CIA when James Perry was pursuing his indexing project, planning to use the Luhn Scanner to

AUTOMATIC TRANSLATION'S WOES

revolutionize indexing, and taking his first steps toward mechanical language translation. Paul knew James and his associate Allen Kent and became involved with aspects of their work as well as other linguistically related efforts the CIA was financing at MIT's Center for International Studies. Paul also managed several CIA-sponsored projects for compiling practical basic glossaries in several languages for scientific fields including metallurgy, an atomic bomb–related topic. Metallurgy was also one of the prime targets of James Perry's "semantic" file-building efforts.

In contrast to Perry's theory-based work, Howerton's glossary and translation projects were pragmatic.[4] Paul trusted practical approaches that got the job done, such as the simple word-to-word dictionaries in foreign travel guides. Paul, however, soon became a respected expert in basic linguistics, computers, and allied technologies—and in information and management issues. He was knowledgeable about the most advanced ideas in all those fields and was a leading advocate for the application of cutting-edge methods. Paul even worked to establish a fellowship program at the agency so that its librarians could study with experts such as Don Swanson, who was a leader in applying computerized information-mining techniques. Swanson took ideas such as Paul's early visions for literature research to new heights and became noted for using data techniques as substitutes for clinical research.

Paul Howerton earned a reputation at the agency as a solid project manager and a science diplomat. He was chosen to be the CIA's advisor to the nation's prestigious Science Advisory Committee. That brought him into contact with the country's leaders in library and information science. He also served as the CIA's representative to the group coordinating the federal libraries' efforts to make all Soviet science and technical information available to America's researchers.[5] As he fulfilled those functions, he deepened his relationship with information experts such as Hans Peter Luhn.

SIMPLE IS GOOD, MAYBE, GEORGETOWN TRANSLATION

It was no wonder that the agency tapped Paul, rather than James Perry, to evaluate the flood of machine translation proposals that reached the agency in the mid-1950s. The Massachusetts Institute of Technology, the Battelle Memorial Institute, Leon Dostert's Georgetown University, the University of Pennsylvania, and the Bunker-Ramo and TRW companies of Los Angeles, among others, requested generous funding while promising immediate results. Some of the proposals centered on Warren Weaver's dream of systems based upon a few general "laws" of language; others were more down to earth. Given his practical (non-theoretical) orientation to machine translation, Paul's selecting Dostert of Georgetown to lead the CIA's effort was predictable. Dostert had been an important part of the Office of Strategic Services, had provided critical translation services for the military brass, and ran language training courses for the intelligence agencies. As well, for Paul and many others, Dostert's rather simple dictionary approach, one that relied on a word-to-word computer file and just a few simple rules, seemed much more sensible than the type of theoretical linguistic approach advocated by Zellig Harris, and his student Noam Chomsky, at the University of Pennsylvania. There was another reason for favoring Dostert. He and Georgetown University had been close to the intelligence community for decades.

In 1958, as Paul Borel was dealing with the threatening consultant's report on Intellofax, Howerton signaled he had good news about the agency's investments in automatic translation. The Dostert–Georgetown University project announced it was about to pass a critical first-stage test although it was to be limited to translation in a narrow field of scientific specialization. Delayed until June 1959, the rather impressive translation of several hundred lines of Russian scientific text in organic chemistry by the Georgetown computerized GAT system pleased the agency. Although the resulting English translation was admittedly crude, and while some ad hoc methods had been used,[6] the CIA decided to join with others, such as the National Science Foundation (NSF), and invest much more in the Georgetown project. The air force and army also helped Dostert's work by providing free computer time. It seems that the National Security Agency had helped even more during Dostert's early automatic translation years. A 1954 report cited the agency as having a machine using a dictionary and six rules of grammar for Russian-to-English translation.[7]

Paul Howerton was increasingly optimistic and believed that within a few years Dostert's team would have systems for six more scientific disciplines and in a short time, economics.[8] With modern computers, he stated, 50,000 words an hour might be translated, compared to 1,800 a day by human translators. Howerton was also hopeful that optical character readers and high-speed printers would soon be available to overcome the input-output limitations to machine translation systems. The military and the NSF, with ambitions like Howerton's, had been supporting some ten optical reader projects and as many for printers.

THE GREAT TRANSLATION CENTER

Others shared Howerton's upbeat views and his newest crusade—to create a great national translation center. One group from Dostert's project, led by Ariadne Lukjanow, asked the CIA for two million dollars a year for a proposed for-profit company that would apply Lukjanow's code matching technique method using computer time purchased from a private Washington, D.C., firm. Dostert joined in with his own proposal for a national linguistics and translation center at his university. The ITEK Corporation also had its visions (at times supported by grants from the NSF) as did James Perry's group then at Western Reserve University. IBM had an even greater dream: it thought a copy of the special-purpose computer it was developing in partnership with the air force (with IBM contributing several million dollars) could handle all the nation's needs for translation, and that a project it was financing at the Baird Atomic company was about to produce a high-grade optical character recognition machine to overcome the text input problem. Besides that, Leon Dostert's hope for automatic input had a well-funded program to train people with vision problems to turn spoken Russian into computerized text using unique typewriters, a new IBM–air force machine, the Stenowriter, that was a much-upgraded semicomputerized version of a court stenographer's steno-machine.[9] There was better techno-news for MT by 1959. The air force–IBM project had led to the ongoing translation of Russian newspapers and there were signs that other languages, such as Chinese, might soon be mechanically translated. The huge IBM–air force project seemed to be going so well that there were plans for a public demonstration of the newest, third version of IBM's special-purpose Mark computer at the coming 1964 World's Fair in New York City.

IBM believed its large investments in mechanical translation were about to result in a profit-making business serving private as well as government needs. Meanwhile, the air force supported work at centers such as the RAND military think tank in California that appeared to be making great progress in developing more sophisticated translation methods than those wired into the IBM–air force computer. A large conclave at UCLA in February 1960 reflected the high level of optimism among researchers from across the country. [10]

AFTER GREAT HOPES, THE PROBLEM IS RECOGNIZED: LANGUAGES ARE NOT LOGICAL

But there had been hints that all was not well. The NSF, for example, gave indications that it had lost faith in the immediate appearance of fully automated and adequate machine translations. It suggested that it might shift its support to the kind of long-term research that targeted the fundamentals problem of language that, it believed, had to be solved before any worthwhile automatic translation was possible. Reflecting that, the foundation had reduced its funding for the Georgetown project in 1958 while increasing its support of Zellig Harris's theory-oriented work at the University of Pennsylvania. The foundation gave $700,000 to Dostert's group to help it wind down its NSF work but $9 million to Harris's team. [11]

The NSF had company in fearing that machine translation's challenges would not easily yield to a few basic laws, or even to a few dozen rules for each language. Just the problems of multiple meanings and syntax demanded hundreds of highly particularized and special computer instructions, even for specialized subsets of languages. The simplest, and crudest, of automated systems were dependent on those language- and context-specific rules and on huge computer memories to hold the rules as well as the thousands of word stems, suffixes, and prefixes.

A description of two challenges in Dostert's first 1954 system gives a flavor of the work needed to handle even simple translations. The Russian term *gyeneral mayor* had to be reversed to arrive at the proper translation in English, "major general." [12] To arrive at "major general" was not easy as there was no general-law solution. The correct translation was accomplished by attaching a rule 21 to the Russian word *gye-*

neral as stored in the machine, and by attaching a rule 110 to the Russian word *mayor*. The computer program gave the instruction that whenever 110 was encountered, look for another rule associated with an adjacent word, and if 21 were found, reverse the two associated words. Another problem that Dostert's team had to overcome was identifying the correct meaning of terms. For example, the Russian word *nauka* means "science" in English while the Russian word *o* can mean either "about" or "of." The proper English translation of *nauka o* is "science of," not "science about." To identify "science of" in the computer's Russian–English glossary "*nauka*/science" had to have affixed to it the rule-sign 241, and *o* had to carry the rule-sign 141. The computer's translation program had to specify that whenever it encountered the rule-sign 141, it was to go back and look for 241. If 241 was encountered, the correct English translation, "science of," was identified. Otherwise, the program would signal "not found" or point to the "about" translation. That and much more complexity was required to deal with even simpler problems. One translation system that was based on near word-to-word translations changed the Russian word *kondensatsija* (condensation) into *horsedensatsija* since *kon*, the first part of that Russian word, could mean horse and because the second part was not in the translation dictionary. [13]

In most computerized translation systems of the period the software programs needed a great deal of help. There had to be costly human editing of texts before and after the machine translations, and after the human interventions the machine translations remained imperfect.

The growing realization that translation was a much more difficult problem than had been imagined was leading to serious questions about the worth of any language mechanization. Especially threatening were complaints about the high cost of automation relative to human translations, the tens of millions of dollars "wasted" on faulty machine translations, and the many overlapping programs. A minimum estimate of government expenditures in translation work from 1956 to the mid-1960s was $140 million. There were at least four major efforts at constructing large Russian–English computer-based dictionaries, and by the mid-1960s there were more than a dozen machine translation projects in the United States with interest growing in Europe. [14]

DOSTERT AND FRIENDS UNDER PRESSURE—CONGRESS AND TECHNICAL DISAPPOINTMENTS

Emotion-charged protests about machine translation reached the American Congress, but mechanical translation's friends, such as the CIA, had prepared to meet the critics. A four-day-long congressional hearing was conducted in May 1960. Eleven administrators and experts at government-supported projects, including Dostert, testified. The result was a two-hundred-page report that indicates the hearing was designed to defend mechanical translation against its detractors. There was no negative testimony, even by researchers such as Victor H. Yngve of MIT who would at times be a public critic of many projects that promised immediate translations. He was also known to give warnings about what he viewed as exaggerated claims of the worth of any mechanized translation research.

An additional but somewhat embarrassing feature of the hearing was that two members of the committee were Georgetown graduates who knew of Dostert's work. For whatever reason, Congress refrained from taking negative action and the CIA, unlike the NSF, continued Dostert's funding. The agency's contributions to his work over the years would total $20 million. But the hearing had worried the NSF, and the military's intelligence arms and the civilian critics were not silenced.

To appease those who objected to duplication and waste, the Joint Automatic Language Translation Group was created. The NSF and the National Academy of Sciences were granted representation. Including the NSF was a necessity. Since 1958 it had been given increasing responsibilities for all aspects of science information. There had been political reasons for that. To meet criticisms that the military and intelligence agencies were not transparent, and were not sharing their human- and machine-produced translations with the public, coordinating power over government projects was being shifted to the foundation. It also began programs to support and synchronize the many human translation services that aided America's science journals.

EVEN THE CIA HAD ENOUGH, TO THE STENOWRITER AND SYSTRAN

Much to Paul Howerton's surprise and disappointment, after the victory at the congressional hearing the CIA initiated an internal review of progress at Georgetown and other sites. As a result, it turned down an opportunity to join the major IBM–air force project and then, to Dostert's dismay and anger, in March 1963 stopped supporting his Georgetown project, complaining somewhat bitterly about huge expenditures that had led to few useful results.

The agency did not abandon all machine translation, however. But its new policies may have been the reason Paul Howerton took an early retirement. The CIA's first commitment after the cancellation of Dostert's project was a technical and methodological backward step. In the same year the Georgetown support ended, the agency contracted with IBM for the use of its Stenowriter system. The Stenowriter had been under development for years, at first intended to be just an input device for recording spoken English translations of foreign documents into the IBM–air force Mark machine. It was a specially constructed court-reporting, shorthand, phonetic-based device upgraded to connect to a computer with a stored dictionary of English words. A typist used the special keyboard to enter "sounds" and created a paper tape that was read into a computer. The computer matched those sounds to the English terms stored in its memory, then printed the English text. The sound-to-English Stenowriters would, it was claimed, save much time and money once their operators became proficient.

Building the glossary for the system had taken years of effort, and an advanced version of the Stenowriter was planned. It was to use Russian as its input language. However, even that advanced version of the Stenowriter system was not a true full translator. It was only to be an aid to humans. It was to just print the Russian and equivalent English words without any attempt at making sense of the translation. To the disappointment of the CIA, even the original English-language Stenowriters did not prove as cost saving for translation as expected. One report stated that after some time they were used only to "record meetings."[15]

The CIA was not the only agency facing translation disappointments. In the early 1960s even the air force, the most generous supporter of MT, developed qualms about its investments. Despite its IBM AN/

GSQ-16 Mark II machine beginning operation at its Dayton, Ohio, information center, it was concerned that its translation projects were damaging its reputation in Washington. The first Mark required both pre- and postediting and had some reliability issues, and then, after debates, the air force and IBM had to invest in the development of a second and improved version. It was delivered in 1964 and remained in operation until 1970, used for Russian-language materials. An anticipated contract for a third version of Mark was not signed because the air force decided to use one of IBM's general-purpose computers and a software package, Systran, instead of the hardwired Mark. The Systran software was developed by Peter Toma, who had moved from the Dostert project to the Los Angeles area in 1958 where his work was supported by air force grants to his LATSEC company. Its SERNA–Systran would later become the first successful commercial translation product.[16]

THE NATIONAL ACADEMY OF SCIENCES, ALPAC, AND THE END OF ONE GOLDEN AGE

Despite various cost-saving attempts, the air force's and other translation projects remained political targets during the 1960s. Continuing criticisms led the military and the CIA to seek a comprehensive review by a neutral and esteemed body of machine translation experts, as well as by those in the new field of computational linguistics that was developed out of the earlier theoretical language explorations. In 1964, the National Academy of Sciences was formally requested to review all projects and methods. It responded, quickly turning responsibilities over to the National Research Council (NRC). The council created the Automatic Language Processing Advisory Committee (ALPAC), appointing seven scientists led by the acclaimed John R. Pierce of Bell Telephone Laboratory (Bell Labs). The group began two years of study funded by the CIA and the military.

ALPAC's committee members were unlike those who testified at the congressional hearings of 1960. ALPAC's members were academics with rather traditional views of what research should be, not practitioners. The committee's leader, Pierce, had earned a Ph.D. in engineering from Caltech, then went to the famous Bell Labs for the remainder of his long career, much of it spent leading its research teams as well as working with luminaries such as Claude Shannon. Pierce was no enemy of applied science but, like Bell Labs itself, he was a devoted friend of theory and long-term, abstract research. He shared that orientation with other ALPAC members. John Carroll, a Harvard psychologist, Eric Hemp, a university of Chicago linguist, and Alan Perlis, a Caltech artificial intelligence professor, all believed laws and explanations should come before applications. Even those members who had ties to immediate and applied machine translation work had academic points of view. Charles Hockett was a mixture of anthropologist and theoretical linguist while Anthony Oettinger of Harvard put as much energy into developing the theory of machine translation as he did to his massive automated Russian–English dictionary.

The mix of those who testified before the 1964 committee was also different from those who gave reports at the congressional hearing. Dostert was not called by ALPAC, nor were the military's representatives—but some already known critics deliberately were. Five leaders of the organizations representing professional human translators testified, and two men from the great Arthur D. Little efficiency/managerial company talked about the economics of translation that favored translation by humans. Surprising, two interrelated operations, that of the American Institute of Physics and Earl Coleman's Consultant's Bureau (later Plenum Press) that had been producing translations of science publications at relatively low cost, were not emphasized in the testimony.

Some MT stakeholders were heard from. Seven men who had some links to applied projects, including Gilbert King, now of ITEK, and three from IBM, voiced their opinions but they seemed to have made the least impact on the committee of any who gave evidence. What they had to admit about the history of their projects may well have had a negative effect. As well, Paul Garvin, who had moved from Dostert's project to the Bunker-Ramo Corporation, seems to have been forced to confess that achieving good translations was too much of a challenge for the technology and the methods of the era.

None of the testimony seems to have changed any minds. Given the committee members' backgrounds, the ALPAC's conclusions were predictable. In 1966, it announced that automatic translation was and would likely continue to be a failure. The committee stated the some

$140 million invested in it since the mid-1950s was a waste and the translations that had emerged were of poor quality and cost far more than human translations. Most of the methods that had been employed or explored were at dead ends, and there were no worthwhile automated translation projects on the horizon, even at the far horizon of the 1980s. In addition to heaping special criticism on the air force's Mark project, ALPAC's report implied there should be no more investments in any projects aimed at immediate results. There was a coda, however. Being academics, they recommended investing $20 million a year for the next few years in computational linguistics, the new version of Warren Weaver's dream of a theory-based science of translation. Work at four or so prestigious centers was recommended.

Given the stature of the ALPAC committee, its report had an impact. IBM, ITEK, and Gilbert King left the translation field, although IBM continued to develop its Stenowriter for the commercial market, work that was passed to a company led by Herbert Avram, an ex NSA-CIA analyst and world chess champion.[17] No other machine projects were begun despite the old Georgetown group launching a public counteroffensive.

The committee did not win all its battles, however. The NSF and other government agencies refused to provide the massive support to theoretical computer linguistics ALPAC had recommended. Academic linguists faced a decade of funding drought. The only trickle of funding came from the air force, which very, very quietly spent some three million dollars a year subsidizing projects that sought new ways to obtain immediate results.[18] Meanwhile, another theoretical-based field related to translation faced its own troubles. In the early 1960s, computer-based artificial intelligence (AI) methods had seemed about to revolutionize information retrieval. Then, by the mid-1960s, evaluations of the field led to a succession of less than complimentary reviews—and the termination of many funding initiatives.

University-based linguistics, AI, and MT were not the only fields to suffer during the later 1960s. As the panic over Soviet science eased, and with the need to finance an increasingly costly war in Vietnam, all academic scientists correctly feared their golden age of funding of abstract, even applied, research was ending.

A FRUSTRATED AGENT, ANOTHER NEW KIND OF PROFESSOR

Paul Howerton had not been called on to defend the CIA's translation work at the 1960 congressional hearing or during ALPAC's investigation, but he knew that MT was under fire. That frustrated him. Although still highly regarded at the CIA, he decided to retire in 1962 at the young age of forty-six, after just ten years' service. He quickly established himself as a consultant on computers and management in America and Europe and did well despite the social and economic problems of the decade. He also joined a venture to establish a new kind of for-profit information company, Information for Industry. Its publishing division began as a cooperating group of consultants intending to act as an advanced special library/research service for those who could not afford to fund their own staff of researchers. For example, the company's information branch filled in gaps in government information by providing timely indexes to patents and specialized science reports, often using innovative methods such as Uniterms and citation analysis. The parent company had larger projects, including planning its own version of a scaled-down Walnut microfilm machine. [19]

Paul edited a series of books on information science topics for the company, and he and others in the group wrote practical guides for information managers. Howerton and his colleagues were also visionaries. They wrote or edited works on the most advanced ideas in computing, information science, and translation, including those of Douglas Engelbart, who is regarded as the father of modern human-computer interfaces. Paul continued his private consulting work, but much of his time after 1962 was spent as a new type of academic. He became a professor and administrator at Washington, D.C.'s, American University, helping to establish a program in the still-being-defined fields of information science and information management. Being a new area without established academic or intellectual credentials, its professors came directly from private industry or, like Paul, from government service. Although without high-level degrees, or socialized into university culture, they were given academic status. With only a Ph.B. degree he may often have felt uncomfortable and estranged from the traditional professorial community.

232   CHAPTER 13

Paul was not alone in being an outsider brought into academia. Two old acquaintances, James Perry and Allen Kent, found themselves in a similar position.

NOTES

1. CREST, "History of the Library." The CIA took on the air force's large Treasure Island translation team at the Library of Congress, but that did not help much.

2. On Paul and his brother Robert James, *Who's Who in the South and Southwest* (Chicago: Marquis Who's Who, 1975) and Paul Wasserman and Janice W. McLean, *Who's Who in Consulting* (Detroit: Gale Research Co., 1973).

3. http://www.globalsecurity.org/wmd/facility/rocky.htm.

4. Paul Howerton, ed., and Alexander Akhonin, comp., *Russian–English Glossary of Metallurgical and Metal-Working Terms* (Cambridge: Massachusetts Institute of Technology, 1955); Paul Howerton, "The Parameters of an Operational Machine Translation System," *Mechanical Translation* 6 (1961): 108–12; Paul Howerton, ed., *Information Handling: First Principles* (Washington, DC: Spartan Books, 1963); Paul Howerton and David C. Weeks, *Vistas in Information Handling Volume I: The Augmentation of Man's Intellect by Machine* (Washington, DC: Spartan Books, 1963).

5. CREST, "Scott Adams," January 7, 1959, "History of Consolidated Translation Survey."

6. Bozena Henisz-Dostert, R. Ross Macdonald, and Michael Zarechnak, *Machine Translation* (The Hague: Mouton, 1979); Jacob Orstein, "Mechanical Translation," *Science* 122 (October 21, 1955): 745–48; W. John Hutchins, *Early Years of Machine Translation: Memoirs and Biographies of Pioneers* (Philadelphia: John Benjamin, 2000); Michael D. Gordon, *Scientific Babel: How Science Was Done Before and After Global English* (Chicago: University of Chicago Press, 2015), esp. 213–66.

7. CREST, "Mechanical Translation Report," 1954; Hutchins, *Early Years*, the Georgetown Project.

8. James M. Lufkin, "Human vs. Machine Translation of Foreign Languages," *IEEE Transactions on Engineering Writing and Speech* 8, no. 1 (1965): 8–14; James M. Lufkin, "What Everybody Should Know about Translation," *IEEE Transactions on Professional Communications* PC-18, no. 1 (March 1975): 22–28. A 1957 international survey of sci-tech publishing and translation was quite optimistic about MT's future: UNESCO, *Scientific and Technical Translating* (Paris: UNESCO, 1957).

AUTOMATIC TRANSLATION'S WOES

9. Gregory John Downey, "Constructing 'Computer-Compatible Stenographers': The Transition to Real Time Translation in Court Reporting," *Technology and Culture* 47, no. 1 (January 2006): 1–16; Gregory John Downey, *Closed Captioning* (Baltimore: Johns Hopkins University Press, 2008).

10. H. P. Edmundson, ed., *Proceedings of the National Symposium on Machine Translation: Held at the University of California, Los Angeles, February 2–5, 1960* (Englewood Cliffs, NJ: Prentice Hall, 1961).

11. National Research Council, Automatic Language Processing Advisory Council (ALPAC), *Language and Machines: Computers in Translation and Linguistics* (Washington, DC: NAS-NRC, 1966), 107–12.

12. CREST, "Linguistic Aspects of Translation," 1954; "701 Translator," IBM, January 8, 1954, http://www.ibm.com/ibm/history/exhibits/701/701_translator.html. One of Dostert's groups secured contracts with the Atomic Energy Commission and EURATOM, but little is known about the quality of the work.

13. Jeffrey S. Gruber, *Lexical Structures in Syntax and Semantics* (Amsterdam: North Holland, 1976).

14. National Research Council, ALPAC, *Language and Machines*. Estimates of the amounts invested vary widely, from tens of millions to more than $150 million. See also Edmundson, *Proceedings of the National Symposium*.

15. Downey, *Closed Captioning*.

16. J. A. Moyne, ed., *Machine Translation Programming Paper 1: General Analysis Technique* / Serna System (Washington, DC: Georgetown University Institute of Languages and Linguistics, June 1959).

17. Downey, *Closed Captioning*.

18. On the air force's contributions and the worrisome status of theory-based translation and retrieval, see Eric de Grolier, *On the Theoretical Basis of Information Retrieval Systems* (Paris: OAR, September 1965).

19. Howerton and Weeks, *Vistas in Information Handling.*

14

A COLD WAR INFORMATION CAREER

James Perry's and Allen Kent's lives and careers would have been very different if they had begun their search for new jobs in the mid- or late 1960s rather than in the early 1950s. Fortunately, after they lost their positions with the Massachusetts Institute of Technology (MIT) and the Central Intelligence Agency (CIA), science information and American higher education were beginning their golden ages. Both were on paths to becoming major industries. But within a decade colleges and science information became political targets.

In 1953, the future had seemed rather bleak for Perry and his colleagues Allen Kent and Madeline Berry. The three were out of work and their record as successful soft-money academics had suffered. Perry was forty-six years old, an age when most men of the era had an established career and were building a retirement nest egg for themselves and their wives. Kent, at thirty-one, was also at a life stage where being settled in was common. Berry was thirty, with a marriage four years in the future, but not quite sure if James Perry was going to be able to find work for her. In addition to the handicaps of the Scientific Aids to Learning and CIA defeats, Perry's group did not have the best of academic credentials. James had only a chemical engineering master's degree dating from the 1930s and had not worked in his field for a decade. Allen had just a bachelor's degree and it was not from one of the nation's top-ranked universities. His smattering of master's degree work at New York University's night school did not count for much.[1]

235

Madeline's undergraduate degree was from a small Catholic college that was regarded as respectable rather than noteworthy.

Also working against their hope of finding satisfying employment, their recent efforts had not been in a recognized field, not even in special librarianship, the profession that had developed to serve corporate information centers. There were few good opportunities for people like Perry and Kent who claimed to be documentalists or information scientists. There were openings for people familiar with information systems and tabulator usage in the expanding chemical and pharmaceutical industries, but the trio realized taking such jobs would mean becoming employees and losing creative independence.

Academia seemed the only home for their talents, but there were no full-fledged university programs in their specialty, only ones in librarianship. As well, library programs were generally regarded as vocational, not academic. So, they were rarely considered as deserving a place in a university's liberal arts or scientific departments. Abraham Flexner, one of the fathers of the modern American university, and creator of the critical Carnegie Standards used to judge a college department's worth, had declared all library programs in the 1920s and 1930s as being far short of academic respectability.[2] Under such pressures library schools were unlikely to give precious faculty slots to anyone concentrating on something as esoteric and untested as semantic factors. The few graduate programs in library studies that might support research (only six in the nation in the mid-1950s) sought candidates with high-status degrees, something Perry's group did not have.

The trio had only a few things in their favor. They had the beginnings of a reputation as a team capable of managing scientific information systems and Perry had just published a major work on information technology. Very important, Perry had finally gained a pledge from IBM to build a super version of the Luhn Scanner and 101 machines— a powerful device that held the promise of being able to support a large centralized information retrieval system. Critical to the trio's future, the golden age of research and university expansion was beginning. Federal dollars began to flow after the outbreak of the Korean War, even some into science information. The National Science Foundation (NSF) opened its Office of Science Information in 1952, the military was heavily investing in information systems, and a few university presidents sensed that information studies deserved a place in academia because it

A COLD WAR INFORMATION CAREER

might soon have its own federal cash cows. The university leaders were correct about an outpouring of federal dollars for all types of research, and the billions of dollars that reached universities during the decade and a half of unprecedented spending shaped the nature of American universities and the careers of Perry and his friends—and that of all the other new information scientists.

LET THE MONEY AND JOBS FLOW, TO MORE THAN MIT....

By 1950, American higher education was on track to becoming one of the nation's largest businesses.[3] More than federal research dollars was driving the ascent. Enrollments in higher education doubled between 1947 and 1960, doubled again in the next decade, and then kept climbing to another near doubling by the twenty-first century. The number of full-time faculty rose from 250,000 to 450,000 during the 1960s and seven hundred new colleges were established between 1950 and 1970. Constant dollar expenditures in higher education climbed even faster, threefold between 1950 and 1960 and threefold again during the next decade. The income of university-like institutions climbed faster than the number of students—but so did the cost of education. Expenditures per student had remained stable in the 1940s but began to climb in the 1950s. By the end of the 1960s the constant dollar-per-student expenditures were three times what they had been at the end of World War II.

Some of that increase was due to a deeper commitment to university research, much of it to fulfill the Cold War's high-tech needs. From Truman's through Eisenhower's and Kennedy's administrations, America fought technology-based wars and higher education benefited from Vannevar Bush's victory in securing promises that a sizable portion of all government research funding would go to academia.

There were massive expenditures for research and development. In 1946, government research funding had dropped to about half of what it had been during World War II and remained at that level until the Korean conflict; then in the next five years it doubled. Not every federal agency, however, was generous during the 1940s and early 1950s. Close to 90 percent of the research funds were spent by the three major Cold War providers. The military, the Atomic Energy Agency, and the National Advisory Committee for Aeronautics—the precursor of the National Aeronautics and Space Agency (NASA)—were the most generous.

The influence of the federal government in academia increased as its share of all research expenditures (corporate, foundation, and government) climbed to more than half by the mid-1950s when, finally, other than military- and space-related federal research budgets began increasing. For example, the organization Vannevar Bush had designed to hopefully give scientists the power to determine what projects they should work on by the mid-1950s was at last beginning to receive significant funding. In 1951, the National Science Foundation (NSF) had a minuscule budget, less than a million dollars. By 1955, that had increased to more than fourteen million. There was a threefold increase after 1957's fears caused by the launch of the Soviet's Sputnik satellite. In 1960, the agency's yearly budget was more than $150 million—by 1966 it had risen to close to $500 million, but more of NSF's academic research was justified by being related to national security needs.

Research universities and their faculties benefited from the increased federal role. From a sharp drop in higher education's share of federal expenditures in 1946, by the 1960s colleges and universities began taking a rather constant 10 percent of all federal research dollars.

Important to Perry's and his friends' careers, after the harried initial years of the Cold War the federal bounty was spread among an increasing number of institutions and academic researchers, partially because federal and nonprofit institutions were being forced by politics to initiate policies to democratize research spending in the 1960s. Much of the spread of research funding to more colleges was due to lobbying by a new generation of entrepreneurial academics.[4]

HAVING IT BOTH WAYS, MAYBE: CENTERS AND THE BUDGET PROBLEM

The consistent 10 percent share of federal research dollars going to academia and the democratizing movement led to some complications and challenges, ones that became very troubling by the 1970s. The unpredictable level of government spending in any specific field made planning for university research facilities and faculty-staffing levels dif-

A COLD WAR INFORMATION CAREER 239

ficult. As well, when there were reductions in funding, universities could be left with expensive departments that had once been self-supporting. A popular institutional alternative was created to avoid such problems, but it was not always successful.

Universities created "centers" for specialized research that depended on their staff's fund-raising abilities, not on a university's budget. The earlier soft-money policy that had shaped James Perry's years at MIT during the 1940s was extended to departments. The vision was that such centers and their nonpermanent staff would aid a university's mission and reputation but could be disbanded in hard times. In addition, the federal government had also used its version of centers to link academia and the Cold War's demands.

A version of the old form of independent organizations that performed services for the government, such as the Red Cross, was developed. These new nonprofit organizations could compete for government and private grants, at times billions of dollars' worth, without having the tax burdens of commercial organizations. The MITRE, Systems Development, and Rand Corporations, and the Stanford Research Institute, for example, utilized faculty talents while keeping universities at a safe distance from projects that might sully a university's ivory-tower reputation—or budget. The government also looked to freestanding older research organizations, such as the Battelle Memorial Institute, that called on academics' talents.

For universities, and for the government, there were good reasons for relying on the supposed budgetary flexibility provided by centers and nonprofits. After the mid-1960s, defense-related spending stalled and overall government research expenditures dropped almost 4 percent in real-dollar value between 1965 and 1970. There was a rebound, but not at the same pace as before, at least until there was a burst of research and development funding in the early 1980s. However, after the previous 1960 highpoint, and despite the Department of Health, Education, and Welfare's policy of shifting its research to university-related centers, the government's share of all research funding continued began to drop, to one-quarter by the 1990s.

That meant universities and researchers, even the highly subsidized medical research centers, necessarily became involved in a new competitive politics of higher education that included ethical issues related to business-sponsored research.

SCIENCE INFORMATION, DEMOCRATIZING RESEARCH, WANNABE UNIVERSITIES

Before then, the universities of the 1950s had faced their own types of struggles, many of them because the surge of federal research support had political implications, even for science information. By the later 1950s, control of science information once again became a politically divisive issue. There were conflicts reminiscent of the immediate post–World War II's struggles over Henry Wallace's populist research and information policies, as well as the 1920s debates over what type of science information should receive philanthropic support.

A related fundamental issue arose because government research spending in the 1950s had followed a logical path: spending research dollars where there was the greatest chance for quick results. That led to concentrating spending in the few best science universities that had established a track record during World War II. In 1960, six universities accounted for a third of funding, twenty took almost 80 percent. With federal funds playing a critical role in financing any research (and faculty salaries and equipment), and with conducting research so critical to an institution's reputation, distributing the federal dollars over more and more institutions became a politicized cause. There was success. By the end of the 1950s the NSF and even private organizations, such as the Ford Foundation, began extensive programs to create more "centers of excellence" in the sciences and technology. Even the military agencies joined in the drive to extend research and development funds to more institutions.

With those and other incentives, an increasing number of higher education's leaders believed their institutions could begin to share in the federal and private generosity. But to do so meant becoming dependent on faculty grantsmen who had to vie against a growing number of competitors. With the funding declines of the 1970s, that put many smaller institutions that had begun their expensive research adventures in the late 1950s and early 1960s (with more hope than resources) in financial jeopardy. Even with the "centers" strategy, they struggled to support an increased number of research faculty and the expensive equipment and buildings they needed to allow competition for research funds.[5]

Another unintended consequence of the policies of academia's golden age of research became one of the causes of the campus protests of the 1960s and 1970s. The issue of how much teaching research professors should do would even impact James Perry's career. Teaching, the professed central function of even research universities, seemed to have a diminished importance as research funding and enrollments grew. The number of students per faculty member had doubled during the 1960s as universities attempted to restrain costs while investing in research. As irritating to students, more and more research-oriented professors spent their time on their projects rather than in the classroom, forcing others, usually graduate students and ill-paid part-time instructors, to assume their teaching load.

PERRY AND FRIENDS, SCIENCE INFORMATION IN THE GOLDEN AGE, BATTELLE

Fortunately for James Perry, Allen Kent, and Madeline Berry, their search for work began at the front edge of America's Cold War research boom.[6] As well, by the mid-1950s it seemed America would always be in another type of golden age, an age of ideological consensus. The labor strife of the postwar years had subsided, the threats of internal Communism seemed to have retreated (partly due to government prosecutions), and university research had few political enemies.

Despite their lack of academic credentials, given the abundance and political calm of the 1950s it is surprising that Perry's group did not immediately find steady work in 1953. Their first job was short lived and was for a small private research organization, Bjorksten Research Laboratories in Madison, Wisconsin. Johan Bjorksten was a genius Ph.D.-holding chemist who had left his research position with an Eastman Kodak subsidiary to create a for-profit research organization to serve business clients. Perry advised Bjorksten on organizing his laboratory's files but was not asked to stay on. Then, before the year was out, Perry and his two collaborators seemed to finally have a possibility of a prestigious home. They connected with D. B. Thomas, an energetic and ambitious new administrator at the Battelle Memorial Institute, one of the nation's leading independent research organizations.

242   CHAPTER 14

Originally planned as philanthropy in the 1920s, Battelle had become one of the nonprofits that were acting much like a business. By the 1950s it was accumulating huge financial surpluses. The institute had a long record of performing impressive contract research for businesses and of sponsoring profitable developments such as Xeroxing. It had also built a track record in information processing and had a history of performing science information contract research for the government, as well as for private industry.

The institute had been generously endowed in the 1920s by the Battelle family, whose fortune stemmed from Ohio's then new steel industry. The institute's grand facility was built next to Ohio State University's campus in Columbus so faculty might help it to fulfill Battelle's mandate to apply science to practical problems. The institute's plans succeeded. It climbed from a staff of thirty to six hundred by 1941. During the next fifty years the workforce increased to sixteen thousand. The institute also became wealthy, so much so that in the 1960s the Internal Revenue Service demanded it return to behaving more like a charity than a profit-making enterprise that had incorrectly benefited from being given a tax-free status.[7]

Metallurgical research and turning science into products had always been the institute's forte. Its first customers were from Ohio's then burgeoning steel industry. Its initial operating head, 1929–1934, was H. W. Gillette, a man who was well schooled in the practical applications of science. He was regarded as America's first professional metallurgist. He had trained at Cornell University, one of the nation's original and leading schools of technology, and had assisted Thomas Edison, the master of applied research. Gillette then worked at the national government's Bureau of Mines, married into the famous Pratt family, and was called to establish Battelle's programs. Gillette was an example of the technologist as a political and social progressive. Like Frederick Winslow Taylor, he believed that science could solve economic and labor problems.

Clyde Williams, the institute's next leader, was also viewed as a father of scientific metallurgy. He was so highly regarded that Vannevar Bush had appointed him to lead the National Defense Research Committee's metallurgical section during World War II. Bush then gave him and the Battelle Institute a major role in developing the technology for the atomic bomb. Williams's influence continued after the war. He was

A COLD WAR INFORMATION CAREER

on the Joint Research and Development Committee that Norman Ball supervised, he headed the National Research Council's metals committee, and he was a founding member of the board for the air force's academic think tank, the Rand Corporation. As well, under his direction the institute became a major player in the development of atomic energy, including the system for the world's first nuclear submarine. The institute was so important and trusted that it could build its own reactor near its campus. In the next decades, Battelle became the manager of most of the nation's nonmilitary atomic facilities, was among the top one hundred military contractors, and built an international presence. The institute also remained a trusted science information center for government agencies, including the CIA.

THE PERRY CONNECTION, SEMANTIC FACTORS REBORN

In the mid-1950s, D. B. Thomas, the institute's next manager, needed an outside team to fulfill a contract with an old institutional friend of Perry's, the Aberdeen Proving Ground, where the army tested its weapons. Aberdeen wanted an advanced system for its reports. Perry heard of Thomas's need and convinced him and the Proving Ground that his semantic factors and automation (that envisioned an improved Luhn Scanner) were the keys to success. Perry was awarded a three-year contract, gained the title of a "documentation engineer," and set himself, Kent, and, especially Madeline Berry, to work on the army's project. There was much more than the Aberdeen contract that made the connection between Perry and the institute's D. B. Thomas seem to have been "made in information heaven." Both men had backgrounds in applied chemistry and both had grand information dreams.

Importantly, Thomas wanted the institute to share in more of the Cold War's research bounty. He already had information-related contracts with the CIA, one to develop an information machine for the air force, and many to have the institute's one hundred librarians serve as science information analysts for the other military services—even working on secret projects. Such rather famous librarian/information scientists as Herbert Ohlman and Jack Belzer were employees. In fact, Battelle had already become one of the nation's largest science information operations, acquiring and analyzing thousands of journals and research papers from around the world. The institute's librarians had developed their own impressive methods and professional culture and they had created huge files on many topics. The institute's holdings on titanium were regarded as a national resource. But Thomas wanted more, much more.

THE GREAT SCIENCE INFORMATION CENTER, PERRY'S GREAT MACHINE, ANOTHER DISAPPOINTMENT

Thomas and Perry soon had plans for creating a great mechanized, for-pay, profit-making science information center at Battelle, one intended to serve the entire nation. Thomas quickly went public about his information ambitions and his views about the market potential for science information. He told the press the annual cost of searching for metallurgy information alone was $84 million and all sci-tech information retrieval cost more than $20 billion.[8] Thomas was not hesitant in declaring that Battelle wanted a large share of that business. It was the institute's established record as a government contractor, its already successful information analysis programs, its atomic connection, and Thomas's ambitions that led to Perry's grand, but short-lived, hope to establish a national semantic factors information center at the institute, one centered on his hoped-for super-Luhn information machine. Unfortunately for James Perry, despite Battelle's great success, it was still unwilling to put anyone on staff unless they and their projects were likely to be self-supporting. That requirement also led to another worry-filled stage in Perry's and Kent's careers.

In 1953, while Madeline Berry concentrated on finishing the project at the Aberdeen Proving Ground, Perry and Kent began a search for the funding needed for their and Thomas's great science information center and jobs for Perry's team. They canvassed Washington and the nation's professional organizations. Perry eventually found two major sponsors and a few minor ones in the chemical industry.

Surprisingly, the most beneficent sponsor was the CIA, the organization that a year before had cast him out. The other major supporter was the academic/industry-based American Society for Metals. Perry had approached the CIA with a new idea soon after James Madison An-

A COLD WAR INFORMATION CAREER

drews had canceled Perry's first indexing contract. Perry's idea was to show that the metallurgical literature, which was so important to atomic programs, could be indexed and easily retrieved with the promised new enhanced version of the Luhn Scanner. The CIA turned him down at first—but Perry persevered, stressing his new relationship with Battelle, the nation's metallurgical center. Perhaps because of the power of the CIA's influential science group that monitored atomic science and technology, Perry's connection to the American Society for Metals, and his link to the respected Battelle Institute, the CIA's administrators relented.

The CIA used the Society for Metals as a cover and agreed to a five-year contract to begin in 1955. Important to Perry's future, the CIA awarded the contract to Perry, not the institute. The project was to explore the feasibility of machine searching of the metallurgical literature using the semantic factors system and the promised super-Scanner from IBM. That called for the creation of a computer-friendly database. The grant was worth at least a half million dollars. The generosity came despite the agency's own ongoing retrieval research, including the Minicard-related explorations of the logic of advanced selection methods. Perry may also have thought the agency would reconsider using his semantic factors for all its major databases.[9]

At Battelle, Thomas signaled he would welcome Perry and his newly found research dollars, at least temporarily. Then, the happy news of the CIA-backed grant was soon followed by a string of disappointments. Conflicts with the head of the already existing science information programs at the Battelle Memorial Institute came first. The institute had many of its own contracts, including ones with the CIA. Allen Kent reported that the institute's chief librarian resented Perry's intrusions and lobbied to have him fired. That frustration was followed by something that had the potential to immediately kill Thomas's great for-profit information service dream.

IBM announced that it was not going to create the improved version of the Luhn Scanner that Perry had helped design and that was to serve as the basis for the Aberdeen and CIA work—and Battelle's national for-profit center. That decision also endangered Battelle's information contract with the air force. Despite Perry's pleas, IBM continued to refuse to invest in developing his device, concentrating instead on turning its general-purpose electronic computers into information processors.

In a few years the company would backtrack on that decision, but not to Perry's advantage. IBM designed and built, with some of its own money, and much from the Office of Naval Research,[10] a special electromechanical system for Mortimer Taube, Perry's classification system competitor. The Taube-IBM COMAC was a relatively affordable machine that automated Taube's Uniterm system.

With 1954's news of the IBM cancellation of the super-Scanner, Perry and Kent were fired—after only a year at Battelle. Berry was informed that once she completed the Aberdeen project, she, too, would be out of work. There seemed only one bit of good news: the CIA did not cancel the five-year "metals" information contract and Thomas allowed Perry to keep it. That meant that Perry still had a bargaining chip. He had a half million dollars of soft money in hand for the five-year CIA/ASM-financed experiment in mechanized information retrieval—but he needed an institutional home.

COMING TOGETHER, IN CLEVELAND: SHERA AND PERRY AND FRIENDS

Perry had sensed that Thomas was disappointed with him well before his team was dismissed, and he had been searching for other opportunities. He did not have to look far. Less than a hundred miles away, in Cleveland, Ohio, were two men with great ambitions for Western Reserve University. Their dream for college education in Cleveland was in direct contrast to those who had gone to Cleveland after World War II with hopes of building a "people's college" to replace elitist and research-oriented higher education.

Western Reserve was a traditional college trying to adjust to a new era. One of the men guiding that search was John Schoff Millis, the university's new president. The other was the librarian Jesse Hauk Shera, who had been Wilmarth Sheldon Lewis and Annie Burr Lewis's favorite when the young Jesse had worked under Wilmarth at the Coordinator of Information/Office of Strategic Service's (OSS) information center during World War II. Millis had been called to Western Reserve in 1949 to pull the college out of financial, academic, and personnel

A COLD WAR INFORMATION CAREER

difficulties. To reduce debts and expenses, Millis had ended the plan for a fourteen-story, block-long downtown campus for the common man's Cleveland College, and concentrated on turning Reserve into a modern research university. He began reshaping undergraduate departments, upgrading faculty, and, significantly, increasing graduate offerings. [11]

One of Millis's toughest challenges was Reserve's library school. [12] It had started in the early 1900s with great hopes and a large endowment from the Carnegie Foundation. That endowment, unfortunately, was slammed by the Great Depression. The school had always run deficits, except during a short burst of post–World War II GI Bill–subsidized enrollments, and faculty salaries and morale had been low since the great crash of 1929. Despite having some nationally recognized faculty, such as Helen Focke, who had begun one of the nation's first courses in documentation, when Millis took charge of the university, the library school's reputation and its rather traditional vocational curricula did not seem worthy of being part of a research university. For example, the school had not taken advantage of Robert C. Binkley's cutting-edge work on microfilm systems for the social sciences during the 1930s when he was a history professor at Western Reserve. Supporting a doctoral program or sustaining its master's program in librarianship seemed impossibilities. As well, the school's faculty did have the grantsman's skills needed in the new age of higher education. Those skills were especially important because philanthropies, such as Carnegie's, had turned away from endowing library schools and a new surge of lobbying to have the federal government subsidize forward-looking and ambitious library schools seemed on the verge of success.

JESSE SHERA, AGAIN

It took some time for Millis to form a strategy for the library school, but he did it. He decided to import new talent, even if that meant paying higher salaries, and having the library's programs turn toward expensive doctoral education. He was determined to find the means to ensure the school could embrace the latest techniques and technologies so that its future graduate programs would succeed. Sensing that federal dollars might be available, he became interested in the scientific information problem and began to build a new faculty with the skills needed to carve a place in the emerging field of information retrieval.

Millis's first major library "catch" was Jesse Shera, who had been at the nation's very prestigious graduate library school at the University of Chicago since he left the OSS in 1944. Shera, although near legally blind, had made a name for himself as a humanistic philosopher of information and librarianship but also as an advocate for library mechanization and new approaches to classification to solve the nation's science-information overload problem. He also was a leader of the most important professional organizations and a dynamic force in the American Documentation Institute.

Millis thought Shera the perfect man to move the department away from vocationalism and create the seventh graduate library program in the nation that could meet Flexner standards. Millis also had confidence in Shera's ability to make all parts of the library school self-supporting. To help him in that, Shera convinced Millis to hire other forward-looking librarians who researched and published and who were significant and highly visible members of professional organizations. One of the most important of them was Margaret Egan, who had also been at the University of Chicago's Graduate Library School.

After that, when Shera heard of Perry's difficulties, he thought he had a great opportunity to go further and make the Reserve "the" cutting-edge library school in the nation. Important, Shera knew he had to do so without plunging the school into debt. That called for generating financing for research from outside the university. James Perry and Allen Kent seemed the men to do that and to establish an information science version of a research center while Shera created a graduate library program. At the same time, Millis imagined he could use to Perry to establish a nonprofit information processing center that would generate an ongoing income stream for the university. Because it was to be one those disposable "centers," Millis was sure it would never become a permanent burden.

WILL THERE BE TWO CULTURES AT THE RESERVE AS AT THE OSS?

Although Shera was an advocate for advanced methods (at times even condemning traditional classification methods such as the Universal Decimal Classification)[13] he remained oriented to an older genteel academic culture like that of his mentor Wilmarth Sheldon Lewis. So, his first plan for the school's doctoral program followed a rather humanistic path. One-half of all class hours were to be in other departments and many of the school's own offerings were oriented toward academic subjects such as the sociology of knowledge (social epistemology). Sadly, programs such as that were intellectually valid but hardly likely to attract grants from federal agencies or generate enrollments. The new grant givers wanted prestige-generating research, and the new students sought vocational and job-getting training.

Reacting to the realities of student demand and grant makers' preference for useful knowledge, Shera created a special master's program in medical librarianship that attracted many dollars from government agencies, such as the Public Health Service, and that led to immediate job placements as federal dollars were driving an expansion in medical research and medical libraries. But Shera still needed ways to finance more general information research, although he remained committed to a program with traditional intellectual foundations for his doctoral program.

To Millis, James Perry seemed to have the answer to his and Shera's needs because of James's information center vision and his CIA contract. Shera also had faith in Perry as an academic, partly because of their joint work in the American Documentation Institute and because of Perry's participation in the symposiums on the information problem that Shera began holding as soon as he took the job at Western Reserve. Shera was also aware of Perry's long publication record and, along with John Millis, believed it overrode Perry's lack of a doctoral degree.

The cancellation of the new Luhn device did not worry Millis. He was sure that Perry's fund-raising abilities would soon lead to a better machine and to a profitable information center. As a result, with the five-year CIA metallurgical funds in hand, and with the expectation that James would fund all his Reserve work through more grants, Perry and Kent were brought to Cleveland to establish the library school's Center

250   CHAPTER 14

for Documentation and Communication Research. There was an extra
bonus for both men, one that seemed to give them academic status. As
well as being directors of the center, they were made associate professors in the library school. However, they were not given the protection
of tenure.[14] For personal reasons, Madeline Berry decided not to join
Perry in Cleveland. She remained on the East Coast, soon married, and
became a mother before working for the National Science Foundation's
important science information program.

THE GREAT INFORMATION CENTER, II

Perry and Kent got off to a flying start after they moved to Cleveland.
There was a series of books promoting their versions of documentalism,
major symposiums that attracted the CIA and other experts, and an
energetic search for contracts and grants. Kent took the lead in creating
radically new curricula in documentation/information science at the library school, a curriculum that became far different from Shera's humanistic one. Despite that swing to a new sort of vocationalism, Perry
and Kent seemed to be meeting all of Millis's and Shera's expectations
for an academically respectable operation, one that would, perhaps, go
beyond being merely self-supporting. Especially pleasing was Perry's
promise to quickly provide Reserve with a very advanced replacement
for the Scanner. He called it the Automatic Selector.

Soon, Perry and Kent were bringing in almost two-thirds of the
library school's income through grants from government agencies, professional organizations, and corporations. There were also contracts for
services, including ones with the CIA, the air force's research centers,
and the General Electric Corporation's information systems division.

Shera approved it all, at least for a while. He published enthusiastic
salutes about the Perry-Kent center and its potential to develop methods for the new types of group-based science activities that were not
well served by typical library methods. His great expectation was that
the center's research would lead to the theories that could make library
and information education be regarded as truly scientific and worthy of
academic status. He also foresaw Perry's and Kent's work leading to a
happy uniting of traditional librarianship and documentation and to the

A COLD WAR INFORMATION CAREER

finalizing of a coherent and nationally recognized curriculum for the new information science.[15]

Although oriented to academic research, Shera also accepted Perry's moneymaking contract work providing practical advice and services to his clients. Jesse did not go as far as Perry in salutes to the Cleveland center, however. Although he liked the pep and push of men like Perry, Shera must have been a bit put off when Perry and Kent wrote that their center would redo all the fundamentals and cure the methodological backwardness of librarians and library schools such as the one at the University of Chicago.[16]

There was more than such talk. Work on the CIA-financed machine-based "metals" retrieval project began early on. The first step was not an exciting one, but it was a necessity. A huge file of searchable abstracts had to be created before any viable tests could be conducted and before a retrieval service could begin generating fees. The absence of such a large body of machine-readable data had frustrated Vannevar Bush since the 1930s. Despite all his influence, he had been unable to finance the creation of a suitable test file. Perry believed he would soon have the first one in the world. He envisioned creating a core of his special telegraphic abstracts with semantic factors indexing for fifteen thousand articles from metallurgical journals and hoped to soon have the funds to add twenty-five thousand more from periodicals in related fields. There also were ambitions to build files for and to provide services in legal fields, education, medicine, and, perhaps, history. There was, however, a significant limit to Perry's ambitions: he was not going to provide any full text to his customers, just lists of the titles of articles retrieved through the search of his abstracts.[17]

Creating the new searchable "metals" special abstracts file soon proved more time consuming than expected. Perry took a short cut. Instead of using the full text of articles already published, existing abstracts were used whenever possible—something that traditional indexers found very questionable. As well, rather old-fashioned technology had to be used for the first stages of all the telegraphic abstracts work. The new abstracts were put onto tabulator cards as a first step to placing them on paper tapes to be read by the promised Reserve Automatic Selector machine.

Perry's team refined the semantic abstracts system but the full test of its worth awaited that searching device. For several years tests had to be conducted with a limited database and handheld edge-notched cards.

THE POOR MAN'S SCANNER AND CONTINUED HOPE, THE GREAT SCIENCE INFORMATION CENTER, III

Perry had to put a high priority on obtaining a high-speed retrieval machine. He desperately needed it to fulfill his obligations to Millis, Shera, and the CIA. Without it, he would be unable to start his center and likely lose his job. He still believed that general-purpose electronic computers would never be much more than calculating devices, but he was unable to find any manufacturer willing to step in to fill the void left when IBM turned away from constructing the improved Luhn super-Scanner.

Perry decided to build his own! How he financed the construction of his Automatic Selector remains unknown, but it is clear he took a low-cost path, perhaps thinking a demonstration prototype might convince some company to invest in a high-speed, full-scale model. Despite the allure and fast-paced development of microfilm machines such as Mini-card, and of general-purpose electronic computers, Perry chose to use slow, old-fashioned, electromechanical relays, a huge set of plugboards for setting up the devices' procedures, and a slow paper tape reader as the hardware for his machine. When at its best, his Selector could process only thirty abstracts per hour. An electronic version using late-1950s transistors and magnetic tapes was expected to do a hundred thousand in the same time. Despite his room-size machine's limitations, and its piece-by-piece construction its design had, according to Allen Kent, some features that were very advanced, such as allowing the use of all Boolean combinations and testing on multiple terms on a single run.

Those features helped Perry gain several important patents, Kent reported, ones that led to an agreement that promised to soon allow Perry's center to at last fulfill its older promises—and much more.[18] Through his contacts with the documentalist Cloyd Dake Gull, who had moved from the Library of Congress's military reports projects to work with the General Electric Company (GE) on its far-reaching computer and information systems projects,[19] Perry obtained a promise from GE

A COLD WAR INFORMATION CAREER

to build, at a very low price, a true electronic special-purpose information computer based on his relay machine's architecture.[20] Significantly, because he did not plan to provide any full text, Perry did not ask GE to include any features such as the automatic creation of Langan aperture cards.

The vision of having the powerful GE machine led Millis, Perry, and even Shera to grander entrepreneurial ambitions for Western Reserve. They were soon lobbying for hundreds of millions of dollars in subsidies to launch the Reserve's first steps toward becoming "the" one great center for the retrieval of all science information in the nation. They planned well, using one of their NSF grants to survey all existing machine-based retrieval projects, to finalize their design, and to write a report to the government they hoped would lead to millions of dollars for Western Reserve. In 1958, Perry's goals seemed realistic because another phase of the Cold War was leading to promises of massive government support for science information and attention to the need for a redoing of America's science information systems.

Perry and Kent's attempt to leverage the fright caused by the Soviet Union's launching of a space satellite would involve them and Western Reserve in a new politics of information, to a split between them and Jesse Shera, to the decline of Perry's center, and to Perry and Kent being forced to leave Cleveland.

NOTES

1. Western Reserve press release, May 1955.

2. Charles C. Williamson, *Training for Library Service: A Report Prepared for the Carnegie Corporation of New York* (New York: Carnegie Corporation, 1923).

3. Thomas Snyder, ed., *120 Years of American Education: A Statistical Portrait* (n.p.: NCES, January 1993).

4. Roger L. Geiger, *Research and Relevant Knowledge: American Research Universities since World War II* (New York: Oxford University Press, 1993), chap. 9.

5. Hugh Davis Graham and Nancy Diamond, *The Rise of American Research Universities: Elites and Challengers in the Postwar Era* (Baltimore: Johns Hopkins University Press, 1997).

6. John R. Thelin, *A History of American Higher Education* (2nd ed.) (Baltimore: Johns Hopkins University Press, 2011), 280.

7. George A. Boehm, *Science in the Service of Mankind: The Battelle Story* (Columbus, OH: Battelle, 1986); http://www.ohiohistorycentral.org/w/Battelle_Memorial_Institute.

8. In 2006 constant dollars.

9. CREST, "Perry Metals," 1954–1955.

10. Mortimer Taube, "The Comac: An Efficient Punched Card Collating System for the Storage and Retrieval of Information," in *Proceedings of the International Conference on Scientific Information Washington, D.C. Nov. 16–21, 1958*, vol. 2, NAS-NSF (Washington, DC: NAS-NSF, 1959), 1245–54.

11. C. H. Cramer, *Case Western Reserve: A History of the University, 1826–1976* (Boston: Little, Brown, 1976); Darwin H. Stapleton, "The Faustian Dilemmas of Funded Research at Case Institute and Western Reserve, 1945–1965," *Science, Technology & Human Values* 18, no. 3 (1993): 303–14.

12. C. H. Cramer, *The School of Library Science at Case Western Reserve University: Seventy-Five Years, 1904–1979* (Cleveland, OH: School of Library Science, 1979).

13. H. Curtis Wright, "Jesse Shera, Librarianship, and Information Science," Occasional Research Paper 5 (School of Library and Information Science, Brigham Young University, 1958); CWR, Papers of Jesse Hawke Shera (1943–1983); Jesse H. Shera, "Documentation: Its Scope and Limitations," *Library Quarterly* 21 (January 1951): 13–26; Jesse H. Shera, *Sociological Foundations of Librarianship* (New York: Asia Publishing House, 1970).

14. Western Reserve press release on the center, May 1955.

15. Jesse H. Shera, Allen Kent, and James W. Perry, *Information Resources: A Challenge to American Science and Industry* (New York: Press of Western Reserve University, Interscience, 1958); Jesse H. Shera, "New Tools for Easing the Research Burden of Historical Research," *American Documentation* 10, no. 4 (October 1959): 274–77; Alan M. Rees, "The Aslib-Cranfield Test of the Western Reserve University Indexing System for Metallurgical Literature: A Review of the Final Report," *American Documentation* 16, no. 2 (April 1965).

16. Jesse H. Shera, "Librarianship in a High Key," *ALA Bulletin* 50, no. 2 (February 1956): 103–5.

17. Eventually the file had one hundred thousand entries.

18. A search of patent files did not reveal those patents.

19. General Electric was planning a huge computer utility system and in 1969 established a center in Cleveland.

20. Allen Kent, "The GE-250," *College Composition and Communication* 11, no. 2 (May 1960): 75–77.

Part III

Information's Troubled Golden Age to the Era of Open Access

15

SPUTNIK'S NEW POLITICS OF INFORMATION

While James Perry and Allen Kent were completing a National Science Foundation (NSF)–sponsored report on centralized information services, and buffing up their ambitious plans for a for-fee, nationwide science information hub at Western Reserve University's Center for Documentation and Communication Research, the Soviet Union sent a small twenty-three-inch sphere with a beeping radio beacon into space. That October 1957 launch of the Sputnik satellite had not been predicted by the Central Intelligence Agency's (CIA) experts, and America's leaders were unprepared for the near panic about an apparent triumph of Communist science and technology over that of the Western world. Although the ideological aspects were muted during the age of consensus, Sputnik intensified the Cold War policy debates that had reemerged in 1956 when Soviet Russia suppressed the revolt in Hungary as the West stood helpless.

Although Stalin had died in 1953, and his brutal policies denounced by Nikita Khrushchev three years later, the Soviet actions in 1956 indicated that Russia was continuing its old foreign policies. The Hungarian revolt and the guilt-raising inability of the United States to aid the uprising (although it had seemed to have encouraged it through such efforts as Radio Free Europe's propaganda broadcasts) primed America for a reexamination of its policies and powers. The inability to do no more than resettle Hungarian refugees and the apparent failure of the rollback policy to free the bloc countries embarrassed the CIA and America's leaders.

Sputnik added to the national depression caused by the Hungarian debacle. Then, America's December 1957 televised botched Vanguard rocket launch led to a sense that the nation's expensive science and technology programs had failed. Unable to reveal the nation's far more advanced satellite and space efforts, such as the work on the Corona spy satellites that would be launched in 1959 (or even of the already operational U2 spy planes), and despite tiny satellite launches beginning in January 1958, America's leaders had few resources to deal with an outpouring of condemnation of the nation's science and technology systems—and its educational institutions.

Two generations of achievements by scientists and educators, such as Vannevar Bush, the members of the National Academy of Sciences, and the wealthiest philanthropies that built what they believed were now the best research universities in the world, were criticized as inadequate, as were the government's efforts in advanced technological development. Even the National Science Foundation faced disapproval, especially from those who, like Henry Wallace, had tried to make all science part of government programs that were directed toward economic development and social welfare programs rather than defense.

THE VINITI CHALLENGE

America's supposed space failures seemed to also be a result of science's information problems. The nation's information providers, private as well as public, were harshly criticized—although they had been hailed as having become the world's most advanced after World War II. One reason for the condemnation of America's scientific journals and abstract and indexing organizations was that a science information version of Sputnik had been discovered: the Soviet Union's huge All Soviet Institute for Scientific and Technical Information (VINITI) was a centralized abstracting service for all scientific fields. With its main headquarters in Moscow, it had two thousand full-time employees, twenty thousand volunteers, and almost one hundred branches throughout the Soviet bloc.

SPUTNIK'S NEW POLITICS OF INFORMATION 259

Its top-down structure had been completed in 1952,[1] giving it the kind of control the Americans believed was needed to provide some two million timely abstracts a year. It appeared that VINITI had been able to coordinate all the Soviet information providers, unlike the situation in the United States where even the government's information systems had grown independently and where the attempts to make them compatible were not meeting expectations. The attempts by the military's ASTIA, the Office of Technical Services, and the Special Libraries Association's Government Science Information Systems initiatives, and the many interagency coordinating committees, had not led to integrated systems. As well, the five hundred nonprofit and for-profit science information services seemed to be exemplars of inefficiency in comparison to VINITI.

VINITI also appeared to have overcome the language translation problem, at least in terms of classification and indexing. It used the numeric Universal Decimal Classification system the West had generally abandoned so that all members of the multilingual Soviet bloc could be accommodated. In contrast, the organizations in the Western world used several languages and classification systems and suffered from continuing nationalistic complications. American information leaders such as Jesse Shera even feared the Soviets would be the first to have advanced machines for information retrieval and full-text translation.

MONEY WILL DO IT, MAYBE

In reaction to Sputnik, a "space race" and an "information race" were launched. The United States began investing billions of dollars in space technology, including the Apollo project to land a man on the moon. Apollo would cost 5 percent of the nation's budget for more than a decade and created a new era of big, expensive, project-oriented science, one that rivaled the atomic bomb project of World War II. There also was an outpouring of proposed solutions for the perceived weaknesses of America's information, education, and governmental research systems.

The Sputnik uproar provided an opportunity to achieve long-sought information goals—although they sometimes were ones that had little relationship to the space race. Among those ready with solutions were

260 CHAPTER 15

James Perry's Western Reserve group and Hubert Humphrey, the rising young liberal Democratic senator from Minnesota. Perry thought he could finally have his huge central information center; Humphrey believed he could achieve his friend Henry Wallace's old dream of having science bow to the "will of the people," rather than to the demands of monopolistic corporations, the military, or a scientific elite that focused on esoteric subjects that had little relevance to daily life. One of Humphrey's hopes was to create a cabinet-level Department of Science that could be used as a counterbalance to the military's dominant role in determining research priorities and what he saw as the National Science Foundation's elitist academic biases.

INFORMATION AND IDEOLOGY IN CLEVELAND

Perry and Humphrey began their crusades immediately after Sputnik's launch. Although the National Science Foundation (NSF), the National Academy of Sciences, and the American Documentation Institute had been planning the largest meeting on science information systems ever held since 1956, Perry, Shera, Kent, and Millis decided not to wait for that November 1958 international conference in Washington, D.C. They secured an NSF grant and organized a meeting of more than 150 influential leaders in science information to take place in Cleveland in February 1958. The more active participants formed the Council on Documentation Research. Meanwhile, Humphrey began setting up congressional hearings to be held just three months later in Washington, D.C. During both the Cleveland meeting and the congressional hearings, the renewed ideological battle with Communism was a given. Despite the acceptance of many of the New Deal's programs, concerns about creeping Socialism would be voiced at the meeting and hearings.

The Cleveland conclave had a title befitting both Perry's old agenda and the Sputnik crisis: "Information Resources—A Challenge to American Science and Industry."[2] The meeting was held under the umbrella of that Council on Documentation Research created to serve as a postconference advocacy group. Jesse Shera was the formal leader of the meeting, but Perry seems to have set the agenda. He and Shera quickly gained the attendees' agreement that an information emergency existed, that an era of the decline of the West in research had begun,

SPUTNIK'S NEW POLITICS OF INFORMATION

and that unprecedented levels of additional funding were needed to solve both of those crises. There was no sense of relying on the older sponsors of science information, the major philanthropic foundations—government was the target, they declared. Early on, the Council on Documentation Research's representatives agreed to lobby the National Academy of Sciences, the National Research Council, and government officials to devise a politically savvy action agenda.

Perry did not hesitate at the general meeting. He presented a grandiose plan for the multimillion-dollar national, one-stop information center at Western Reserve. He called it the National Center for the Coordination of Scientific and Technical Information. It would, he said, serve as more than a machine-based retrieval center. It would coordinate all the science information services, supervise the adoption and use of the semantic factor classification and telegraphic abstracts, and would conduct research into all phases of science information. Perry was enthusiastic about his semantic factors becoming the lingua franca of science in the Western world although it was based on English words and although France had already demanded that any international system use its language as well as English. Perry made it clear that he regarded the Universal Decimal Classification (UDC) and similar systems as artificial, unfriendly, and inefficient, although the Soviets considered the UDC as essential.

Perry went too far with his proposals. Worse for him, his implicit criticisms of the existing abstracting and indexing services that scholars had relied upon since the emergence of the modern scientific infrastructure in the late nineteenth century backfired. Those private organizations felt threatened, more than the government services. Fearing that Perry's plan could lead to his center absorbing them, the nonprofits' leaders acted. Although the larger nonprofit services were already in the process of forming their own umbrella organization, the National Federation of Science Abstracting and Indexing Services (NFSAIS), at an NSF-sponsored gathering in Philadelphia, all the old services' representatives in Cleveland protested Perry's plans.[3]

THE NFSAIS'S CRUSADE FOR A PLURAL SYSTEM

Beginning with fourteen of the largest services (with *Biological Abstracts* in the lead), NFSAIS soon enrolled most of the nation's some five hundred science-related private abstracting and indexing organizations. Miles Conrad, the editor of *Biological Abstracts* and NFSAIS's leader, thought the organization could prevent encroachments by government services, or the likes of Perry's, by lobbying, by eliminating redundancies in coverage, and by encouraging the sharing of resources.

NFSAIS quickly found some important allies in its battle to preserve a plural science information system, one with a mix of government, nonprofit, and for-profit providers. John Green of the Department of Commerce and the leaders of the National Academy of Sciences helped NFSAIS's cause. Later, as new pressures hit them, the traditional non-profit academic publishers joined in NFSAIS's struggle. After a long wait they formed the Association of Learned and Professional Society Publishers in 1971.[4]

Well before then, and before NFSAIS became active, other protests had led to alterations in Perry's ambitions. He reduced the scope of his proposed center. By the end of 1958's Cleveland meeting Perry had to back away from his original proposal for a single provider and from his criticisms of the existing services. The meeting's summary gave explicit recognition to the value of America's unique mixed (plural) system and admitted that the Soviet centralized model would not be a good fit with Western traditions. At that point, Perry put emphasis on his proposed center's potential to help coordinate (with the aid of the American Documentation Institute) all of America's services to fill in gaps in the coverage of scientific and technical literature. He emphasized his center's potential to integrate literature from many disciplines to satisfy interdisciplinary and mission-oriented needs.

A STAR IS BORN IN CLEVELAND

Despite Perry's retreat, his, Shera, and Kent's visions remained grand. They foresaw Western Reserve erecting a building larger than its new library for their center; a yearly payroll of some thirty-five million dollars; coordinated regional centers; and, a government subsidy of twenty-five million dollars a year for a decade when, they were sure, the center would become more than self-supporting. They also planned an expanded version of the American Documentation Institute's old Bibliophile service, a microfilming center that would supply copies of any scientific article to distant customers. When communications technology was ready, the center was also to coordinate the creation of such innovations as teletype networks.[5] All that meant that even Perry's scaled-down center would be a giant compared to the existing nongovernmental providers. It would be twenty times the size of *Biological Abstracts* and three times that of *Chemical Abstracts*, America's and the world's abstracting giant.

The Cleveland group had reasons to be optimistic about the center's realization because they had become information science's first media stars. Two weeks before the Cleveland meeting a local newspaper reporter interviewed Allen Kent and wrote an eight-column story about Western Reserve's national center plan. The article included an admiring section on the great retrieval machine.[6] The story was picked up by the largest American newspapers, wire services, and popular magazines—even by the foreign press. One consequence was that Allen Kent was called upon to host a visiting Soviet delegation that had heard of the Reserve's work and, soon, he was asked to spend a month in the Soviet Union. Within a year, other important American information leaders, such as John Green of the Office of Technical Services, Miles Conrad of *Biological Abstracts*, and Dale Baker of *Chemical Abstracts*, made information pilgrimages to Moscow as part of President Eisenhower's push for détente.[7]

On Kent's return from Russia he wrote a glowing review of VINITI and seemed unconcerned about possible criticism for admiring a Communist achievement, or about his article's seeming turn-away from Perry's recent promise to preserve America's plural information arrangement. Kent's VINITI review included strong hints that Western Reserve could provide America with a comparable solution to its information crisis.[8] Kent and Perry also prepared a moving picture film about the future Cleveland center to use for fund-raising purposes. Allen then drafted a long article on "A Machine That Does Research" that was soon published in the popular *Harper's Magazine*.[9]

An important result of the newspaper stories about the Western Reserve project was a phone call to Cleveland from Senator Hubert

264   CHAPTER 15

Humphrey, the liberal Democrat, who was pursuing his own science agenda.

MORE POLITICS OF SCIENCE AND INFORMATION

Hubert Humphrey was not from the working class, but he was not a child of the secure middle class.[10] His family's precarious status had shaped his sympathy for the poor. Born in 1911 to the family of a pharmacist whose Minneapolis business suffered during the Great Depression, Hubert entered the University of Minnesota but left and earned a pharmacist's license at age twenty. He worked in his father's store for six years and then decided to obtain his college degree, but not in pharmacology or medicine. He chose political science. He never explained why he chose the faraway Louisiana State University for his studies, why he returned to Minneapolis when World War II began, or why he took rather mundane bureaucratic jobs and then a position as an untenured college instructor. It is clear, however, that he became devoted to politics rather than academia and that he was a left-leaning liberal. At age thirty-two, and exempt from the draft due to disabilities, he ran for mayor of Minneapolis but was defeated. He did not abandon politics, however. He won the 1945 mayoral race, staying on for three years until he was elected to his first of three terms in the United States Senate. By then, 1948, he had become a major force in the liberal wing of the Democratic Party and a friend and colleague of the founders of the Americans for Democratic Action (ADA), the liberal organization led by some of America's most respected intellectuals.

Humphrey might have become more than just a leftist liberal had his 1944 attempt to unite the radical Minnesota Farmer-Labor Party and the state's Democratic Party not been nearly undermined by what he believed was a Communist plot. That was one of the reasons why he felt comfortable being close to Reinhold Niebuhr and Arthur Schlesinger Jr. of the ADA, the men who were instrumental after World War II in the crusade against Communism, and why Humphrey had no regrets over supporting 1950s legislation that outlawed the American Communist Party.

Hubert first arrived in Washington just in time to witness the defeat of Henry Wallace's campaign to make science a handmaiden of "the people." Humphrey, however, remained a New Dealer and was not afraid of government action. In 1957, when he was leading the Senate Committee on reorganization of government operations, he and his assistant Walter Reynolds, who had aided Henry Wallace's earlier science efforts, and John Green of the Department of Commerce's Technical Information Service, decided the time was right for another attempt to make the federal government's science programs efficient and focused on social needs.

Humphrey's proposed Science and Technology Act of 1958 was far reaching. A cabinet-level department would be created and most all civilian agencies that conducted science activity, including the Atomic Energy Commission, and what became the National Aeronautics and Space Administration, would be transferred to it with, as Henry Wallace had envisioned, the Department of Commerce holding the policy and bureaucratic strings. Even the National Science Foundation was to be made a part of the new bureaucracy, perhaps as less than an equal partner with a reenergized Office of Technical Services (OTS). The foundation's supporters worried that Humphrey's plan would lead to amateurs and politicians rather than scientists determining what research to conduct and what funding priorities would be.

As Humphrey and Reynolds were drawing up their science policy legislation, and preparing hearings on it, they became aware of the so-called information problem and the various proposals to cure it. Even though they were left leaning and supporters of small business, they were drawn to the idea of a centralized science information facility, perhaps one to be run by the government. When they read of Western Reserve's machine and Perry's plans, they thought they had found a viable plan. Jesse Shera and John Millis were contacted. They agreed to provide all the information from their February conference and began preparing to testify at Humphrey's scheduled May 1958 hearing. As they were doing so, word of Humphrey's ambitions for a unified science department and, it seemed, an allied central information service, reached others with different information visions and political orientations.

FOR APPLIED SCIENCE, NOT FOR THOSE PESKY PROFESSORS

The May 1958 congressional hearings opened with a statement by Humphrey that protested too much. He made a short reference to all the complaints about America's existing information systems, ranging from the inability of the academic journals and indexes to provide timely coverage to the inefficiencies of government providers. He then acted like a politician and spent much time declaring that his hearing did not presume that the nation's information system needed any significant reform or that his committee was in favor of shifting federal dollars to a centralized or socialized system.

After that, he essentially turned the first day of the hearings over to Jesse Shera who presented, along with Perry and Kent, the Reserve's plan. They showed their promotional film. Shera also offered reports, some prepared by members of Humphrey's staff, that painted a very bleak picture of the state of the American science information system. The nation was wasting hundreds of millions of dollars a year because of a lack of access to previous research and, at best, only 30 percent of the world's science literature was being indexed, usually too late, they asserted. They reported that in many cases it was cheaper to do research than to find the previous literature on a problem. One memorable and oft-cited supposed fact in their reports was that a 1950s five-year-long American research project on automatic translation machines had wasted more than one million dollars because a very important article with the solution to a circuit design problem had been published in a Soviet journal before the American project began, but was not discovered until its conclusion.

One very long report cited by Shera was authored by Jennie and Herschel Clesner of Humphrey's staff. It criticized all the government agencies and was especially hard on the academically oriented Library of Congress and the National Science Foundation. The Clesners had extremely harsh words about the foundation because, they claimed, it was the major force blocking the creation of an efficient and unified national system. That was an implicit criticism of the academic professor types and of organizations such as NFSAIS that represented their interests.[11]

After presenting the documents Shera also protested too much. He stated he was against any slavish imitation of VINITI or any threats to America's existing unique services but continued on to support a centralized system outside of, but using, government support. He let friends know that he was also in favor of the creation of a new independent National Institute of Documentation if Humphrey's great science department was established.

Others who had been at the Cleveland meeting went further in support of information centralization and government's role in it during their congressional appearances. Merritt L. Kastens of Stanford University's great research center, the Stanford Research Institute, was also in favor of a centralized system that would perform many coordinating as well as operational functions. Based on studies by his colleagues (such as the soon to be famous Charles P. Bourne and Douglas Engelbart) he estimated the center would need a yearly budget four hundred times larger than that of *Biological Abstracts*. Presumably, his National Technical Information Service would be based near the Stanford campus. Although Kastens accepted a greater role for government than had Shera, it was not a total one. He pointed to the invaluable work being done by the almost five thousand independent special libraries that had emerged in industry and government since World War II and emphasized how the Stanford center could serve their applied-science needs, especially by processing the technical reports the academic providers were unable to handle or the OTS provide.

Perhaps he and the Cleveland group were not aware the National Science Foundation and the Council on Library Resources had just given a million-dollar start-up grant to the National Bureau of Standards to begin to establish its version of a centralized science information operation, or, that one of the newest items in Humphrey's legislative proposal was a provision that another agency planned to be under the Commerce Department, the Bureau of Technical Services (a vastly expanded version of John Green's OTS), was to have the power to establish a comprehensive system.

There were additional voices at the 1958 hearing that supported the goal of creating greatly enhanced systems to serve applied and big science's needs. Eugene Jackson was one of the nation's most influential new special librarians. He had the perfect background to lead some of the most important government and industrial research information centers. He began his career as an engineer, and then obtained a library degree just before being drafted during World War II and sent to work as an army technical librarian in Europe. He was then assigned to Dayton, Ohio, to run the air force's new information center where he became an expert in handling reports. Then, he became the head of the precursor to NASA's information services. By the time of the Humphrey hearings, he led the impressive General Motor's library at its research center in Michigan. He testified that a great national center would aid all industrial research laboratories, that it would bolster the American economy, and that corporations such as General Motors would be such a center's best customers.

Another advocate for more government help for applied research and development was Mortimer Taube, one of the first men to become an information millionaire. After a long career as a government librarian, including working on the Library of Congress's secret projects, he had devised his Uniterm system and formed Documentation Inc., a for-profit company that processed and distributed reports and other materials for major government agencies such as NASA, as well as for private corporations—all on a contract basis. His first interaction with Hubert Humphrey had been to submit a proposal for a costly study of how to unite all the government agencies and the major private organizations. His testimony at the hearing was a bit different. He spoke against any fears of "socialized" information, and he called for more government investment in information systems—with a subtext that because of their efficiency it was for-profit services such as his that should be most generously supported.

FOR THE COMMON SCHOLAR, OPEN ACCESS BEFORE ITS TIME, AND FOR PURE SCIENCE

There were other advocates at the hearings, ones who were not always oriented to information for applied and big science's needs. Nor were they in favor of the centralization and "socialization" of information services, or of Humphrey's plans for a people's Department of Science. The range of opinions was reminiscent of that of the 1920s struggle that had caused so much pain for science publishers such as Herbert Haviland Field. There were representatives of the interests of traditional academic research scholars and of typical college instructors who just needed to keep aware of the major trends in their field. There was also a subtle but very influential voice that represented somewhat of a throwback, the lone genius researcher.

Some of those who testified for the recognition of the needs of those in "old science" must have startled James Perry. James D. Mack, a librarian at Pennsylvania's Lehigh University, had worked at the Western Reserve center and was on the committee that organized the February meeting in Cleveland. He had explored the potentials of teletype and facsimile transmission for the Reserve's program and for libraries in general.[12] He spoke, he implied, for the typical university library's needs. He was for increased support for the established academic indexing and abstracting services. He argued against Shera and Perry's proposed centralized and mechanized operation because it had the potential to undermine the older providers. He did not want to leave a typical academic library with no choice but to subscribe to an expensive service that would call for submitting requests and waiting for a response. He said that if there was to be a new role for the federal government it should be that of giving additional funds to the major nonprofit indexing and abstracting services that provided affordable hard-copy volumes that individual libraries could control and that were accessible to their patrons.

Mack was not alone in trying to protect the traditional services and scholars. Some of the most powerful men in the library and the science information field came to their defense and questioned the need for any great central facility. Evan Jay Crane of *Chemical Abstracts*, Miles Conrad of *Biological Abstracts*, and Elmer Hutchisson of the American Institute of Physics (all NFSAIS supporters) were also among the very few who began publicly questioning the "information crisis" premise that pointed to the inadequacy of the services provided by nonprofit organizations.[13]

As well, Quincy Mumford of the Library of Congress (LC) was direct in his letter to Humphrey's committee. He rejected the claims that the LC failed to collect foreign science information, citing facts showing that the library had the nation's, perhaps the world's, largest collection, one gained through some sixteen thousand exchange programs. Mumford asserted the library held more than 60 percent of all Soviet and bloc science and technology publications and that it even had a vigorous program to acquire technical reports from America's agencies. (He did not mention the ongoing CIA-LC relationship or that the library was also the recipient of the extra periodicals the CIA's Foreign Documents Division was collecting.) Mumford also rejected the claim that what the library had on its shelves sat unused. He stated the library had its own science division (it held over one million items and had a staff of more than seventy-five) and had accepted millions of dollars from the military agencies to translate the books and articles in its collection.

He then became confrontational. He objected to any plan, such as Humphrey's, for a science department that would take the exchange program away from the library. It was illogical, he said, to set up a new agency, such as a National Library of Science under the president, and leave Congress's library holding millions of orphaned items.

Evan Jay Crane of the Chemical Abstracts Service (CAS) was a bit more subdued in his long letter to Humphrey. He sidestepped mentioning some financial problems that his and other nonprofits had faced since World War II. But Crane made it clear that he saw no information crisis and that he was against any proposal that would undermine the independent services. He had a bundle of statistics to demonstrate how CAS had overcome challenges during the Great Depression. He emphasized the success of CAS's post–World War I program creating the type of cooperative international abstracting system favored by the Rockefeller Foundation and the League of Nations. With volunteers from around the world, and a staff of two hundred in the United States, CAS, he said, was publishing ten thousand abstracts a month and had become the West's premier chemical information service—one that outshone the Soviet system, especially because CAS now indexed all its abstracts, something not usually done in the Eastern Bloc.

Those indexes, once declared superfluous for all but university teaching, were now seen to be so valuable that CAS had put aside an amount more than its annual budget to finance a ten-year cumulative index. Crane was also very proud because CAS was, he claimed, able to cover almost 100 percent of the world's chemical literature, and at a low cost because, over its fifty-year life, it had carefully maintained its reputation as an impartial institution without a tinge of nationalism. Crane implied that a government service might not be able to maintain such cooperation because of continued nationalistic and Cold War fears.

Miles Conrad, the head of *Biological Abstracts* (*BA*), and NFSAIS, put many of the same ideas forward, but more forcefully. Although he could not claim as much coverage of the world's biological and agricultural literature as CAS's for chemistry, he asserted that *BA*'s coverage was more than adequate and as good as or better than VINITI's. He then hinted that seeking complete coverage of all journals and reports was more than a bit of a fool's errand. Most important work appeared in a relatively small subset of publications, he stated. Like Crane, Conrad skipped over some problems and emphasized how important *BA*'s international volunteer-based system based on the traditional norms of pure academic science was and how much damage might be done if a government organization replaced it.

He also emphasized how efficient and speedy *BA*'s operations were. He was proud that *BA* was following the new international standards for author written abstracts, although many academic purists still demanded abstracts written by information professionals in every field a document touched upon. Conrad did skirt an underlying issue about international cooperation. He stated that while the International Council of Scientific Unions' science information program, the postwar version of the 1920s Institute for Intellectual Cooperation, was making some headway, most bibliographic and abstracting services were still creatures of their own nations and even the long-sought goal of a postcard exchange program for the prepublication announcement of articles remained unfulfilled.

As had Crane, Conrad stressed that America's independent academic services were now on a sound financial basis. He took special aim at those who, he said, claimed they were already government operations because they relied on so many subsidies to survive. He admitted that *BA* had taken some monies from the government, but only to speed up its operations and in an amount totaling less than 7 percent of its budget. He acknowledged that *BA* and the other services would accept more financial help, but only to accelerate processing, not for survival needs.

When Conrad put on his hat as the leader of NFSAIS, he became a more effective defender of the independent nonprofit services. He had tables showing that America's major indexing, abstracting, and listing services covered 55 percent of all the world's sci-tech publications. If

INFORMATION FOR THE ACADEMIC LITTLE GUY

Elmer Hutchisson, another academic publisher, shared in Crane's and Conrad's defenses of the older services—but he had a much different focus, one reminiscent of Burton Livingston's tussle with the National Research Council in the 1920s. Although Hutchisson had participated in applied and group projects since World War II, he spoke not for the pressured academic researcher who needed and could afford indexes and abstracts, but for the more typical individual college professor–teacher who wished only to keep up with the latest developments in a field of study. Hutchisson's testimony must have been a surprise because he represented the nonprofit American Institute of Physics and he and many other American physicists were heavily involved in big science. He declared that the traditional academic journals, not indexing and abstract services, were the ones in need of and deserving of subsidies. He spoke against a torrent of uncritical citations and abstracts that overwhelmed a scientist. What was needed, he said, were more quality journals provided at low cost that featured evaluative review articles composed by the best men in each field.

After outlining the common scholar's needs, Hutchisson launched into an advocacy of the expansion of an early version of the "gold" open access argument of the twenty-first century. He stated that the cost of publishing the many excellent articles in physics had skyrocketed since World War II and the number of articles per issue had increased. To be able to keep subscriptions at an affordable level, a page-charge policy had been instituted by many journals. Authors or their institutions were asked to pay a fee, then as much as $150 a page, to cover the cost of publication. Hutchisson complained that while universities and corporations usually agreed to the charges, many government agencies, perhaps for legal reasons, were reluctant to do so. So, Hutchisson asked Humphrey's committee to recommend that page charges (dissemination subsidies) be made an integral part of every government research program so that the typical professor or student could have access to the best of America's research.

SPUTNIK'S NEW POLITICS OF INFORMATION

Another contributor to Humphrey's meeting was more delicate than others when objecting to Humphrey's proposals for the science department and an American VINITI. But William O. Baker was such an important man in American science's politics that even his guarded criticisms had great influence. Baker was not only the leader of Bell Laboratories, the nation's most advanced corporate research center, but a member of the Republican-oriented President's Science Advisory Committee (PSAC). Baker was leading his own panel on the information problem for President Eisenhower.

What Baker told Humphrey was in plainer language in his PSAC report, but in both instances his points were that America's traditional science information services should be aided, not diminished in any way; that the National Science Foundation should remain focused, as Vannevar Bush had wanted, on the individual research scientist's needs and priorities; that the cure for the science information overload was the government's helping to coordinate the existing services; that scientists did not want to be excluded from the information process by bureaucrats; and, most important, all efforts should be focused on helping the individual scientist's "genius." Baker, of course, had no liking for a unified science department.

MORE OBJECTIONS TO PERRY'S AND HUMPHREY'S AMBITIONS

The traditional science advocates were not the only ones reacting to Sputnik and plans like Perry's and Humphrey's. The military had its new science initiative, one that would later have a great impact on all type of information processing. In 1958, President Eisenhower had the Department of Defense create its Advanced Research Projects Agency (ARPA, later DARPA), mandating it to pursue high-risk, adventurous research to be overseen and conducted by university researchers, such as those at MIT.[14] ARPA spawned its Information Processing Technology Office (IPTO) in 1962 as a successor to its older command and control research center. With its vast resources, the IPTO laid the foundation for high-speed nationwide computer networking (ARPANET) and computerized information processing, although few of its researchers or leaders were information professionals. Most were computer sci-

274   CHAPTER 15

entists and engineers who were creating their own niche in the science information field.

In addition to the military, government science information providers, many times under direct pressures from a seemingly endless series of presidential and congressional investigations following Baker's PSAC report,[15] began to organize to fend off the threat of a centralized service. The process began informally in the 1950s with heads of the major agencies voluntarily cooperating to try to establish common standards. Then, after the President's Science Advisory Committee once again demanded action, the Committee on Scientific and Technical Information (COSATI) was created in 1962. It had more resources for reforming government systems than earlier panels but had a difficult battle and had to endure much criticism as it sought ways to achieve coordination.

Humphrey's 1958 hearings and efforts such as COSATI did not lead to radical changes, and the opinions expressed at the historic November 1958 science information conference in Washington suggested the United States would look to technology and methods, not politics, to solve its science information problems.

NOTES

1. United States Senate, *Science and Technology Act of 1958, Hearings before a Subcommittee of the Committee of Government Operations, United States Senate Eighty-Fifth Congress, Second Session, on S.31026*, May 2, 6, and 7, 1958 (Humphrey Committee).

2. Jesse H. Shera, Allen Kent, and James W. Perry, *Information Resources: A Challenge to American Science and Industry* (New York: Press of Western Reserve University, Interscience, 1958).

3. *New York Times*, February 1, 1958.

4. Robert Heller & Associates, *A National Plan for Science Abstracting and Indexing Services* (Philadelphia: NFAIS, 1963); M. Lyne Neufeld et al., *Abstracting and Indexing Services in Perspective: Miles Conrad Memorial Lectures 1969–1983* (Philadelphia: NFAIS, 1983).

5. Allen Kent and James W. Perry, *Centralized Information Services: Opportunities and Problems* (New York: Interscience, 1958); on ADI, http://www.loc.gov/rr/scitech/trs/trsadi.html//.

6. National Council of Jewish Women, interview with Allen Kent, May 12, 1993.

7. *New York Times*, November 9, 1959.

8. Allen Kent and A. S. Inerall, "Soviet Documentation: A Trip Report," *American Documentation* 10, no. 1 (January 1959): 1–19. Informative on other reports on Soviet information and computer efforts is: Nicholas Lewis, "Peering through the Curtain: Soviet Computing through the Eyes of Western Experts," *IEEE Annals of the History of Computing* 38 (January–March 2016): 34–44. THE CIA's CREST files contain many surveys of Soviet computer achievements.

9. Allen Kent, "A Machine That Does Research," *Harper's*, April 1959, 1–6.

10. Charles Lloyd Garrettson III, *Hubert H. Humphrey: The Politics of Joy* (New Brunswick, NJ: Transaction, 1993).

11. Shera submitted the Clesners' report without a full citation (p. 23) but it seems to have been a version of their "Technical, Scientific, and Engineering Information as a Factor in Competitive Coexistence," *Federal Law Journal* 17 (November 3, 1957): 236.

12. Kent and Perry, *Centralized Information Services*, 47.

13. A. G. Oettinger, "An Essay in Information Retrieval: The Birth of a Myth," *Information and Control* 8 (1965): 64–79.

14. Sharon Weinberger, *The Imagineers of War: The Untold Story of DARPA* (New York: Knopf, 2017).

15. Harold Wooster, "Historical Note: Shining Palaces, Shifting Sands: National Information Systems," *JASIS* 38, no. 5 (September 1987): 321–35.

16

AN AMERICAN INFORMATION CENTURY?

Five months after the conclusion of Senator Humphrey's 1958 hearings, the National Defense Education Act (NDEA) was made law in October, just a month before the great international science information conference was to begin. The NDEA would have a profound impact on higher education and information services. It had become law after many months of sometimes rancorous congressional negotiations, ones with overtones of antielite populism, and after complaints by liberals that the supposed Sputnik and American science crises were being used to undermine the kind of Progressive education that reformers such as John Dewey had advocated since the turn of the century.[1]

In reaction to Sputnik, the NDEA promised generous amounts for loans and grants to students to pursue university-level science education and millions for enhanced science research and graduate programs—but not for Progressive programs in such things as "life adjustment." The NDEA also included subsidies to encourage foreign language instruction (not including traditional academic "frills" such as Latin or Greek) and programs that would increase science teaching at all educational levels. The act also sponsored experiments in radio and television science instruction. While it precluded aid for the humanities, the act supported some social sciences, such as area studies and sociology, that promised solutions to Soviet and third-world problems.

The NDEA made science information a national priority. A high-level Science Information Council was established to ensure progress. A range of stakeholders were appointed to represent the many views on information systems, including Western Reserve's John Millis, who favored centralized programs for applied science, and Bell Lab's William O. Baker, who spoke for traditional researchers' needs. The NDEA also had provisions for a greatly enhanced National Science Foundation (NSF). In one year, NSF's budget was increased threefold and the allocation for its information section doubled.

WHAT WAS THE NSF TO BECOME?

There were indications that such increases for the NSF would continue in the future—although the NDEA was ambiguous on important questions about NSF's policies. Was Bush's dream of a self-directed but federally funded academia to be the NSF's goal? Or, would the foundation become "the" substitute for a Humphrey- and Wallace-like Department of Science, turning away from supporting abstract academic science? Would the foundation's enlarged Office of Science Information Services have the power to coordinate all the government science information services? Could and should the foundation create its own central science information center? If not, would it support outside centralized facilities such as Perry's or would it focus on bolstering the old organizations?

There were a few hints the agency might be allowed to follow its original mandate of supporting university-based old science and that it would continue to keep its hands off the government's information services. But there were also indications that populist policies like Henry Wallace's might triumph. The NSF was ordered to support engineering research and education for practical knowledge. Hubert Humphrey wanted more. His scheduling of additional congressional hearings suggested that if his cabinet-level department and information center was not established, the NSF would be forced to act as a substitute.

In contrast, William O. Baker's report for the White House [2] and a presidential-ordered Bureau of the Budget study gave additional ammunition to those opposed to Humphrey's plans. The bureau declared both ideas uneconomic and contrary to the rules of government organization. It and Baker's report gave priority to support for the traditional role of the NSF.

NSF'S STRUGGLE FOR INFORMATION INDEPENDENCE AND THE GREAT CONFERENCE

Fortunately for the professor types, Alan Tower Waterman, the long-time head of the NSF, was an academic, through and through. Waterman was a Princeton graduate in physics and a professor at Yale before working for Vannevar Bush as a research manager in the Office of Scientific Research and Development (OSRD) during World War II. After the war, he was a civilian program manager for the dollar-rich Office of Naval Research that quietly became the nation's largest sponsor of abstract research during the 1940s and early 1950s. In 1950, when Waterman agreed to lead the NSF, he used its small allocations to sponsor academic science and traditional information programs. Waterman's choice for the man to head the strengthened Office of Science Information Services after the sudden death in 1957 of Alberto F. Thompson, its previous leader, also suggested the NSF would follow its established policies. Burton Adkinson, Thompson's successor, had served in the Office of Strategic Services (OSS) after receiving a degree in physical geography from Clark University. He then returned to spend a decade at the Library of Congress, leading its research and exchange sections. He was active in the established library organizations such as the Special Library Association and the International Federation for Documentation.

Despite such indications that academic science would be favored, when the long-planned NSF-sponsored Washington, D.C., International Conference on Scientific Information had its first session on November 16, 1958, the future of America's information policies remained uncertain.[3] But trends reflected in the meeting's papers and discussions included three certainties: the United States was now the Western world's information giant; true information internationalism remained just a dream; and indexing and classification methods and technologies were on the brink of major changes.

The conclave's presentations made it appear that it would be an American, not a British or French or German, "information century," and that it was the end of the era of the dominance of semantic factor–like sophisticated classification and indexing systems. The meeting's presentations also indicated that a new wave of information efficiency, empowered by technology, was emerging. To most attendees, technology and methods, not any radical policy changes, were the solutions to the science information crisis.

A NEW NATIONALISM AND A PROFESSION-DEFINING MEETING

The Washington meeting was the first major international information conference ever to be held in the United States. There had been a string of symposiums on science information after World War II, but the important ones had been in England and France, ranging from the Royal Society meeting in 1948 to the Dorking Conference of 1957.[4]

The five-day Washington meeting dwarfed them in size and funding. Generous dollars came from the NSF, the American military, the American government's civilian departments, and some three dozen large corporations. There were one thousand registrants, more than seventy papers, and a sixteen-hundred-page report. Most of the attendees and presenters were from the United States but there were many from the other modern nations. Soviet Russia sent some of its VINITI leaders while England was represented by its most respected experts in science information. Cyril Cleverdon, B. C. Vickery, D. J. Foskett, and J. E. L. Farradane, as well as important newcomers like Karen Sparck-Jones, traveled to Washington. Even J. D. Bernal, Britain's radical-leftist "Red information scientist" who usually voiced his disdain for capitalism, made the trip to America. Jacques Samain (inventor of the Filmorex microform retrieval machine) came from Paris to speak on France's National Centre for Scientific Research information work. Reflecting the worldwide disentrancement with Marxism after the 1956 revelations about Stalin's brutalities and, then, the Soviet invasion of Hungary, Bernal's contribution included nothing about science information "for the people" and Samain refrained from any nationalistic complaint about the United States' anticolonialism policies that had alienated France's leaders.

The American attendees included a few professionals from traditional libraries, but most were of a new breed of information experts in government and industrial information centers. Universities such as MIT that had been involved with science information and automatic translation projects sent representatives. Leon Dostert and Zellig Har-

AN AMERICAN INFORMATION CENTURY? 281

ris were among the many involved in machine translation that came to Washington. There were also men from the Central Intelligence Agency (CIA) and the National Security Agency (NSA), who listed themselves only by their home addresses in the Washington suburbs. All the West Coast's rapidly expanding aero industries sent their computer experts, including Don Swanson. The major computer corporations paid for many of their information experts to attend. Established figures, such as H. P. Luhn of IBM and Claire Schultz of Remington Rand, were joined by younger researchers such as Phyllis Baxendale of IBM's research center in Northern California that served the space industry.

There also were policy makers and science philosophers at the meeting. The famed William O. Baker, John Tukey, Derek J. de Sola Price, and Chauncey D. Leake listened to presentations and made informal comments. Surprisingly, Vannevar Bush, Warren Weaver, and Claude Shannon did not appear, nor were their ideas the focal point of the discussions.

There were some leaders of the new generation of for-profit information services in attendance. Mortimer Taube, Calvin N. Mooers, and Saul Herner were there as well as Eugene Garfield, the struggling young information entrepreneur.[5] Predictably, James Perry, Allen Kent, and Jesse Shera stayed for the entire meeting, at times wrangling with a rather cynical Ralph Shaw. They did not, however, use the meeting's formal presentations to advance their proposed center's cause, perhaps because of prior agreements to keep the meeting nonpolitical.

WE WILL BE OBJECTIVE

The sessions began with contributions that were restricted to professional concerns about typical library and information problems. The first papers reviewed the major existing classification methods and studies of user behavior. The meeting moved to a discussion of the international abstracts/indexing problem, but without making a choice between what one commentator posed as the only three alternative solutions to the science information crises: a centralized VINITI-like system; the purely voluntary cooperative International Council of Scientific Unions approach; or, the older Western pluralistic model of large specialized services, such as Chemical Abstracts, mixed with smaller independent nonprofit, government, and for-profit services. Other papers and panels indicated there were still those who were committed to realizing the old dreams of cooperative, nonprofit worldwide information systems, such as those found in the idealistic dreams of Paul Otlet and H. G. Wells, but those papers and comments did not include any practical solutions.

There were also some discussions that anticipated an issue that arose again and again in the 1960s: Were scientists or information professionals to play the dominant role in designing and managing science information services?

TRADITIONS AND HIERARCHY BE DAMNED

The conference then began concentrating on technical matters, such as techniques for superimposed coding and on the use of Zipf and other word frequency systems. The participants who were using punch-card technologies contributed several papers on superimposition, something Luhn worked on. The problem he and others faced was that cards had room for only a limited number of code areas. Several papers put forward techniques for imposing several codes in a single space. There were also some contributions on topics that fit with information efficiency, but not with Perry's semantic factors or any other elegant intellectual approach to organizing or retrieving information.

The meeting's emphasis was on greater innovations than superimposed coding. The first hints of the possibility of a fundamental and widespread change in information methods came from the representatives from England. Their presentations were somewhat of a surprise. While England's Dorking Conference of the previous year had emphasized the value of traditional comprehensive classification methods, with an emphasis on universal factor approaches, in 1958 there were cautions about the worth of any general scheme. The grand Universal Decimal Classification that many European nations still favored was treated as outmoded and even factor and colon systems must, the British commented, yield to limited ones designed for special fields.

Frederick Jonker, an American colleague of Mortimer Taube, joined in and became philosophical about the issue. He declared the old hierarchical methods and even colon/aspect classifications fit the nine-

AN AMERICAN INFORMATION CENTURY? 283

teenth century when the world seemed stable and science was focused on categorizing everything. Today's world was different, he asserted, and he demanded the use of new information methods, ones that fit an ever-changing world that was not hierarchical. Any new method, he stated, must also respond to the needs of a new era of information democracy where diverse viewpoints on any subject had to be acknowledged. After laying that foundation, he emphasized that fixed, single categorization systems like Dewey's, Bliss's, or even Ranganathan's were clearly unsuited to the new worlds of applied science and engineering. Amazing technologies, he hinted, were to soon allow powerful new cost-saving methods that could deal with diversity.

Hans Peter Luhn did more than hint. He gave a demonstration of the power of computers and of methods that relied on the contents of documents rather than "outside" categories or information professionals' judgments. He showed his KWIC indexes and his much more radical method to create abstracts by using computers and simple algorithms on the full text or just the abstracts of articles. His ideas pointed the way to a great leap in information efficiency.

While computers in 1958 were not yet ready, and while using word counts on full text awaited an era when publications were composed on computers, others besides Luhn were exploring information retrieval methods that skirted the need for indexes, abstracts, and, especially, costly human intervention. Their innovations went beyond the experiments that had begun in the early 1950s using electronic computers to select documents based on their index entries. Karen Sparck-Jones of England, who had previously been devoted to methods like Ranganathan's, gave a paper at the 1958 meeting that showed the similarity of methods for automatic translation and information retrieval. She predicted they both would soon be applied in real settings. The young scholar Victor H. Yngve of MIT gave a presentation that was more direct and boastful about machine-based, full-text searching's potentials.

Other participants were busy developing more advanced approaches, all based on complex mathematical algorithms, not expensive and fallible human judgments. Coming from institutions with large budgets and the most advanced computer facilities, Edmund Stiles of the National Security Agency, M. E. Maron of the defense contractor TRW, and Phyllis Baxendale of IBM's San Jose center reported on studies showing that sophisticated probabilistic algorithms and fast computers with large memories would soon replace humans in the abstracting and retrieval processes.

The fulfillment of such dreams awaited a revolution in computer power, but two others at the 1958 meeting had ideas for methodological alternatives that were already, or about to become, operational. Although the two were very different men from almost opposite backgrounds, they both had been motivated by the call for methods that matched the way new applied scientists thought. One was well known; the other was about to make his mark.

NEW METHODS FOR SCIENCE INFORMATION, EFFICIENCY TRUMPS ELEGANCE

One of the most famous of the first new systems was Mortimer Taube's previously described Uniterms. Taube came from a solid middle-class family that could help him attend the prestigious University of Chicago to study philosophy and then to obtain a Ph.D. in the subject at the University of California at Berkeley in 1935. It seems that Taube was deeply influenced by the illustrious Alfred North Whitehead. Despite having written an impressive dissertation titled "Causation, Freedom and Determinism: An Attempt to Solve the Causal Problem through a Study of Its Origins in Seventeenth Century Philosophy," Taube received no academic job offers. As a stopgap he obtained a library degree at Berkeley in 1936, then worked in a series of insecure library and lecturing positions around the country for eight years. The jobs were not demanding and gave him time to pursue his philosophical interests. He also studied the newest approaches to logic. Well before the era of the new math, Taube became a crusader for the use of the Boolean logic that became so important to computer circuitry, software, and, later, to information searching techniques that depended on statistics.[6]

Taube put all his academic studies to good use, but not in a way that could secure him a philosophy professorship. As soon as he began his library career he published noteworthy articles on traditional library subjects while also becoming recognized as a leader in new library techniques. In 1944, he finally landed a permanent job, one at the Library of Congress (LC). He was soon recognized as a classification

AN AMERICAN INFORMATION CENTURY? 285

expert and as a proficient manager. As described above, he worked on the military's large-scale bibliographic projects at the library during and after World War II. Finding that existing classification methods did not fit the materials, and needing to speed production, he developed what became his Uniterm Coordinate Indexing. It was based on techniques that had been gradually developing for more than a decade, and it had some echoes of the facet items appended to the hierarchical codes in Dewey's and the Universal Decimal Classification's (UDC) systems.

Using his experience in dealing with scientific and technical documents, his training in the new math's logic, and his education as a philosopher, Taube refined the previous "term" methods. He added in his sharp business mind. As a result, as the government increasingly contracted out its classification-indexing work during the early 1950s, Taube founded the for-profit company Documentation Inc., and became the first science information millionaire.

WORDS, WORDS, NOT CONCEPTS

Taube had not invented his terms system on his own. Innovators in England had been using an approach like Uniterms since the mid-1930s. Articles about such methods had appeared in professional journals in the 1930s. As well, before the end of World War II a commercial system for small collections with a technology to partially automate term-based retrieval had been developed. The Batten system used punched sheets that were slid over each other in a way much like that done by the codebreakers of World War II. In Batten's optical coincidence system, the punched sheets were manipulated across each other until light appeared through an appropriate combination of holes. Those coincidences indicated the desired items. That system was displayed at the important Royal Society conference on science information in 1948. Before then, in 1947, an American, Calvin Mooers (Watson Davis's son-in-law) had created his own version of a terms system. Other systems similarly designed for very small document collections appeared in the 1950s.[7]

Mortimer Taube's key innovations came after he became convinced that term methods might be modified to become useful for larger collections, although there were no affordable high-speed machine technologies for such systems.[8] Of great importance, even without advanced technologies, term methods were labor saving and cost effective. Term methods took less time and called for less subject-matter expertise.

There were shortcomings to term systems, especially ones that relied on words from within documents rather than the concepts in a classification system, but Taube was an information pragmatist and was willing to forgo features that allowed protections against such things as "man bites dog" and the lack of a universal terminology to achieve efficiency. Processing speed, cost savings, and searching flexibility were his goals. Taube's Uniterm method was in ways a bare-bones system, but a flexible one. Multiple terms were not combined into a full index entry. They were brought together only when a request was made. They were "postcoordinated." The system's multiple independent entries allowed a user to request a search using any desired combination of the terms. In such systems, a request could be made, for example, for all documents indexed for asthma, bedding, mites, and East Coast; or, for asthma, mold, and Massachusetts. Such flexibility was a practical impossibility with traditional methods or even subject-classified card-form bibliographies. No book or card catalog could contain all the possible cross-links among the indexing words.

Taube's version of a terms system was organized like the index to a book. Individual terms were listed along with the indicators for the documents that contained them. At first, Taube used a primitive technology. Each indexing term had its own large paper index card with documents' identifying numbers listed on it. To find items, the several related term cards were pulled then examined by eye to find the document identifiers that were on all the pulled cards. With a relatively small file that was not a forbidding task, but to realize its potential, the term method needed the power of technologies such as IBM's electro-mechanical collators and sorters and, later, electronic computers.

The technical challenge was not the number of terms (they stabilized at some thirty thousand in the largest systems) but identifying the documents' identification numbers. For a solution to that, Taube turned to mechanization. With so many government agencies poised to use terms systems, there seemed to be a market for an affordable special information machine. So, IBM consented to build COMAC, a clever but ungainly enhanced special-purpose collator system, for Taube.

AS THEY PROBABLY THOUGHT, A HORATIO ALGER INFORMATION SCIENCE STORY

Another and more revolutionary method that threatened James Perry's semantic factors success and that challenged the traditional indexing and abstracting services was brought to life by Eugene Garfield. His method was perhaps the closest to meeting Bush's demands for "association" and arguably the most efficient and the flexible of the substitutes for traditional classification/indexing. Although Garfield's citation indexing did not reach the market until the mid-1960s, and while it was oriented to traditional academic publications, it had been a bother to Perry and Kent well before then.

Eugene Garfield was an unusual man with a background very different from Mortimer Taube's. Garfield came from an odd background for a librarian, for an information scientist, or for an information entrepreneur. He was from a second-generation New York City Jewish immigrant family that was part of the respectable but near-poor working class. The family had, however, a strong intellectual bent. Eugene might have become a Communist because a few of his relatives did have ties to 1930s radical organizations, and to aggressive labor unions such as Big Bill Haywood's IWW, but he was too young (born 1925) to be recruited by his leftist relatives during the heyday of American Communism. Eugene never became a radical, but he always had an underlying commitment to social justice. One of his later information goals reflected his sympathy for less fortunate scholars. He wanted to find a means to aid scientists ill treated by the peer review process of his time. (One of his solutions, citation indexing/ranking, became essential to the success of Google, the giant of the Internet.) Garfield also had strong beliefs about the moral obligations of science and scientists, partly because he was influenced by the writings of J. D. Bernal, England's "Red scientist."[10]

Eugene's early manhood was almost a classic Horatio Alger rags, but with little riches, story. He attended New York City's neighborhood public schools, at times taking such vocational subjects as typing and printing. During his school years he endured some health issues, as well as having to work at rather menial jobs to help support his family. Partly because of the burdens of work and health, Eugene was not an academic marvel as a teenager. But that did not dampen his enthusiasm for learning. When a family member gave him a few books about chemistry, it sparked an interest that lasted a lifetime and, although having little free time, he satisfied his deep appetite for learning through long visits to New York City's libraries. After completing high school, Eugene made a rather unusual decision. He risked his future and the little money he had and decided to be the first Garfield to go to college. He had developed ambitions to be, like James Perry, a chemical engineer, but he did not choose Cornell, or the nearby Brooklyn Polytechnic College that Joe Becker had attended—although Eugene might have received some financial aid from those schools. Rather, he moved across the country to the University of Colorado and enrolled in its engineering department. Surprisingly, he soon left and spent a few months in California building ships for the war effort. He returned to New York to try to join the merchant marine but the army drafted him. He was on his way to becoming an officer but a medical problem soon led to an honorable discharge. Eugene was adrift again.

A bit of America's version of Socialism then gave him some latitude. The government had decided to subsidize military veterans as they pursued further education through the GI Bill.

FINDING HIS WAY AND SEARCHING FOR AN INFORMATION NICHE, JAMES PERRY, ONCE AGAIN THE 101

Garfield's college choice this time was Columbia University and, oddly, the study of the French language. That lasted only a few months. Then, he was off to the University of California at Berkeley to enter a premedical program. Although he was living on his meager government income, he took on the responsibility of marriage and fatherhood. Within a short time, there was a divorce. He again dropped out of school and headed back to New York, now carrying the responsibility of a young child. The twenty-one-year-old reenrolled at Columbia, this time as chemistry major. He did well in the program but his 1949 degree did not guarantee a good job. He decided to continue his chemistry studies,

AN AMERICAN INFORMATION CENTURY?

this time at the University of Pennsylvania. His luck turned on him again. He was injured in an auto accident and had to withdraw from the program. He was also out of money. He had to take a job as a salesclerk while studying Gregg shorthand in hopes of a secretarial position if he failed as a chemist.[11] He then secured a position as a laboratory assistant. It was not well paying but it involved him in some interesting bibliographic challenges. He soon quit, however. At age twenty-five he seemed to be destined for a permanent "rags" status.

Luck then intervened. While on his way to interview for a low-paying job as a medical-chemical secretary, Garfield encountered James Perry, who was then at MIT's chemical information project and working for the CIA. That meeting led Garfield to a stint as a junior researcher at the Johns Hopkins Welch Medical Library's great forward-looking effort to modernize the army's medical information systems. It was one of the few advanced government-sponsored information projects of the time and was using the sophisticated IBM 101 statistical tabulating machine.

Eugene learned a great deal about the device, statistical analysis, librarianship, and advanced classification ideas. Then, some frictions led his wanderlust to take hold once more. After just two years at Johns Hopkins, Garfield was again without much money and had no job in sight. He decided to return to New York and to again become a college student. He enrolled in Columbia University's library school and earned a master's degree in 1954—at age twenty-nine.

While pursuing the degree he wrote a seminal paper on his idea for citation indexing, a fundamentally new way to recover information. It was different from all previous approaches, even terms. However, it did have some precursors in the legal field, and M. M. Kessler of MIT's Technical Information Project would soon produce his version of citation indexing for sci-tech literature.[12]

CITATIONS VERSUS CLASSIFICATION

Garfield believed that using the references (citations) to other works in a publication could serve as the most efficient and least expensive way to "index" and retrieve information. His Columbia thesis, and his 1955 paper, "Citation Indexes for Science: A New Dimension in Documentation through Association of Ideas,"[13] introduced his first thoughts on the method. Significantly, and reflecting Garfield's tendency to always be somewhat of an outsider, the seminal article was not published in a library or even a documentalists' journal. Perhaps without him realizing the importance for his career, the article appeared in the prestigious and widely read *Science* magazine.

The article was not a mere techno-statement. It was a salute to the importance of shaping bibliographic systems to help scientists to expand their visions and concepts by facilitating the association of ideas—something, he asserted, no traditional subject, term, or classified system (such as Dewey's or the Universal Decimal Classification) could do. No indexer or classifier, Garfield stated, could possibly anticipate all the possible uses of a publication. Therefore, old-fashioned indexing, by its nature, would always be biased. Citation indexing was unbiased because it traced all connections in an article, he claimed.

Citation indexing had more advantages, Garfield asserted. It provided the benefits of the specific identification of the many ideas in an article while avoiding the related high cost of separate indexing. Furthermore, he believed that with progress in automation the cost of citation indexing would soon be lowered and it certainly would be much faster than that of services dependent on the judgment of professional indexers. Labor cost would be low because only basic subject-area classification and rather routine logging of citation identifiers would be required. High school graduates could be the new indexers. Most important, Garfield was certain that his methods would lead to weekly or, at worst, biweekly bibliographies, not ones that took months or years to complete.

Garfield soon realized that citations could serve many other needs. His social idealism was reflected by his concept of an "impact factor" that could be calculated from the number of times a publication was cited by others. That statistic would be, he believed, an objective measure of an author's contribution to science. It could overcome what Garfield saw as a tendency for those in science's elites to gain undeserved recognition and overlook the contributions of outsiders.

He may have not imagined, in the mid-1950s, that new and very important information fields would emerge from citation indexing, including bibliometrics and scientometrics, or that he and his methods would lead him to become associated with academic luminaries such as

Robert Merton and Chauncey Leake, both of whom foresaw that citation analysis could be used to define the actual intellectual parameters of a scientific field. Garfield did, however, soon realize that his impact factor could be a means for librarians to decide what journals to add to their collections.

Unluckily, Garfield did not have the funds to start his citation service. In early middle age he remained without a worthwhile job. His future was not bright. He could not even find a slot as a soft-money academic. There was one suggestion of a possibly better future, however. He had been working on developing an innovative, quick, and cost-effective method of indexing the literature of chemistry, including patents. His chemical ideas were not as radical as those concerning citation indexing, but his methods seemed to fit the needs of an industry in a great hurry to overcome its information crisis.

Garfield's chemical information concepts gained the attention of executives in the Philadelphia area's expanding chemical industry—but they only supported some part-time consulting work for him. To supplement his consulting income, Garfield began thinking of resuscitating his ideas for quick current journal-content notification services. At the same time, he enrolled in Zellig Harris's linguistics program at the University of Pennsylvania, seeking a Ph.D. How much Garfield knew of Harris's connection to the CIA's machine translation work is unknown.

IF THE NONPROFITS CAN'T AND THE GOVERNMENT WON'T . . .

While surviving on income from unpredictable consulting work, Garfield took his chemical information and citation indexing ideas to the major nonprofit bibliographic services. *Chemical Abstracts* and *Biological Abstracts* seemed too busy catching up with their backlogs of traditional offerings to explore any far-reaching alternatives. Eugene did not give in. After borrowing money, he converted a shed into an office. The thirty-year-old then spent hours each week indexing articles for several versions of his *Current Contents*. That publication was aimed at scientists and managers in corporate research centers. Sparsely indexed, *Current Contents* used the table of contents of the latest journal issues in each field to keep busy researchers and executives up to date. The series proved somewhat of a success. Garfield was not rich, but now he could at least support himself. However, it was not until the end of the 1950s that the good side of the Horatio Alger story began to emerge.

Garfield had not given up on creating a timely product for information on new chemical compounds. He finally secured a pledge of support from several corporations and added *Index Chemicus* to his small for-profit company's publications list. The *Index* was a different product than *Chemical Abstracts* or *Biological Abstracts*: it was not a substitute for full abstracts but it had a great advantage. Garfield got the *Index* to researchers' desks in weeks, not months. One study showed that Garfield's service was three times faster than those of the established abstract providers. In the mid-1960s, a *Biological Abstracts* item appeared thirty-two weeks after the initial publication of an article while it took *Chemical Abstracts* twenty-seven weeks to report on a publication. Garfield and his small staff were taking just eight weeks.

Just as he was gaining success in the corporate and applied-research markets, an opportunity finally appeared for Garfield to gain a place in the prestigious academic nonprofit information sector. It had taken outside help and some time for the opportunity to appear. Joshua Lederberg, the 1958 Nobel Prize–winning molecular biologist, contacted Garfield about the ideas in Eugene's *Science* article. Lederberg was fascinated by the potentials of citation indexing. He saw it as a means of tracing the history and the actual, not predefined, boundaries of a field of study. Also, important to him, one could search using citations without being constrained by the decisions of an arbitrary classifier. Using his standing as a Nobel winner, and his new position at Stanford University, he obtained grants from the federal government's National Institutes of Health (NIH) and the National Science Foundation (NSF) to apply Garfield's ideas. The grants enabled Eugene to build a citation index to the literature of genetics.

In hopes of more government grants, Garfield changed the name of his firm to the Institute for Scientific Information (ISI) and envisioned turning it into a provider of all types of science information services, but on a scale much smaller than Perry and Kent's visions for Western Reserve.[14] For a moment it seemed Garfield's operation was to join the ranks of the celebrated nonprofit academic bibliographic services. That was not Garfield's fate, however. A little thing would change informa-

AN AMERICAN INFORMATION CENTURY?

tion's history. The NIH terminated the institute's grant, soon followed by the NSF's cancellation of its funding because, Eugene was told, new government policies forbade funding for-profit companies.

Unable or unwilling to found a nonprofit firm, to find a job in academia, or to create a center at a university, Eugene's operation remained a small and struggling for-profit company that had corporations and chemical companies, not academics, as its major customers. His older products continued as his mainstays while the citations projects were once again put on his hold list. However, citation indexing remained a threat to Perry, Kent, and Shera, who had maintained their hopes of establishing their great centralized information center at Western Reserve University.

Although disappointed, Garfield did not abandon his citation method ambitions. It took years of patience, courage, and perseverance. In 1964, when he was nearing forty, his *Science Citation Index* became a regular publication. Over time, his offerings became essential to academic researchers in science and the social sciences. They also attracted the interest of leading historians and sociologists of science. As well, academic administrators embraced citation indexing, seeing it as vital for several reasons. Among them was that counts of citations to a professor's articles appeared to be an unbiased measure to be used in tenure and promotion decisions. Such impersonal and seemingly objective measures of contribution seemed a way for the bureaucracies at the now giant universities to counter growing complaints about the peer review process.

Garfield's tenacity eventually led him to the "riches" side of the Horatio Alger story. His ISI soon had its own multimillion-dollar building; he became a millionaire; and, he became one of the founding members of the Information Industry Association, which would play a significant role in the ongoing battles over "socialized" and, later, "capitalistic" information systems.

NOTES

1. Barbara Barksdale Clowse, *Brainpower for the Cold War: The Sputnik Crisis and the National Defense Education Act of 1958* (Westport, CT: Greenwood, 1981), 39.

2. President's Science Advisory Committee (PSAC), *Improving the Availability of Scientific and Technical Information in the United States* (Baker Report), 1958.

3. NAS-NSF, *Proceedings of the International Conference on Scientific Information, Washington, D.C. Nov. 16–21, 1958*, vol. 2 (Washington, DC: NAS-NSF, 1959).

4. *Proceedings of the International Study Conference on Classification for Information Retrieval Held at Beatrice Webb House, Dorking, England, 13–17th May 1957.*

5. American University, *Machine Indexing: Progress and Problems: Papers Presented at the Third Institute on Information Storage and Retrieval, American University 1961* (Washington, DC: Center for Technology and Administration, 1961).

6. *New York Times*, Mortimer Taube obituary, September 7, 1965, p. 39.

7. Robert S. Casey and James M. Perry, eds., *Punched Cards: Their Applications to Science and Industry* (New York: Reinhold, 1951); Jose-Marie Griffiths and Donald W. King, "US Information Retrieval Systems, Evolution and Evaluation (1945–1975)," *IEEE Annals of the History of Computing* 24, no. 3 (July–September 2002): 35–54.

8. Mortimer Taube, *Studies in Coordinate Indexing Vol. 1.* (n.p.: Documentation Inc., 1953); Frederick G. Kilgour, "The Origins of Coordinate Searching," in *Historical Studies in Information Science*, ed. Trudi Bellardo Hahn and Michael Buckland (Medford, NJ: Information Today, 1998), 107–15.

9. Mortimer Taube, "The Comac: An Efficient Punched Card Collating System for the Storage and Retrieval of Information," in *Proceedings of the International Conference on Scientific Information, Washington, D.C. Nov. 16–21, 1958*, vol. 2, NAS-NSF (Washington: NAS-NSF, 1959), 1246.

10. B. Cronin and H. B Atkins, *The Web of Knowledge: A Festschrift in Honor of Eugene Garfield* (Medford, NJ: Information Today, 2000). Paul Wouters, *The Citation Culture* (n.p.: n.p., 1999), has a concise biography of Garfield and the creation of his citation system.

11. Eugene Garfield, "Autobiographical Sketch," *Journal of Information Science* 27, no. 2 (2001): 119–25.

12. M. M. Kessler, *Comparison of the Results of Bibliographic Coupling and Analytic Subject Indexing* (Cambridge, MA: Massachusetts Institute of Technology, 1963).

13. Eugene Garfield, "Citation Indexes for Science: A New Dimension in Documentation through Association of Ideas," *Science* 122, no. 3159 (1955): 108–11.

14. CHF, interview with Eugene Garfield, 1987.

17

THE PLURAL INFORMATION SYSTEM SURVIVES, WITH DIFFICULTY

While Eugene Garfield was creating a new for-profit science information service, information populists continued their fight to expand the reach of government services, and academic entrepreneurs such as James Perry and Allen Kent struggled to maintain their versions of profit-making nonprofits.

Hubert Humphrey had failed to establish his science department for "the people" or a centralized information service in the late 1950s, and Perry and Kent were unsuccessful in getting all they wished. All the information populists would gain in the next few years were half-a-loaf victories. Their achievements included some additional funds for John Green's Office of Technical Services, a pledge by the government's information agencies to find ways to cooperate, and, eventually, promises by the National Aeronautics and Space Administration (NASA) and the Atomic Energy Commission (AEC) to establish distribution centers for their unclassified reports, ones that would transfer knowledge directly to the public. The National Science Foundation (NSF) was strengthened, but it seemed intent on serving traditional, not applied, science.

The results disappointed the liberal Democrats but they did not give up. Humphrey continued with hearings through the 1960s, but he was not the only active science information politician. In 1963, Roman Pucinski, another midwestern Democratic politician, put forward a proposal for a huge government-run science information center based at John

Crerar Library in his hometown of Chicago, not in Cleveland. He wanted his center to be much more powerful and all-encompassing than the one Perry envisioned.

THE PLURAL MIX SURVIVES

Pucinski lost his battle because of the opposition of what he labeled "scientific elitists" and "capitalistic" for-profit providers. Whatever the cause, the United States never had a VINITI imposed on it. The nation's pluralistic science information system of a rather disorganized mix of nonprofit, for-profit, and ill-coordinated government services remained intact. So, the Western Reserve group still had a chance to overcome its defeats of the late 1950s, the National Science Foundation could continue to reinvigorate the traditional nonprofit science information providers, and for-profit companies had room to develop.

The NSF had fared much better than Perry. Although its reinvented Office of Science Information Services (OSIS) had not been made the overseer of all science information systems, it was given a great deal of money to fix America's science information systems by coordinating the nation's indexing and abstracting services and by eliminating government inefficiencies. It had so much that despite knowing of the military's huge investments in information technologies, it began funding a wide range of projects.

Between 1958 and 1974, when the politics of science led to an almost 50 percent cut in the funds for the foundation's information programs, the OSIS invested hundreds of millions of dollars in the traditional academic science information organizations and in information science research. Combined with the military expenditures, and those of the Advanced Research Projects Agency, the NSF's grants created information science's golden age of the 1960s.

FOR OLD SCIENCE

As Elmer Hutchisson and William O. Baker desired, by the early 1960s the NSF's leaders were doing as much as they could to support the old nonprofit information services, even providing more aid to the National

Federation of Science Abstracting and Indexing Services (NFSAIS). As well as the direct help, after a few grants the NSF decided to stop funding for-profit organizations.

That was one of the reasons why the Information Industry Association was formed. It members objected to government funding of nonprofits such as *Chemical Abstracts* that "unfairly" competed with commercial services. They also fought against the nonprofits and government providers by lobbying for the expanded use of value-added contracting services for distributing government information.

Additional federal dollars did go to for-profit translation services because of the NSF's responsibilities to advance and coordinate the sci-tech translation efforts, but the established larger nonprofit academic information companies were the major recipients of the NSF's dollars, including journal publishers. Tens of millions went into subsidizing the dissemination of information through page charges and through direct subsidies to academic journals.[1] Page charges were made part of grants, sometimes as much as $1,500 a page. The OSIS also financed new technologies for the nonprofits.

The foundation's dollars and the National Defense Education Act's (NDEA) student-subsidy programs also underwrote the creation of many of the new university-based information science programs. They usually arose out of established library departments that had been enlivened by the NSF's new favorites, mathematically oriented faculty who seemed to be making their craft a "science." Along with dollars from military agencies, especially the air force, the NSF's grants also built a cadre of university-based information researchers. In addition, the NSF's funds helped to give new life to the American Documentation Institute. It became the American Society for Information Science.[2]

As E. J. Crane and Miles Conrad had demanded in their testimony at the 1958 congressional hearings, the major nonprofit indexing and abstracting organizations received NSF help to expand their services and to modernize, including computerizing their operations. Between NSF funding and contract work for government agencies, some of the larger services, such as *Biological Abstracts* (BIOSIS), *Chemical Abstracts* (CA), and *Engineering Index* (EI), soon had as much as a quarter of their income coming from the government. It was, for example, the NSF's prodding, and dollars and the technical expertise of the National Security Agency's Ronald Wigington, that brought *Chemical Abstracts* into the computer age.[3]

WHO WILL COORDINATE? JOE BECKER?
THE MARKETPLACE?

The NSF's policies did not please everyone, however. Senator Humphrey was criticizing the foundation for not using its powers to coordinate all science information services, including the government's. The NSF's refusal to take advantage of the chance to set up its own information VINITI-like center was an irritant.[4] As well, throughout the 1960s and early 1970s, there was another tug-of-war between those demanding support for the "old science" information providers and those wanting more resources for government agencies—and new for-profit companies. There was at least one panel or committee hearing each year (thirty within twenty years) ranging from the COSATI attempt to bring order to the government agencies and to provide support to applied-science mission-oriented systems, to the National Academy of Sciences SATCOM report that echoed William O. Baker's demand that the country maintain a pluralistic system that paid special deference to traditional science's needs.

Meanwhile, another voice had joined the information debate. During the later years of the 1960s Great Society's social welfare programs, the federal concern over information access extended to general libraries and their patrons. The long-sought National Commission on Libraries and Information Science (NCLIS) was created in 1970. It was led, perhaps ironically, by the CIA's old friend Joe Becker. It had a mandate that included increasing popular access to science information, but its members were never sure of how to achieve that goal. Then, in the mid-1970s, America's stressed economy led to the commission's reorientation. The NCLIS switched from emphasizing federal subsidies to supporting the growth of nonprofit and for-profit computer network services. That came just as the Office of Technical Services (now the National Technical Information Service [NTIS]) endured budget reductions.

TROUBLES IN CLEVELAND

Before then, in 1959, hopes in Cleveland reawakened. Given the national attention to the plans for the great Western Reserve information center, Kent's well-advertised trip to Russia to view its VINITI information system, and the NSF's new sizable budget, Perry and Shera expected their calls for additional funding would be well received by the foundation. One hurdle to realizing all the potentials of their grantsman's skills was soon overcome. There had been some complaints about the close relationship between Perry and Kent and Madeline Berry Henderson after she had moved to a policy-shaping position at the foundation. Fortunately, those conflict of interest complaints were dismissed.

There was another problem that was not as easy to solve. Early on, questions were being raised about a history of wasteful government investments in retrieval systems, as well as in machine translation projects. In response to that, and to criticisms of "socialized" information, Perry and Kent put aside their adventurous plan for their huge center and submitted a proposal to the NSF for a smaller but still very ample long-term grant for their information retrieval projects. The CIA-sponsored metallurgical database that had been under development for so long was to be the centerpiece.

By the end of 1959, the Reserve's proposal was approved—but with rather threatening complications caused by the foundation having to meet demands to ensure that all its information investments were sound and objectively evaluated. Perry and Kent had to agree to a complex and rather demeaning evaluation of their work. That disappointment was accompanied by a greater frustration: the Luhn super-Scanner fiasco was repeated! General Electric informed Perry and Kent it was not going to build the grand special-purpose 250 computer it had promised. It made the announcement just as Kent was penning an article proclaiming its great powers.[5] It took the threat of a lawsuit to convince the company to provide one of its general-purpose computers, the 225, and very expensive long-delayed software that imitated the special-purpose 250.

There were potentials for more embarrassments. Although Perry and Kent's team had spent five years on the CIA-metallurgy project, had declared their metals information retrieval system a success, and had advertised it as ready for commercial use, the foundation declared that the first year of its planned multiyear funding had to be devoted to an examination of the powers of the semantic/telegraphic abstract system. Kent, if not Perry and Shera, took that in stride. There was no other choice if they wanted continued funding, and they may have known that similar demands were to be made on other recipients of foundation dollars, such as the Chemical Abstracts Service.

TWO CULTURES, ONCE MORE, AGAIN: SHERA AS A WILMARTH LEWIS VERSUS THE ENTREPRENEURS

There was an additional problem that made it difficult to meet the foundation's demand for a thorough evaluation of the center's methods: the once happy association between Perry and Shera had broken down and Shera's relationship with Kent was tense. Shera had come to worry about Perry's center being too entrepreneurial, producing too little science of information, and neglecting teaching. There were some confrontations, and by late 1959 the soft-money Perry was on his way to the University of Arizona's engineering department—with a grant from the army signal corps to use his factors system to index Fort Huachuca's engineering and, perhaps, its intelligence documents.

Allen Kent was left with all the administrative as well as research burdens at the center. With some trepidation, in early 1960 Kent accepted a generous $700,000 from the National Science Foundation (NSF) for the Reserve's part in the proposed yearlong evaluation program. Then, the work stalled. Including the time needed to prepare for the test, it took not one but more than three years before the effort's final report was made public in 1964. By that time, after he had additional clashes with Jesse Shera, Kent had decided to leave Western Reserve for a more welcome home in Pittsburgh, Pennsylvania.

More than the conflicts with Shera had caused Kent's frustrations and his flight from Cleveland. In late 1959, the NSF decided to require that Kent agree to much more than a self-study. It wanted a validating outside agency to be involved, probably to Kent's professional humiliation. It called on the National Academy of Sciences, not Kent, to design and conduct the Reserve's evaluations. Other information centers' systems were to be used as comparative benchmarks. The academy passed the request to the new Office of Documentation at the National Research Council that was headed by Karl F. Heumann, a specialist in chemical information. He had led the council's Chemical-Biological Coordination Center and had been a researcher at *Chemical Abstracts*. Heumann put together a team of experts to devise a plan for the tests. He hired independent professionals to conduct evaluations of the retrieval power of the several test participants' methods, and to compare each of them to those of Western Reserve. The council then contacted the management/efficiency consulting firms, Stanford Research Institute and Arthur Anderson & Co., asking them to survey user responses and to evaluate the operational efficiency of Kent's operation.

THE THREATENING CRANFIELD EVALUATION

Kent began polishing his metallurgical database, the semantic factors and telegraphic abstracts' retrieval methods, and the techniques used on the Rapid Selector searching machine (and its hoped-for replacement from General Electric). At the same time, the information groups at the John Crerar Library, the Franklin Institute, and the Department of Commerce's Office of Technical Services prepared for their allied experiments in retrieving metallurgical information. The National Science Foundation soon called on Cyril Cleverdon of England's aeronautical information service, whose work had been financed by the foundation since 1957, to include at least a quick study of Western Reserve's system in his larger comparative test of all types of retrieval methods.

Turning to Cleverdon was perhaps one way for the foundation to avoid becoming entangled in a relationship with potentially dangerous ethical issues. General Electric's information group, led by Cloyd Dake Gull, who had worked with Perry on the Selector and various methods projects, had sought financing to compare General Electric's Unitermlike methods with Perry's factors. Given that General Electric was a major contender for government contracts (including automating the National Library of Medicine), and had links to Western Reserve, funding its proposed test seemed unwise.

Cyril Cleverdon, in contrast, was not involved in any controversial projects and was internationally respected. He became famous, some say infamous, for the formalization and quantification of the "recall" and "precision" criteria that were to become the foundation for evaluating retrieval systems. Recall was based on a prior evaluation of the contents of a file of documents. In recall's most objective form, impartial experts with a search question in hand tagged all the relevant items in a file—items that, for example, answered a request for documents dealing with the chemistry of high-grade steel that had been published since 1950. Then, a retrieval method was applied to the file using the same question. The percent of all the prejudged relevant items retrieved was that method's recall score. Precision was the percent of all the retrieved items from a search that were judged to answer the search question. A low recall score meant that important items had been missed. A poor precision score meant a user would have to examine many useless documents.[6]

THE RESERVE'S EMBARRASSMENT, THE QUESTIONS PROBLEM, AND MORE

Constructing effective recall and precision tests was not easy. Problems ranged from the determination of what were relevant items to how to phrase search questions. Kent's Reserve and the other centers' staffs wrangled over those issues while preparing for the NSF's evaluation. The tests began in 1962, but not without encountering more problems and conflicts.

It was Kent's duty to select a random set of user questions that would serve as a thorough test base for the various parallel searches. He and his staff did not perform as expected. The National Research Council's experts were upset when Kent's staff pulled back their first list, claiming, somewhat apologetically, that it was not a typical question set. Kent submitted another. The council did not like that and ordered the first selection to be used. Then, the council realized those questions were not typical document retrieval queries but ones asked by engineers and designers for the kinds of facts usually found in reference and textbooks. However, by the time that was understood, the council's supervisory committee decided it was too late to begin anew.

That was followed by another embarrassment: the evaluators had expected that all the participants would submit every item they retrieved because a full submission was critical to any measures of preci-

THE PLURAL INFORMATION SYSTEM SURVIVES, WITH DIFFICULTY   303

sion. They were more than a bit disappointed when Kent's people reported they had postedited their list of retrieved items, by hand, eliminating many items they felt were irrelevant. For example, their run for one of the search questions flagged 8,505 documents. After Kent's group examined them, they decided only 630 were relevant and included only them in their report of recalled items.[7] Another procedural disappointment came when the council's evaluators found Western Reserve's team had failed to build an index listing all of the articles and documents in their files. That made comparisons of the results of the various searches very difficult. The council's investigations had also discovered that all types of operations-related housekeeping procedures at Reserve's center were below standard. The Reserve's excuse was that many of the deficiencies had been caused by the late arrival of General Electric's 225 computer. That did not satisfy the council.

Kent and his group became angry when they read the NSF's assessment. The evaluation team's (and Cleverdon's) conclusions were so negative that Kent thought of launching a major protest. The council's final report gave Western Reserve very low marks on everything. The relevancy power of their machine searches was too low and the irrelevancy rate was too high, 50 percent in many searches. As well, despite the center's generous funding by many sponsors, the data files had been poorly maintained and, perhaps most galling, Kent's staff had failed to use the most powerful parts of the telegraphic/semantic factor systems (such as role indicators) during their searches. On top of those criticisms, the council-sponsored surveys of previous users of the Reserve's system yielded only a 50 percent satisfaction level—and few scientists reported interest in the system that, supposedly, had been designed especially for them.

THE TERM SURPRISE, THE BREAKUP

Later results from Cleverdon's larger study of all the major classification methods did little to help semantic factors. Cleverdon's team found that a plain (and inexpensive) method was as good as all others. Mortimer Taube's simplest version of Uniterms did as well as sophisticated versions of the Universal Decimal Classification or any factor- or facet-based system.

By the time the council's report on the Reserve was made public, Allen Kent already had a new job, partly because both he and James Perry had managed to escape any blame for the shortcomings of the Reserve's operations. Although their careers were not ended, the remaining group at Western Reserve had to go on the defensive, as well as to adjust to a combination of declining funding and widespread use of improved computer technology that weakened Western Reserve's advantage. The center continued through the 1960s, but with minimal financial support and without a large moneymaking retrieval service.

Meanwhile, Jesse Shera had continued to press for the modernization of library methods—despite his return to a focus on the humanistic and sociological aspects of information. Some of the Reserve's 1960's library school faculty, such as William Goffman,[8] did cutting-edge work in quantitative information science. Shera also arranged a visiting professor's position at the school for Andrew Booth, England's pioneer in mechanical translation and computer applications.[9] But the Reserve's library school and information research center entered years of deficits, ones that became increasingly difficult to manage as the university dealt with the financial consequences of its overexpansion as it had sought to join the ranks of the top-tier research universities. Telegraphic abstracts and semantic factors had an even less happy future. They both fell out of favor. No indication of their use after the early 1960s has been discovered.

In contrast, James Perry settled into a comparatively quiet and rewarding life after more than twenty years of being an insecure soft-money academic. His 1960 appointment to a regular faculty position in the University of Arizona at Tucson's engineering department as a systems engineer allowed him to escape many of the agonies of constant grant seeking and publication, but the relative peace of his new setting did not that mean Perry had a perfect life. He had to face health and marital issues. He passed away in 1971, at age sixty-four, a year after he had divorced his first wife and married Jessica Melton, an ex–Western Reserve faculty colleague who had moved to the University of Arizona's library school.

A UNIVERSITY BUILDER'S INFORMATION DREAM

Allen Kent's post-Cleveland life was long and action filled. He lived until 2014, age ninety-two. That was some fifty years after he had moved to Pittsburgh and to a college campus that had to confront more difficult challenges than Western Reserve's. Kent arrived at the University of Pittsburgh (Pitt) as its new leader was attempting to change the college into a nationally ranked research institution.

Pitt had been a downtown streetcar college. It was as much an adult learning center as a university. In the early 1950s, Pittsburgh's wealthy civic leaders, with the rich Mellon family in the lead, decided to revitalize Andrew Carnegie's old steel town. A part of that multibillion-dollar undertaking was hundreds of millions of dollars for Pitt.

Edward Harold Litchfield, a very energetic and imaginative managerial wunderkind, was appointed chancellor in 1956 with an assignment to create a true university. He had academic, diplomatic, and business experience, as well as a bent toward entrepreneurship. One of his strategies was to have Pitt begin to share in the surge of Cold War research funding and the other federal dollars that he believed would soon pour into higher education because of the Great Society programs. They did flow. Federal programs would provide ample funds for medical research and even for library schools through initiatives such as the National Defense Education Act and the Library Services and Construction Act. Those programs were of special importance to science information and the growth of library schools. Allied federal library careers and training initiatives financed more than 1,000 doctoral degrees and 2,800 master's degrees in library and information science between 1963 and 1989.[10]

Betting on continued local and federal support, Litchfield began building, but also tearing down. He launched expensive plans for the acquisition of swaths of downtown Pittsburgh as sites for new buildings, especially ones for graduate education, his favorite. Establishing graduate programs meant reshaping Pitt's faculty. A third of the old teaching staff, those without Ph.D.s and solid records of grant getting, were persuaded to leave. That "deadwood" was replaced with well-credentialed grantsmen. With what he believed was a promise of never-ending subsidies from the Mellon family and their friends, salaries well above Pitt's old levels were offered to new faculty. As had Frederick Terman at Stanford University, Litchfield made them aware of his visionary plans and of his expectation that they would always make financial contributions to the university, whether they were in the regular faculty or working in his new centers.

Litchfield seemed to be on a roll. Within a few years he doubled the number of faculty and, reflecting the shift to graduate education, reduced the student-to-faculty ratio by one-third. His policies also changed the student body. The percent of out-of-state students increased threefold as ill-prepared local students were directed to the area's junior colleges. A source of great pride, the income from federal grants increased tenfold during Litchfield's tenure, reaching an astounding level of one-half of the university's budget.

Such success was not threat-free, however. Perhaps because of unfortunate negotiations, the federal grants were not a pure blessing. A requirement that the university contribute its own funds to each project accompanied many of the grants. That soon led to an overall loss for Pitt. Partly because of that, the cost per student soon doubled and tuition was increased 300 percent during the 1960s. Pitt's great dependency on federal dollars also left it vulnerable to swings in the federal largesse.

As early as 1961, five years after Litchfield arrived, Pitt was running a small yearly deficit. Litchfield saw that as only a short-term problem, one that would be disappear once all his expensive changes matured into functioning programs. He refused to retreat from his expansionist policies, ones that had extended to information programs. He financed a huge new library building and agreed to take on the responsibility for the long-struggling Carnegie Library School of Pittsburgh when the State of Pennsylvania covered the expense of the initial transfer year. Litchfield began reforming the school. He lured Harold Lancour from the very successful graduate library program at the University of Illinois with a generous offer and set him to reshaping the old Carnegie curricula, and to creating a graduate program that fit with an age of information retrieval. In a few years, the library school had one of the nation's largest enrollments.

Litchfield had begun envisioning another and more grandiose information project well before his library school began operation. His dream for a great moneymaking Knowledge Availability Systems Center (KASC) was more imaginative than what Perry and Kent had been

THE PLURAL INFORMATION SYSTEM SURVIVES, WITH DIFFICULTY

pursuing since the 1940s. The computerized center was to deliver all types of information to paying customers and, Litchfield advertised, it would be a boon to Pennsylvania's industries and research institutions.

THE GREAT SCIENCE INFORMATION CENTER IV, KASC

Looking for someone to turn his KASC concepts into a functioning operation, Litchfield contacted Allen Kent, just as Kent's relationship with Jesse Shera had reached a low point, and before the difficulties at the Reserve's center became apparent. In 1963, after a brief meeting with Litchfield and perhaps unaware of Pitt's financial challenges, Kent accepted an appointment in the library school and the responsibility for the Knowledge Availability Systems Center. Jack Belzer, the computer specialist, and one of his coworkers in Cleveland were also hired. For the first time in his life Kent had what seemed to be a protected job and, perhaps to his surprise, he had a regular faculty appointment despite holding only an undergraduate degree. That may have caused some dissatisfaction among the new advanced-degree-holding faculty, but Litchfield thought it was necessary for Kent to have full faculty status if he was to guide the information work in many of the campus's other departments and centers. Litchfield had planned to have the Knowledge Center work with Pitt's Space Research Coordination Center and the psychology, education, and engineering departments to make sweeping changes in all realms of information processing. Kent's team was even seen as competent to evaluate programs in computerized instruction. Allen's attention was, however, directed to KASC and to his role in the library school.

With Lancour's help, Kent began shaping a program in the new and still undefined field of information science. He did well. Within a decade, Kent created one of the first Ph.D. programs in the new field, taking advantage of the federal programs that subsidized advanced library career training. Those programs were especially generous during the 1960s and early 1970s.[11] Kent soon became involved in much more than curriculum building and the Knowledge Center. He began another round of editing important works on information methods and technology while holding series of conferences on theoretical and applied information science. He and Litchfield invited the best and brightest of the newest breed of information specialists to Pitt. The most influential information managers in the federal government were honored guests.

Kent's energy was boundless. He was a tireless fund-raiser for KASC. He continued his participation in Joe Becker's EDUCOM, advised the White House on national programs for library and information automation, and held many positions in professional organizations. More important, the problems with the NSF's 1959 Western Reserve grant did not spill over to harm Kent's years at Pitt. He became a renowned grantsman.

Within a few years, in 1969, his funding efforts were aided by Anthony Debons, a man who had an insider's knowledge of information science grant making. Debons had status as a Ph.D. psychologist and had a deep appreciation of electronics and engineering. He was and would remain one of the most loyal advocates of Claude Shannon's and Warren Weaver's mathematical approaches to information. Debons had applied that and his psychological expertise to building advanced information and communications systems for the military.

One reason for Kent hiring Debons was that Debons had spent most of his career as a high-level supervisor of the air force's generous grants for information systems and mechanical translation. Debons had been an important figure at the air force's Wright Field information complex and at its Rome, New York, advanced research center that had sponsored many information research projects, including some of James Perry's. Debons was also influential in NATO's European information programs and had an international reputation in the technologies that combined computers with complex graphics displays. He was also regarded as an expert in all aspects of command-and-control systems. After leaving the air force in the mid-1960s, Debons acted as a consultant for military contractors—then, he ventured into academia.

Unfortunately, Debons had a rather disheartening experience in the psychology department at the University of Dayton that was located near the air force's Wright Field research center. His very, very innovative information science program combined the best of information methods and theories with psychology and an appreciation of the most sophisticated display technologies. Despite that, it failed to attract enough students. By 1969, he was out of work. Debons's misfortune proved a boon to Allen Kent, who had just convinced the Pennsylvania

THE PLURAL INFORMATION SYSTEM SURVIVES, WITH DIFFICULTY 309

government's grant administrators that a doctoral-level program in information science was essential to the state's economic development. He secured a technology development grant, hired Debons, and established his Ph.D. programs in information science. Meanwhile, Kent's grantsman's wizardry had proven vital to the survivals of all the library and information programs at Pitt.

KENT SURVIVES, LITCHFIELD DOES NOT

Kent's fund-raising skills were needed. Just two years after Kent had moved to Pittsburgh, Litchfield's university was bankrupt! The leaders of the Mellon philanthropies did not rescue the college although they attempted to save the older independent Mellon Research Institute that was also in financial difficulty.[12] Litchfield was forced to resign, the university had to go to the state government for the funds to pay past-due salaries, and a program of budgetary stringency was imposed. Floors were not cleaned, lightbulbs were turned off, and the heat was turned down. It was only Kent's entrepreneurial and fund-raising skills, and luck, that saved the Knowledge Center and the library program from early deaths.

He had convinced the state that information and Pitt deserved another of its grants for technology development, but much more was required for the center's survival. Fortunately, Kent's needs matched those of the National Aeronautics and Space Administration (NASA) as it was trying to respond to Henry Wallace–like populist demands. Because of the continuing complaints that Cold War science was not being made useful to the common man, NASA sought ways to distribute its hundreds of thousands of declassified reports to the public. Finding that existing government services, such as the OTS/NTIS, were overwhelmed, NASA's leaders decided to create a new engineering information version of Wallace's agricultural services. NASA announced it would create a new form of the old agricultural stations' freestanding regional distribution centers.

Unfortunately, NASA's information program had to be self-financing. Not receiving the Great Society's federal support that had gone to ERIC, the national educational database, and the National Library of Medicine's Medline, NASA's and similar new Atomic Energy Commission centers were expected to pay for themselves after a few years. They had to be aggressive and each center had to convince civilian customers to purchase their information products.

The ramifications of the demand that the centers quickly become self-supporting were not immediately noticed. But, as during the OTS/NTIS's early years, the charges the NASA's centers had to impose would mean they would serve large corporations much more frequently than Wallace's vaunted small businessman.[13] Kent did not worry about that. He was perhaps the first in line with a proposal to NASA for establishing one of their centers. He received a half-million-dollar grant for the first year of the KASC's NASA work and a promise of four more years of the same if the center showed indications it was becoming self-supporting.

Kent became the KASC's first salesman and quickly secured promises from major steel and chemical companies to be regular paying customers. He convinced NASA to let him guide its other regional information hubs. He coordinated the use of their mainframe computers, and he supervised the training of their many salesmen-consultants. Kent also began winning grants from other government agencies, including the National Science Foundation, the National Institutes of Health, and the State of Pennsylvania for KASC's research work on a range of information problems. Kent made explorations into the possibilities for health, pharmacy, and legal information systems—even a student-manned human simulation of the retrieval process. However, the income from the NASA grants remained the centers' mainstay, even while Kent was channeling some of the proceeds from KASC's work to Pitt's information school program.

The dependency on NASA proved to be a serious weakness, one that almost killed the center. Kent built an aggressive sales and consulting organization and was pleasing his corporate customers by incorporating information from databases that Pitt's library was buying from for-profit companies, but by the end of the fifth and final year of NASA's funding, the center had failed to become self-supporting. All of Kent's programs were in danger; there had not even been enough income to finance his desired special-purpose retrieval computer, or for exploring any esoteric classification and retrieval methods.

SAVING KASC

Although Pitt had escaped the riots and upheavals of antiwar and New Left movements, by 1968 KASC was in serious trouble. But Kent once again worked his grantsman's magic. He saved the center from closing by convincing NASA to continue its support—and for twenty more years. But even with that and Debons's help, new computer-online technologies allowed the rise of for-profit providers that made the center's other services noncompetitive. It became a specialized, not general-purpose, operation.

Surprisingly, the usually ingenious Kent was unable to exploit two developments that might have made KASC an example of a successful university-based, freestanding entrepreneurial adventure. John Horty, a law professor at Pitt, had been one of the first to explore the full-text searching of legal documents. Originally supported by the air force, his work migrated to the private sector and, eventually, to highly profitable firms such as Lexis. Horty left Pitt in 1967 to establish his own Aspen system before Kent had an opportunity to bring him or Pitt's older chemical information service into KASC.[14]

Despite Kent's knowledge of the advances in computer and communications technologies, and despite his role in developing Pitt's own NSF financed in-house, online bibliographic system (one that was the first to use the *New York Times'* computerized retrieval system), KASC became somewhat of a techno- and business model dinosaur, one heading for extinction.

In contrast, Kent and Debons's graduate information school prospered, even after the federal subsidies for library and information science education began to decline in the late 1960s, gradually dropping to one-tenth of the yearly subsidies of 1963.[15] Debons's creative approach to information education and his and Kent's skills at fund-raising go far in explaining the library school's programs popularity and survival, even during the challenging economic times of the 1970s.

A NEW AMERICAN ECONOMY, A PAINFUL ONE

By the end of the 1970s, survival was a challenge for higher education—especially for high-cost programs such as graduate information science.

Information programs' difficulties were only a small part of higher education's malaise. Higher education's and the American economy's golden ages were over. The economy was nearing the end of the American century as foreign competition, the federal government's struggle to finance "guns and butter," and the Middle East's control of the cost and flow of oil pushed an already overburdened economy into a decade of stagflation and changes in the government's education policies.

There was a new American economy. It led to significant reductions in state and federal contributions to universities. That compounded a decline in the growth of the student-age population and it was feared that 10 percent of the institutions in America's vastly overexpanded college and university system would have to close. Even major research universities, such as the University of Michigan, were in deep financial trouble and there were worries that America's hard-won place as the home of the world's best research universities would be lost to a resurgent Europe.

In reaction, American higher education began a long and at times agonizing search for a new organizational model. Its leaders turned to business-oriented approaches and went further away from the ideals of the universities of the early twentieth century than had the entrepreneurial institutions of the 1960s.[16] Science information also faced wrenching challenges when federal support began to decline in the early 1970s. The NSF, for example, had to reduce its subsidies to scientific journals and information research. At the same time, military investments leveled off.

Meanwhile, new technologies and related methods were changing the nature of the science information industry while the new economic conditions were undermining the balanced plural science information system. Unlike the situation in the 1920s, the private philanthropies were unable, or unwilling, to step in with significant long-term aid for nonprofit science information. There was only one major private philanthropic project, a third version of the MIT Scientific Aids to Learning (SAL) project, and it contributed little. With the government and the philanthropies retreating, other providers, for-profit ones, began taking the lead in a new science information industry.

NOTES

1. Useful on the history of page charges is J. Merton England, *A Patron for Pure Science: The National Science Foundation's Formative Years 1945–57* (Washington, D.C.: National Science Foundation, 1983).

2. *American Documentation* 16, no. 3 (1965): passim.

3. Ronald L. Wigington and James L. Wood, "Standardization Requirements of a National Program for Information Transfer," *Library Trends* 18 (1969–1970): 4342–445; Robert V. Williams, "Interview with Dale Baker," Chemical Heritage Foundation, ca. 2000.

4. Harold Wooster, "Historical Note: Shining Palaces, Shifting Sands; National Information Systems," *JASIS* 38, no. 5 (September 1987): 321–35; Walter L. Reynolds, "The Senate Committee on Government Operations and Documentation," *American Documentation* 12, no. 2 (April 1961): 93–97.

5. Allen Kent, "The GE-250," *College Composition and Communication* 11, no. 2 (May 1960): 75–77.

6. Cyril Cleverdon, "Report on the Testing and Analysis of an Investigation into the Comparative Efficiency of Indexing Systems," Cranfield College of Aeronautics, Cranfield, England, 1962; Mortimer Taube, "A Note on the Pseudo-mathematics of Relevance," *American Documentation* 16, no. 2 (April 1965): 69–72; Tefko Saracevic, "Research on Relevance in Information Science: A Historical Perspective," in *International Perspectives on the History of Information Science and Technology*, ed. Toni Carbo and Trudi Bellardo Hahn (n.p.: ASIS&T, 2012), 49–60; Phyllis A. Richmond, "Review of the Cranfield Project," *American Documentation*, October 1963, 307–11.

7. National Academy of Sciences—National Research Council, *The Metallurgical Searching Service of the American Society for Metals, Western Reserve University: An Evaluation*, NAS Pub. 1148 (Washington, DC: NAS, 1964).

8. William Goffman, "The Ecology of Medical Literatures," *American Journal of the Medical Sciences* 263, no. 4 (1972): 267–73.

9. Gordon C. Barhydt, *Western Reserve University Index of Educational Resources* (Cleveland, OH: Western Reserve, 1964).

10. Edward G. Holley and Robert F. Schremser, *The Library Services and Construction Act: An Historical Review* (Greenwich, CT: JAI Press, 1983).

11. The Higher Education and Libraries Act and amendments 1963– were critical to all library programs.

12. J. W. Servos, "Changing Partners: The Mellon Institute, Private Industry, and the Federal Patron," *Technology and Culture* 35, no. 2 (April 1994): 221–57.

13. James G. Williams, *Governance of Special Information Centers: The Knowledge Availability Systems Center at University of Pittsburgh* (Urbana:

University of Illinois Graduate School of Library and Information Science, n.d.).

14. Charles P. Bourne and Trudi Bellardo Hahn, *A History of Online Information Services 1963–1976* (Cambridge, MA: MIT Press, 2003), 229.

15. Redmond Kathleen Molz, *The Federal Roles in Support of Academic and Research Libraries* (Chicago: ALA, 1991).

16. George Keller, *Academic Strategy: The Management Revolution in American Higher Education* (Baltimore: Johns Hopkins University Press, 1983).

18

A NEW INFORMATION ERA

The American Information Century's Challengers

The Knowledge Availability Systems Center at the University of Pittsburgh might have had a longer and happier life if Allen Kent and Anthony Debons had been able to cultivate the leaders of America's new large-scale information sponsoring philanthropy of the 1950s and 1960s. Unfortunately for them, a group at the Massachusetts Institute of Technology (MIT) applied its well-honed powers of grantsmanship and reached into the pockets of the Ford Foundation before others.

In the mid-1960s, MIT began what amounted to a third generation of the Vannevar Bush–inspired Scientific Aids to Learning project (SAL) of the 1930s. This new SAL became a last hurrah for large-scale nonprofit support of science information projects for a generation. MIT's men did not advertise their version of Shera's or Perry's dreams of a permanent information research laboratory as a reincarnation of SAL1 or SAL2, but what became known as INTREX was another attempt to show that libraries needed a revolution propelled by scientists and technologists, not by librarians or even information scientists. Following a national trend of deferring to applied scientists for problem solving, INTREX looked to engineers and physicists to drive a new era in science information—one powered by computers and using methods that had little to do with traditional indexing or classification techniques.

315

The first SAL of the 1930s had been allowed to wither as World War II began. It had achieved little. The second attempt came after the war ended. It was amply funded by the Carnegie interests, the traditional supporters of library causes. James Perry, and to a lesser extent Allen Kent, had been briefly associated with the last phases of the SAL's second incarnation, but even with their contributions SAL2 also failed to meet expectations. MIT, busy with many Cold War technology projects, including cutting-edge computer developments and automatic translation explorations, then backed away from library causes for a decade until its administrators decided the institute needed another library. They began a fund-raising drive for more than buildings. Alongside the library project was an initiative to finance INTREX. It was the INTREX effort that linked the institute with the new giant American philanthropy, the Ford Foundation—a creation of the Ford Motor automobile fortunes.[1]

The foundation was established in the mid-1930s but came into its own in late 1947 when the senior Henry Ford's bequest turned the foundation into the nation's wealthiest philanthropy. During the 1940s and early 1950s the foundation was led by humanists who focused on financing broad social programs. After Sputnik, Ford's administrators bowed to the advice of applied-science-oriented leaders such as Warren Weaver. They and MIT's officials turned the foundation's attention to improving engineering education in the nation's top universities.

Librarians believed the foundation's new initiative included them. Ford began receiving pleas for help to libraries and information science. In 1956, to stop the many library advocates from pestering it, the foundation began generously funding the Council on Library Resources (CLR). The nonprofit CLR was a new organization that represented the nation's most important general research libraries. The CLR's connections convinced the foundation to channel all its library and information efforts through it. The CLR received tens of millions of dollars from the foundation over the next twenty years.[2]

The foundation's information goals were to increase library efficiency and control costs, especially in science and technology libraries. Technological innovation was the centerpiece of its plans. Although Verner Clapp, the CLR's first president, was a humanist, technology and efficiency also became the major goals of the council. Clapp soon funded many library technology projects, including the Library of Con-

A NEW INFORMATION ERA

gress's creation of the MARC national standard for computer-based cataloging. He also helped the library begin developing its own computerized catalog under the direction of the National Security Agency's ex-employees Sam Snyder and Henriette Avram.[3]

A LIBRARY LABORATORY IN CAMBRIDGE, NOT CLEVELAND OR NEW YORK

The council's advisors, including Warren Weaver, wanted more than aid to traditional libraries. They demanded that Clapp create a "laboratory" that could define the "library of the future."[4] They had Clapp establish a set-aside for such a laboratory in the CLR's budget. As a result, in 1961 Clapp had a multimillion-dollar fund for "the" library laboratory for the nation. He first turned to the general-purpose New York Public Library. The foundation's advisors did not like that. They pushed the CLR to use a more technologically experienced center that could serve Cold War needs. Clapp searched for other sites and people—but he did not seek out Perry or Kent. He hired J. C. R. Licklider, a psychologist/computer scientist who was at an MIT spinoff, the BB& N consulting firm. Clapp gave Licklider $2 million for a two-year series of critical "experiments."

Licklider published *Libraries of the Future* in 1965, although he had conducted few if any experiments and had not begun creating a laboratory. His work may have, however, helped him develop ideas for the precursor of the Internet, the American government's ARPANET.

Clapp, the council, and the Ford Foundation were disappointed because Licklider produced only ideas, but groups within MIT promised a technology-based solution if they were granted the CLR's remaining laboratory funds. One of MIT's groups was led by William N. Locke, an administrator in charge of the institute's library project. He had worked on one of the few operating SAL2 projects during the 1940s, speech recognition. Another MIT group had grander library and information ambitions than Locke's. Carl Overhage, a high-tech professor who had just moved from MIT's Cold War Lincoln Laboratory center to the institute, was ready with his own information ambitions. In 1963, he returned to the institute and created his version of an information laboratory, one separate from Locke's library effort and

Licklider's explorations. Overhage was optimistic despite sensing that federal research dollars were becoming harder to obtain. He was given a faculty slot in MIT's engineering department and a go-ahead for his laboratory project, but only when he could raise from outside sources the some $36 million[5] he predicted he would need for just the initial four years of experiments by his team of some fifty helpers, mainly graduate students.

Overhage, accustomed to funding levels of the most critical years of the Cold War, was soon disappointed. All he could acquire was what he considered a pittance. The National Science Foundation (NSF) and the private MIT-linked Sloan Foundation gave $120,000. A last-minute grant of more than $500,000 came from the Independence Foundation, perhaps the one in Boston that seems to have had ties to the Central Intelligence Agency (CIA). Overhage did not use the money to launch his project, however. He spent most of it on a conference at the Woods Hole institute to gain national academic approval of what he would soon call Project INTREX. The participants at the conference shared Overhage's orientation to information reform. Only seven of the nearly fifty attendees were librarians. There was little attention to methods and, surprisingly, Vannevar Bush's "association" was not a prominent subject at the meeting.

After the 1965 Woods Hole meeting, Overhage did somewhat better as a fund-raiser. Although the older large private foundations, Carnegie and Rockefeller, had pulled back from their predominant early twentieth-century roles in the library world, they remained targets. Overhage was rebuffed by the Rockefellers, but the reluctant Carnegie managers finally pledged $1.25 million spread over two years. Then, the NSF and the military's Advanced Research Projects Agency (ARPA) promised $4.5 million. The ARPA contribution may have been helped by Licklider becoming a high-level administrator at the agency. With an additional $300,000 from the offices of the American Publishers Association for explorations of automating newspaper archiving, Overhage had almost $6 million in hand and began establishing his library laboratory in MIT's Electronic Systems department—not its library. But Overhage wanted and needed more. Surprisingly, the Council on Library Resources held back for a time. Then, just as the Carnegie and NSF grants were ending, the council saved the day. It gave Overhage $6 million in 1968 and more in 1970 and 1972. Including the $2 million it had given

A NEW INFORMATION ERA 319

Licklider, the council's contributions to INTREX (mainly Ford Foundation monies) came to about one-half of what Overhage would spend during the six active years of the project.

That huge amount did not indicate that INTREX had a kinder fate than Perry's center at Western Reserve or Kent's KASC. In 1972, the final evaluation of the third version of SAL led the council to end its relationship with INTREX. The council concluded that the project's leaders had made some technological contributions but had turned away from the needs of all types of research libraries to focus on hardware development and sci-tech information problems. No grand system had been created, and the never-completed large file of article indexes and abstracts needed for valid retrieval experiments was one that was only suited for group and mission-oriented sci-tech research.

Because of this failure to create a grand information center, the development of America's modern library came in increments and through gradual technological improvements, not through a single large program. As important, the science information infrastructure of the later twentieth century evolved in new political and economic contexts.

TECHNOLOGY, MARKETS, EDUCATION AS BUSINESS, AND THE FOR-PROFIT INFORMATION ERA

In the late 1960s, while INTREX was winding down, and as the ideologically driven outbursts by the New Left were subsiding, America was beginning to face critical economic challenges, ones that would cause troubling realignments in society as well as in higher education and the science information industry. As the advantage in heavy industry and manufacturing shifted to rapidly developing Asia, information and information technologies seemed to be the best hope for the American economy. Significantly, at the same time as America focused on information, Europe was on a path to becoming the dominant force in general and scientific publishing and, partly a result of higher education's plight, the nation's science information infrastructure was beginning to undergo a transformation—one as deep as that in its colleges and universities. As America's colleges dealt with their wrenching economic woes, becoming more like businesses to survive, the nation's for-profit science information providers began to outdistance the nonprofit and government publishers and services.[6] The severity of the changes in science information would be unrecognized for two decades—but the forces leading to the unbalancing of the plural American information system, and the resurgence of Europe as a science information power, had been at work since the 1970s.

The expansion of the for-profit science information sector in the United States came first. Many of the factors leading to the rise of the nation's for-profits were related to government policies and economic trends, but technology played a critical role. The appearance of improved communications networks and powerful computers, as well as the regular encoding of information (such as indexes and abstracts and science articles) in computer readable form, were important.

The first steps in the science information industry's transformation came as new types of for-profit corporations appeared, developing computerized publishing operations and what became known as "online" information systems.[7] The new online business has its own fascinating history. Computer-communications advances and the shareable computer-readable databases that became common allowed information to be stored on central computers, then, searched by many users using local terminals at great distances. During the 1970s, and for the next few decades, those online systems were rather crude, relying on modifications of teletype terminals and primitive CRTs (cathode ray tube displays) and special and rather costly communications networks. Those early online systems were limited in other ways. They provided only bibliographic information, not full text, and they required a skilled librarian to manipulate their rather difficult searching programs.

Meanwhile, aided by a few state and federal subsidies aimed at increasing higher education's efficiency, college libraries were struggling to establish their own special type of networks for cataloging data. After years of turmoil, those efforts led to the giant national nonprofit but fee-charging Online Computer Library Center (OCLC) that also became a reference resource for academics.[8] That success was surprising as it had proven more difficult than expected to create and maintain special-purpose online systems for academic libraries when only small subsidies came from civilian governments and philanthropic "angels." Greater than predicted investments were needed for hardware and for designing software for the academic systems, as well as for those aimed at serving commercial customers.

A NEW INFORMATION ERA

While there was little federal money for online academic library systems, the military agencies and their contractors were still benefiting from the Cold War. Not surprisingly, the United States' large missile companies (and allied universities such as Stanford) that had access to the most powerful computers became the major forces in the development of the first general-purpose online information systems of the mid-1960s.

DIALOG AND ADDING VALUE

One of the first significant for-profit systems for sci-tech information was originally designed for the in-house use of the National Aeronautics and Space Administration (NASA) and its contractors. It morphed into an important type of information provider, the value-added, for-fee company. The Dialog service offered an unlimited number of networked customers access to the multiple databases stored on its central computers. The datasets were not specially created, but cost-free ones from the government or, later, those contracted from indexing and abstracting services. Dialog and similar providers "added value" by reformatting and delivering information in digital form, and by providing a retrieval program. At first, Dialog's emphasis was on bibliographic information, but it and other services moved to full text as soon as it was technically feasible.

Roger Summit was among the first to envision the potentials of this new type of sci-tech information business. Roger, a young Stanford University psychology and management-science graduate, worked at Lockheed's missile-space center near Palo Alto, California, but not as one of the many special librarians employed in the aerospace industry.[9] Although not a librarian, Summit came to believe he could turn the bibliographic searching software and computer networking technologies the company was developing for the government into a moneymaking consumer product. Under his guidance, Lockheed began by competing for contracts for processing and delivery systems of government databases. At the time, contracting out the processing and electronic delivery of government science information seemed a way to save the taxpayers money. Expanding government centers such as the Office of

Technical Services during an era of government frugality had little support.

There were limits to what the online services could do, however. In the 1960s, and for at least the next twenty years, the consumers of online information were large corporations and universities that could afford the expensive computer-communications systems, not Henry Wallace–like citizens.[10] But Roger Summit had no worries about populist complaints when he began obtaining rights to freely use a wide range of government databases on his for-profit Dialog system. In 1967, for example, he won a value-added contract to reformat and distribute the new U.S. Department of Education's ERIC database.[11] He soon added the bibliographic files of other government agencies. Sensing that with a wide spectrum of data there would be a greater chance of attracting enough paying subscribers to make his online system profitable, he added the Chemical Abstracts Service's files to his bundle of offerings. That addition brought some legal complications, ones highlighting problems of government involvement in science publishing. Because so much of Chemical Abstracts' work was government funded, there was a demand that its products be considered part of the public domain and, therefore, freely accessible to other providers than Dialog. Eugene Garfield was one of the major players in such battles.[12]

The legal tussles did not stop Summit. He continued acquiring rights to bibliographic information, including those for a range of academic journals. Then, he extended his reach by paying royalties for more types of databases. But after five years of operation Lockheed worried that Summit's service was never going to be profitable. Customers were difficult to find and hold before computers and network connections became widespread consumer items.[13]

Lockheed was about to close the operation. Roger then made a bold move. He changed Dialog into an independent company. He had a few years of rough going. It was not easy to gain new subscribers or the capital needed to sustain his business. But, with the help of the increased research needs in corporations, he patiently guided the business to prosperity. He also became a leader in the for-profit bibliographic industry.

Importantly, because the government decided not to create more than a few of its own online services, Dialog became a greater value-added provider of government databases while adding proprietary in-

A NEW INFORMATION ERA

formation to its offerings. That, plus the spread of the company to Europe, paid off. Sixteen years after Dialog became a private company, Summit sold it for a billion dollars to an integrated American information corporation. Then, like other science information companies, it became an article of trade bouncing to and from among European and American investors.[14]

BECOMING FOR-PROFIT BY NECESSITY, BRS

There were other high-tech science information for-profits with different origins than Dialog's. The Biomedical Research Service was the product of the post–World War II expansion of the American higher education system, as well as of the drive to make every college meet the very expensive criteria for research universities. In the 1950s, New York's government decided to establish public universities across the state, ones that would provide the same level of education as the respected Columbia and Cornell, but at affordable tuitions. Problems soon arose. The founders of such new state institutions had not anticipated the high cost of modern universities. The system's administrators soon had to economize, while at the same time struggling to achieve equality among its campuses. In reaction to the escalating cost of libraries, the government created the hopefully efficient Bibliographic Retrieval Services (BRS) in 1968. It was an initially state-subsidized all-campus telecommunications network and value-added provider of such items as the National Institutes of Health's MEDLINE and the bibliographic products of *Biological Abstracts.*

Each of New York's member campuses was to share in the cost and the system was expected to be self-supporting. BRS had a good start but it unexpectedly required subsidies amounting to more than the charges levied on the campuses it served. The economic woes of the 1970s then hammered it. The state withdrew its financial support. In a desperate attempt to save the service, BRS's managers converted it into an independent nonprofit in 1975. That did not work. BRS was stranded and needed capital to survive.

There were no philanthropic foundations willing to help BRS or other innovative online, nonprofit systems. Even the originally well-subsidized OCLC library cooperative cataloging organization that was building the first true national catalog (later, the first international catalog) had tough going in the 1970s. The old philanthropies, even the Ford Foundation, were not willing to provide it or the BRS with further aid.

Desperate, in 1976 BRS's managers reorganized as an American for-profit corporation and attempted to sell stock. Being for-profit and independent lasted just four years. Reflecting the rise of the European economy, a Dutch corporation assumed control. But BRS's saga did not end there. In another few years, as the United States fell into one of its worst recessions, BRS became part of perhaps the strangest stories in the history of science information.

CHALLENGING THE AMERICAN INFORMATION CENTURY

The United States' lead in the creation of online services and its dominance in scientific publishing after World War II made it seem that there was going to be an uncontested American science information century. That proved untrue, although the nation's early start gave it a long-lasting advantage in the new computer-dependent field of quantitative information science and advanced search and retrieval methodology. Giants in those new research fields, such as the physicist Don R. Swanson and the computer scientist Gerard Salton, grew up alongside computers during the 1960s and 1970s. They helped fashion a framework for a next generation of information innovators. Science publishing had a less favorable later twentieth-century history in the United States. It took decades, but America's postwar advantage was successfully challenged.

World War II had severely damaged Europe's science information businesses, but as soon as the war ended plans were made for a rebirth—and despite Socialist traditions, for-profit firms were to play the dominant part. One reason for that was, in contrast to the United States where individual science disciplines had relied upon their professional societies to publish journals, many European nations, especially Germany, had always used for-profit companies.[15] With Germany, the world's old science information leader restrained by its occupiers' policies, there were opportunities to take over its markets.

Britain was the first to reinvigorate its science journal publishing industry. It did it through a very unusual process that eventually led to the huge Pergamon Press. The story began in 1945 when England's leading scientists pleaded to their government for help in creating a British science publishing company to fill in the void left by Germany's once world-dominant firms, such as Springer Verlag, being forbidden to sell their works outside of Germany. The British government had a nationalistic reason for listening to its scientists: it feared the United States' publishers would undercut England's unless there was immediate action.

The government did not establish a service but gave aid to Butterworth, one of England's largest traditional publishers, to create a new series for science information. The series emerged under the rubric of 1947's new Butterworth-Springer company. A critical part of the government's help for Butterworth was waiving many regulations to allow the company to bring to England a "Nazi" scientist who had been one of Springer-Verlag's best salesmen and an ace recruiter of articles from Europe's most important scientists. That man, Paul Rosbaud, was chosen to lead Butterworth's new science effort.[16] Also important to the Butterworth story was a mysterious young Czechoslovakian.

LUDVIK OR ROBERT?

Ludvik Hoch left a small Jewish village in Czechoslovakia in 1939 when he was just sixteen. After briefly serving with the Czech resistance against Germany's invasion, he fled to France. After serving in the French army, Ludvik made another escape from the Germans. He managed to reach England. Once across the channel he joined the British army. He did well, serving as a language expert. Some cryptic comments indicate that he also worked for the British Foreign Service. That phrase points to intelligence operations. He decided to make England his home and soon changed his name to the very British, Ian Robert Maxwell, became a captain in the British army, and was awarded its Military Cross for heroism.[17]

When Germany surrendered, the British assigned Maxwell to what became the center of espionage in the world, Berlin. He was there when Soviet intelligence was attempting to penetrate every Allied organization. It is known that he first worked as a translator and interrogator, but his public persona was the editor of *Der Berliner*. He must have been involved in more, perhaps including his own private version of obtaining intellectual reparations. Still in the British army, and working for the Allied Control Commission, he began helping the struggling German science publishing houses to obtain scarce materials. He soon had his own special business partnership with the Springer publishing interests.

There was more going on. He began a series of international balancing acts. He seems to have been able to arrange for the Czechs to become the major arms supplier to Israel in 1948, while at the same time maintaining good relations with the Soviets and the British—although both nations worried about Israel's expansion. Maxwell continued to be an Israeli asset for the rest of his life while still befriending the Soviets, the British, and their allies. He helped convince Russia to allow the emigration of hundreds of thousands of Jews to Israel. As well, there are credible reports that one of Maxwell's spin-off firms in the United States appropriated a critical software package that made him millions of dollars and gave Israeli intelligence access to many other governments' vital secrets. The software purchased from Maxwell's firm had built-in (trapdoor) access points for Israel's Mossad intelligence agency.

Well before then, during the 1940s, Maxwell had sensed there was a new and profitable line of business emerging. He envisioned new markets for science information and academic publishing and sensed a great opportunity for a dynamic entrepreneur like himself. Although near penniless when he returned to England in the late 1940s, by 1951 Maxwell was on his way to becoming a billionaire, a member of Parliament, and an international power broker.

The key to his success was building a near monopoly over scientific journals in many fields, an advantage gained through following Rosbaud's example of very aggressive recruitment of papers, through adept marketing, and through the creation and acquisition of journals. Maxwell's first step had been to help Rosbaud obtain the rights to be the exclusive British and American distributor for all the publications of Germany's Springer publishing house after the Allied governments launched their effort to turn West Germany into an industrial giant to showcase capitalism. The new policies included relaxing restrictions on

A NEW INFORMATION ERA

its publishing industry. Maxwell made similar licensing agreements with the Soviet and satellite nations' publishers, being blocked from a gaining a monopoly over Soviet bloc publications only by the adroit bargaining of Earl Maxwell Coleman, the founder of what became Plenum Press.

Maxwell deepened his reach into other educational materials. When Butterworth and Rosbaud decided to end their relationship, Maxwell stepped in with financial help and, a few years later, bought out Rosbaud, thus gaining full control of what became Pergamon Press.[18] Following that, he acquired other major publishers in the West. His control of science and academic publishing became so tight that he was accused of manipulating the world price of journals and textbooks. His pattern of rather predatory business behavior had perhaps been one reason for Butterworth, then Rosbaud, cutting loose from him.

Maxwell did not stop with his Pergamon Press scientific offerings, other academic journals, or with Soviet bloc materials. He invested in newspapers and television-cable networks in England and continental Europe. He even joined the Central Intelligence Agency–sponsored consortium for the translation of Soviet scientific publications. Significant, he, as did other investors of the time, viewed scientific information as a part of a larger and profitable business opportunity. To them, science information was a commodity, a product, as were textbooks and business news.

Yet, Maxwell seems to have had some special affection for scientific information and for science's role in developing information methods. In the early 1960s he established, along with many other related publications, a prestigious information science journal and soon recruited some of the outstanding figures in American and continental information science to guide what became *Information Processing and Management*. There was much more on his business agenda.

WHAT HAVE J. PAUL GETTY AND ARMAND HAMMER TO DO WITH SCIENCE INFORMATION?

There were other unusual connections shaping science information into an industry. As in the case of Robert Maxwell, Roy Thomson (the First Baron Thomson of Fleet Street) was an unlikely man to be in England's

House of Lords, to build a multibillion-business conglomerate, or to corner the market on biological and zoological bibliographic services. He wasn't a scientist; he wasn't part of the well-educated liberal world that Wilmarth Lewis had known; and, if his early business ventures are an indicator, he should have ended up as an obscure owner of a few rural, small-town Canadian newspapers and a tiny radio station or two. But in the 1920s, armed only with a private-business-college education, burdened with poor eyesight, and having just a few hundred dollars in capital, Thomson launched what became a brilliant career. He soon bought more local newspapers, ice-cream cone businesses, hairstyling companies, and whatever else seemed to guarantee a profit. He had some help along the way. A good friend and early partner was the fellow Canadian Jack Kent Cooke. Cooke left Canada and migrated to America where he managed to get overnight citizenship so he could begin a phenomenal career in cable television and ownership of teams in the new cash-cow business of professional football. Although an American citizen, he was a "Brit" at heart and probably felt national pride when he purchased a true icon of the United States' once unchallenged industrial might, the Chrysler Building.[19]

While his friend Cooke was busy with his Canadian and United States interests, Roy Thomson moved from Canada to Scotland so he could enter the television industry in England. He purchased major newspapers there, even the fabled *Times of London*, and then a string of papers in the United States. He accumulated great riches and received a peerage as he became an international business and investment giant. He also had mystery-laden Middle Eastern dealings with the strange Soviet-connected Armand Hammer. Hammer and his father had been one of the first, if not the first, Americans to arrange trade deals with the Soviet Communists after the revolution of 1917 and, later, became secret conduits for both information and funds between Russia and America.[20]

Thomson made another friend, J. Paul Getty.[21] Getty, an Oxford University–educated American from an ultrarich oil-industry family, had put aside his youthful bad habits to become one of the world's richest men. He had made shrewd oil deals throughout the world, including a 1949 agreement with Saudi Arabia. He decided to move to England and to a baronial estate, a setting that fit his status aspirations. He and Roy Thomson met there and agreed to take a great adventure together. In 1968, they poured millions into North Sea oil explorations—they soon reaped hundreds of millions in profits.

A BETTER INVESTMENT OPPORTUNITY THAN OIL: ACADEMIC INFORMATION

Roy Thomson was pleased, but he was a shrewd businessman who knew that conditions always change. So, he trained his son to be ready to guide his companies into new ventures and technologies. Soon after Sir Roy's death in 1976 times did change, and so did Thomson's corporation. Oil was turning out to be an unpredictable business, and a risky one, as Middle Eastern nations began acting on their own. In reaction, Roy's son looked for investments that would provide predictable as well as high returns. Taking his firm public, and raising huge amounts of capital, the younger Thomson proceeded to go after the most profitable sectors of the information business.

He first acquired financial and health information companies, then publishers of college and professional books. He would tell interviewers that academic publishing was a great opportunity because college attendance was growing, as were the number of professionals. Both had to have an ever-changing product, information. He was prescient. He had entered a very rewarding market.

Thomson soon had a major share in American textbook publishing and its business-related research companies. He moved much of his company's administrative staff to New York City, sought more funds on the stock market, and additional acquisitions. Gale research, Macmillan, other textbook publishers, and major law publishing companies, including West Publishing, were brought under the Thomson umbrella.

His company was soon a billion-dollar information enterprise, but its managers wanted it to grow larger and to have a greater force in economic globalization. Thomson merged with the English news giant Reuters, purchased Dialog, and acquired other popular online database providers. Thomson continued to prosper and had revenues in the tens of billions of dollars by the opening of the twenty-first century. One of the reasons for the conglomerate's continued success was its move into the field of specialized science information and online science databases. A first step came in 1992. Thomson purchased Eugene Garfield's already giant Institute for Scientific Information of Philadelphia. Its scientific bibliographies, its citation indexes (using information footnoted in articles), and its retrieval methods that predated the best web search engines had become a vital segment of America's and the world's science infrastructure.[22]

Thomson did not rest with acquiring for-profit science information companies, however. By 2007, Thomson, as had Maxwell, speeded the transformation of the old nonprofit science information sector and the redoing of the 1960s' American plural information system. Thomson gained control of the world's two major bibliographic operations in biology. He purchased *Biological Abstracts*, the Rockefellers' great post–World War I hope for international nonprofit biological information. England's old gentlemanly *Zoological Record* came next.

Thomson had protected all its biological information-market flanks. Garfield's service fulfilled the needs of those who wanted citations and links; the other two publications satisfied those who stood by abstracts. Because of Thomson's policies, the once tiny American and British abstracting and citation services had become part of a for-profit corporation with annual revenues of billions of dollars. The Thomson empire also gained income from value-added contracts with the United States' Patent Office to deliver its information. Henry Wallace and E. U. Condon had once tried to make that office the center of a great Socialistic system to provide free information to the common man.

NOT A REALM OF GENTLEMEN SCIENTISTS, BUT OF MULTINATIONAL CONGLOMERATES

Thomson's adventures were just one part of the rise of the multinational information conglomerates that came to dominate a sixteen-billion-dollar-a-year market for sci-tech periodicals by 2014.[23] Decades after Germany's giant Springer revived and gained independence (it ranked second in the world in science publishing by 2000), it mated with Kluwer and Bertelsmann. Then, a group of British investors rode in to take them over and spurred their new organization's efforts in Asia, even in Communist China.[24] The venerable Dutch firm Elsevier,[25] already on the path to becoming the world's largest science publisher, grew even faster when it merged with Britain's Reed in 1992.[26] Elsevier's reach

A NEW INFORMATION ERA

soon extended to America where it purchased LexisNexis (the legal and general information online service), ChoicePoint (the huge computerized identity and credit rating service), and even Bowker, the revered American library service provider. Reflecting the turbulence in the new information industry, Bowker was later purchased by America's Cambridge Information Group.[27]

In the United States, *Chemical Abstracts* remained an independent nonprofit but it had become a $300-million-a-year business with relationships with German and Japanese companies that were so close it was hard to tell who owned who, or if the service remained nonprofit in fact as well as in legal form. Its executives had six-figure salaries and its fees became so high that small research universities had to contract for less inexpensive versions of its database with restrictions that prevented access until the close of regular business hours.[28] Meanwhile, older library service companies began to expand into journal publishing with England's Taylor and Baker becoming a major international presence. The venerable John Wiley merged with England's Blackwell to be able to remain a force in scientific publishing. While not focused on science information, England's Pearson PLC became the world's largest publisher, taking over some of America's major firms.

In addition, libraries had become dependent on a few large service-providing "aggregators" who value-added hundreds of journals and indexing and abstracting offerings from many sources. Those aggregators were not limited to providing science information. They were frequently businesses that dealt with all types of information including legal, financial, and even weather data.[29] One of the largest of such multiproduct aggregators did remain in American hands. EBSCO is an Alabama corporation with its information "campus" located in Ipswich, Massachusetts, an old colonial coastal fishing village.

EBSCO grew from a small magazine subscription service for the American armed forces, and a manufacturer of such things as fishing lures, to become one of the important players in worldwide general online academic database delivery. It had yearly revenues of two billion dollars a year by 2015. It was even absorbing databases once supplied by the nonprofit OCLC.[30] There was another American exception, Cambridge Information Group (CIG). It appeared in the 1970s after rescuing the old Cambridge Scientific Abstracts (CSA) company that had failed as a small niche operation. CIG's business took off in the late

1990s and within a decade was large enough to purchase ProQuest, another huge information provider, for more than two hundred million dollars. It also absorbed Bowker, the revered American library publisher that had been shunted to and from various owners.[31]

One indicator of the end of American dominance in science information is American Society for Information Science changing its name to the Association for Science Information and Technology and holding some of its annual meetings abroad.

ORDERLY, YES, AFFORDABLE, NO

For some, the new information conglomerates were an acceptable version of economic globalization and a necessarily high-capital rationalization of what had become a science information industry. There were assertions that integration seemed to bring badly needed order, cost savings, and optimal pricing of journals and bibliographic services.

The need for large firms that could afford expensive computers and allied technologies was often mentioned. As early as the 1980s, for example, Vladimir Slamecka, one of Mortimer Taube's colleagues and a leader at the important information center at Georgia Tech University, went further. Citing the slumping American economy, the decline of America's science capabilities, and the rise of Europe's research and publishing industries, he deemed the consolidation of science information services a necessity for America's welfare.[32] Other spokesmen for the new international corporate order claimed it provided innovators a chance to turn fresh ideas into realities and that it would prevent disastrous failures of undercapitalized ventures. Some also thought the new system had its own balance.

Although dominated by a few large corporations (by 2014 five companies published more than one-half of all scientific articles), there were claims there were enough firms in the market to allow competition that prevented the ills of monopoly or stifling oligopolies.[33] To others, the new system was out of balance, undemocratic, and inefficient—badly so.

By the mid-1990s the financial pressures on higher education, and what many regarded as price gouging by the new information companies, led to reactions that were reminiscent of the efficiency movement

A NEW INFORMATION ERA

of the late nineteenth century, the antimonopoly crusades of the early twentieth century, and, to a degree, the left-leaning ideological battles of the 1930s and 1960s.

NOTES

1. M. M. Kessler, *Comparison of the Results of Bibliographic Coupling and Analytic Subject Indexing* (Cambridge: Massachusetts Institute of Technology, 1963).

2. Deanna B. Marcum, "Reclaiming the Research Library: The Founding of the Council on Library Resources," *Libraries and Culture* 31, no. 1 (Winter 1996): 113–24; Deanna B. Marcum, "Automating the Library: The Council on Library Resources," *IEEE Annals of the History of Computing* July–September 2002, 2–13.

3. Henriette Avram, http://liswiki.org/wiki/Henriette_D._Avram; Lawrence Buckland, *The Recording of Library of Congress Bibliographic Data in Machine Form: A Report Prepared for the Council on Library Resources, Inc.*, November 23, 1964.

4. Colin B. Burke, "The Ford Foundation's Search for an American Library Laboratory," *IEEE Annals of the History of Computing*, July–September 2002, 56–74.

5. In 2006 constant dollars.

6. John J. Regazzi, *Scholarly Communications: A History from Content as King to Content as Kingmaker* (Lanham, MD: Rowman & Littlefield, 2015), 185.

7. Charles P. Bourne and Trudi Bellardo Hahn, *A History of Online Information Services 1963–1976* (Cambridge, MA: MIT Press, 2003).

8. K. Wayne Smith, *OCLC Online Computer Library Center Inc.: Furthering Access to the World's Information for 30 Years*, Newcomen Publication Number 1502 (n.p.: OCLC, 1997).

9. Melvin S. Day, interview by Robert V. Williams, the Chemical Heritage Foundation, 1997; Madeline B. Henderson, ed., *Interactive Bibliographic Systems: Proceedings of a Forum Held at Gaithersburg. Md. Oct. 4–5, 1971* (n.p.: U.S. AEC Office of Information Services, 1973).

10. Moshe Farjoun, "The Dialectics of Institutional Development in Emerging and Turbulent Fields: The History of Pricing Conventions in the On-Line Database Industry," *Academy of Management Journal* 45, no. 5 (October 2002).

334 CHAPTER 18

11. Delmet J. Trester, *ERIC: The First Fifteen Years 1964–1979; A History of the Educational Resources Information Center* (Washington, DC: Government Printing Office, 1979), ERIC ed195289.

12. Day, interview.

13. Bourne and Hahn, *History of Online Information Services*.

14. LexisNexis Academic, passim.

15. Einar H. Fredriksson, ed., *A Century of Science Publishing: A Collection of Essays* (Amsterdam: ISOS, 2001).

16. H. Kay Jones, *Butterworths: History of a Publishing House* (London: Butterworth, 1980); Fredriksson, *Century of Science Publishing*; Arnold Kramish, *The Griffin* (New York: Houghton Mifflin, 1986); https://en.wikipedia.org/wiki/Paul_Rosbaud.

17. Bernard Fry, "Robert Maxwell and Information Processing," *Information Processing and Management* 24, no. 3 (1988): 215–17; Gordon Thomas and Martin Dillon, *Robert Maxwell, Israel's Superspy: The Life and Murder of a Media Mogul* (New York: Carroll and Graf, 2002).

18. Jones, *Butterworths*.

19. Russell Braddon, *Roy Thomson of Fleet Street* (London: Collins, 1965); Susan Goldenberg, *The Thomson Empire* (n.p.: Kampmann, 1984).

20. Steve Weinberg, *Armand Hammer: The Untold Story* (Boston: Little, Brown, 1989); Edward Jay Epstein, *Dossier: The Secret History of Armand Hammer* (New York: Random House, 1996).

21. Ralph Hewins, *The Richest American: J. Paul Getty* (New York: Dutton, 1960); Russell Miller, *The House of Getty* (New York: Henry Holt, 1985); J. Paul Getty, *As I See It: The Autobiography of J. Paul Getty* (Englewood Cliffs, NJ: Prentice Hall, 1976).

22. LexisNexis passim; *Globe and Mail*, April 9, 1992; *Philadelphia Inquirer*, January 13, 2004.

23. Bill Cope and Mary Kalantzis, "Journal Prices, Oligopoly Concentration in Journals, Signs of Epistemic Change," *First Monday*, April 6, 2009; Bill Cope and Angus Phillips, eds., *The Future of the Academic Journal* (Oxford, UK: Elsevier/Chandos, 2014); Sheila Webber, "The Global Electronic Information Industry: Squeezing Out the Middle Ground," *Proceedings of ASIS Annual Meeting* 35 (1998): 179–89.

24. John Cox, "Globalization, Consolidation and the Growth of Giants; Scholarly Communication, the Individual and the Internet," *Serials Librarian* 40, nos. 1–2 (2002): 105–16.

25. Cornelis D. Andriesse, *Dutch Messengers: A History of Science Publishing, 1930–1980* (Leiden, Netherlands: Brill, 2008).

26. GlobalData—History, February 13, 2013, http://www.lexisnexis.com.proxy-bc.researchport.umd.edu/hottopics/lnacademic/.

A NEW INFORMATION ERA

27. An indication of the commercialization of science publishing, Bowker was later purchased by America's Cambridge Information Group, which also bought the small but significant Cambridge Scientific Abstracts Company.

28. Interviews with University of Maryland librarians, 2014.

29. Carol Tenopir, "Not Just Science Anymore," *Library Journal* 126, no. 20 (December 2001): 45–46; V. Larivière, S. Haustein, and P. Mongeon, "The Oligopoly of Academic Publishers in the Digital Era," *PLOS ONE* 10, no. 6 (June 10, 2015), doi:10.1371/journal.pone.0127502.

30. Wayne Jones, *E-serials: Publishers, Libraries, Users, and Standards* (New York: Haworth, 1998).

31. Cambridge Information Group, http://www.ulib.niu.edu/publishers/CIG.htm.

32. Vladimir Slamecka, "Trade-Offs in the International Flow of Science and Technology Information" (Washington, DC: U.S. Dept. of Commerce, September 1980).

33. Secretary of State for Trade and Industry (UK), *Reed Elsevier PLC and Harcourt General, Inc.: A Report on the Proposed Merger* (n.p.: n.p., 2001).

19

ANOTHER SERIALS CRISIS, OPEN ACCESS, THE RETURN OF IDEOLOGY

Well before there was a public awareness of the concentration in the publishing industry, or of the for-profits' rise, there were signs of another science information crisis. By the 1980s, the torrent of science publications, the escalating cost of searching them, and the pressures on university finances led to a rather desperate search for relief. The new "serials crisis" shared much with previous ones, but it had special problems and it arose in unique technological, ideological, and legal settings. The reactions to it had an unexpected level of intensity as economic globalization made science and information vital to America's economic welfare, as well as to its defense.

The protests about the serials crisis of the late twentieth century began in reaction to severe practical difficulties. There was the escalating financial burden of building and maintaining expanding journal collections—and there were concerns over the difficulties in accessing government-sponsored information. Cost was a major issue. The average per-journal subscription price was increasing multiple times faster than the cost of living. Experts claimed the price of science journals rose 400 percent between 1980 and 1990, with 8–10 percent annual increases afterward. Growths for bibliographic services were matching that.[1] Several prestigious science and medical journals' yearly subscriptions cost more than $10,000. Adding to the problem, the number of journals appeared to be on the way to doubling, as was the number of articles in each issue.

338   CHAPTER 19

Even America's affluent universities were overwhelmed. Given the pressures on university budgets since the 1970s, and the trend toward libraries receiving an ever-diminishing percentage of higher education's expenditures, library administrators were compelled to decrease the percentage of the world's publications on their shelves. Even so, there was a growing library maintenance burden as the number of well-regarded scholarly journals in science, technology, and medicine published in America alone approached seven thousand and as maintaining a year's run of a single journal was calculated to be $1,000.

There were more than economic problems. Complaints included ones over the overly long time between the submission of an article and its publication, sometimes as much as a year, and there were conflicts within university communities over favoritism. With the cost of science and medical journals rising faster than that in other fields, and with science departments typically being the source of most of the critically needed grant income, scientists' requests for subscriptions tended to dominate library budgets. As a result, science journals were crowding out those in the humanities and social sciences. The favoring of science periodicals also meant that journal holdings were pushing out books. Library budgets seemed another unacceptable consequence of academia's "two cultures," scientists versus humanists.

The problems and conflicts intensified during the 1990s, frustrating faculties, administrators, and the tax-paying public. By the opening of the twenty-first century the crisis became political. There were calls for congressional investigations. There was so much frustration that in 2003 several library groups organized themselves into the Information Access Alliance to lobby against cartels, aggressive sales practices, "bundling" that forced subscribers to pay for unwanted journals, and the deepening copyright restrictions that made interlibrary loans too expensive.[2]

OLD SCIENCE THREATENED: IS INTELLECTUAL PROPERTY THEFT?

The calls for government action were prompted by more than practical concerns about science journals. There were some ideologically driven complaints about broader issues, ones with the flavor of the information protests of the 1940s. There was outrage over trends indicating that research, even in prestigious universities, was becoming part of a new era of commercialized intellectual property. The shift had been encouraged by government actions such as the Bayh-Dole Act of 1980 that allowed the patenting of the results of government-sponsored research. The act was part of the search for ways to encourage joint corporate-university ventures that would provide income to higher education.[3]

The complaints about commercialization had merit, as did those generated by signs that the old ethic of a free flow of science and other information was in danger. As the American economy became increasingly dependent on its service sectors, information and artistic production were given more and more protections, ones that made access more expensive. Copyright shields were being extended to ninety-five years, even for research publications. Computer software was gaining patent as well as copyright protection, and many types of artistic work were being considered as permanent property.

A DIVIDED ACADEMIA

There was more that threatened old science's open culture. Vannevar Bush's dream of having universities gain income from patents on faculty research seemed to have been realized, leading to fears of secrecy about research results and worries that inquiry would be driven by the profit motive, not Flexner-like pure scientific inquiry or even Henry Wallace's quest for socially useful knowledge. Keeping research secret was not confined to the big science academic fields. The oversupply of academics in the humanities and spiraling publish-or-perish demands led, for example, to dissertations being kept from public view until their authors could turn them into published books, ones justifying awarding increasingly difficult-to-obtain professorships.[4]

There was disagreement over the consequences of the changes. Some of the discontented echoed the "people's" science arguments of the Henry Wallace years. But supporters of university commercialization and for-profit information services developed their own arguments. As early as the 1980s, led by for-profit publishers and journal suppliers, there were renewed public battles to prevent "information Socialism." For example, an effort by the National Science Foundation to underwrite a central computerized facility that would handle all the editing

340   CHAPTER 19

and publication chores for the small nonprofit science journals died under opposition from for-profit organizations.[5]

But the protestors did not retreat. They became increasingly vocal, complaining about for-profit mergers and acquisitions. They protested the emergence of an oligopoly in science publishing, one that would soon lead to three firms publishing close to 50 percent of all science-technical-medical papers and to rising profit margins for the largest firms—margins that were higher than those for corporations in the lucrative chemical and high-technology fields. One major publisher was said to have achieved close to a 40 percent profit margin by 2009.

Meanwhile, library administrators were trapped because there were no substitutes for an article. Libraries were captive markets; they had to subscribe to journals or pay exorbitant fees for individual articles.

There were many types of proposed solutions to libraries being captives. Some of the proposals fit the long history of science information's pragmatic technical adjustments; others had a radical tinge. The emerging Internet technology played a role, but mutations of older political ideologies were what turned the battles into emotionally charged crusades. Liberation, open access, open societies, and, especially, open culture became the public face of the serials crisis.

Open access's advocates demanded no-cost access to all science information—for everyone. Liberation and open culture looked to something broader: the end of all forms of intellectual and artistic "repression" in the West, as well as the newly liberated Soviet bloc. Free accesses to music, art, and literature, as well as science information, were the goals.

REFORM IN NEW POLITICAL AND TECHNOLOGICAL CONTEXTS

The reform proposals were varied, as were their advocates. What began in the early 1990s as a version of the early 1900s Progressive era's mild information efficiency movement changed into one that had the idealism and Socialistic slant of Henry Wallace's times. It threatened America's plural science information system as much as the for-profit surge had. The progression from practicality to ideologically driven demands can only be sketched here.

ANOTHER SERIALS CRISIS, OPEN ACCESS, THE RETURN OF IDEOLOGY   341

Significantly, the new information reformers labored in unique contexts, including ideological ones. During the 1980s, global capitalism was ascending while the older left ideologies were disintegrating. At the end of the decade, it seemed that the Red cause had collapsed as Communist rule in Eastern Europe crumbled.[6] That was followed by the breakdown of the Soviet Union and by China's welcoming of capitalists' factories within its borders. As well, by the mid-1990s the United States' spurt of New Left aggressive radicalism of the Vietnam War era had become a curiosity.

In Europe, the replacement for the New Left was a rather ambiguous "green" political movement that emphasized environmental and peace issues spiced with some egalitarianism. In America, a set of well-subsidized political organizations, such as ACORN, were at the time rather inconspicuously forwarding a Progressive social agenda through more evolutionary than revolutionary means as they emphasized "identity" issues over Marxism.

The American mainstream had, in contrast, a faith in politically middle-of-the road, efficiency- and technology-based reform, especially in the information industry. Technological change was playing a major role. By the mid-1990s, computers and computer networks were widely available consumer items in the West. The great and world-spanning Internet soon followed. Within two decades, millions of people became linked together through inexpensive home computers and network connections enabled by a rewiring of the world because of the phenomenal carrying power of fiber-optic cables. There were also signs of researchers finally making breakthroughs in automatic translation, speech recognition, and artificial intelligence after the old law-based approaches had been abandoned, replaced by statistical methods utilizing the powers of supercomputers and huge collections of data on what people did, not on supposed laws.[7] The new technologies had the potential to reduce cost and increase access.

Some of those confronting the serials crisis utilized the new technologies in a practical way, with a goal of preserving the plural information system. For example, in 1993 Johns Hopkins University's press began the nonprofit, online focused Project Muse to act as a journal aggregator, providing services to small journals with subscription rates for libraries at prices lower than those charged by large for-profit companies. A year later, Stanford University set up its similar HighWire Press.[8]

342   CHAPTER 19

There were also somewhat radical and politically driven reactions in the 1990s, ones that touched many nerves. Prodded by interest groups, and another drive for government efficiency, a digital initiative within the federal government began. It had the goal of making all in-house federal reports available on the Internet, free of charge, bypassing value-added services and the old depository library program that depended on expensive print, microfiche, and computer disk media. But less disruptive alternatives prevailed.

PRAGMATIC EFFICIENCIES

There was a more traditional response that focused on nongovernmental information. Surprisingly, it was led by a humanist of the eastern liberal establishment and funded by the conservative Mellon Foundation. The Mellons had decided to fill the void left by the withdrawal of the older philanthropies from sponsoring science information.[9]

After William Bowen resigned from the presidency of Princeton University in 1988, he was asked to head the Pittsburgh-centered Mellon Foundation that had spent so much on developing the University of Pittsburgh. Bowen brought with him a deep concern over higher education's economic woes. He quickly turned his attention to the serials crisis, especially the cost of maintaining collections. Large academic libraries were running out of space, and the cost of binding and storing back copies of journals was financially draining. After a few years at the foundation, Bowen gave the go-ahead to explore what was for then a technically radical solution. Significantly, it was one that did not rely upon government support or on any fundamental legal or institutional changes, despite having a grander vision than older solutions like Watson Davis's.[10]

Bowen decided to establish an independent nonprofit, but self-sustaining, organization to copy back runs of journals and place their full text in a media that could allow libraries to have copies in a space-saving format besides microfilm. He soon went further and committed to a computer-based, network- and user-accessible, full-text archive. That was a gamble because digital copying faced significant technical challenges in the early 1990s. Nevertheless, Bowen and Kevin Guthrie, his aide, were prescient and JSTOR (Journal Store) came to life in 1995,

ANOTHER SERIALS CRISIS, OPEN ACCESS, THE RETURN OF IDEOLOGY 343

years before other scholarly full-text digital programs, such as Google Books or the HathiTrust, appeared.[11]

Bowen and the foundation did not plan JSTOR as a charity, it was not to be open access, and it was not to endanger America's existing system. Supported by subscription charges to participating libraries, with royalty payments when needed, it was designed to protect the income of the journal publishers, many of whom already felt financially hard pressed.

Unexpectedly, the service quickly proved to be more than a way to save shelving space and maintenance costs. JSTOR became a favored resource for scholarly research. The Mellon Foundation soon decided to go beyond Bowen's original visions. It founded the Portico project to computer archive new electronic journals, even if they were not to be on JSTOR, so they would not be lost as was the case with so much of electronic publishing. The foundation's managers also moved the organization into other advanced library initiatives, including some that would aid the open access cause. They financed the creation of software at the Massachusetts Institute of Technology that allowed universities to electronically archive faculty publications. The foundation also supported the OAIster project at the University of Michigan to facilitate the use of online author and university repositories. Mellon's library policies later became a bit more radical. The foundation helped finance PLOS (Public Library of Science), one of the first open access journal adventures.[12]

Another liberal but more politically charged reaction to the cost of serials appeared in the 1990s. Like JSTOR, its goal was to reduce costs while preserving the nonprofit segments of America's information system. This time, the response was by librarians. In 1998, the Association of Research Libraries (ARL), an organization representing the one hundred largest research libraries in the United States, decided to form the Scholarly Publishing and Academic Resources Coalition (SPARC). Its strategy was to use the influence and knowledge of its members to incubate low-cost but high-quality traditional journals to compete with those of the established publishers and to find ways to reduce the cost of science publication through creating alternatives to such things as the expensive prepublication review process. Another goal was to educate librarians, academics, and, especially, policy makers about the science information problem. The coalition also became one of the leaders in

344 CHAPTER 19

the battle against a new type of "predatory" journal. With escalating pressure to publish, journals with little or no circulation that charged high fees to authors and published all submitted articles became a temptation for academics—usually to their disappointment.[13]

As SPARC was pursuing its moderate goals, others were pushing radical alternatives, ones that had some traces of the New Left's ideology—but not its vocabulary. Some of those proposals went far beyond rebalancing the plural system.

MOVING BEYOND PRAGMATIC SOLUTIONS, STEP BY STEP

It wasn't until he was in his forties that Paul Ginsparg, an American theoretical physicist, emerged as one of the voices representing a new generation of a bit more than liberal American scientists. Paul had a touch of J. D. Bernal in him and was for liberating science information, but he was not a member of the more aggressive group that one commentator labeled as the shock-troop "abolitionists" of the information world. Paul never became as radical as reformers such as Pat Brown, Stevan Harnad, Lawrence Lessig, or Aaron Swartz—and he never became as famous as Peter Suber.[14] Paul's contribution was to use his access to advanced computers and computer networks to create his arXiv worldwide service to make the preliminary drafts of academic papers (preprints) freely available to anyone with access to what became the web. That was a great extension of the old habit of scientists sending their manuscripts to favored colleagues for comments. The service did not directly threaten journals because the final published version of an article remained under copyright protection. But Paul's arXiv was a step toward universal free access to all science information, something others were soon advocating.

Peter Suber was among those advocates. He was a young philosophy professor at a small midwestern Quaker college who made a connection that led him to be the most recognized spokesman for what became known as the open access movement. A critical step came when Suber received a sizable grant from the Open Society Foundation created by the American George Soros.[15] Soros, an aggressive multibillionaire

ANOTHER SERIALS CRISIS, OPEN ACCESS, THE RETURN OF IDEOLOGY 345

hedge-fund operator, had escaped as a young man from Budapest in Communist Hungary in the late 1940s.

Soros had been using his hard-won and controversial fortune to undermine Communist rule in Europe. After the upheavals of 1989, he spent millions helping to create civil, open society institutions to replace the totalitarian ones of the Communist era. Like the conservative Rockefeller Foundation at the end of World War I, Soros wanted to rebuild liberated Europe's scientific information systems and to provide ongoing access to the best scientific information in the West. But Soros was not a conservative and his interests included more than science information and the nations that had cast off Communism. Soros also spent millions through institutions such as the San Francisco–based Tides Foundation, ACORN, and the left wing of the Democratic Party to "open up" every aspect of American society. Soros never proclaimed a formal ideology, but it was clear that his ideas constituted a new kind of leftist activism, one without traditional Communist doctrine that tacitly accepted capitalism. [16]

Peter Suber was not as radical as Soros, but he lobbied for government and private information policies that would make science information free to consumers. He did not openly denounce the idea furthered by Stevan Harnad, another Hungarian immigrant, that authors should bypass all journals and institutions by placing their articles on the web without prior review. Harnad's option was called "green" because there were to be no fees at any publication stage. In contrast to Harnad, Peter emphasized what seemed a more realistic and less disruptive solution. Authors would pay for publication in journals that would, in turn, charge no subscription or access fees to readers. That became known as the "gold" option. It was a version of the old idea behind "dissemination" grants in Cold War government contracts. Although it placed a burden on authors, especially those in fields not supported by outside funds, it seemed a way to satisfy the journal industry and librarians. [17]

Another reformer made gold and the government open access policies ideological. Harold Varmus was a young, Nobel Prize–winning geneticist. Ironic for an open access leader, he had worked at the University of California in San Francisco, one of the nation's most entrepreneurial and patent-rewarded educational institutions, before moving on to head the National Institutes of Health. Harold came together with

346 CHAPTER 19

Pat Brown and Michael Eisen (other radical Bay Area scientists who had tried to launch a worldwide boycott of high-priced, for-profit publishers) to create competitors to the leading science journals. With start-up help from the Mellon and other foundations, they created the "gold" Public Library of Science (PLOS) journals. PLOS's founders hoped its journals would quickly become self-supporting and force the traditional journals to lower their prices.

Varmus, a loyal and well-connected liberal Democrat, then spearheaded a campaign that involved government action, one that was a greater threat to the publishing establishment than was PLOS.[18] He became the public face of a program that went beyond the information policies of Henry Wallace or Hubert Humphrey. His goal was to have the full-text (not just bibliographic information) of every publication tied to government-financed, nonclassified research placed on a government website, such as PubMed, with free access for the public. That ultragreen proposal became a highly charged political issue that led to public displays of the ideological premises of both left and right.[19]

BEYOND ACCESS, CULTURE

More was to come as science's open access movement merged with what became known as the open culture crusade. Open culture's original battles were against restrictions on the use of music and computer software and the censorship of the web. Its most visible figures were part of a cluster of young instant Internet millionaires who had more than a tinge of the old hippie and computer hacker culture in their ideological veins.[20] Not surprisingly, their homes were in San Francisco, California, and Cambridge, Massachusetts, centers of the Internet-based new capitalism.

John Perry Barlow, Brewster Kahle, Carl Malamud, Aaron Swartz, and Lawrence Lessig, along with other supporters of the Electronic Frontier Foundation (EFF), gave time and much money to keeping the Internet free of any restrictions and became leaders in the net neutrality movement to prevent unequal treatment of Internet transmissions. They soon began working to make all types of information free.

Kahle founded the Internet Archive of San Francisco; Lessing led the struggles against restrictive copyright laws through his Creative

Commons organization. Barlow was a founder of the EFF and was an aggressive advocate of the rights of computer and software hackers. Malamud devoted much time to downloading and making public government information, as well as music that was not legally public.[21]

Many of those West Coast radicals found a welcome at Harvard University's Berkman Center for Internet and Society. It had been conducting its own "access" campaign, one that went further than Harnad's academic self-publishing plan. Under Stuart Shieber, the legal niceties required to compel faculty to publish all their articles on a university's free-access website were put into place. That victory was acclaimed by information's left wing while arousing worries about the future of the traditional publishers.

Others sought more than forcing faculty members to bypass regular journals.[22] The young Aaron Swartz, another Internet millionaire and one of Lessing, Malamud, and the Harvard center's associates, took open access, even open culture, to a new level. After attending a George Soros–sponsored event in Europe, he returned to America, applied his hacking skills, and illegally downloaded the contents of the private-property JSTOR. He was arrested and began making public statements sounding much like those of a 1930s Marxist. He declared that all intellectual property is theft. Then, in January 2013, he committed suicide.[23]

Swartz instantly became a martyr to the information liberation movement, and to the open access and open culture causes, just as John Reed had been martyred by the Reds of the 1920s and the liberals of the 1940s.

OLD COMRADES DID NOT FORGET

Aaron's death, combined with Edward Snowden's 2013 disclosure of the American National Security Agency's secret phone and Internet spying, led to an EFF class action lawsuit against the government, one that revealed the ideological complexity of the open movements. It also indicated that Marxism had not been entirely forsaken. The EFF's open culture entourage, including groups allied against gun laws and for legalized marijuana, was joined by some older faces of the ideological and political left. The coalition was reminiscent of those of the radical 1930s and Henry Wallace's era. The Unitarian Church of Los Angeles, the Unitarian Service Committee, the National Lawyers Guild that had been the legal mainstay of the Communist Party for two generations, the Soros and Tides Foundation–linked ACORN Active Media group, the American Civil Liberties Union, and the Washington, D.C.–based anticopyright Public Knowledge organization joined the lawsuit.[24]

NOTES

1. Lee C. Van Orsdel and Kathleen Born, "Journals in the Time of Google," *Library Journal*, April 15, 2006; Lee C. Van Orsdel and Kathleen Born, "Reality bite2: Periodicals Price Survey 2009," *Library Journal*, April 15, 2009; Donald W. King and Frances M. Alvarado-Albertorio, "Pricing and Other Means of Charging for Scholarly Journals: A Literature Review and Commentary," *Learned Publishing* 21, no. 4 (October 2008): 248–72; Donald W. King and Carol Tenopir, "Some Economic Aspects of the Scholarly Journal System," *Annual Review of Information Science and Technology* 45, no. 1 (2011): 295–366.

2. Theodore C. Bergstrom et al., "Evaluating Big Deal Journal Bundles," *PNAS* 111, no. 26 (2014): 9425–30, doi:10.1073/pnas.1403006111.

3. Daniel S. Greenberg, *Science for Sale: The Perils, Rewards, and Delusions of Campus Capitalism* (Chicago: University of Chicago Press, 2007).

4. Harvard University instituted such a policy, http://www.gsas.harvard.edu/current_students/the_phd_dissertation.php.

5. Bill Cope and Mary Kalantzis, "Signs of Epistemic Disruption," *First Monday* 14, no. 4 (April 2009).

6. John Patrick Diggins, *The Rise and Fall of the American Left* (New York: Norton, 1992).

7. Widespread practical applications awaited the second decade of the new century, but the later 1990s saw the research breakthroughs. Outlines of the history of the new AI may be found in such works as: Xuedong Huang, James Baker, and Raj Reddy, "Historical Perspective of Speech Recognition," *Communications of the ACM* 57, no. 1 (January 2014): 94–103; Robert D. Hof, "AI Hits the Mainstream," *MIT Technology Review* 119, no. 3 (2017): 62–66; and Nello Cristianini, "Intelligence Revisited," *New Scientist* 232, no. 3097 (October 29, 2016).

8. HighWire Press was sold to a for-profit investment firm in 2014.

ANOTHER SERIALS CRISIS, OPEN ACCESS, THE RETURN OF IDEOLOGY   349

9. David Hammack and Helmut J. Anheier, *A Versatile American Institution: The Changing Ideals and Realities of Philanthropic Institutions* (Washington. DC: Brookings, 2013).

10. Roger C. Schonfeld, *JSTOR: A History* (Princeton, NJ: Princeton University Press, 2003).

11. https://en.wikipedia.org/wiki/HathiTrust.

12. Andrew Albanese, "Can Public Library of Science Grow? Scientists Not Following Pledge, but Librarians Hope for Attitude Change," *Library Journal* 127, no. 6 (April 1, 2002): 20–21.

13. http://www.arl.org/sparc/about/index.shtml; http://sparceurope.org/scientists-foundations-libraries-universities-and-advocates-unite-and-issue-new-recommendations-to-make-research-freely-available-to-all-online/.

14. G. Taubes, "Publication by Electronic Mail Takes Physics by Storm," *Science* 259, no. 5099 (1993): 1246–48.

15. Michael T. Kaufman, *Soros: The Life and Times of a Messianic Billionaire* (New York: Knopf, 2002); David Horowitz and Richard Poe, *The Shadow Party: How George Soros, Hillary Clinton and Sixties Radicals Seized Control of the Democratic Party* (Nashville, TN: Thomas Nelson, 2006).

16. Richard Poynder, "George Soros Gives $3 Million to New Open Access Initiative," *Information Today* 19, no. 4 (April 2002): 20–21.

17. Peter Suber, *The Case of the Speluncean Explorers* (London: Routledge, 1998); Peter Suber, *Open Access* (Cambridge, MA: MIT Press, 2012).

18. Albanese, "Can Public Library of Science Grow?"; Harold Varmus, "Autobiography," http://nobelprize.org/nobel_prizes/medicine/laureates/1989/varmus-autobio.html.

19. M. Carl Drott, "Open Access," in *Annual Review of Information Science and Technology*, ed. Blaise Cronin (Medford, NJ: Information Today, 2006); John Willinsky, *The Access Principle: The Case for Open Access to Research and Scholarship* (Cambridge, MA: MIT Press, 2005); Charles W. Bailey Jr., "Transforming Scholarly Publishing through Open Access: A Bibliography," n.d., http://digital-scholarship.org/tsp/transforming.htm; M. Laakso, P. Welling, H. Bukvova, L. Nyman, B. C. Björk, and T. Hedlund, "The Development of Open Access Journal Publishing from 1993 to 2009," *PLOS ONE* 6, no. 6 (2011), http://www.ncbi.nlm.nih.gov/pubmed/21695139, accessed August 27, 2015; on FASTR act: http://www.sparc.arl.org/advocacy/national/frpaa#sthash.Wa2aLpuJ.dpuf; by Suber on government open access: http://dash.harvard.edu/bitstream/handle/1/4725009/suber_sabo.htm?sequence=1; on opposition to government open access: http://techcrunch.com/2012/02/15/the-dangerous-research-works-act/.

20. Fred Turner, *From Counterculture to Cyberculture: Stewart Brand, the Whole Earth Network and the Rise of Digital Utopianism* (Chicago: University of Chicago Press, 2006).

21. Lawrence Lessig, *Free Culture: How Big Media Uses Technology and the Law to Lock Down Culture and Control Creativity* (New York: Penguin, 2004); Carl Malamud, *Exploring the Internet: A Technical Travelogue* (Englewood Cliffs, NJ: Prentice Hall, 1992).

22. N. Medeiros, "Harvard, NIH, and the Balance of Power in the Open Access Debate," *OCLC Systems & Services*, 2008, 137–39; https://osc.hul.harvard.edu/policies/.

23. Lawrence Lessig, *The Boy Who Could Change the World: The Writings of Aaron; With an Introduction by Lawrence Lessig* (New York: New Press, 2015); Justin Peters, *The Idealist: Aaron Swartz and the Rise of Free Culture on the Internet* (New York: Scribner, 2016).

24. On the lawsuit: https://www.eff.org/cases/first-unitarian-church-los-angeles-v-nsanewfrpmweb/lawsuiteffetc.

BIBLIOGRAPHY

Major archival sources: Case Western Reserve University, Shera Papers; Columbia University Archives, Carnegie Foundation; Lewis Walpole Library, Lewis Papers; U.S. National Archives, RG165, 226, 263, CIA CREST as at U.S. National Archives.

Addicott, Kenneth K. "Museums for the Army." Ph.D. diss., Teachers College, Columbia University, 1944.

Adkinson, Burton W. *Two Centuries of Federal Information.* Stroudsburg, PA: Dowden, Hutchinson & Ross, 1978.

Albanese, Andrew. "Can Public Library of Science Grow? Scientists Not Following Pledge, but Librarians Hope for Attitude Change." *Library Journal* 127, no. 6 (April 1, 2002): 20–21.

Alvarez, David. "American Clandestine Intelligence in Early Postwar Europe." *Journal of Intelligence History* 4, no. 1 (2004): 7–24.

———. "Behind Venona: American Signal Intelligence in Early Cold War." *International and National Security* 4, no. 2 (Summer 1999): 179–86.

Amato, Ivan. "A Century of CAS." *Chemical and Engineering News* 85, no. 24 (June 11, 2007): 38–39.

American National Biography. Vol. 9, "James Newton Gunn."

American University. *Machine Indexing: Progress and Problems: Papers Presented at the Third Institute on Information Storage and Retrieval, American University 1961.* Washington, DC: Center for Technology and Administration, 1961.

Andriesse, Cornelis D. *Dutch Messengers: A History of Science Publishing, 1930–1980.* Leiden, Netherlands: Brill, 2008.

Anonymous. *Automation of ASTIA.* Arlington, VA: ASTIA, 1960.

———. *The Center for Scientific Aids to Learning: An Interim Report to the Carnegie Corporation of New York.* Cambridge: Massachusetts Institute of Technology, February 1, 1951.

———. *Large Capacity Memory Techniques for Computing System.* N.p.: ACM, 1962.

———. "Machine Techniques for Information Selection." CREST. 6 10 and 12 1954.

———. *Proceedings of the International Study Conference on Classification for Information Retrieval Held at Beatrice Webb House, Dorking, England, 13th–17th May 1957.*

———. "Technical Information Activities of the Department of Defense." *Science*, n.s., 114, no. 2973 (December 21, 1951): 653–61.

———. *Who Was Who in America*, vol. 5 (1969–1973). New Providence, NJ: Marquis-Who's Who, 1973.

Ash, Lee, ed. *Who's Who in Library Service*. 4th ed. N.p.: Shoe String Press, 1966.

Avco Corporation Electronics and Ordnance Division, Cincinnati 41, Ohio. *Technical Investigations of Addition of a Hardcopy Output to the Elements of a Mechanized Library: Final Report 20 Sept. 1961*.

Bailey, Charles W., Jr. "Transforming Scholarly Publishing through Open Access: A Bibliography." N.d. http://digital-scholarship.org/tsp/transforming.htm.

Ball, Norman T. "Making a Classification System." In *Punched Cards: Their Applications to Science and Industry*, edited by Robert S. Casey and James W. Perry, 379–92. New York: Reinhold, 1951.

———. "Ratification of Constitutional Amendment by State Conventions." *George Washington Law Review* 2 (1934): 216–21.

———. "Research or Available Knowledge: A Matter of Classification." *Science*, n.s., 105, no. 2715 (January 10, 1947): 34–36.

———. *The Special Committee on Technical Information* [Booklet]. Washington, DC: National Military Establishment Research and Development Board, 1949.

Barhydt, Gordon C. *Western Reserve University Index of Educational Resources*. Cleveland, OH: Western Reserve, 1964.

Batchelder, R. W. "The Scope and Value of the Microcard." *Special Libraries*, May–June 1952, 157–61.

Beard, R. L., and Karl F. Heumann. "The Chemical-Biological Coordination Center: An Experiment in Documentation." *Science*, n.s., 116, no. 3021 (November 21, 1952): 553–54.

Becker, Joseph, and Robert M. Hayes. *Information Storage and Retrieval*. New York: Wiley, 1967. First published 1963.

Bergstrom, Theodore C., Paul N. Courant, R. Preston McAfee, and Michael A. Williams. "Evaluating Big Deal Journal Bundles." *PNAS* 111, no. 26 (2014): 9425–30. doi:10.1073/pnas.1403006111.

Black, Alastair, Dave Muddiman, and Helen Plant. *The Early Information Society: Information Management in Britain before the Computer*. Hampshire, UK: Ashgate, 2007.

Blum, John Morton, ed. *The Price of Vision: The Diary of Henry A. Wallace 1942–1946*. Boston: Houghton Mifflin, 1973.

Boaz, Martha. *Modern Trends in Documentation: Proceedings of a Symposium Held at the University of Southern California April 1958*. London: Pergamon, 1959.

Boehm, George A. *Science in the Service of Mankind: The Battelle Story*. Columbus, OH: Battelle, 1986.

Bogg, S. Whitmore. "Library Classification and Cataloging of Geographic Material." *Annals of the Association of American Geographers* 27, no. 2 (June 1937): 49–93.

Borel, Paul Arnold. *Along the Way: Fragments from My Three Score Years*. Great Falls, VA: River Bend House, 1986.

Borko, Harold. "Measuring the Reliability of Subject Classification by Men and Machine." *American Documentation* 15, no. 4 (1964): 268–73.

Bourne, Charles P., and Trudi Bellardo Hahn. *A History of Online Information Services 1963–1976*. Cambridge, MA: MIT Press, 2003.

Bower, Tom. *Maxwell: The Final Verdict*. London: HarperCollins, 1995.

Bowker, Geoffrey C., and Susan Leigh Star. *Sorting Things Out: Classification and Its Consequences*. Cambridge, MA: MIT Press, 1999.

Braddon, Russell. *Roy Thomson of Fleet Street*. London: Collins, 1965.

Bradley, Mark A. *A Very Principled Boy: The Life of Duncan Lee, Red Spy and Cold Warrior*. New York: Basic Books, 2014.

Brugioni, Dino A. *Eyes in the Sky: Eisenhower, the CIA, and Cold War Aerial Espionage*. Annapolis, MD: Naval Institute Press, 2010.

Buckland, Lawrence. *The Recording of Library of Congress Bibliographic Data in Machine Form: A Report Prepared for the Council on Library Resources, Inc*. November 23, 1964.

BIBLIOGRAPHY

Bukharin, Oleg A. "The Cold War Atomic Intelligence Game, 1945–70: From the Russian Perspective." *Studies in Intelligence* 48, no. 2 (2004).

Burke, Colin B. "The Ford Foundation's Search for an American Library Laboratory." *IEEE Annals of the History of Computing*, July–September 2002, 56–74.

———. *Information and Intrigue*. Cambridge, MA: MIT Press, 2014.

———. *Information and Secrecy: Vannevar Bush, Ultra, and the Other Memex*. Metuchen, NJ: Scarecrow Press, 1994.

———. "Librarians Go High-Tech, Perhaps: The Ford Foundation, the CLR and IN-TREX." *Libraries & Culture* 31, no. 1 (Winter 1996): 125–29.

———. "A Rough Road to the Information Highway. Project INTREX: A View from the CLR Archives." *Information Processing & Management* 32, no. 1 (January 1996): 19–32.

Bush, Vannevar, Erich Bloch, and Daniel J. Kevles, eds. *Science, the Endless Frontier: A Report to the President on a Program for Postwar Scientific Research*. Washington, DC: National Science Foundation, 1990.

Casey, Robert S., and James M. Perry, eds. *Punched Cards: Their Applications to Science and Industry*. New York: Reinhold, 1951.

Central Intelligence Agency Office of Central Reference. *Document Classification: Papers Presented at the Conference on Philosophy of Document Classification in OCR*. N.p.: Office of Central Reference, January 1960.

Clesner, Jennie, and Hershel Clesner. "Technical, Scientific, and Engineering Information as a Factor in Competitive Coexistence." *Federal Law Journal* 17 (November 3, 1957): 236.

Cleverdon, Cyril. "Report on the Testing and Analysis of an Investigation into the Comparative Efficiency of Indexing Systems." Cranfield College of Aeronautics, Cranfield, England, 1962.

Clowse, Barbara Barksdale. *Brainpower for the Cold War: The Sputnik Crisis and the National Defense Education Act of 1958*. Westport, CT: Greenwood, 1981.

Condon, Richard A. "Mechanized Image Systems." In *Data Acquisition and Processing in Biology and Medicine*, edited by Kurt Enslein with John F. Kinslow, 179–88. Vol. 4, *Proceedings of the Rochester Conference*. Oxford, UK: Pergamon, 1966.

Consolazio, William V., and Margaret C. Green. "Federal Support of Research in the Life Sciences." *Science*, n.s., 124, no. 3221 (September 21, 1956): 522–26.

Cope, Bill, and Mary Kalantzis. "Journal Prices, Oligopoly Concentration in Journals, Signs of Epistemic Change." *First Monday*, April 6, 2009.

———. "Signs of Epistemic Disruption." *First Monday* 14, no. 4 (April 2009).

Cope, Bill, and Angus Phillips, eds. *The Future of the Academic Journal*. Oxford, UK: Elsevier/Chandos, 2014.

Costello, J. C. "Uniterm Indexing: Principles, Problems and Solutions." *American Documentation* 12, no. 1 (1961): 20–26.

Cox, Gerald J., C. F. Bailey, and R. S. Casey. "Punch Cards for a Chemical Bibliography." *Chemical and Engineering News* 23, no. 18 (September 25, 1945): 1623–26.

Cox, John. "Globalization, Consolidation and the Growth of Giants: Scholarly Communication, the Individual and the Internet." *Serials Librarian* 40, nos. 1–2 (2002): 105–16.

Cramer, C. H. *Case Western Reserve: A History of the University, 1826–1976*. Boston: Little, Brown, 1976.

———. *The School of Library Science at Case Western Reserve University: Seventy-Five Years, 1904–1979*. Cleveland, OH: School of Library Science, 1979.

Crawford Report, Task Force of the President's Special Assistant for Science and Technology. "Scientific and Technological Communication in the Government." April 1962.

Cristianini, Nello. "Intelligence Revisited." *New Scientist* 232, no. 3097 (October 29, 2016).

Cronin, B., and H. B. Atkins. *The Web of Knowledge: A Festschrift in Honor of Eugene Garfield*. Medford, NJ: Information Today, 2000.

Culver, John C., and John Hyde. *American Dreamer: The Life and Times of Henry A. Wallace*. New York: Norton, 2000.

Darling, Arthur B. *The Central Intelligence Agency: An Instrument of Government to 1950*. University Park: Pennsylvania State University Press, 1990.

de Grolier, Eric. *On the Theoretical Basis of Information Retrieval Systems*. Paris: OAR, September 1965.

Diggins, John Patrick. *The Rise and Fall of the American Left*. New York: Norton, 1992.

Donaldson, Scott. *Archibald MacLeish: An American Life*. Boston: Houghton Mifflin, 1992.

Downey, Gregory John. *Closed Captioning*. Baltimore: Johns Hopkins University Press, 2008.

———. "Constructing 'Computer-Compatible Stenographers': The Transition to Real Time Translation in Court Reporting." *Technology and Culture* 47, no. 1 (January 2006): 1–16.

Doyle, Lauren B. "Indexing and Abstracting by Association." *American Documentation* 134 (1962): 378–90.

Drott, M. Carl. "Open Access." In *Annual Review of Information Science and Technology*, edited by Blaise Cronin. Medford, NJ: Information Today, 2006.

Edmundson, H. P., ed. *Proceedings of the National Symposium on Machine Translation: Held at the University of California, Los Angeles, February 2–5, 1960*. Englewood Cliffs, NJ: Prentice Hall, 1961.

Edmundson, H. P., V. A. Oswald, and R. E. Wyikys. *Automatic Indexing and Abstracting of the Contents of Documents*. Los Angeles: Planning Research Corporation, October 31, 1959.

Elliott Committee Report. Select Committee on Government Research 88th Congress. 1964.

England, J. Merton. *A Patron for Pure Science: The National Science Foundation's Formative Years 1945–57*. Washington, DC: National Science Foundation, 1983.

Enslein, Kurt with John F. Kinslow. *Data Acquisition and Processing in Biology and Medicine. Vol. 4, Proceedings of the Rochester Conference*. Oxford, UK: Pergamon, 1966 .

Epstein, Edward Jay. *Dossier: The Secret History of Armand Hammer*. New York: Random House, 1996.

Farjoun, Moshe. "The Dialectics of Institutional Development in Emerging and Turbulent Fields: The History of Pricing Conventions in the On-line Database Industry." *Academy of Management Journal* 45, no. 5 (October 2002).

Fischer, George L., et al., eds. *Symposium on Optical Character Recognition*. Washington, DC: Spartan Books, 1962.

Ford, Clellan S. *Human Relations Area Files, 1949–1969: A Twenty-Year Report*. New Haven, CT: Human Relations Area Files, 1970.

Foskett, A. C. *The Universal Decimal Classification: The History, Present Status and Future Prospects of a Large General Classification Scheme*. London: Linnet Books, 1973.

Foskett, D. J. "The Construction of a Faceted Classification for a Special Subject." *Proceedings of the International Conference on Scientific Information, 1958*. Washington, DC: NSF-NAS, ca. 1958.

Fredriksson, Einar H., ed. *A Century of Science Publishing: A Collection of Essays*. Amsterdam: ISOS, 2001.

Fry, Bernard. "Robert Maxwell and Information Processing." *Information Processing and Management* 24, no. 3 (1988): 215–17.

Garfield, Eugene. "Autobiographical Sketch." *Journal of Information Science* 27, no. 2 (2001): 119–25.

———. "Citation Indexes for Science: A New Dimension in Documentation through Association of Ideas." *Science* 122, no. 3159 (1955): 108–11.

———. "Preliminary Report on the Mechanical Analysis of Information by Use of the 101 Statistical Punched Card Machine." *American Documentation* 5, no. 1 (January 1954): 7–12.

Garfield, Eugene, and Emik A. Avakian. "AMFIS—The Automatic Microfilm Information System." *Special Libraries* 48 (1957): 145–48.

Garrettson, Charles Lloyd, III. *Hubert H. Humphrey: The Politics of Joy*. New Brunswick, NJ: Transaction, 1993.

Geiger, Roger L. *Research and Relevant Knowledge: American Research Universities since World War II*. New York: Oxford University Press, 1993.

BIBLIOGRAPHY

Getty, J. Paul. *As I See It: The Autobiography of J. Paul Getty.* Englewood Cliffs, NJ: Prentice Hall, 1976.

Gimbel, John. *Science, Technology and Reparations: Exploitation and Plunder in Postwar Germany.* Stanford, CA: Stanford University Press, 1990.

Glenn, Bess. "The Taft Commission and the Government's Record Practices." *American Archivist* 21, no. 3 (July 1958): 277–303.

Goffman, William. "The Ecology of Medical Literatures." *American Journal of the Medical Sciences* 263, no. 4 (1972): 267–73.

Goldenberg, Susan. *The Thomson Empire.* N.p.: Kampmann, 1984.

Goldstine, Herman H. *The Computer from Pascal to von Neumann.* Princeton, NJ: Princeton University Press, 1980.

Gordon, Michael D. *Scientific Babel: How Science Was Done Before and After Global English.* Chicago: University of Chicago Press, 2015.

Graham, Hugh Davis, and Nancy Diamond. *The Rise of American Research Universities: Elites and Challengers in the Postwar Era.* Baltimore: Johns Hopkins University Press, 1997.

Greenberg, Daniel S. *Science for Sale: The Perils, Rewards, and Delusions of Campus Capitalism.* Chicago: University of Chicago Press, 2007.

Griffiths, Jose-Marie, and Donald W. King. "US Information Retrieval Systems, Evolution and Evaluation (1945–1975)." *IEEE Annals of the History of Computing* 24, no. 3 (July–September 2002): 35–54.

Gruber Jeffrey S. *Lexical Structures in Syntax and Semantics.* Amsterdam: North Holland, 1976.

Haines, Joe. *Maxwell.* Boston: Houghton Mifflin, 1988.

Hammack, David, and Helmut J. Anheier. *A Versatile American Institution: The Changing Ideals and Realities of Philanthropic Institutions.* Washington, DC: Brookings, 2013.

Hart, David M. *Forged Consensus: Science, Technology, and Economic Policy in the United States 1921–1953.* Princeton, NJ: Princeton University Press, ca. 1998.

Hayes, Robert M. "Joseph Becker: A Lifetime of Service to the Profession of Library and Information Science." *Bulletin of the American Society for Information Science and Technology* 22, no. 1 (October–November 1995): 24–26.

Heaps, Jennifer Davis. "Clio's Spies: The National Archives and the Office of Strategic Services in World War II." *Prologue* 30, no. 3 (Fall 1998): 195–207.

———. "Tracking Intelligence Information: The Office of Strategic Services." *American Archivist* 61, no. 2 (Fall 1998): 287–308.

Heller, Robert, and Associates. *A National Plan for Science Abstracting and Indexing Services.* Philadelphia: NFAIS, 1963.

Henderson, Madeline B., ed. *Interactive Bibliographic Systems: Proceedings of a Forum Held at Gaithersburg, Md. Oct. 4–5, 1971.* N.p.: U.S. AEC Office of Information Services, 1973.

Henderson, Madeline M., John S. Moats, and Mary Elizabeth Stevens. *Cooperation, Convertibility, and Compatibility among Information Systems: A Literature Review.* Washington, DC: National Bureau of Standards, GPO, June 1966.

Henisz-Dostert, Bozena, R. Ross Macdonald, and Michael Zarechnak. *Machine Translation.* The Hague: Mouton, 1979.

Hewins, Ralph. *The Richest American: J. Paul Getty.* New York: Dutton, 1960.

Himwich, Williamina A., Eugene Garfield, Helen O. Field, John M. Whittock, and Sanford V. Larkey. *Final Report on Machine Methods for Information Searching.* Baltimore: Johns Hopkins University, 1955. http://garfield.library.upenn.edu/papers/26.html.

Hof, Robert D. "AI Hits the Mainstream." *MIT Technology Review* 119, no. 3 (2017): 62–66.

Holley, Edward G., and Robert F Schremser. *The Library Services and Construction Act: An Historical Review.* Greenwich, CT: JAI, 1983.

Hollings, Christopher. *Scientific Communication across the Iron Curtain.* New York: Springer, 2016.

Horowitz, David, and Richard Poe. *The Shadow Party: How George Soros, Hillary Clinton and Sixties Radicals Seized Control of the Democratic Party.* Nashville, TN: Thomas Nelson, 2006.

Howerton, Paul, ed. *Information Handling: First Principles.* Washington, DC: Spartan Books, 1963. http://userpages.umbc.edu/~burke//.

———. "The Parameters of an Operational Machine Translation System." *Mechanical Translation* 6 (1961): 108–12.

Howerton, Paul, ed., and Alexander Akhonin, comp. *Russian–English Glossary of Metallurgical and Metal-Working Terms.* Cambridge: Massachusetts Institute of Technology, 1955.

Howerton, Paul, and David C. Weeks. *Vistas in Information Handling Volume I: The Augmentation of Man's Intellect by Machine.* Washington, DC: Spartan Books, 1963.

Huang, Xuedong, James Baker, and Raj Reddy. "Historical Perspective of Speech Recognition." *Communications of the ACM* 57, no. 1 (January 2014): 94–103.

Hunt, Lynda. *Secret Agenda: The United States Government, Nazi Scientists, and Project Paperclip, 1945 to 1990.* New York: St. Martin's, 1991.

Hunter, Vera Gadberry. "Survey of the Office of Technical Services U.S. Dept. of Commerce, June 1945–August 1952." M.A. thesis, Catholic University, June 1953.

Hutchins, W. John. *Early Years of Machine Translation: Memoirs and Biographies of Pioneers.* Philadelphia: John Benjamin, 2000.

Jayroe, Tina J. "A Humble Servant: The Work of Helen L. Brownson and the Early Years of Information Science Research." *Journal of the American Society for Information Science and Technology* 63, no. 10 (2012): 2052–61.

Jeffreys-Jones, Rhodi. "Antecedents and Memories as Factors in the Creation of the CIA." *Diplomatic History* 40, no. 1 (January 2016): 140–54.

Jones, H. Kay. *Butterworth: History of a Publishing House.* London: Butterworth, 1980.

Jones, Wayne. *E-serials: Publishers, Libraries, Users, and Standards.* New York: Haworth, 1998.

Kaser, Richard T., and Victoria Coz Kaser. *BIOSIS Championing the Cause: The First 75 Years.* Philadelphia: NFAIS, 2001.

Katz, Barry. "The Arts of War: 'Visual Presentation' and National Intelligence." *Design Issues* 12, no. 2 (Summer 1996): 3–21.

———. *Foreign Intelligence: Research and Analysis in the Office of Strategic Services.* London: Oxford University Press, 1989.

Kaufman, Michael T. *Soros: The Life and Times of a Messianic Billionaire.* New York: Knopf, 2002.

Keller, George. *Academic Strategy: The Management Revolution in American Higher Education.* Baltimore: Johns Hopkins University Press, 1983.

Kent, Allen. "Exploitation of Recorded Information. I. Development of an Operational Machine Searching Service for the Literature of Metallurgy and Allied Subjects." *American Documentation* 11, no. 2 (April 1960): 173–88.

———. "The GE-250." *College Composition and Communication* 11, no. 2 (May 1960): 75–77.

———. "A Machine That Does Research." *Harper's*, April 1959, 1–6.

Kent, Allen, and A. S. Inerall. "Soviet Documentation: A Trip Report." *American Documentation* 10, no. 1 (January 1959): 1–19.

Kent, Allen, and James W. Perry. *Centralized Information Services: Opportunities and Problems.* New York: Interscience, 1958.

Kent, Allen, J. W. Perry, and M. M. Berry. "Machine Literature Searching V: Definition and Systemization of Terminology for Code Development." *American Documentation* 5, no. 3 (August 1954): 166–72.

Kessler, M. M. *Comparison of the Results of Bibliographic Coupling and Analytic Subject Indexing.* Cambridge: Massachusetts Institute of Technology, 1963.

Kilgour, Frederick G. "The Origins of Coordinate Searching." In *Historical Studies in Information Science*, edited by Trudi Bellardo Hahn and Michael Buckland, 107–15. Medford, NJ: Information Today, 1998.

BIBLIOGRAPHY 357

King, Donald W., and Frances M. Alvarado-Albertorio. "Pricing and Other Means of Charging for Scholarly Journals: A Literature Review and Commentary." *Learned Publishing* 21, no. 4 (October 2008): 248–72.

King, Donald W., and Carol Tenopir. "Some Economic Aspects of the Scholarly Journal System." *Annual Review of Information Science and Technology* 45, no. 1 (2011): 295–366.

Kramish, Arnold. *The Griffin.* New York: Houghton Mifflin, 1986.

Kruzas, Anthony Thomas. "The Development of Special Libraries for American Business and Industry." Ph.D. diss., University of Michigan, 1960.

Kuhns, Woodrow. "The Beginnings of Intelligence Analysis in CIA: The Office of Reports and Estimates; CIA's First Center for Analysis." *Studies in Intelligence* 51, no. 2 (2008). https://www.cia.gov/library/center-for-the-study-of-intelligence/csi-publications/csi-studies/studies/vol51no2. Accessed April 2017.

Kuipers, J. W. "Microcards and Microfilm for a Central Reference Service (of Eastman Kodak Co.)." Presented before the Micro Documentation Symposium, Division of Chemical Literature, at the 116th meeting of the American Chemical Society in Atlantic City, September 18–23, 1949.

Laakso M., P. Welling, H. Bukvova, L. Nyman, B. C. Björk, and T. Hedlund. "The Development of Open Access Journal Publishing from 1993 to 2009." *PLOS ONE* 6, no. 6 (2011). http://www.ncbi.nlm.nih.gov/pubmed/21695139. Accessed August 27, 2015.

Langer, William L. *In and Out of the Ivory Tower: The Autobiography of William L. Langer.* New York: Neale Watson Academic, 1977.

Larivière, V., S. Haustein, and P. Mongeon. "The Oligopoly of Academic Publishers in the Digital Era." *PLOS ONE* 10, no. 6 (June 10, 2015). doi:10.1371/journal.pone.0127502.

Lessig, Lawrence. *The Boy Who Could Change the World: The Writings of Aaron Swartz; With an Introduction by Lawrence Lessig.* New York: New Press, 2015.

———. *Free Culture: How Big Media Uses Technology and the Law to Lock Down Culture and Control Creativity.* New York: Penguin, 2004.

Lewis, Annie Burr. *Dancing on a Sunny Plain.* West Port, CT: Yale University, 2012.

Lewis, Jonathan E. *Spy Capitalism: ITEK and the CIA.* New Haven, CT: Yale University Press, 2002.

Lewis, Nicholas. "Peering through the Curtain: Soviet Computing through the Eyes of Western Experts." *IEEE Annals of the History of Computing* 38 (January–March 2016): 34–44.

Lewis, Wilmarth Sheldon. *One Man's Education.* New York: Knopf, 1967.

Liebert, Herman W. "Wilmarth Sheldon Lewis (1895–1979)." *Yale University Library Gazette,* 54, no. 4 (April 1980): 198–200.

Light, Jennifer S. "Facsimile: A Forgotten 'New Medium' from the 20th Century." *New Media and Society* 8, no. 3 (2006): 355–78.

Lockmiller, David A. *History of the North Carolina State College of Agriculture and Engineering.* Raleigh, NC: Edwards & Broughton, 1939.

Lowenthal, Mark M. *U.S. Intelligence: Evolution and Anatomy.* 2nd ed. Westport, CT: Praeger, 1992.

Lufkin, James M. "Human vs. Machine Translation of Foreign Languages." *IEEE Transactions on Engineering Writing and Speech* 8, no. 1 (1965): 8–14.

———. "What Everybody Should Know about Translation." *IEEE Transactions on Professional Communications* PC-18, no. 1 (March 1975): 22–28.

MacKay, Neil. *The Hole in the Card: The Story of the Microfilm Aperture Card.* St. Paul: Minnesota Mining & Manufacturing, 1996.

Malamud, Carl. *Exploring the Internet: A Technical Travelogue.* Englewood Cliffs, NJ: Prentice Hall, 1992.

Marcum, Deanna B. "Automating the Library: The Council on Library Resources." *IEEE Annals of the History of Computing,* July–September 2002, 2–13.

———. "Reclaiming the Research Library: The Founding of the Council on Library Resources." *Libraries and Culture* 31, no. 1 (Winter 1996): 113–24.

Maron, Melvin Earl (Bill), and John L. Kuhns. "On Relevance, Probabilistic Indexing, and Information Retrieval." *Journal of the ACM* 7, no. 3 (July 1960): 216–44.

McReynolds, Rosalie, and Louise S. Robbins. *The Librarian Spies: Philip and Mary Jane Kenney and Cold War Espionage*. Westport, CT: Praeger, 2009.

Meadows, A. J., ed. *The Origins of Information Science*. London: Taylor-Graham, 1987.

Meckler, Alan Marshall. *Micropublishing: A History of Scholarly Micropublishing in America, 1938–1980*. Westport, CT: Greenwood, 1982.

Medeiros, N. "Harvard, NIH, and the Balance of Power in the Open Access Debate." *OCLC Systems & Services*, 2008, 137–39.

Melton, John L. "The Semantic Code Today." *American Documentation* 1, no. 2 (April 1962): 176–81.

Miksa, Francis L. *The Development of Classification at the Library of Congress*. Champaign: University of Illinois, Graduate School of Library and Information Science, ca. 1984.

Miksa, Shawne D. "Pigeonholes and Punchcards: Identifying the Divisions between Library Classification Research and Information Retrieval." Ph.D. diss., Florida State University, 2002.

Miller, Russell. *The House of Getty*. New York: Henry Holt, 1985.

Mindell, David A. *Between Human and Machine: Feedback, Control, and Computing before Cybernetics*. Baltimore: Johns Hopkins University Press, 2002.

Molz, Redmond Kathleen. *The Federal Roles in Support of Academic and Research Libraries*. Chicago: ALA, 1991.

Montague, Ludwell Lee. *General Walter Bedell Smith as Director of Central Intelligence: October 1950–February 1953*. University Park: Pennsylvania State University Press, 1992.

Moyne, J. A., ed. *Machine Translation Programming Paper 1: General Analysis Technique / Serna System*. Washington, DC: Georgetown University Institute of Languages and Linguistics, June 1959.

NAS-NSF. *Proceedings of the International Conference on Scientific Information, Washington, D.C. Nov. 16–21, 1958*. Vol. 2. Washington, DC: NAS-NSF, 1959.

National Academy of Sciences—National Research Council. *The Metallurgical Searching Service of the American Society for Metals, Western Reserve University: An Evaluation*. NAS Pub. 1148. Washington, DC: NAS, 1964.

National Council of Jewish Women. Interview with Allen Kent. May 12, 1993. http://images.library.pitt.edu/cgi-bin/i/image/image-idx?view=entry;cc=ncjw;entryid=x-ais196440.233.

National Research Council, Automatic Language Processing Advisory Council (ALPAC). *Language and Machines: Computers in Translation and Linguistics*. Washington, DC: NAS-NRC, 1966.

Neufeld, M. Lyne, et al. *Abstracting and Indexing Services in Perspective: Miles Conrad Memorial Lectures 1969–1983*. Philadelphia: NFAIS, 1983.

Newhard, Nora. "The Unitarian Service Committee: Under the Direction of Dr. Robert C. Dexter, 1938–1944." Honors thesis, Clark University, 2009.

Nyce, James M., and Paul Kahn, eds. *From Memex to Hypertext: Vannevar Bush and the Mind's Machine*. Boston: Academic Press, 1991.

Oettinger, A. G. "An Essay in Information Retrieval: The Birth of a Myth." *Information and Control* 8 (1965): 64–79.

Office of Scientific Intelligence. *The Original Wizards of Langley: A Symposium Commemorating 60 Years of S&T Intelligence Analysis*. Washington, DC: CIA, ca. 2008.

Orne, Jerrold. "Library Division of the Office of the Publication Board." *Special Libraries*, September 1946, 203–9.

Orstein, Jacob. "Mechanical Translation." *Science* 122 (October 21, 1955): 745–48.

Osborn, Andrew D. "From Cutter to Dewey to Mortimer Taube and Beyond: A Complete Century of Change in Cataloging and Classification." *Cataloging and Classification Quarterly* 12, no. 3/4 (1995): 35–50.

Pascal, Zachary G. *Endless Frontier: Vannevar Bush, Engineer of the American Century*. Cambridge, MA: MIT Press, 1999.

Perry, James W. "Determination of the Iodine Content of the Public Water Supplies of North Carolina as a Possible Explanation of the Lack of Goiter among the Inhabitants." M.A. thesis, North Carolina State College of Agriculture and Engineering, 1928.

BIBLIOGRAPHY

———. "Machine Translation of Russian Technical Literature: Notes on Preliminary Experiments." CREST. 1952.

———. "The Mechanism of Oxidation of Linseed Oil." M.A. thesis, Massachusetts Institute of Technology, 1931.

———. *Scientific Russian: A Textbook for Classes and Self-Study.* New York: Interscience, 1950.

Perry, James W., and Allen Kent. *Tools for Machine Literature Searching: Semantic Code Dictionary, Equipment, Procedures.* New York: Interscience, 1958.

Peters, Justin. *The Idealist: Aaron Swartz and the Rise of Free Culture on the Internet.* New York: Scribner, 2016.

Peterson, Michael. "Before Bourbon." NSA Center For Cryptologic History. N.d.

Pietsch, H. E. "Future Possibilities of Applying Mechanized Methods to Scientific and Technical Literature." In *Punched Cards: Their Applications to Science and Industry,* edited by Robert S. Casey and James M. Perry, 437–55. New York: Reinhold, 1951.

Pinelli, Thomas E. *NASA DOD Aerospace Knowledge Diffusion Research Project Report # 11, Chronology of Selected Literature Reports, Policy Instruments, and Significant Events Affecting Federal Scientific and Technical Information (STI) in the United States.* DOD, Indiana University, January 1992.

Poynder, Richard. "George Soros Gives $3 Million to New Open Access Initiative." *Information Today* 19, no. 4 (April 2002): 20–21.

President's Science Advisory Committee (PSAC). *Improving the Availability of Scientific and Technical Information in the United States* (Baker Report). 1958.

Rahm, Alan J. "The Minicard System for High Speed Data Retrieval." N.p.: Recordak Corporation, 1960.

Rayward, W. Boyd, ed. *European Modernism and the Information Society: Informing the Present, Understanding the Past.* Burlington, VT: Ashgate, 2008.

———. *The Universe of Information: The Work of Paul Otlet for Documentation and International Organization.* Moscow: Published for International Federation for Documentation (FID) by All-Union Institute for Scientific and Technical Information (VINITI), 1975.

Rees, Alan M. "The Aslib-Cranfield Test of the Western Reserve University Indexing System for Metallurgical Literature: A Review of the Final Report." *American Documentation* 16, no. 2 (April 1965).

Regazzi, John J. *Scholarly Communications: A History from Content as King to Content as Kingmaker.* Lanham, MD: Rowman & Littlefield, 2015.

Reynolds, Walter L. "The Senate Committee on Government Operations and Documentation." *American Documentation* 12, no. 2 (April 1961): 93–97.

Richards, Pamela Spence. "Aslib at War: The Brief but Intrepid Career of a Library Organization as a Hub of Allied Scientific Intelligence, 1942–1945." *Journal of Education for Library and Information Science* 29, no. 4 (Spring 1989): 279–96.

———. "Gathering Enemy Scientific Information in Wartime: The OSS and the Periodical Reproduction Program." *Journal of Library History* 16, no. 2 (1981): 253–64.

———. *Scientific Information in Wartime: The Allied German Rivalry, 1939–1945.* Westport CT: Greenwood, 1994.

———. "The Soviet Overseas Information Empire and the Implications for Its Disintegration." In *Proceeding of the 1998 Conference on the History and Heritage of Science Information Systems, ASIS-CHF,* edited by Mary Ellen Bowden, Trudi Bellardo Hahn, and Robert V. Williams, 206–13. Medford, NJ: Information Today, 1999.

Richmond, Phyllis A. "Review of the Cranfield Project." *American Documentation,* October 1963, 307–11.

Saracevic, Tefko. "Research on Relevance in Information Science: A Historical Perspective." In *International Perspectives on the History of Information Science and Technology,* edited by Toni Carbo and Trudi Bellardo Hahn, 49–60. N.p.: ASIS&T, 2012.

Satija, M. J. *Manual of Practical Colon Classification.* New Delhi: Sterling, 1984.

Schonfeld, Roger C. *JSTOR: A History.* Princeton, NJ: Princeton University Press, 2003.

BIBLIOGRAPHY

Schultz, Claire K. *H. P. Luhn: Pioneer of Information Science.* New York: Spartan Books, 1968.

Schulz, Hedda, and Ursula Gregory. *From CA to CAS Online.* Berlin: Springer-Verlag, 1988.

Secretary of State for Trade and Industry (UK). *Reed Elsevier PLC and Harcourt General, Inc.: A Report on the Proposed Merger.* N.p.: n.p., 2001.

Servos, J. W. "Changing Partners: The Mellon Institute, Private Industry, and the Federal Patron." *Technology and Culture* 35, no. 2 (April 1994): 221–57.

Shannon, Claude Elwood, and Warren Weaver. *The Mathematical Theory of Communication.* Urbana: University of Illinois Press, 1949.

Shera, Jesse H. "Documentation: Its Scope and Limitations." *Library Quarterly* 21 (January 1951): 13–26.

———. "Librarianship in a High Key." *ALA Bulletin* 50, no. 2 (February 1956): 103–5.

———. "New Tools for Easing the Research Burden of Historical Research." *American Documentation* 10, no. 4 (October 1959): 274–77.

———. *Sociological Foundations of Librarianship.* New York: Asia Publishing House, 1970.

Shera, Jesse H., Allen Kent, and James W. Perry. *Information Resources: A Challenge to American Science and Industry.* New York: Press of Western Reserve University, Interscience, 1958.

Simpson, Christopher, ed. *Universities and Empire: Money and Politics in the Social Sciences during the Cold War.* New York: Free Press, 1998.

Slamecka, Vladimir. "Trade-Offs in the International Flow of Science and Technology Information." Washington, DC: U.S. Dept. of Commerce, September 1980.

Smith, Bruce L. *American Science Policy since World War II.* Washington, DC: Brookings Institution, 1989, 1990.

Smith, K. Wayne. *OCLC Online Computer Library Center Inc.: Furthering Access to the World's Information for 30 Years.* Newcomen Publication Number 1502. N.p.: OCLC, 1997.

Snyder, Thomas, ed. *120 Years of American Education: A Statistical Portrait.* N.p.: NCES, January 1993.

Stapleton, Darwin H. "The Faustian Dilemmas of Funded Research at Case Institute and Western Reserve, 1945–1965." *Science, Technology & Human Values* 18, no. 3 (1993): 303–14.

Stewart, Robert K. "The Office of Technical Services: A New Deal in the Cold War." *Knowledge Creation Utilization and Diffusion* 15, no. 1 (September 1993): 46–77.

Stout, Mark. "The Hazards of Private Spy Operations: The Pond: Running Agents for State, War, and the CIA." *Studies in Intelligence* 48, no. 3 (2004): 69–82. https://www.cia.gov/library/center-for-the-study-of-intelligence/kent-csi/vol48no3/pdf/v48i3a07p.pdf. Accessed February 12, 2015.

Suber, Peter. *The Case of the Speluncean Explorer.* London: Routledge, 1998.

———. *Open Access.* Cambridge, MA: MIT Press, 2012.

Tatarchenko, Ksenia. "Cold War Origins of the International Federation for Information Processing." *IEEE Annals of the History of Computing* 32, no. 2 (April–June 2010): 46–57.

Taube, Mortimer. "The Comac: An Efficient Punched Card Collating System for the Storage and Retrieval of Information." In *Proceedings of the International Conference on Scientific Information, Washington, D.C. Nov. 16–21, 1958,* 1245–54. Vol. 2., NAS-NSF. Washington: NAS-NSF, 1959.

———. *The Minicard System: A Case Study in the Application of Storage and Retrieval Theory.* N.p.: NITS AD137472, ca. 1957.

———. "A Note on the Pseudo-mathematics of Relevance." *American Documentation* 16, no. 2 (April 1965): 69–72.

———. *Studies in Coordinate Indexing Vol. 1.* N.p.: Documentation Inc., 1953.

Taube, Mortimer, and Harold Wooster, eds. *Information Storage and Retrieval: Theory, Systems, and Devices.* New York: Columbia University Press, 1958.

Taubes, G. "Publication by Electronic Mail Takes Physics by Storm." *Science* 259, no. 5099 (1993): 1246–48.

BIBLIOGRAPHY

Tenopir, Carol. "Not Just Science Anymore." *Library Journal* 126, no. 20 (December 2001): 45–46.

Thelin, John R. *A History of American Higher Education.* 2nd ed. Baltimore: Johns Hopkins University Press, 2011.

Thomas, Gordon, and Martin Dillon. *Robert Maxwell, Israel's Superspy: The Life and Murder of a Media Mogul.* New York: Carroll and Graf, 2002.

Thompson, Thomas. "The Fifty-Year Role of the US Air Force in Advancing Information Technology: A History of the Rome, New York Ground Electronics Laboratory." N.p: n.p., n.d.

Trester, Delmet J. *ERIC: The First Fifteen Years 1964–1979; A History of the Educational Resources Information Center.* Washington, DC: Government Printing Office, 1979. ERIC ed195289.

Troy, Thomas F. *Donovan and the CIA: A History of the Establishment of the Central Intelligence Agency.* Washington, DC: Central Intelligence Agency, 1988.

True, Alfred Charles. *A History of Agricultural Experimentation and Research in the United States, 1607–1925.* Washington, DC: U.S. Department of Agriculture, 1937.

Turing, Alan M. *Mechanical Intelligence.* New York: Elsevier Science, ca. 1992.

Turner, Fred. *From Counterculture to Cyberculture: Stewart Brand, the Whole Earth Network and the Rise of Digital Utopianism.* Chicago: University of Chicago Press, 2006.

UNESCO. *Scientific and Technical Translating.* Paris: UNESCO, 1957.

United States Senate. *Science and Technology Act of 1958, Hearings before a Subcommittee of the Committee of Government Operations, United States Senate Eighty-Fifth Congress, Second Session, on S.31026.* May 2, 6, and 7, 1958 (Humphrey Committee).

Van Orsdel, Lee C., and Kathleen Born. "Journals in the Time of Google." *Library Journal,* April 15, 2006.

———. "Reality bite2: Periodicals Price Survey 2009." *Library Journal,* April 15, 2009.

Vance, John K. "Philosophy of Classification." CREST. 1959.

Varlejs, Jana. "Ralph Shaw and the Rapid Selector." In *Proceeding of the 1998 Conference on the History and Heritage of Science Information Systems, ASIS-CHF,* edited by Mary Ellen Bowden, Trudi Bellardo Hahn, and Robert V. Williams, 148–55. Medford, NJ: Information Today, 1999.

———. "The Technical Report and Its Impact on the Post–World War II Information Systems." In *History and Heritage of Scientific and Technical Information Systems,* edited by W. Boyd Rayward and Mary Ellen Bowden, 89–99. Medford, NJ: Information Today, 2004.

Vickery, B. C. *Faceted Classification Schemes.* New Brunswick, NJ: Graduate School of Library Service, Rutgers, the State University, 1966.

———. "The Structure of Semantic Coding: A Review." *American Documentation* 10 (July 1959): 234–41.

Waller, Douglas. *Wild Bill Donovan: The Spymaster Who Created the OSS and Modern American Espionage.* New York: Free Press, 2011.

Wang, Jessica. "Liberals, the Progressive Left, and the Political Economy of Postwar American Science: The National Science Debate Revisited." *Historical Studies in the Physical and Biological Sciences* 26, no. 1 (1995): 139–66.

———. "Science, Security and the Cold War: The Case of E. U. Condon." *ISIS* 83 (1992): 238–69.

Wasserman, Paul and Janice W. McLean. *Who's Who in Consulting.* Detroit: Gale Research Co., 1973.

Warner, Michael. "Salvage and Liquidation." CIA Library. April 15, 2007. Updated June 27, 2008. https://www.cia.gov/library/center-for-the-study-of-intelligence/csi-publications/csi-studies/studies/96unclass/salvage-and-liquidation.html.

Webber, Sheila. "The Global Electronic Information Industry: Squeezing Out the Middle Ground." *Proceedings of ASIS Annual Meeting* 35 (1998): 179–89.

Weeks, David C., Mildred Benton, and Mary Louise Thomas. *Universal Decimal Classification.* Washington, DC: U.S. Air Force Office of Scientific Research, 1971.

Weinberg, Steve *Armand Hammer: The Untold Story.* Boston: Little, Brown, 1989.

BIBLIOGRAPHY

Weinberger, Sharon. *The Imagineers of War: The Untold Story of DARPA.* New York: Knopf, 2017.

Wiener, Norbert. *Cybernetics; or, Control and Communication in the Animal and the Machine.* Cambridge, MA: MIT Press, 1948.

Wigington, Ronald L., and James L. Wood. "Standardization Requirements of a National Program for Information Transfer." *Library Trends* 18 (1969–1970): 4342–445.

Williams, James G. *Governance of Special Information Centers: The Knowledge Availability Systems Center at University of Pittsburgh.* Urbana: University of Illinois Graduate School of Library and Information Science, n.d.

Williams, Robert V. "Hans Peter Luhn and Herbert M. Ohlman: Their Roles in the Origin of Keyword-In Context/Permutation Automatic Indexing." *JASIST* 61, no. 4 (2010): 835–49.

———. "The Use of Punched Cards in US Libraries and Documentation Centers, 1936–1965." *IEEE Annals of the History of Computing* 24, no. 2 (April–June 2002): 16–33.

Williamson, Charles C. *Training for Library Service: A Report Prepared for the Carnegie Corporation of New York.* New York: Carnegie Corporation, 1923.

Willinsky, John. *The Access Principle: The Case for Open Access to Research and Scholarship.* Cambridge, MA: MIT Press, 2005.

Wilson, Leonard S. "Lessons from the Experience of the Map Information Section, OSS." *Geographical Review* 39, no. 2 (April 1949): 298–310.

Winks, Robin, *Cloak & Gown: Scholars in the Secret War, 1939–1961.* New Haven, CT: Yale University Press, ca. 1996.

Wooster, Harold. "Current Research and Development in Scientific Documentation." In *Encyclopedia of Library and Information Science*, ed. Allen Kent and Harold Lancour, vol. 16 (New YorkL Marcel. Decker, 1971): 336–365.

———. "Historical Note: Shining Palaces, Shifting Sands: National Information Systems." *JASIS* 38, no. 5 (September 1987): 321–35.

Wouters, Paul. *The Citation Culture.* N.p.: n.p., 1999.

Wright, H. Curtis. "Jesse Shera, Librarianship, and Information Science," Occasional Research Paper 5, School of Library and Information Science, Brigham Young University, 1958.

INDEX

101 IBM advanced tabulator, 141, 143, 289
1401 IBM computer, 212
360 IBM computer line, 210, 212–213, 214
3M company, 71, 103
5202 computer, 180

Aberdeen Proving Ground, 145, 243, 244, 245
Abstracts/Precis at COI, 29
ACORN, 341, 345, 347
Addicott, Kenneth, 77–79, 108, 117; Intelligence Subject Code, 82, 85–86, 93, 97–101, 105–106, 110–112; mechanization, 82, 98–102, 103–104
ADI. *See* American Documentation Institute
Adkinson, Burton, 22, 31, 278
Advanced Research Project Agency (ARPA-DARPA/IPTO), 262, 273, 317, 318
AEC. *See* Atomic Energy Commission
AEGIS Already Existing General Information System, 214
Air Force Documents Division, Dayton, OH (CADO), 181
Air Force Foreign Technology Division, Dayton, OH, 181
ALPAC, Automatic Language Processing Advisory Committee, 228–230

American Chemical Society (ACS), 91, 145, 146–147, 153–154, 169
American Documentation Institute (ADI), 89–90, 91, 159; *American Documentation*, 159
American Information Century, 279, 324; challenges to, 325–331
American Society for Information Science & Technology (ASIS/ASIS&T), 85, 215, 297, 332
American Society of Metals (ASM), 245, 246
AN/GSQ-16. *See* Mark computers
Andrews, James Madison, 97, 106–108, 137, 175, 190, 194, 197, 218; alternatives to Intellofax, 140, 176, 183; budget and policy problems, 137–138, 139, 175, 176, 178; consultants' reports, 191–192; Intelligence Subject Code, 108–109, 112, 180; James Perry, 153, 161, 169, 173; Minicard, 192–193, 194
Aperture cards, 56, 59, 63–64, 65, 70, 71, 178, 207
Apollo program, 262
Applebaum, William, 41, 42, 44
Army Medical Library. *See* Surgeon Generals Library
ArXiv, 344
ASM. *See* American Society of Metals
Aspect systems, 31

364 INDEX

Association of Research Libraries (ARL), 343

ASTIA, 196, 259

Atomic Energy Commission (AEC), 86, 295

Auchincloss family, 10, 65

Automatic Selector, 250, 251, 252

Automatic translation. *See* Mechanical Translation

Automation Development Group, 203

AVCO, 182

Avram, Herbert and Henriette, 230, 317

Bagnall, John, 83, 217, 218

Baker, Dale, 263

Baker, William O., 273, 274, 278, 281, 296, 298

Ball, Norman T., 86–92, 97, 137, 155, 158, 161, 214; Intelligence Subject Code, 92–93, 110–111

Bancroft, Hubert Howe, 20, 23

Barlow, John Perry, 346

Batchedler, Richard W., 39, 61, 68

Bateman, Otto, 56

Battelle Memorial Institute, 179, 181, 222, 239, 241–242, 243–246

Batten System, 285

Baxendale, Phyllis, 281, 283

Bayh-Doyle Act, 339

Becker, Joseph "Joe", 82–85, 102, 161, 215, 298, 308; computers, 205–206, 209, 210, 211, 212

Belzer, Jack, 244, 307

Benson-Lehner Flip, 207

Berkman Center for Internet & Society, 347

Bernal, J.D., 125, 280, 287, 344

Bibliofilm / Auxiliary Publication, 90

Bibliometrics, Scientometrics, 221, 290

Binkley, Robert C., 94n13, 247

Biographics / biographies group, 19, 30, 40, 105, 179, 182, 207

Biological Abstracts, 132, 133, 262, 263, 267, 269, 271, 300, 323, 330

Biomedical Research Service (BRS), 323–324

Bissel, Richard, 183

Bjorksten, Johan, 241

Booth, Andrew, 304

Borel, Paul, 194–195, 197, 209, 212, 215; computers, 205, 210–211, 212, 214; mechanical translation, 217, 218; Minicard, 204, 205, 206, 207, 209

Bourne, Charles O., 267

Bowen, William, 342–343

Brahn, Josephine, 198

Bremen, Florence, 51, 55, 64, 67

Bridges, Harry, 93n4

Brown, Pat, 344, 346

Brownson, Helen L., 91, 92, 214

Burchard, John E., 147, 148–149, 157–158

Bureau of Technical Services, 267

Bush, Vannevar, 25, 75, 80, 82, 88, 90, 91, 104, 120, 121, 130, 138, 148, 157–158, 159, 176, 315, 339; classification as association, 24, 25, 92; Joint Research & Development Board, 76, 81, 86; NDRC/OSRD, 25, 75, 242; NSF and science information policy, 121, 127, 129, 237, 238, 273, 278; rapid selectors, 62, 89, 126, 129, 140, 142, 155, 159, 180, 182, 190

Butterworth, 325, 327

CADO, 181

Cambridge Investment Group (CIG), 330, 331

Cambridge Scientific Abstracts (CAS), 331

CAPRI, 211, 212, 214

Carnegie foundations, 25, 61, 80, 91, 130, 148, 149, 157, 159, 160, 247, 318

CAS. *See Chemical Abstracts*/Chemical Abstract Service

Casey, William, 47, 66, 71

Censorship Office, 19, 29, 31, 50

Census Bureau, 99, 141

Center for Documentation & Communication Research, 257

Center for International Studies at MIT, 160, 161, 221

Centers, as university strategy, 161, 174, 239, 240

Central Information Division (CID), 8–9, 32, 35, 41, 57, 68; conflicts at, 42–43, 44, 45; culture of and classification system, 26–27; information culture,

INDEX

change at, 37, 40, 41, 43–44; review of, 43. *See also* Wilmarth Sheldon Lewis; John Langan; Intellofax; aperture cards

Central Intelligence Agency (CIA), 81, 97, 137, 257, 260; science information and translation, 27, 84, 327

Central Intelligence Group (CIG), 68, 76–77, 80–81, 94n5, 98, 101–106; new classification system (ISC), 80, 81, 82, 85–86, 92, 105–106; new retrieval system, 82, 98, 100, 101–104; Office of Research & Estimates, 77

Chemical Abstracts/Chemical Abstracts Service (CAS), 132–133, 219, 263, 269, 270, 281, 291–292, 297, 299, 300, 322, 331

Chemical notation systems, 145, 154

CHIVE, 205, 209, 211, 212

Chomsky, Noam, 222

CIA. *See* Central Intelligence Agency

CID. *See* Central Information Division

CIG. *See* Central Intelligence Group

Citation Indexing, 26, 206, 231, 287, 289–290, 291, 292–293, 330

Civil Service Commission, 8

Clapp, Verner, 10, 89, 197, 316, 317

Classification Experts. *See* Melvil Dewey; Herbert H. Field; Paul Otlet; S. R. Ranganathan

Classification / indexing/ retrieval systems, major types. *See* Aspect systems; Citation Indexing; Colon classification; Decimal Classification; Facet classification; Library of Congress (LC); Subject headings; Uniterm

Classification Team at COI, 20

Clesner, Jennie & Hershel, 263, 275n11

Cleverdon, Cyril, 280, 301, 303

CLR. *See* Council on Library Resources

CODIB. *See* Committee on Documentation

COI. *See* Coordinator of Information

Coleman, Earl, 229, 327

Collection and Dissemination group, 101

Colon classification, 31, 110, 139, 156, 193, 282

COMAC, 246, 286

Committee on Classification, 90

Committee on Documentation (CODIB), 197, 203, 211

Concentration in publishing / retrieval industries, 329–332, 340

Condon, Edward. U., 126, 128, 330

Connor, Robert D. W., 9

Conrad, Miles, 262, 263, 269, 271, 297

Controlled Vocabulary, 164, 178, 200

Cooke, J. Kent, 328

Coon, Carleton S., 107, 108

Coordinator of Information (COI) creation of, 5–6, 7, 8. *See also* Central Information Division

Corona Satellites, 139, 178, 206, 258

COSATI, 274, 298

Council on Documentation Research, 260

Council on Library Resources (CLR), 316–317

Crane, Evan J., 269, 270, 272, 297

Creative Commons, 346

Current Contents, 291

Cybernetics, 147

DARE, 209

Davis, Watson, 90, 130, 285

Debons, Anthony, 308, 311, 315

Decimal Classification, 11, 13–14, 15, 16

Defense Intelligence Agency, 193, 199, 215

Denebrink, Commander Francis, 20

Department of Agriculture and information systems, 60, 90, 122, 129, 140, 159, 189, 192

Department of Commerce, 88, 118, 120, 125, 126, 262, 264–265, 301

Department of Defense science group, 92

de Rochemont, Richard & John, 47, 51–52, 52n4, 71

De Sola Price, Derek, 281

Deston, Raymond, 43–44, 57

Dewey, Melville (Melvil), 11

Dexter Folder Co., 69

Dialog, 206, 321, 322

Division of Special Information, 8, 9, 21, 22

Documentalism / Documentalists, 90, 144, 149, 197, 236, 252, 290

Documents Intelligence Section, 32

INDEX

Donovan, William, 4, 7, 20, 31, 33, 70, 75, 76; COI/OSS, plans for, 5–7, 37; CID, 7–9; communists, 22
Dorking Conference, 280, 282
Dostert, Leon, 222, 223, 224, 226, 227, 232n2, 280
Dulles, Allen:, 138, 176, 207–208, 209
Dyson, G. Malcom, 154

Eastman Kodak (Eastman), 60, 70, 71, 103, 141, 180, 181, 182–183, 184–186, 193, 194, 195, 197, 206–208, 241
Eberstadt, Ferdinand, 138, 176
Ebsco, 331
Edge-notched cards, 67, 89, 142, 145, 154, 157, 165, 252
EDUCOM, 215, 308
Efficiency movement & information, 12, 13, 44, 57
Egan, Margaret, 248
Egbert, Lawrence Deems, 20, 23, 34, 35, 43
Eisen, Michael, 346
Electronic Frontier Foundation (EFF), 346
Elsevier, 330
Engelbart, Douglas, 231, 267
Engineering Index, 297
ERIC, 322

Facet classification, 156, 157, 165, 296
Farmington Plan, 23, 117
Farradane, J. E. L., 280
FBIS. *See* Foreign Broadcast Information / Intelligence System
FDD. *See* Foreign Documents Division
FDR. *See* Roosevelt, Franklin D.
FIAT. *See* Field Information Agency Technical
Field Information Agency Technical (FIAT), 83, 117–118, 119, 126
Field, Herbert H., 14, 93, 268
Film'n File / Filmsort, 65, 68, 69–70
Filmorex, 184, 280
Finch, William G. H., 102–103
Fixed Field coding, 142, 184, 185
FMA Filesearch, 207
Focke, Helen, 247

Ford Foundation, 159, 206, 236, 315, 316, 317, 318, 324
Foreign Broadcast Information / Intelligence System (FBIS), 179
Foreign Documents Division (FDD), 81, 84, 138, 217, 270
For-profit information services, 281, 295, 297, 319–320, 323, 324, 337, 339–340
Foskett, D. J., 280
Frankfurt Scholars, 6
Franklin Institute, 301
Fulbright. J. William, 125
Full Text systems, 321, 342, 346

Garfield, Eugene, 129, 146, 281, 287–289, 330, 346. *See also* citation indexing; Institute for Scientific Information
General Electric (GE), 102, 107, 196, 212, 250, 252, 254n19, 299, 301
Generic searching, 93, 110, 112, 140, 156, 164, 166, 177, 185, 197–198, 201
Georgetown University, 88, 222, 224, 226, 227, 230
Getty, J. Paul, 328
Gillette, H. W., 242
Ginsparg, Paul, 344
Goffman, William, 304
Goldberg, Emanuel, 62
Google Books, 343
Green, John C., 88, 126, 127, 128, 190, 262, 263, 264, 295
Grombach, John "Frenchy", 33, 68
Groves, Leslie, 86, 126
Gull, Cloyd Dake, 252, 301
Gunn, James N., 13
Guthrie, Kevin, 342

Hamilton, Neil, 48
Harnad, Stevan, 344, 345, 347
Harris, Zellig, 222, 224, 291
Hathi Trust, 343
Hayes, Robert, 205, 212
Henderson, Madeline Berry, 154, 162, 165, 169, 174, 235, 241, 243, 244, 249, 299
Herner, Saul, 281
Heumann, Karl F., 131, 301
Hierarchical classification, nature of, 13; objections to, 25, 31, 156. *See also*

INDEX 367

generic searching
Higher Education, 174, 241; adopts
business model, 312, 338–339;
entrepreneurial, 174, 240, 312;
expansion, 75, 237, 238, 240, 277;
financial problems, 311–312, 332, 338,
342; information programs and
science, 277, 305, 321
HighWire Press, 341, 348n8
Hooton, Earnest Albert, 107–108
Horty, John, 311
Howerton, Paul William, 217, 218–220,
231; translation, 220, 221–222, 223,
224
Howerton, Robert, 220
Human Relations Area Files, 105
Humphrey, Hubert, 125, 259–260, 264,
265; science and information policies,
259–260, 262–266, 267, 278, 295, 298
Hutchisson, Elmer, 269, 272, 296
Hyman, Julius, 219
HYPO, 180

IAC. *See* Intelligence Advisory Boards
and Committees
IDC. *See* Interdepartmental Committee
for the Acquisition of Foreign
Publications
Ideology & information policy, 119, 120,
121, 125, 127, 338, 340, 344, 345,
346–347
Index Chemicus, 292
indexing: deep and shallow, 26, 31, 56, 97,
110, 164, 184, 190, 191, 196, 211, 215
Industrial Register at CIA, 178, 182
Information cost, escalation of, 60, 272,
337, 338
Information cultures, 21, 35, 37, 45,
147–148, 266, 268; information needs,
269, 272, 273
Information Industry Association, 290,
297
Information Race, 259
Information socialism, 121, 127, 128, 129,
339
Information theory, statistical, 147–148,
156
Institute for Scientific Information (ISI),
278, 292, 329

Integrated intelligence information
system, requests for, 33–34, 80
Intellectual Reserve, 7–8
Intelligence Advisory Boards and
Committees (IAC), 193, 194–195, 208
Intelligence classification systems,
uncoordinated, 16, 33. *See also*
Intelligence Subject Code
Intelligence Publications Index (IPI), 179
Intelligence Subject Code (ISC), 82, 109,
113n1, 137, 161, 179; nature of,
110–112, 179; objections to and
revisions, 86, 97, 109, 110, 113n10,
139, 192, 195; 1960 new version of,
198, 199–201, 204; CIA abandons, 214
Intellofax hardware system, 101–105, 112,
113n5, 138, 140, 176, 204, 209–210,
214
Intellofax as retrieval system, and
criticisms of, 105, 137, 139, 169, 176,
183, 190, 191, 193, 203, 204, 205, 209.
See also Intelligence Subject Code
(ISC)
Interdepartmental Committee for the
Acquisition of Foreign Publications
(IDC), 22, 84
International Conference on Scientific
Information 1958, 279–282
International Council of Scientific
Unions, 271, 281
Internet Archive, 346
Internet-Web Tycoons & Open Access,
346
INTREX, 315–316, 318–319
IPI. *See* Intelligence Publications Index
IPTO. *See* Advanced Research Project
Agency
ISBN, 131
ISC. *See* Intelligence Subject Code
ISI. *See* Institute for Scientific
Information
ITEK, 206–208, 229–230

Jackson, Eugene, 267
Jenkins, David, 93n4
John Crerar Library, 94n9, 179, 296, 301
Joint Automatic Language Translation
Group, 226

368 INDEX

Joint Research & Development Board, 76, 81, 85, 86, 91, 92, 243
Jonker, Frederick, 282
Journals, economic problems of, 131–133
JSTOR, 90, 342–343, 347

Kahle, Brewster, 346
Kastens, Merritt L., 267
Keeney, Philip, 22
Kent, Allen, 46, 118, 162–163; Aberdeen and Battelle, 243, 244, 245, 246; MIT and CIA, 161, 162, 164–165, 173; politics of information, 257, 260, 263, 266, 281; University of Pittsburg and KASC, 305, 307–308, 309–310; Western Reserve, 248, 250, 251, 262–263, 293, 299, 300, 302–303
Kent, Sherman, 89, 204
Keppel, Frederick, 61
Kessler, Mike, 206, 289
Kilgore, Frederick, 22
King, Gilbert, 182, 205, 229, 230
Kirkpatrick, Lyman, 208, 209
Kluckhon, Clyde, 21
Knowledge Availability Systems Center (KASC), 306, 308, 310, 311
Kuipers, J. W., 181
Kluwer, 330
KWIC, 177, 186n4, 283

Lancour, Harold, 306, 307
Langan, John, 46–52, 53n21, 64, 66–67, 68–69, 70, 72n1; at OSS, 55–70; information methods, 56–58, 63–64; information businesses, 65–66, 67–68, 69, 71–72. *See also* aperture cards; Sheldon Wilmarth Lewis; William Casey; Richard & John de Rochemont
Langer, William B., 5, 9, 26, 39, 41, 45, 57
Larkey, Stanford V., 143
LATSEC, 228
LC. *See* Library of Congress
Leake, Chauncey, 281, 291
Lederberg, Joshua, 292
Lee, Dudley Parker, 39
Lee, Duncan, 6
Leghorn, Richard, 207–208
Lessig, Lawrence, 344, 346
Lewis, Annie Burr, 10–11, 12, 66, 246

Lewis, Wilmarth Sheldon, 9–12, 19, 23, 24, 26–29, 33, 35, 37; alienation and resignation from OSS, 35, 41, 42, 44. *See also* John Langan; Archibald MacLeish; Jesse Shera; Raymond Deston
Lexis/Nexis, 311, 331
Libraries Services and Construction Act, 305
Library of Congress (LC), 15, 16, 23, 60, 84, 94n9, 103, 121, 129, 269, 316; COI/OSS/CIA, 7–8, 17n8, 179, 232n1
Licklider, J. C. R., 159, 160, 317–318
Litchfield, Edward H., 305–306, 307–308, 309
Livingston, Burton, 272
Locke, Wm. N., 159, 317
Lockheed, 206, 321, 322
Look magazine, 68
Lotka, Alfred J., 148
Lowenhaupt, Henry S., 86, 182
Luhn, Hans Peter, 97, 98–102, 194, 281, 282, 283; Scanner, 141–143, 154, 169
Lukjanow, Ariadne, 223
Lundahl, Arthur C., 182–183

MacCarthy, George L., 60
Mack, James D., 269
MacLeish, Archibald, 7–8, 9, 11, 17n8, 23
MacLeish, Kenneth, 20, 23
Malamud, Carl, 346, 347
Manners, Joan (aka Lorna Brown, Lorna Langan), 48, 49, 50, 55, 66–67
Map sections COI/OSS, 22, 31, 39, 41
MARC, 316
March of Time, 47, 51, 52n4
Mark computers, 181, 223, 227–228, 229
Maron, M. E., 283
Marshall Plan, 92, 128, 162
Massachusetts Institute of Technology (MIT), 147, 148–149, 161, 206, 220, 273, 280, 289, 312. *See also* Vannevar Bush; Scientific Aids to Learning; Intrex; James Perry
Massing, Hede, 6
Mathematical Reviews, 61
Maverick, Maury, 125
Maxwell, Robert, 325–327
McBee Co., 65, 70

INDEX

McCullum, A. H., 108
McSpadden, George, 58
Mechanical Translation (MT), 76, 173, 181, 206, 221–222, 223–225, 227, 230, 233n12; objections to, 225–226, 228–230
Medline, 309, 323
Mellon foundations, 305, 309, 342, 343, 346
Mellon Research Institute, 309
Melton, Jessica, 304
Memex, 25
Merton, Robert, 291
Metallurgical / Metals file, 244–245, 251, 299, 301
Microcard, 61, 62, 65, 68
Microfilm, 22, 39, 59–61, 89, 90, 94n13, 123, 127, 168, 178, 180, 182, 189, 247, 262; problems with, 35, 61–62. *See also* aperture card Eastman Kodak; Microcard; Minicard; Rapid Selector; Recordak; Vernon Tate; Walnut
Millis, John Schoff, 246–248, 249, 253, 260, 265, 278
Minicard, 71, 180–181, 182–183, 191, 192–193, 195, 203; technical nature, 184–186, 194; conflicts over, 174, 190, 193, 194, 195–196, 204, 206–208, 209
MIT. *See* Massachusetts Institute of Technology
MITRE, 239
Montgomery, James A., 43
Mooers, Calvin, 281, 285
MT. *See* Mechanical Translation
Mumford, Quincy, 269
Murdock, George P., 105

NAS. *See* National Academy of Sciences
NASA. *See* National Aeronautics & Space Agency
National Academy of Sciences (NAS), 90, 130, 226, 228, 258, 260, 261, 298, 300
National Aeronautics & Space Agency (NASA), 206, 210, 237, 268, 295, 309–311, 321
National Archives of U.S., 22, 39, 60, 61, 63–64, 89, 157
National Bureau of Standards, 122, 126, 140, 267

National Center for the Coordination of Scientific & Technical Information, 261, 263
National Commission on Library & Information Science (NCLIS), 298
National Defense Education Act (NDEA), 277–278, 297
National Institute of Health (NIH), 292
National Intelligence Authority, 76–77
National Inventors Council, 88, 89, 119
National Library of Medicine, 301, 309
National Research Council (NRC), 131, 228
National Science Foundation (NSF), 129, 219, 223, 224, 226, 230, 236, 238, 253, 260, 261, 278, 292, 297, 299, 300, 303, 311, 318; information policies protect "old science", 278, 279, 295, 296, 297, 298
National Security Agency (NSA), 210, 230, 280
NCLIS. *See* National Commission on Library & Information Science
NDEA. *See* National Defense Education Act
New Left, 311, 319, 341, 344
Net Neutrality, 346
NFAIS, NFSAIS, 261, 262, 266, 271, 297
NIH. *See* National Institute of Health
NODEX, 177
NRC. *See* National Research Council
NSA. *See* National Security Agency
NSF. *See* National Science Foundation

OAIster, 343
OCLC, 320, 323, 331
OCR. *See* Office of Central Reference
Oettinger, Anthony, 229
Office of Central Reference (OCR), 175–176, 178, 189, 205, 209, 210–211, 212–213, 214; reviews of, 190–192, 192. *See also* Intellofax; Intelligence Subject Code; Minicard
Office of Science Information (NSF)(OSIS), 236, 278, 279, 296, 297
Office of Scientific Information of CIA (OSI), 137–138, 139, 140, 165, 182, 209, 212, 218

370　　　　　　　　　　　　　　　　　　　　**INDEX**

Office of Scientific Research &
　Development (OSRD), 25, 75, 76, 91,
　121, 131, 148, 158, 279
Office of Strategic Services (OSS):
　origins, powers, end of, 6, 33, 35, 37,
　41, 68, 76
Office of Technical Services (OTS/NTIS),
　119–121, 122, 126, 128, 265, 267, 298,
　309
Ohlman, Herbert, 244
Online systems, 206, 311, 320–321, 322,
　323, 324, 329, 331, 341, 343
Open Access, 340, 343, 344, 346, 347
Open Culture, 339, 340, 346, 347
Open Society, 340, 344–345
Optical coincidence testing, 62, 141–142,
　142, 143, 169, 170, 285
OSI. *See* Office of Scientific Information
　of CIA
OSIS. *See* National Science Foundation
　Office of Science Information
OSS. *See* Office of Strategic Services
OSRD. *See* Office of Scientific Research
　& Development
Otlet, Paul, 14–15, 60, 92, 105, 112, 131,
　281
Ottemiller, John H., 22, 45, 77
Outline of Cultural Materials, 105
Overhage, Carl, 317–318

Patent Office, 88, 89, 90–92, 254n18, 330
Patents and higher education / open
　access, 121, 339, 345
Pearson Publishing, 331
Pergamon Press, 325, 327
Perry, James, 144–145, 174, 235–236,
　241, 289, 304; at Battelle and
　Aberdeen, 241, 243, 244–246; at CIA,
　161–162, 165, 169, 173; and Luhn,
　154, 169; mechanical translation, 160,
　161, 162, 173, 220; at MIT and ACS
　connection, 146–147, 153–155, 157,
　159, 160–161; at Western Reserve,
　information center, Sputnik crisis,
　249–253. *See also* Semantic Factors
Photoscopic memory, 181
Physical Review, 133
PIC section, 178, 182, 183, 195, 204, 206,
　212

Pictorial Records groups, 38–39, 55, 63
Pierce, John R., 228
Plenum Press, 229, 327
PLOS. *See* Public Library of Science
Plural Information System, 262, 263, 281,
　296, 298, 312, 320, 330, 340, 341, 344
the Pond. *See* Grombach
Portico, 343
Presentation Branch, 38, 52
President's Science Advisory Committee
　(PSAC), 273, 274
Project MUSE, 341
ProQuest, 332
PSAC. *See* President's Science Advisory
　Committee
Public Library of Science (PLOS), 343,
　346
Publications Board, 153
PubMed, 346
Pucinski, Roman, 295, 296

QUICK, 177

Rabinow, Jacob, 141
Ranganathan, S. R., 89, 110, 156, 199,
　282, 283
Rapid Selector(s), 25, 89, 99, 129, 140,
　141, 153, 155, 159, 160, 180, 190, 301
Ream, Louis: B., 41, 42, 43, 44, 45
Recall, Precision, 301–302
RECON, 206
Recordak, 60
Reed publishing, 330
Relativ index, 24, 111, 200
Research & Analysis group, 5, 6, 8, 19, 20,
　25, 26, 43, 44, 76, 77, 101
Research and Estimates group, 77
Research Funding, Golden Age and
　decline of, 236, 241, 296, 311
Reynolds, Walter, 264, 265
Richards, Atherton, 37–38, 52, 66, 67–68,
　69–70, 71, 72
Rider, Fremont, 62, 68
Rome NY, Air Force research center, 181,
　308
Roosevelt, Franklin D., 3, 5, 7, 25,
　124–125
Rosbaud, Paul, 325, 326, 327
Ross, Colonel Frank, 20

INDEX

Ruggles, Richard, 140, 180, 181, 182, 183

SAL. *See* Scientific Aids to Learning
Salton, Gerard, 324
Samain, Jacques, 184, 280
Scanner. *See* H. P. Luhn
Schultz, Claire, 281
Science Citation Index. See Citation Indexing
Science Information Council, 277
Science Service, 60, 90
Scientific Aids to Learning (SAL), 149, 153, 157–160, 161, 174, 312, 315–316. *See also* Intrex
Scott, Eugene, 90
SDC. *See* Systems Development Corporation
Semantic Factor System, 157, 163–169, 221, 245, 251, 261, 279, 304; at CIA, 161, 165, 173; evaluation of, 301, 302–303
Serial Searching, limitations of, 58, 62, 99, 182, 184, 207
Serials Crisis, 91, 127, 337–338, 341, 342
Shannon, Claude, 147–148, 156, 157, 228, 281, 308
Shaw, Ralph, 123, 126, 189–190, 192, 281; review of OCR, 190–192, 197, 211
Shera, Jesse, 21–22, 45, 90, 304; break with Perry & Kent, 300; COI-OSS, 22, 31, 35, 40, 44–45; Sputnik information crisis, 259, 260, 265, 266–267, 281; Western Reserve, 248, 249, 250, 253, 262
Slamecka, Vladimir, 332
Slidell, Atherton, 63
Snowden, Edward, 347
Snyder, Sam, 317
Social Science Research Council, 7, 61, 94n13
Socialism/Communism and information policy, 121, 122, 127, 128, 129, 260, 288, 339
Soft-money academics, 143, 157, 173, 235, 239, 246, 291, 300
Soros, George, 344–345, 347
Space Race, 259
SPARC, 343
Sparck-Jones, Karen, 280, 283

Special Libraries Association / special libraries (SLA), 94n9, 259, 267, 279, 321
Special Register at CIA, 178, 190, 202n13, 211, 212
Springer / Springer-Verlag, 325, 326, 330
Sputnik and reactions to, 91, 238, 257, 258, 259, 260, 273, 277, 316
State Department, 3, 6, 13, 16, 33, 68, 76, 77, 79, 84; COI-OSS and ISC, 27, 34, 80, 85, 86, 105, 110, 200
Stenowriter, 223, 227, 230
Stewart, Irwin, 157–158
Stiles, Edmund, 283
Strong, General George V., 33, 80
Suber, Peter, 219, 344, 345
Subject headings, 16, 93, 112, 133, 139, 154, 179
Subject Intelligence Code (SIC), 215
Subject Terms at COI/OSS, 26, 28, 110
Summit, Roger, 321–322, 323
Superimposed coding, 142, 155, 282
Surgeon Generals Library, 129
Swanson, Donald (Don), 205, 221, 281, 324
Swartz, Aaron, 344, 346, 347
Systems Development Corporation (SDC), 211
Systran, 227

Tabulators and cards for retrieval, 28, 52, 56, 57, 58, 59, 63, 79, 85, 99, 100, 101, 104, 110, 129, 131, 142, 145, 167, 177, 178, 181, 205, 212, 251. *See also* 101 IBM Advanced Tabulator
Taft Commission, 12, 16
Taft, Wm. Howard, 12
Target Intelligence Committee (TICOM), 117
Tate, Vernon, 22, 39, 61, 63, 89, 149, 155, 157, 158, 161
Taub, Mortimer, 139, 196, 210, 246, 268, 281, 284, 285, 332. *See also* Uniterm
Tauber, Maurice. F., 90
Taylor, Frederick W., 12, 242
Telegraphic Abstracts, 157, 167, 168, 251, 300, 301, 303, 304
Terman, Frederick, 305
Thomas, D. B., 241, 243–244, 245, 246

Thompson, Alberto, 91, 279
Thomson, Roy, 327–330
TICOM. *See* Target Intelligence Committee
Tides Foundation, 345, 347
Translation (human), 84, 94n9, 232n1, 297
Tukey, John, 281
Turner, Frederick Jackson, 76
Tyler, Dr. A. W., 180–181, 182, 183, 195

U2, 138, 179, 182–183, 204, 258
UCLA, University of California Los Angeles, 205, 211, 218
UDC. *See* Universal Decimal Classification
Unit Record, 58, 59, 62, 99, 184
United States Intelligence Board, 176, 197, 203, 208
Uniterm, 139–140, 198, 284, 285–286, 303
UNIVAC, 196, 212
Universal Decimal Classification (UDC), 11, 15, 89, 105, 110, 183, 198, 249, 259, 261, 282, 285, 290, 303
University of Pennsylvania, 221, 224, 269, 289, 291
University of Pittsburgh, 305–306, 309, 311; information school, 307, 311. *See also* Knowledge Availability System Center; Kent Allen; Litchfield, Edward; Mellon foundations

Value-added provider, 297, 321, 322, 323, 330, 331, 342
Vance, John K., 113n10, 198–199

Varmus, Harold, 345–346
Veilleux, Mary, 198
Vickery, B.C., 280
VINITI, 258–259, 263, 267, 271, 280, 281, 299
Voge, Adolph, 93

Wallace, Henry, 120, 122–125, 128, 189
WALNUT, 176, 206, 207
Washington Document Center (WDC), 83–84, 217
Waterman, Alan T., 279
WDC. *See* Washington Document Center
Weaver, Warren, 148, 217, 221, 229, 281, 308, 316, 317
Weeks, David, 198
Wells, H.G., 282
Welch Medical Library and project, 129, 143, 289
Western Reserve University / Case Western Reserve, 189, 246–248, 253, 261, 262–263, 265, 279. *See also* Kent, Allen; Millis, John Schoff; Perry, James; Shera, Jesse
Wiener, Norbert, 147, 148, 157
Wigington, Ronald, 298
Williams, Clyde, 242
Wiswesser, Wm. J., 154

Yale University, 7, 9, 11, 20, 21, 22, 45, 105, 140, 279
Yngve, Victor H., 226, 283
Young, George, 20, 23

Zipf, George K., 148, 282

ABOUT THE AUTHOR

Colin B. Burke is a historian who has researched and published on the history of higher education, quantitative methods in history, American political history, the history of computers, the history of information, the history of nonprofit organizations, and intelligence history.

Among his honors, he has been the Eugene Garfield Fellow at the Chemical Heritage Foundation, a Research Fellow at the Yale PONPO Center, the Scholar in Residence at the National Security Agency, a Fellow of the Social Science Research Council, and the Fulbright Scholar in Warsaw during the year when Poland ousted the Communists. He has received research grants from many government and private agencies. Among his works related to the history of education, information, libraries, and intelligence are: *American Collegiate Populations: A Test of the Traditional View*; *Information and Secrecy: Vannevar Bush, Ultra, and the Other Memex*; *The Secret in Building 26*; "History of Information Science"; *It Wasn't All Magic: The Early Struggle to Automate Cryptanalysis*; and *Information and Intrigue*.

Lightning Source UK Ltd.
Milton Keynes UK
UKHW010313011220
374421UK00001B/13